Managing IP Networks with Cisco Routers

Managing IP Networks
with Cisco Routers

Scott M. Ballew

O'REILLY™

Cambridge · Köln · Paris · Sebastopol · Tokyo

Managing IP Networks with Cisco Routers
by Scott M. Ballew

Copyright © 1997 O'Reilly & Associates, Inc. All rights reserved.
Printed in the United States of America.

Editor: Mike Loukides

Production Editor: Jane Ellin

Printing History:

October 1997:   First Edition.

This book is printed on acid-free paper with 85% recycled content, 15% post-consumer waste. O'Reilly & Associates is committed to using paper with the highest recycled content available consistent with high quality.

ISBN: 1-56592-320-0   [7/98]

Table of Contents

Preface

There are many good books on system administration, whether for UNIX, Windows, or what have you. There are also many good books on administering different network services, such as the Network File System, the Domain Name System, the World Wide Web, and many email systems. There are even excellent books explaining the theory behind computer networks or exploring the detailed operation of network protocols. But until now there really hasn't been a book on how to administer a network of IP routers—a book that covered the details that are part of the day-to-day operation of a network from a hands-on perspective. That is why I wrote this book. I hope you find it a useful part of your library.

Intended Audience

Because so many network administrators find themselves given the task of managing a network of IP routers, or possibly charged with the task of building such a network from the ground up, they are my primary audience. I assume that these readers have a basic familiarity with networking concepts and technologies, though not necessarily a familiarity with the specifics of IP networking.

This book is also useful to information systems managers who are trying to assemble a staff of network administrators to implement a new network, or migrate an existing bridged network of IP machines to use routers. While these readers probably are not as interested in the nuts and bolts of router configuration, they need a basic understanding of network and router management so they can select prospective employees and understand what their employees are doing.

Finally, this book is useful to readers who are curious about how IP networks work from a practical point of view, rather than a theoretical understanding of the protocols,[*] even if they aren't directly involved in network administration.

---

[*] An excellent theoretical presentation of the Internet Protocols can be found in *Internetworking with TCP/IP, Volume 1*, by Douglas Comer, available from Prentice Hall.

What's in This Book?

So what is in this book? Before I answer that question, let me list a few things that are *not* in this book. First, this is not a book detailing the inner workings of the IP protocols. Many good books already do that, and I have great respect for their authors. It also is not intended to be an exhaustive resource on Cisco routers, nor a replacement for Cisco's documentation. The documentation for the Cisco Internetwork Operating System is thousands of pages long, and I am not about to deceive myself and you by claiming that this book can replace that information. My goal is to augment your documentation, not replace it. It is also not intended as a cookbook giving recipes for all of your unique network requirements. Such a book would not be possible. Every network is unique in some way, and there are nearly an infinite number of possible network configurations. Finally, this book is not intended to give you the *only* way, nor is it necessarily going to show you the *best* way, to solve your network problems. What this book *is* intended to do is to give you a good, solid background in the many aspects of designing, building, and operating a network of IP routers.

In Chapter 1, *The Basics of IP Networking*, I present a brief introduction to how IP networks work. While not an exhaustive description of the protocols, it should give everyone a common background that forms the basis for later discussion. Topics include how IP addresses are structured and used; subnets, supernets, and masks; private and public addresses; the IP routing algorithm; and domain names and the Domain Name System.

Next, in Chapters 2 and 3, I explore the issues surrounding the design of your IP network. While you may not have the luxury of starting from scratch, the topics covered in these chapters help you to identify areas where your current network may be deficient and help you to plan what your network should be moving toward. Topics in Chapter 2, *Network Design—Part 1*, include defining your goals; network architecture; media selection, including a brief survey of common LAN and WAN media; and different physical topologies and their strengths. These are mostly the theoretical side of network design. The discussion continues in Chapter 3, *Network Design—Part 2*, with topics such as the differences between hubs, switches, and routers; the placement of routers in your network; network mask selection and subnet assignment strategies; proxy ARP, its uses and pitfalls; and redundancy and fault tolerance in your network design. It finishes with a brief discussion of how multi-protocol routing affects your network design.

Chapter 4, *Selecting Network Equipment*, discusses what you should be considering as you evaluate and select equipment for your network. It starts with a discussion of what an IP router is, and what the trade-offs are for various types of routers. From there, it focuses on the criteria you should be considering as you evaluate your prospective equipment vendors: functionality, interoperability, and reliability, to name just a few.

In Chapter 5, *Routing Protocol Selection*, we begin moving away from design issues. This chapter's discussion of routing protocol selection is a must for any serious network administrator. Topics include static vs. dynamic routing, how dynamic routing protocols are classified, and the trade-offs between the different classes. This chapter ends with a summary of the criteria you might use to select a routing protocol for your network.

Once you have a routing protocol in mind, Chapter 6, *Routing Protocol Configuration*, delves into configuring your routing protocol. I present examples using RIP, EIGRP, and OSPF that cover many common situations. While clearly not an exhaustive set of examples, they should give you enough of the flavor of configuring these protocols for various tasks to get you thinking about how you might meet your specific needs. The examples include propagation of static routes, defining backup static routes, using variable length subnet masks with a classful routing protocol, suppressing and filtering routing information, multi-path routing, and routing with multiple dynamic routing protocols at the same time.

Chapter 7, *The Non-Technical Side of Network Management*, begins a discussion of some non-technical aspects of managing your network of routers. Topics include how you view your network, where its boundaries are, what kinds of staff skills you need, what costs are involved and how you estimate them, and establishing a help desk. Chapter 8, *The Technical Side of Network Management*, continues this discussion by shifting the focus to more technical aspects of network management, such as different ways to monitor your network, troubleshooting techniques, and a survey of tools that you might use to help with these tasks. Finally, we explore some things you can do to avoid trouble in the first place, such as keeping careful records and planning configuration changes.

In Chapter 9, *Connecting to the Outside World*, we talk about connecting your network to the outside world. No, this is not a detailed step-by-step of how to connect to the Internet. Other books already adequately cover that. This chapter discusses the issues and pitfalls surrounding *any* connection to the outside world, whether to the Internet or to a neighboring network. While a connection to the Internet is part of the discussion, it is not the main focus. Instead, when we talk about the Internet, we discuss issues like external routing, whether multiple providers or multiple links to the same provider is a better solution, and Network Address Translator (NAT) technologies. We also explore examples of configuring external routing, whether to the Internet or a neighbor, using the Border Gateway Protocol (BGP).

In Chapter 10, *Network Security*, we explore the role of the network in providing security to connected hosts, or assisting them in maintaining their own security. Topics include an overview of what security is, your need to assess your security needs, and ways to address specific aspects of network security through firewalls, encryption, and designing for privacy. This chapter presents a mix of methods for enhancing security from both within and without your routers including ways to help your routers better protect themselves from attack.

Appendices cover configuring router interfaces, getting RFCs, getting Internet drafts, and obtaining IP addresses. In discussing interface configuration, I present examples showing the most common configurations for Ethernet, Token Ring, FDDI, serial lines (leased and dial-up), Frame Relay, and ATM.

In essence, this book is a hands-on introduction for the novice network administrator. While not necessarily a complete and detailed reference to all aspects of IP router administration, it is a good foundation upon which further knowledge may be built.

What's missing from this book is a discussion of IP multicast routing and the MBONE. This is a topic that I wrestled with throughout the process of writing this book, and almost included many times. But in the end, I decided that it was still a little too fluid to be adequately handled. Even though some networks are providing "production" MBONE service, the truth is that multicast routing is still a research topic. The details change monthly, if not even more frequently, and I felt that anything I said would be out-of-date too soon to justify including it; providing out-of-date information was a worse alternative than providing nothing at all.

Finally, although this book focuses on Cisco routers, and shows all examples using Cisco's Internetwork Operating System (IOS), it's not a piece of Cisco marketing literature.[*] Don't get me wrong—I use Cisco products, and like them. But there are other router vendors whose products are worth your consideration. The decision to focus on Cisco was largely pragmatic: I needed a way to put concrete examples in the book, and Cisco is the dominant router vendor and the vendor I'm most familiar with. I have tried to make the book as even-handed as possible; the techniques and tricks I demonstrate using Cisco's IOS should be applicable to most other modern routers.

---

[*] While I won't discuss Cisco's product line, I will note that they make a few low-end routers that don't use IOS.

We'd Like to Hear from You

We have tested and verified all of the information in this book to the best of our ability, but you may find that features have changed (or even that we have made mistakes!). Please let us know about any errors you find, as well as your suggestions for future editions, by writing to:

> O'Reilly & Associates, Inc.
> 101 Morris Street
> Sebastopol, CA 95472
> 1-800-998-9938 (in US or Canada)
> 1-707-829-0515 (international/local)
> 1-707-829-0104 (FAX)

You can also send us messages electronically. To be put on the mailing list or request a catalog, send email to:

> *info@oreilly.com*

To ask techncial questions or comment on the book, send email to:

> *bookquestions@oreilly.com*

Acknowledgments

No book is ever the work of a single individual. If you doubt me on that, just try writing one! I learned more about this process than I ever thought possible (and maybe more than any sane individual should know). Still, it is not an experience that I regret. I had fun doing it, and I think part of that fun has to do with the way the folks at O'Reilly & Associates worked with me.

Among the people who made this book possible, I have to say that my technical editor, Mike Loukides, certainly helped make this as pleasant an experience as possible. He never once badgered me about my missing a deadline for a chapter, yet he always seemed to know how to drop just the right hint to get me moving again when my determination was flagging. He also provided me with several thought-provoking questions about whether something should or should not be in the book—questions I was too close to see clearly.

I also want to thank Dave Curry, now at IBM, for steering Mike to me in the first place. I had never considered authoring a book before, but when Mike asked Dave about someone who might be able to write this book, Dave gave him my name. I was flattered that Dave thought so much of my skill in networking that he would think of me to write a book on it. Without Dave, I wouldn't be writing this.

I'd also like to thank my technical reviewers who provided me more valuable advice and commentary than I had ever dreamed of. Alex Bochannek (Cisco Systems) provided detailed technical corrections to my example configurations and my descriptions of features of the Cisco IOS. Karl Friesen (Bethel College) provided insight as both a small campus network administrator and an ISP operator. Curt Freeland (Notre Dame) not only provided excellent technical information, but also provided insight as an author. Eric Pearce (O'Reilly) provided a hard-hitting, no-nonsense assessment of where the book was weak. He pulled no punches, and the book is better for it. Finally, Larry Billado (Purdue) provided feedback to me about readability and completeness, as well as where I was getting too detailed or not detailed enough. This kind of input is invaluable since I often stop seeing what is on the page and instead see what I *think* I wrote.

My thanks also go to Professor Douglas Comer for giving me my first opportunity to manage a network while I was just a lowly grad student sitting in his lab. Not only did he educate me in class with his clear description of how the IP protocol suite works, but he gave me an opportunity to apply that knowledge in the operation of the Cypress Network, a research network he had built a few years before. That experience helped to make his classroom presentation real, and fostered my fascination with computer networking until it became a deep love. Thanks, Doug!

Finally, I'd like to thank Gary for putting up with my innumerable requests to read a section and give me his opinion, for tolerating the moments when my confidence in my ability to pull this off waned, and for patiently prodding me to work on my book when it was the *last* thing I wanted to do. And let's not forget Rascal, my dog, who has certainly felt that he has been sorely neglected for the last two years while I worked on this. I owe him many hours of play and attention.

1

The Basics of IP Networking

In recent years, IP networking has gained enormously in popularity, spurred largely by the growth and popularity of the Internet. But the availability of trained network administrators who are able to manage these networks has fallen far behind. Often, already overworked computer support personnel are pressed into service as IP network administrators, and are given responsibility not only for the administration of the hosts and servers on the network, but also for the routers, switches, and hubs that make up the network infrastructure. This is a task for which most are unprepared.

In this book, I seek to fill the void that has been left in the knowledge of many computing professionals as IP networking has come to their organizations. In so doing, I hope that it will be a useful introduction to the tasks, issues, and tools involved in effectively managing a collection of IP routers to form a stable, reliable IP network on which many organizations are coming to depend.

Because the backgrounds of people pressed into service as network administrators are so varied, there will probably be times when you will find the material in this book extremely basic and familiar. This is good, and simply indicates that your background already includes some of this information. But rather than skip over those portions that at first seem well-known to you, I urge you to read them. You may find a different point of view that clarifies something you always found vague or confusing; you may even find some new information that you somehow missed.

For example, this chapter reviews some of the basic concepts of IP networking including addressing; subnets, supernets, and netmasks; the IP routing algorithm; and mapping between names and addresses using the Domain Name System (DNS). It is not intended to be an exhaustive reference on IP, nor is it intended to be a tutorial for those completely unfamiliar with IP networking. Rather, this chapter is intended to ensure that we are all working with the same basic under-standing. If you skip this chapter, you may find that a later portion of the book assumes that you know something you would have learned from this chapter. If you want more details about the inner workings of the IP protocols, I encourage you to read *Internetworking with TCP/IP, Vol. 1,* by Douglas Comer, (Prentice Hall). For a solid grounding in the fundamentals of IP network administration, see *TCP/IP Network Administration* by Craig Hunt (O'Reilly).

After ensuring that we all have a common knowledge base, the next few chapters discuss how to design your network (in practice, this is more likely to mean how to correct the design problems that exist in the network you find yourself main-taining); what to look at when selecting routers; how to select a dynamic routing protocol; and how to configure the routing protocol you have selected. Later chap-ters cover topics like maintaining and operating your network; connecting your network to other networks, including the Internet; and finally how to enhance the security of your network and assist the hosts on your network to defend them-selves against threats from the network.

Throughout this book, you will find examples, techniques, and tips that reference the Cisco *Internetwork Operating System (IOS)*. Don't take this to imply that the information is useless if you don't happen to own Cisco routers. Most of the exam-ples and techniques should be adaptable to any router that supports the necessary protocols. Some of the tips, while not directly translatable to your router, may give you ideas to try with your routers, no matter what their vendor.

Addresses and Networks

In any network, every destination must have a unique identifier that other machines use to send it information. This identifier is usually called an *address*. In some network technologies, an address identifies a particular machine, while in others, such as IP, an address identifies a network attachment point, more commonly known as an *interface*. As a result, a single machine with multiple interfaces may have multiple IP addresses—one for each interface. Interfaces are usually physically distinct connections (i.e., a physical socket into which you plug a network cable), but they can be logical connections that share a common under-lying physical connection. You might see the second case, more formally called *interface multiplexing*, on an attachment to an ATM network. Logically separating the hosts on the ATM network into multiple groups allows you to treat each group as a separate logical network, even though the hosts are physically connected to a single physical network. A device attached to this network could participate in several of these logical networks at the same time simply by estab-lishing the appropriate logical connections, each with its own IP address.

Machines that have multiple addresses are called *multi-homed* machines. All routers are multi-homed; by definition, they route packets between multiple networks. However, not all multi-homed machines are routers. It is possible (and not uncommon) for one machine to have multiple network connections, perhaps because it is a file server shared by several different networks, without providing IP routing services between any of these networks.

The Structure of an IP Address

IP addresses are 32 bits long. We treat this address as a sequence of four bytes, or (to use the terminology of network engineers) four *octets* (8-bit bytes). To write out an IP address, you convert each octet to decimal, and separate the four decimal values with periods. Thus, the 32-bit IP address:

```
10101100   00011101   00100000   01000010
```

is typically written:

```
172.29.32.66
```

This format, known as a *dotted quad,* is convenient for humans; we will use it for most of the discussion in this book. But there will be times when it is more convenient to work with the hexadecimal representation of the 32-bit address because it makes some operations easier to perform or visualize. In hexadecimal, the IP address shown above would be represented as:

```
0xac1d2042
```

Even though an IP address is a single 32-bit value, the collection of all IP addresses is not a flat space. Instead, it consists of a two-level hierarchy of networks and hosts within those networks, each identified by a portion of the IP address: that is, we can divide any IP address into a network number and a host number. In the IP protocol, the network number identifies a collection of machines that are able to communicate directly with each other at layer two of the ISO* network reference model.† This is the Data Link Layer and includes such technologies as Ethernet, Token Ring, and FDDI (Fiber Distributed Data Interconnect), as well as point-to-point lines. IP treats each of these as a single network, whether it is truly a single physical cable, or is composed of multiple segments connected by repeaters, bridges, or switches. It shouldn't be surprising that the host number specifies a particular machine that belongs to the network. Figure 1-1 shows an example.

---

* ISO is the International Organization for Standardization.

† This reference model provides a framework for discussing network systems. Details of its seven layers are available in many networking texts, and will not be discussed here.

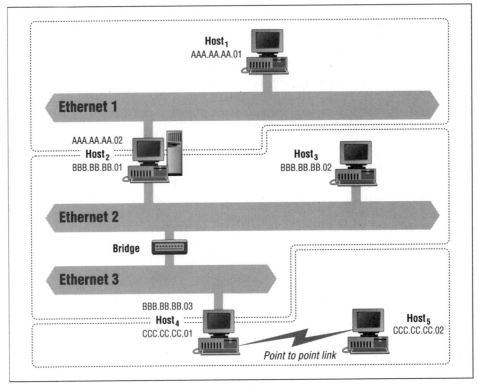

Figure 1-1. Ethernets 2 and 3 are a single network

In Figure 1-1, Ethernets 2 and 3 form a single IP network, even though separated by a bridge, since a bridge is invisible to network-layer protocols like IP.* Host2, Host3, and Host4 all have IP addresses that contain the network number of this bridged Ethernet. The serial link between Host4 and Host5 forms a second IP network, and Host4 and Host5 will have IP addresses that contain the network number for this serial link. Finally, Ethernet 1 is a third IP network, and Host1 and Host2 will have IP addresses that contain this third IP network number. Host2 and Host4 each have two IP addresses; they are multi-homed hosts, and may be routers. The two-level structure of IP addresses will be important later when we talk about routing. For now, it is enough to determine which part of an IP address is the network number and which is the host number.

Putting the network number into an IP address has one important consequence. A host's IP address depends on the network to which it is connected. This implies that if a host is moved to a new network, it must change its address.

---

* A more detailed explanation of the difference between routers and bridges can be found in Chapter 3.

In contrast to other networking technologies such as Novell's IPX, where the address is based on the hardware address of the network adapter, or Apple Computer's AppleTalk, where the address is chosen automatically, IP addresses are assigned and configured manually. While there are protocols like the *Boot Strap Protocol (BOOTP)* and the *Dynamic Host Configuration Protocol (DHCP)* that assist a machine in determining its IP address, the servers for these protocols still require some amount of manual configuration, and many machines do not take advantage of these services. The need to renumber a host manually whenever it moves results in additional maintenance effort.

Network Numbers and Masks

I said above that all IP addresses consist of a network number and a host number on that network. However, where the division between the network number and the host number occurs differs for each network. To allow software in routers and hosts to easily identify where this division occurs for any given address, each address has an associated *network mask*. This mask is a 32-bit number, just like an IP address, where all bits in the network portion of the address are set to 1, and all bits in the host portion are set to 0. For example:

```
11111111  11111111  00000000  00000000
```

indicates that the first 16 bits of the associated IP address represent the network number, and the last 16 bits represent the host number within that network. A computer can extract the network number from an IP address using a simple bitwise *AND* of the IP address with the mask.

Originally, network masks were permitted to have discontiguous 1-bits, this practice has been eliminated partly because it was confusing to humans, and partly to simplify the exchange of routing information. Now, all masks must have all of their 1-bits contiguous. Thus, a mask like:

```
11111111  11111111  00000011  00000000
```

is illegal because the last two 1-bits are not contiguous with the others. This restriction is not a great burden since few masks were ever defined that were not contiguous.

Like IP addresses, network masks are traditionally represented using either the dotted quad or hexadecimal notation. Thus, you might see a mask represented as 255.255.254.0, or as 0xfffffe00, which is how they are more often expressed to software. However, since network masks are always associated with an IP address and have little meaning on their own, a new format is becoming increasingly popular. Because all of the 1-bits are now required to be contiguous, you can talk about a 23-bit mask, and it is clear that you must mean a mask with 23 1-bits, followed by 9 0-bits, or 0xfffffe00 in hexadecimal. This allows for the rather cumbersome statement "the network starting at `192.168.2.0` with network mask `255.255.254.0`" to be more succinctly written as `192.168.2.0/23`. This new notation is called *base address/bit count notation*. While most software still does not allow this format for input, it is becoming increasingly common for output.

In the Cisco IOS, for example, to set the output format for network masks for the current session, you can issue one of the commands in Table 1-1.

Table 1-1. Setting the Netmask Output Format

Command	Resulting Display
terminal ip netmask-format bit-count	192.168.2.0/23
terminal ip netmask-format decimal	192.168.2.0 255.255.254.0
terminal ip netmask-format hexadecimal	192.168.2.0 0xFFFFFE00

Alternatively, you can make the bit-count format the default for all sessions by adding the following lines to your configuration:

```
line con 0
 ip netmask-format bit-count
line vty 0 4
 ip netmask-format bit-count
```

If you'd rather not use the bit-count format, you can substitute `decimal` or `hexadecimal`.

The base address/bit count notation allows you to discuss IP address spaces of virtually any size, from a simple two-host, point-to-point link, to a multimillion-host network. For example, consider the two base addresses shown in Figure 1-2. Because these addresses share a common 23-bit prefix, and are consecutively numbered, it is possible to represent the combined address space using the network number/bit count notation—specifically, `192.168.10.0/23`.

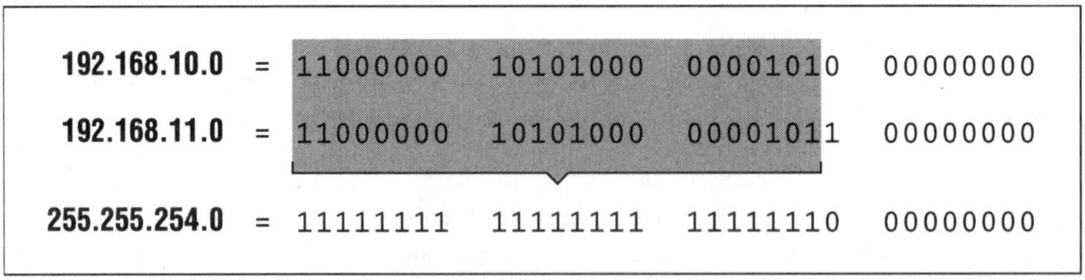

192.168.10.0 =	11000000	10101000	00001010	00000000
192.168.11.0 =	11000000	10101000	00001011	00000000
255.255.254.0 =	11111111	11111111	11111110	00000000

Figure 1-2. Two addresses with a common 23-bit prefix

But not every combination of base address and network mask is valid in this notation. Figure 1-3 shows four addresses that cannot be represented by a single base address/bit count specification. Because these addresses, although consecutive, do not share a common 22-bit prefix, it is not possible to specify a 22-bit mask

that would include them all. If you tried to reference this address space as
`192.168.10.0/22`, you would only include two of these addresses, and two
others not shown. Instead, you would have to use two separate specifications,
`192.168.10.0/23` and `192.168.12.0/23`, which requires two separate
routing table entries, as we will see later in this chapter.

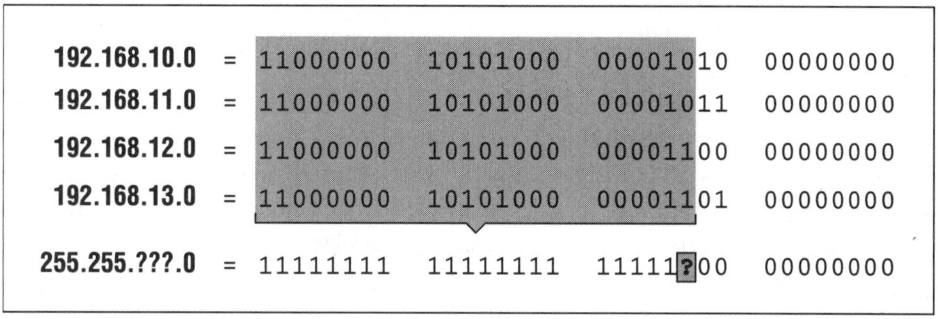

192.168.10.0	=	11000000	10101000	00001010	00000000
192.168.11.0	=	11000000	10101000	00001011	00000000
192.168.12.0	=	11000000	10101000	00001100	00000000
192.168.13.0	=	11000000	10101000	00001101	00000000
255.255.???.0	=	11111111	11111111	11111?00	00000000

Figure 1-3. Four addresses with no common 22-bit prefix

Does `192.168.10.0/22` represent *any* valid address space? Yes and no. If you
apply the mask to the address, you would find that it is the same address space as
`192.168.8.0/22`. So is it important which base address is used in this notation?
Yes! While a computer will correctly determine that `192.168.10.0/22` is the
same as `192.168.8.0` through `192.168.11.255`, even experienced network
administrators will often mistakenly believe that the address space referenced is
`192.168.10.0` through `192.168.13.255`. This is a major difference! This may
result in duplicate address assignment, routing problems, and other mysterious
failures. To reduce confusion, and make the notation unambiguous, convention
dictates that the base address, when masked by the mask specified, *must* have a
host part with no 1-bits. This restriction is so important that all well-written
network software will enforce it and flag any violation as an error.

In general, for some number, N, of contiguous base addresses to have a common
prefix, N must be a power of two, and the last octet containing the network
number (not including any bits of the host number) must be evenly divisible by N.

Classes of IP Addresses

The base address/bit count notation just described allows for a good fit between
the size of the network address space and the actual number of hosts. You can
easily count the hosts on your network, round up to the next power of two, and
request a network number and mask that allow for the hosts you need, with
reasonable room for expansion. But this hasn't always been the case. Before
network masks were generalized, there were *classes* of networks, with implicit
masks associated with them. Although these were largely made obsolete by the

more general *classless* architecture discussed above, the literature and jargon are peppered with references to these classes (they'll even be mentioned from time to time in this book), and some routing protocols, such as RIP, are still intimately aware of them. For these reasons, let's turn back the clock and explore these network classes and the evolution toward the modern, classless architecture in place today.

The designers of IP didn't envision supporting a network the size of today's Internet. They assumed that they would only need to support a few large networks (large computer corporations and major research universities), a medium number of medium-sized networks, and many small networks. Therefore, they created three classes of networks: class A for the largest networks; class B for the medium networks; and class C for the smallest networks. They also wanted to make routing decisions easy, so they encoded the class of the network in the first few bits of the IP address as shown in Figure 1-4.

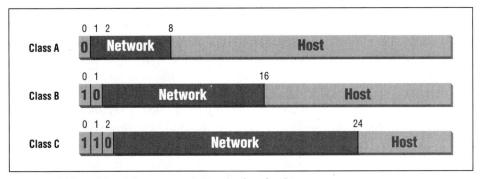

Figure 1-4. The address class is encoded in the first few bits

If the first bit of the address is 0, the network is a class A network. In a class A network, the first octet is the network number, and the remaining three octets identify the host within that network. Because the first bit of the address is fixed at 0, there can be 127 class A networks with more than 16 million hosts each. If the first two bits of the address are 10, the network is a class B network. In a class B network, the first two octets are the network number, and the last two octets identify the host within that network. This allows for 16,384 class B networks (again, observe that the first two bits are fixed) with around 65,000 hosts each. Finally, if the first three bits are 110, the network is a class C network. In a class C network, the first three octets are the network number, and the last octet identifies the host within that network. This allows for approximately 2 million networks with 256 hosts each. Notice how easy it is to look at the first few bits, and then extract the network and host fields from the address. Simplicity was important, because computers at the time had much less processing power than they do today.

As originally defined, addresses for which the first three bits were 111 were called class D addresses, and were reserved for future use. Since that time, researchers have modified this definition so that a class D address is now defined as an address where the first four bits are 1110. These addresses do not represent a single machine, but rather represent a collection of machines that are part of an IP multicast group, and will be discussed in the next section. Addresses beginning with 1111 are now called class E addresses, and are reserved for future use. Presumably, if a suitable use were found for another class of addresses, the definition would be modified so that class E addresses began 11110, and a new class F address would be defined (and reserved for future use) beginning with 11111.*

So how do these network classes relate to their modern classless equivalents? Notice that a class A network effectively has an 8-bit network mask. This means that the class A network 10.0.0.0 would be designated 10.0.0.0/8 in classless notation. Likewise, the *natural* network mask for a class B network is 16 bits long, and that for a class C network is 24 bits long. This results in the class B network 172.16.0.0 becoming 172.16.0.0/16, and the class C network 192.168.1.0 becoming 192.168.1.0/24. However, while it is true that all networks that were formerly known as class B networks have a natural network mask of 16 bits, it is not true that all networks with 16-bit masks are class B networks.†

Consider the network 10.0.0.0/16. This network is using a 16-bit mask, but it is still a class A network (or, rather, a portion of one) because its binary representation still starts with a zero bit. In the same way, the network described by 192.168.0.0/16 is also not a class B network. Instead, it is a collection of 256 class C networks. This distinction is only important when you are dealing with hosts and protocols that are aware of network classes, but then it can be crucial. In classless addressing, a 16-bit mask is a 16-bit mask.

Subnets and supernets

As the designers of the IP protocols gained experience with it, they discovered that the original network classes were of an unwieldy size to be useful for the emerging LAN technologies. For example, it is unreasonable to assign a class B network, with a potential for over 65,000 hosts, to an Ethernet with a limit of 1,200 attachments. The solution they developed is called *subnetting*, and was the first explicit use of network masks.

---

* This seems to be the last bastion of common use of the old class structure for addresses, but it, too, is giving way to the more accurate name *multicast address space*. For those who are purists, you could also represent these addresses as 224.0.0.0/4, or you could just refer to them as the range from 224.0.0.0-239.255.255.255. Use whatever works best for you.

† Nor does an 8-bit mask indicate a class A network, or a 24-bit mask indicate a class C network.

In IP subnetting, bits are taken from the host number of the IP address and used as if they are part of the network number. For example, recall that the class A network 10.0.0.0 has 8 bits of network number and 24 bits of host number. Engineers realized that they could subdivide this network by taking 8 bits of the host number and adding them to the network number, as shown in Figure 1-5. This gave 256 *subnetworks* of approximately 65,000 hosts each. Or, instead, they could take 16 bits from the host number and use them for the subnet, thereby extending the network number in a different way to give around 65,000 subnets of 256 hosts each.

Network	Subnetwork	Host
10	–	27.9.4
10	27	9.4
10	27.9	4

Figure 1-5. Different interpretations of the address 10.27.9.4

There is no requirement that subnet masks fall on 8-bit boundaries. However, many sites use masks that fall on 8-bit boundaries because they make it easier for humans to identify the subnet number. If we take the class A network 10.0.0.0, and do no subnetting, the division between network number and host number falls at the first dot. If we use 8 bits of subnet (i.e., a 16-bit network mask), then the division between the subnet and the host falls at the second dot. If, instead, we used 16 bits of subnet (a 24-bit network mask), then the division falls at the third dot. While computers don't care about such niceties, human beings find such conventions useful. For example, if we were to use a 10-bit subnet on our example network, 10.0.0.0, we get 1024 subnets of 16384 hosts each. However, the division between the subnet number and the host number occurs in the middle of the third octet and is not clearly visible in the dotted quad notation. Consider the addresses 10.1.190.1 and 10.1.191.1. Are they on the same subnet? These two are, but 10.1.192.1 is not. Even the hexadecimal representations don't make it clear. Only the binary representation makes it clear which subnet is which.

A subnet mask always has at least as many 1-bits as the natural network mask for the network's class. This means that a subnet is always smaller than whatever classful network it is part of. When address space exhaustion became a concern several years ago, many observed that there was no technical reason for the mask to be so constrained. Why not let a network mask be larger than a natural class C network mask, and so let a block of class C networks be treated as a single network, or *supernet?* * In fact, why limit this to class C networks? Why not allow contiguous blocks of class B networks to form a supernet as well?

This insight is the basis for *Classless Interdomain Routing (CIDR)*, the current classless architecture. Generalizing network masks to allow both subnets and supernets resulted in a new set of *classless* routing protocols, where previously there had only been *classful* protocols. Classful and classless protocols do not mix well because classless protocols require knowledge of the mask involved, while classful protocols make assumptions about the mask. In controlled situations, however, it is possible to join the two together at the edge of a routing domain. This should be undertaken only as a last resort, and with full knowledge of the consequences.

Broadcast and Multicast Addresses

There are times when a host on an IP network needs to communicate with all of the hosts on the network. Because there is no easy way to determine which other addresses on the network are assigned to hosts, or even which hosts on the network are currently operational, a host might have to send a copy of the message to each and every address on the network. This would be a waste of network capacity and computing resources. To eliminate this problem, IP defines the address 255.255.255.255 as the local network *broadcast* address. In addition to their own unique IP addresses, all IP hosts listen for this broadcast address.

Local network broadcasts work well if the host only needs to send its message to the other hosts directly attached to the same network. However, there are also times when a host needs to send a packet to all hosts on a network to which it is not directly attached. IP defines this as a *directed broadcast*. The address for a directed broadcast is the network number of the target network, with all the bits of the host number set to 1. Thus, the directed broadcast address for the network 10.0.0.0/8 would be 10.255.255.255, and the directed broadcast address for network 172.29.0.0/16 would be 172.29.255.255. Because of the potential for abuse by malicious or ignorant users, most routers can be configured to discard directed broadcasts, and not pass them to the target network. Chapter 10 shows an example of how to do this.

Some older software used 0 bits instead of 1 bits to denote broadcasts. While these *0s broadcast* systems are a vanishing breed, it is possible that you may come across one, especially if you have some older systems at your site. In fact, one major UNIX workstation vendor had its software default to 0s broadcast until

---

* Also known as an *aggregate*, or a *netblock*.

fairly recently. Modern software should accept either form of broadcast, and should be configurable to send exclusively 1s or 0s broadcasts, with 1s broadcast being the default.

Like a broadcast address, a *multicast* address is a single address that represents a group of machines. Unlike a broadcast address, however, the machines using a multicast address have all expressed a desire to receive the messages sent to the address. A message sent to the broadcast address is received by all IP speaking machines, whether they care what it contains or not. For example, some routing protocols use multicast addresses as the destination for their periodic routing messages. This allows machines that have no interest in the routing updates to ignore them with ease. A broadcast, on the other hand, must be examined by all machines, including those not running IP protocols, to determine whether they are interested. This is because where a hardware broadcast facility exists, it is almost always used for sending IP broadcasts even though this results in non-IP speaking hosts receiving the message. They should silently discard it, but it still takes some small amount of processing for them to determine their lack of interest.

Other Special Addresses

Two other special IP addresses should be mentioned. The first of these is the *loopback* address, `127.0.0.1`. This address is defined as the address of the software loopback interface on a machine. The loopback interface has no real hardware associated with it, and does not physically connect to a network. It exists primarily to allow testing of the IP software on a machine without being concerned with whether or not a hardware interface or device driver are working. Alternatively, it may be used as an IP interface on the local machine that is always up and reachable, regardless of the status of interface hardware. For example, this address could be used as a reasonably portable way for client software on a machine to contact server software running on the same machine without having to worry about the local host's external address.

The IP protocol specifications, known as *Requests for Comment,* or *RFCs,*[*] require that this address, and the entire `127.0.0.0/8` network, must *never* appear outside a machine and, if it does, it must be silently discarded by any host or router receiving a packet so addressed. Notice that this address violates the property that IP addresses uniquely identify a host, because every host on an IP network is entitled to use this address for its loopback interface.

The second special IP address is the address `0.0.0.0`. In addition to being used by older software as a local network broadcast address, some routing protocols

---

[*] Instructions for obtaining a copy of the RFCs can be found in Appendix B.

treat this address as a catch-all or *default* route. I will talk more about default routes when I discuss the IP routing algorithm.

Usable Addresses for a Given Network Mask

Until now, I have said that any network using a 24-bit network mask allows for 256 hosts. This is not entirely true. Recall that an address with all 1s in the host portion indicates a broadcast address. Recall also that some older implementations use 0s for broadcasts. Because of this, the addresses with host portions of all 1s and all 0s may not be assigned to a host. This yields 254 usable host addresses. The same restrictions hold true for all other subnetwork masks.

Consider the 31-bit mask 0xfffffffe. This mask would seem to produce a subnet with two hosts on it—ideal for a point-to-point link. However, because we can't have host numbers that are all 1s or 0s, this mask is useless. The correct mask for a network with two usable hosts would be the 30-bit mask 0xfffffffc. The first host on the network has a host number of 1, and the second has the host number 2. The host number 0 is not allowed, and 3 would be the broadcast address.

Likewise, there has been some ambiguity regarding subnets whose subnetwork number is all 0s or all 1s. Some network software doesn't handle these cases properly. Other software requires you to configure it explicitly to allow these two subnets. For example, the Cisco IOS allows the use of subnet 0 if you include the command

```
ip subnet-zero
```

in your configuration. However, this is discouraged because of the confusion that could result from having a subnet and network number that are indistinguishable. This may even cause your dynamic routing protocol to fail! The use of the all 1s subnet is allowed, but should also be avoided. Unless you know that all of your network software supports either or both of these subnets (all 0s and all 1s), you should avoid using them.

Table 1-2 shows the number of subnets and hosts for all subnet masks of three different sized netblocks. For example, if your netblock is 16 bits long, you could use a 25-bit subnetwork mask to obtain 510 subnets of 126 hosts each. However, if your netblock is 20 bits long, the same 25-bit mask would yield 30 subnets of 126 hosts each. Notice that some masks do not produce a useful number of subnets. These are marked with a dash. Similar numbers can easily be derived for other netblock sizes. As you consider your selection of subnetwork masks, keep this table in mind.

Table 1-2. Number of Subnets and Hosts for Various Masks and Netblocks

# bits	Subnetwork Mask	Number of subnets if netblock is			Effective # of Hosts
		16 bits	20 bits	24 bits	
16	255.255.0.0	1	-	-	65534
17	255.255.128.0	-	-	-	32766
18	255.255.192.0	2	-	-	16382
19	255.255.224.0	6	-	-	8190
20	255.255.240.0	14	1	-	4094
21	255.255.248.0	30	-	-	2046
22	255.255.252.0	62	2	-	1022
23	255.255.254.0	126	6	-	510
24	255.255.255.0	254	14	1	254
25	255.255.255.128	510	30	-	126
26	255.255.255.192	1022	62	2	62
27	255.255.255.224	2046	126	6	30
28	255.255.255.240	4094	254	14	14
29	255.255.255.248	8190	510	30	6
30	255.255.255.252	16382	1022	62	2
31	255.255.255.254	32766	2046	126	-
32	255.255.255.255	65534	4094	254	-

Private and Public Addresses

I have said that IP addresses must uniquely identify a host, but I have not defined the scope of this uniqueness. In order to allow an IP address to be used unambiguously by the routing algorithm to determine a path to the destination, an address must be unique among all networks reachable from a given host using the IP protocols. This collection of IP networks is called an *internetwork*. The most well-known example of such an internetwork is the *Internet.*

On the Internet, the way IP addresses are assigned ensures their uniqueness. A central administrative authority known as the *Internet Registry** assigns an entire IP network number to a site connecting to the Internet. No other site will be assigned the same network number. Therefore, as long as the site assigns a

---

* The central registry in the United States has delegated portions of the address space and authority to assign those addresses to regional registries. See Appendix D for information about the registry that serves your area, and how to contact it.

different host number to each host on its network, each IP address will be unique. That is, the Internet Registry ensures that network numbers are unique; individual networks ensure that host numbers are unique within their network. These globally unique addresses are known as *public* IP addresses.

With the explosive growth in connections to the Internet, there has been some concern over the eventual exhaustion of the IP address space. This has led some in the Internet community to propose that a set of IP network numbers be set aside for private addressing by sites. These networks would not be assigned to anyone by the Internet Registry, but would be open for use by any site (connected to the Internet or not) that wished to implement a private address space. IP addresses would be unique within such a private address space, but there is no uniqueness guaranteed between private address spaces. Two private address spaces could easily use the same private network number, and therefore could assign the same IP address to two different hosts. Because private addresses aren't unique, communication between privately addressed networks isn't possible without coordination of address assignments by the respective network administrations. Of course, if two network administrations coordinate their private address assignments in such a way to ensure the uniqueness of addresses, the result is that only one private address space truly exists.

Several classes of enterprises could conceivably benefit from private addresses. Among these are enterprises that are unlikely to connect to the Internet, enterprises that have large numbers of machines that have special security needs and should not be globally accessible, and enterprises that have more machines than they might be able to get a public address space for. An example given by the proponents of private addresses is a large airport that has its arrival and departure displays individually addressable via TCP/IP. It is unlikely that these displays need to be directly accessible from other networks. Another example is a company that has been assigned a small address space, but has many networked computers in a lab or on a factory floor. These computers might need to access central resources in the corporation, but external access by these machines might neither be required nor desired.* In this case, private addresses conserve the organization's limited public address space.

The addresses reserved for private use are listed in Table 1-3. These addresses are not unique across the Internet, but only within the enterprise that chooses to use them. Hosts with private addresses are able to reach all other privately addressed hosts within an enterprise, as well as all publicly addressed hosts within the enterprise, but not hosts in any other enterprises. Likewise, hosts with public addresses

---

* Historically, some people have used the test network, 192.0.2.0/24, for these purposes. The use of the test network for permanent, private address space is discouraged. Instead, use the addresses explicitly reserved for private addressing.

can reach all publicly addressed hosts, whether in their own enterprise or another, as well as those privately addressed hosts within their own enterprise, but not those hosts with private addresses in other enterprises.

Table 1-3. Addresses Reserved for Private Address Spaces

Begin	End	Classless Notation
10.0.0.0	10.255.255.255	10.0.0.0/8
172.16.0.0	172.31.255.255	172.16.0.0/12
192.168.0.0	192.168.255.255	192.168.0.0/16

Figure 1-6 shows three enterprises connected to each other. Enterprises A and B have chosen to use private address spaces for some of their hosts, and public addresses for others. Enterprise C has chosen to use only public addresses. Privately addressed hosts in enterprise A, such as A3, can communicate with all hosts within enterprise A, but not with any hosts outside of enterprise A, no matter how they are addressed. Likewise, a privately addressed host within enterprise B, such as B2, can communicate with any host in enterprise B, whether the publicly addressed B1, or the privately addressed B3, but not others outside. Publicly addressed hosts within A, such as A1, can communicate with all of the hosts in all three enterprises except the privately addressed hosts in enterprise B, and publicly addressed hosts within B can communicate with all hosts except the privately addressed hosts within enterprise A. Finally, the hosts within enterprise C, all of which are publicly addressed, can communicate with the publicly addressed hosts in all three enterprises, but not with the privately addressed hosts in enterprise A or B.

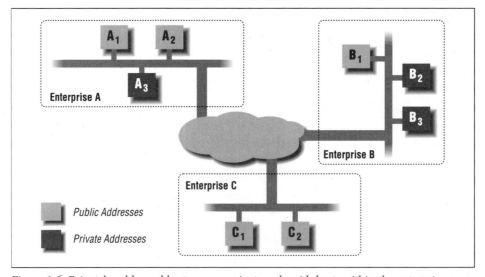

Figure 1-6. Privately addressed hosts communicate only with hosts within the enterprise

Remember that private addresses are not globally unique. In Figure 1-6, A3 could have the same IP address as B3 without problem. Therefore, a set of rules and guidelines must be followed by any enterprise using private addresses. These rules and guidelines are specified in RFC 1918. In summary, they are:

- Routing information about private networks must not be propagated on inter-enterprise links (such as a link to the Internet, or a private link to another enterprise).

- Packets with private source or destination addresses should not be forwarded across such links.

- Indirect references to such addresses (such as Domain Name System resource records) should be contained within the enterprise.

See RFC 1918 for a fuller discussion of these issues. Appendix B provides information on obtaining RFCs.

Private address spaces should be used with caution and with forethought. There are certainly advantages to private addresses, including a much larger address space than an enterprise can obtain from the global address pool, and greater security because privately addressed hosts are, while not completely secured from attacks, certainly much harder to locate and attack from outside the organization. They are not without their disadvantages, however. Chief among these disadvantages are the need to re-address any host when it needs to change from being a private to a public host; the precautions that must be taken to prevent the private address information from leaking out of the enterprise; and the creation of a category of *second class* hosts that are unable to communicate with all hosts in an internet. While the disadvantages can be mitigated through the use of proxy servers or a *Network Address Translator (NAT)*, proxies and NATs add complexity to the network, and introduce another place where mistakes can be made.

This last reason has led many in the Internet community to oppose the use of private addresses. They prefer, instead, that a solution to the address space exhaustion be provided. While this is a fine goal, such a solution is not available yet and does nothing to help enterprises solve their addressing problems today. I believe that, with proper care and understanding, there are appropriate uses for these private address spaces both for enterprises that are connected to the Internet, and those who are unlikely to connect.

In this book, I use private addresses in all examples. There are a number of reasons for this decision: I didn't want irate email from the owner of an assigned network number, and so on. But most important, I wanted to make it clear that you can't cut and paste my examples into your router configuration files. Unlike the examples in other O'Reilly books, router configuration examples must always be adapted to the needs of your local site; they can't be copied verbatim.

The IP Routing Algorithm

In an IP network, each machine makes its own routing decisions. The algorithm used is the same, whether the machine is a router or a host. The sending machine does not have to figure out the entire path through the network to a destination. Instead, it only needs to figure out the next machine, or *hop*, along the path. It then sends the packet to that machine, which is responsible for figuring out the next hop toward the destination. The process is repeated until the packet is finally delivered to the destination machine. Information about the next hop toward a destination is kept in a *routing table*. Each entry in this routing table describes a single IP network, subnet, or host, and the address of the next hop to take to get there.

Traditional (Classful) IP Routing

While most routers and many hosts are capable of routing in a classless IP network, many hosts and some routers still use a routing algorithm that is closely tied to the class of the destination network. This *classful* routing algorithm is:

```
For a given destination IP address:
if I have a host-specific route for this destination
    extract the next hop address from the routing table entry
    send the packet to the next hop address
else
    determine the network number of the destination
    if I have an interface on that network
        determine the subnet mask for the network from my interface
    else
        determine the subnet mask for the network from its class
    endif
    mask the destination address with the mask to get a subnet
    if I have an interface on that subnet
        send the packet directly to the destination
    else if I have an entry in my routing table for the subnet
        extract the next hop address from the routing table entry
        send the packet to the next hop address
    else if I have a default route in my routing table
        extract the next hop address from the routing table
        send the packet to the next hop address
    else
        report that the destination is unreachable
    endif
endif
```

The algorithm first checks for a *host-specific* route. A host-specific route is an entry in the routing table that exactly matches a single IP address. This might be used to designate a machine on the remote end of a point-to-point serial line.

If it doesn't find a host-specific route, the algorithm next tries to determine the subnet mask for the destination network. In the case of a remote network (one that this machine does not connect to directly), it has no knowledge of the subnet mask in use, so simply uses the natural netmask of the network's class. If it does connect directly to the network, it determines the subnet mask from its own interface configuration. This interface may or may not connect to the subnet containing the destination address, but the algorithm assumes that the subnet mask is the same. A consequence of this assumption is that the classful routing algorithm cannot deal with a network that uses different subnet masks in different areas, unless the network is carefully laid out by the network administrator to avoid ambiguous routing entries.

After the algorithm has determined a subnet mask for the destination network, it masks the destination address with this mask to get the subnet number to use as a search key for its routing table. If it determines that it is directly attached to this subnet, it delivers the packet directly. Otherwise, it searches its routing table for an entry for this subnet, and determines the next hop address from the entry found.

As a last resort, the algorithm looks for a *default* route (also known as a *gateway of last resort*). A default route usually has a smart router (one that has more complete routing tables) as its next hop, but the default route could just indicate a router that is closer to a majority of the IP network than the sender.

Finally, if the algorithm is unable to determine a next hop for a destination, it reports the destination as *unreachable*, either directly to the user program (if the sending machine cannot find a next hop), or by using the *Internet Control Message Protocol (ICMP)*.

Classless IP Routing

With the introduction of supernets, the routing algorithm had to be updated to deal with arbitrary portions of the IP address space. Each routing table entry needs to include a destination and a next hop address, plus a mask to indicate the size of the address space described by this entry. Adding this mask to the routing table entries allows for a generalization of the classful routing algorithm into a *classless* algorithm. Implementing the routing table lookup portion of this algorithm is typically more complex than it is for the classful algorithm, but the algorithm itself is much simpler:

```
For a given destination IP address:
search the routing table for the longest prefix match for the address
extract the next hop address from the routing table entry
send the packet to the next hop address
```

```
if no match was found
   report that the destination is unreachable
endif
```

The first difference you will notice is that this algorithm is much simpler and more general than the classful algorithm. Including network masks in the routing table entries allows us to eliminate most of the special cases necessary in the classful algorithm. For example, host-specific routes are now simply entries with a mask of 255.255.255.255. Since these 32-bit masks always match a destination with a longer prefix than any subnet, network, or supernet, they are preferred over the less specific routes, just as they were in the classful algorithm. Likewise, the default route, if present, is simply represented as an entry with a destination address of 0.0.0.0 and a mask of 0.0.0.0. When this mask is used to mask any destination address, the result will be 0.0.0.0, which matches the destination address in the entry. However, this resulting prefix will always be shorter than any more specific route that might exist for a network, subnet, or supernet, so this route is still the route of last resort.

A useful consequence of the "longest match" requirement is that it is possible to have a less specific route, a supernet for example, and a more specific route, a subnet for example, that both match a given destination address, but have different next hop addresses. This allows a machine to have a single summary route that covers most of the supernet, but still have some *holes* that need to be routed differently. While generally useful, you should be careful about creating too many holes in your netblocks or networks because they defeat the goal of having compact, efficient routing tables. Remember, if you have holes in your netblocks or networks, you not only have to have a routing table entry for the supernet or network, but you also have to have entries for each hole.

A final useful consequence of adding masks to the routing table entries is that it is now possible to have different subnet masks in different parts of the network. You still need to make sure that subnet masks are assigned to avoid any ambiguous overlaps, but you are otherwise freed from the requirement to design your network topology to avoid ambiguous routing entries brought on by the use of differing subnet masks. A technique for assigning these *Variable-Length Subnet Masks (VLSM)* will be discussed in Chapter 3, *Network Design—Part 2*.

Routing Table Maintenance

Because each machine in the IP network simply forwards the IP packet to the next hop without computing the entire path to the destination, all of the machines, and especially all of the routers, must have a consistent view of how to get to each destination. In other words, it is essential that their routing tables be synchronized with each other. To understand why, consider what happens if router A and router B both believe that the other is the correct next hop toward the destination 10.0.0.1. When router A receives a packet destined for 10.0.0.1, it will forward it to router B. Router B will consult its routing table and determine that the next hop is router A, and forward it there. The result is known as a *routing loop*, and may involve more than just two routers.

Routing tables may be kept synchronized by different methods. The simplest to understand and implement is *static* routing. In static routing, each router is manually configured with a list of destinations, and the next hop to reach those destinations, by a configuration file stored on stable storage. Making sure that all the routing tables are consistent is left to the network administrator. It is up to the administrator to make sure that no routing loops appear, and that all destinations are reachable from all routers.

The simplicity of static routing is appealing for a small number of destinations, or for *stub* networks that have only one or two paths to the rest of the network, but it is not without its drawbacks. Chief among these drawbacks is that static routing can't adapt to failures in the network or take advantage of alternate paths through the network to a destination. Additionally, when the number of destinations and routers grows beyond a small number, updating the routing tables when the network topology changes becomes prohibitively difficult and time consuming.

A more flexible solution uses a routing protocol that allows the routers to compute their routing tables dynamically, based on information provided by the other routers in the network. Many such routing protocols have been designed and implemented, and I will talk about a few of them in later chapters. In general, the routers speak a protocol that communicates information about the current functional topology of the network. From this information, the router computes one or more next hop routes for each destination, trying to produce a path to the destination that is as close to optimal as possible. If nothing interferes with the flow of routing information between the routers, and if they all implement the protocol correctly, they will all compute routing tables that are consistent with each other.

Between the extremes of static routing and dynamic routing, there is a continuum of routing schemes that are part dynamic and part static. These hybrid schemes strike a balance between the flexibility of dynamic routing and the simplicity of static routing. For example, while it is typical for the routers in a network to use dynamic routing among themselves, the hosts on the individual networks may be configured with a static default route. It is also possible to configure a router to have a few static routes, perhaps to destinations outside of the direct control of the network administrator, and to then *advertise* those routes to the other routers using a dynamic routing protocol. Regardless of the exact scheme chosen, dynamic routing is typically confined to the machines under the direct control of the network administrator, and perhaps a few carefully controlled exchanges with neighboring network administrations, with the bulk of the machines using static routes. My rule of thumb is:

- Use static routing where you *can.*

- Use dynamic routing where you *must.*

Domain Names and the Domain Name System

So far, I have talked exclusively about IP addresses. Addresses are fine for computers, being compact and numeric, but they are difficult for humans to work with and remember. Most people can remember perhaps a few dozen distinct numbers. However, people work well with names, and can remember hundreds of names without difficulty. For this reason, machines in an IP network are given names; these names map to IP addresses.

The Structure of the Domain Name System

Originally, machine names were taken from a flat name space, since there were at most a few hundred machines to name. The master list of names was maintained by a central registry in a file. However, as the Internet grew, it became impossible for the central registry to keep up with adding, changing, and deleting names. Further, it became difficult to select a unique name for a new machine. For these reasons, the Internet engineers designed a new hierarchical name space called the *Domain Name System (DNS)*. The DNS was capable of delegating authority for a portion of the name space to any group, who could then delegate a sub-portion to another group.

In the DNS, all names are composed of a set of words, known officially as *labels*, separated by dots. Any number of labels may be used to form the name of a specific host; in practice, most organizations use between three and six. These labels form a group of trees, with the rightmost label identifying the root of a tree, and each label to the left identifying a branch at a lower layer in the tree. Figure 1-7 shows several *domain names* and the resulting tree structures.

Notice that the label fribitz appears three times, twice at different places in the bar tree, and once in the baz tree. This demonstrates how the DNS provides a solution to the name collision problem. An individual label only needs to be unique among the labels used at a given level of a sub-tree.

Authority for names in the DNS can be delegated to another organization at any branch of a tree, but does not have to be. For example, in Figure 1-8, we see that authority has been delegated from Organization 1 to Organization 2 at the doogle branch, but no delegation has occurred at the foo branch. Likewise, Organization 2 has delegated authority for the schnitzel branch to Organization 3, but has

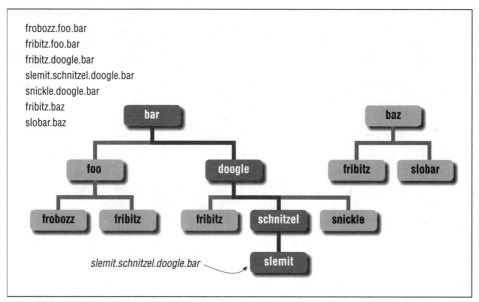

frobozz.foo.bar
fribitz.foo.bar
fribitz.doogle.bar
slemit.schnitzel.doogle.bar
snickle.doogle.bar
fribitz.baz
slobar.baz

Figure 1-7. Domain names form a set of trees

retained authority for the `fribitz` and `snickle` branches. Organization 4 has chosen not to delegate any authority. This ability to delegate authority over portions of the name space allows for greater scaling of the registration process. Rather than having a central authority that is responsible for all host names, authority is given to a local registry to handle the assignment of host names for an organization.

In Figure 1-8, the roots of the two trees are labeled `bar` and `baz`. These are known as top-level or *root* domains. Originally, there were six top-level domains, shown in Table 1-4.

Table 1-4. Original Internet Top-Level Domains

Domain	Meaning
com	commercial organizations
edu	educational organizations (universities)
gov	government (primarily US) organizations
mil	US military organizations
net	network infrastructure organizations
org	organizations, primarily non-profit, that did not fit any the above

However, as is the story with much of the Internet, this list did not scale well to a world-wide network, so the Internet engineers designated new top-level domains.

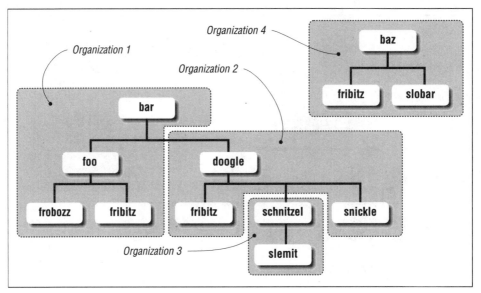

Figure 1-8. Authority may be delegated to another organization at any branch of tree

These domains were defined to be the ISO two-letter country codes as specified in ISO 3166. Most non-US users began to register their new domains and to reregister existing domains in these new country domains. Some countries even *require* their citizens to use them, thereby leaving the original six domains to be occupied primarily by US organizations, even though there is a US country domain.

In addition to these long-standing top-level domains, recent action in the Internet has resulted in the recommendation for the creation of a set of seven additional generic top-level domains (gTLD, in the literature). These names, and their intended purposes, are given in Table 1-5.

Table 1-5. Generic Top-Level Domains (Proposed)

Domain	Meaning
firm	businesses, or firms
store	businesses offering goods to purchase
web	entities emphasizing activities related to the World Wide Web
arts	entities emphasizing cultural and entertainment activities
rec	entities emphasizing recreation/entertainment activities
info	entities providing information services
nom	those wishing individual or personal nomenclature

At present, these new top-level domains have not been implemented. Registrars for these domains are being sought, and the final details of their governance are being ironed out. Those who are interested in learning the latest status of this process can do so on the World Wide Web at *http://www.iahc.org.*

Domain Name Servers

Unlike the original host table, the DNS does not use a static file located on each machine to *resolve* a name into an IP address. Instead, a set of machines on an IP network are designated as *name servers*. No one server has a complete copy of the domain database. Instead, each is authoritative for one or more domains. Typically, an organization designates one or more machines as the authoritative name servers for its domain, and possibly for other domains the organization has agreed to serve. These machines have complete information for the portion of the domain name system delegated to them, and a cache of information that they have recently resolved.

When asked a question about a name it is authoritative for, either by a program on the server machine or by a client machine, the name server answers directly. If it is asked about a name it is not authoritative for, it recursively searches for the information on other name servers and responds with the result of the search. It also puts a copy of the answer in its cache for a time period specified by the name server that gave it the information. Then, if some other program or machine asks about that name, and the information has not expired, the name server answers the question itself, without contacting any other name servers. This results in a significant reduction of traffic to remote name servers.

The ability of a name server to locate a requested name, and its willingness to answer questions about names for which it is not authoritative, means that not every machine needs to run the name server software. Most machines in an organization will be configured to act as a client to a name server running on another machine. For example, a group of workstations will usually be configured to use the name server running on their file server, rather than run a server themselves. The advantages of this configuration are that the workstations are easier to manage and can share the name server's cache.

In order to carry out recursive queries for non-local information, a name server must be configured with additional information. This additional information is a list of the *root* name servers, a small group of name servers that have been designated to carry the information for all top-level domains.

When a local name server is asked about a name for which it has no information, it asks one of the root servers for information about the name. The response from the root server is a list of authoritative servers for the top-level domain containing the name. The local server then asks one of these servers for information about the name, after caching the list of servers for future queries. The server queried may either have the information, in which case it answers, or it may have delegated the information to a subsidiary server, which it tells the local server about. It may also, if requested, ask the subsidiary server for the information requested and send back a response.

The ability of a name server to locate a server that has authority for a desired name, without being preconfigured to know about the structure of the remote name space, means that an organization can exercise nearly complete autonomy in decisions about what name structure to use, and how to delegate portions of this structure among a set of servers. Only the servers that are delegating authority to a subsidiary name server need to know about the delegation. This degree of autonomy and the transparency to the end user has led the DNS to be perhaps the world's largest and most successful distributed database.

Readers who are interested in the details of the DNS protocol and concepts should refer to RFC 1034 and RFC 1035, which are the defining documents of the system. Those who are interested in the maintenance and operation of a name server should refer to *DNS and Bind*, by Paul Albitz and Cricket Liu, available from O'Reilly & Associates.

Most network managers work in terms of network addresses, rather than names; router configurations should *always* be written in terms of addresses. Although names are much easier to memorize and work with in general, a router is often reading its configuration long before a DNS server is available, either because it has not yet been started, or because the router has not yet learned routes to the network containing the server. If you used names in your router configuration, the router might be unable to resolve these names into addresses, and would fail to boot correctly. There's also a good reason that network managers would rather work with numbers: if you have a network problem, there's a good chance that your routers won't be able to contact your name servers. If that's the case, the names aren't going to help you much; in fact, they'll get in your way. When dealing with routing, it's better to think like a router—that is, in terms of IP addresses, rather than names.

2

Network Design—
Part 1

This chapter begins our discussion of the issues surrounding the network design process. Topics covered include specifying networking goals, network architecture, media selection, and physical topology. The next chapter continues this discussion, beginning with the placement of routers in your network. Later chapters talk about equipment and routing protocol selection.

If you have an existing legacy network, no matter how extensive, you may well be asking why you should bother reading a chapter on network design. After all, you are not going to design a new network; you manage an existing network. While few network administrators are fortunate enough to design their networks starting with a blank sheet of paper, you should still go through the exercise of designing your ideal network. Designing your ideal network helps you to figure out what you really want to do, without worrying about the constraints imposed by any legacy network. Once you have your ideal network design in hand, you can go back and start adapting it to the realities of your legacy system and other constraints (such as time or money).

When you are done, you will have two designs in front of you. The first is your ideal network, and the second is reality. Both are important. Your reality-constrained network details what you must do to have a successful network. It clearly spells out the requirements placed on your network in a way that helps you make decisions. In fact, it may actually dictate what some of these decisions must be. Your ideal network design is important for another reason. It helps you keep your goals in mind without the clutter of reality. Therefore, it can help you make a decision that is not dictated by reality. For example, if you need to decide between options A and B, and option A supports your ideal network, but option B does not, then you would select A.

The difference between your two designs is also important. It helps you to identify the compromises you are making. For example, if your ideal network
supports only Token Ring to the desktop, but your reality requires Ethernet
support for a legacy LAN in a department, it becomes clear that you don't want to
add a new Ethernet in another department. Instead, you should work to eliminate
the legacy Ethernet.

Stating Your Goals—An Important First Step

The first part of any network design should be a statement of your goals. These
goals should address the following key elements:

- Functionality—what is the network supposed to do?

- Reliability—how well does it provide the functionality?

- Availability—where is the network accessible, and what percent of the time is
  it up?

- Flexibility—how easy is it to adapt the network to changing needs?

- Cost—how much does the network cost to build and maintain?

Cost includes both the initial investment, as well as the recurring costs. Both of
these cost components can further be broken down into hardware costs, software
costs, maintenance costs, and personnel costs. While it is not important to state
these individual costs as part of your goals, it is important that no one of them be
neglected.

For each of the above questions, there is no right or wrong answer. Rather than
being black and white, these criteria are all shades of gray. Additionally, they are
not completely independent of each other. Typically, by increasing your cost, you
can increase any or all of the others as much as you wish. For example, if you're
willing to spend more, you can build a network with more features, better reliability, and so on. However, it is also true that some of these criteria trade off
against each other. If you wish to increase the functionality of your network, say
by providing support for additional protocols, you may be doing so at the
expense of availability and reliability. Running a second or third protocol may
result in increased instability in your network, either because of software bugs or
because the increased complexity lends itself to more errors. You can, of course,
reestablish your availability and reliability goals by further increasing your costs,
perhaps by building completely separate routing structures for each protocol.
However, it isn't possible to achieve perfection in all of these categories, at least
not for a reasonable price.

Once you have stated the goals for your ideal network, including your overall design objective, you must modify them based on any legacy systems you must support. Typically, a legacy system forces you to increase or extend your design goals. For example, if you must support an existing non-IP protocol in your network, your design will require additional functionality. As I pointed out earlier, this may result in a decrease in your network's reliability and availability, unless you are willing to spend more money.

Now that you have adjusted your goals to account for legacy systems and constraints, you should have two high-level designs before you. The first is your ideal, and the second is reality. Remember, both are important. The first is your ultimate target, while the second represents operational reality. Keep both in mind as you are working on the rest of your design. If you ever find yourself with two or more choices that both achieve the goals of your real network, then rely on your ideal network design to break the tie. This way, when future changes remove one or more of the constraints that caused you to modify your ideal design, you are closer to achieving your ideal network.

Network Architecture—How It All Fits Together

Once your goals are known, you can consider the architecture of your network. A properly designed network consists of three major functional components:

- Core
- Distribution
- Access

The core is your backbone network interconnect system. In a LAN or campus network environment, it is typically high speed and high reliability, and has no users directly attached to it. In a WAN-based network, the core is usually composed of long-haul, high-speed links. This is your high-speed routing system, and so should have few demands placed on it other than routing decisions. Any problems in this part of your network will have an impact on all other parts.

The second component is your distribution system. Depending on the scope of your network, it may consist of building riser cables, inter-building links, or even short- or long-haul WAN links. The distribution system connects the access system, discussed below, with your core. In a LAN environment, the distribution system may be of any speed, depending on the media involved, but is typically some-where between your core and access systems in both speed and reliability. In a WAN environment, the distribution system would be the links from your various sites to your core.

Some support services may reside in this component, such as a *Network Time Protocol (NTP)* server, a DNS server, or other infrastructure support services. This is typically not the best place for user attachments, but may be a good place for a larger file server in a LAN. If a service is placed in this area, try to place it as close to the clients it serves as possible, thereby minimizing the impact of a failure of this service on others. Any problems in this part of your network can impact a major portion of your network, but the scope of these problems will be limited to those access systems directly attached to the problem component, and those who need to access those systems.

The third component is your access system. This is typically the most visible and most extensive component of your network. In a LAN or campus environment, this component includes your network hub equipment (Ethernet hubs, Token Ring concentrators, etc.), the cable from these hubs to the desktop, and possibly the interface cards in your client machines. It may also include building routers (though these are more often thought of as distribution components) or small-office access routers that connect to the corporate WAN. In a WAN environment, the access component is likely to include the LAN segments at each site, along with the hub equipment, dial-up IP servers and modem pools, and possibly small routers at each site. This is the component where you attach users' machines, work group file servers, database servers, etc. Any problems in this area are typically visible only to the work group affected.

As Figure 2-1 shows, the boundaries between these components may fall within a router, or possibly within a network segment. Consider Router1, Router2, and Router3. They straddle the line between the core and the distribution, providing services in each. Likewise, Router4, Router5, and Router6 are straddling the line between the distribution and access components. Depending on the size of your network, or on the operational constraints and goals you have set, some parts of your network will perform duties in two or more of these areas. Consider the network segment indicated connected to Router1 and Router4. It serves both distribution and access functions. When this happens, distribution functions have usually been moved to either the core or the access systems, or both. This is the case with the networks connected to Router2, which have no identifiable distribution component. While not a perfect situation, it is, nevertheless, often a necessity.

Media Selection—What Goes Where?

Ideally, you want to select one, or at most two, media to use in any single functional component. Each additional medium you support requires additional equipment and trained personnel, and limits the flexibility of your network, or increases your costs significantly. To understand why, consider what happens if you need to move a machine from one place in your network to another, perhaps

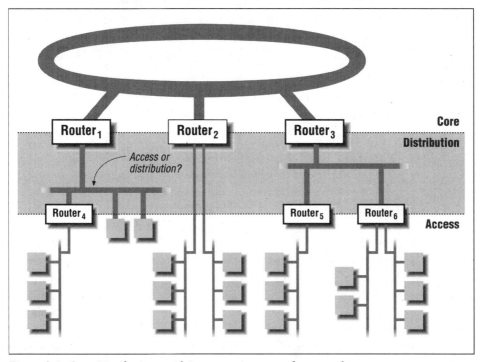

Figure 2-1. Core, Distribution, and Access components of a network

because of an office change. If your access component consists of a single supported medium, the move is easy; you may only need to change the machine's IP address. However, if you have two or more media, you have to worry about whether the machine's current access medium is available in the new location. If it isn't, you have to change the machine's hardware interface to match the medium available at its new location. The alternative is to provide access to all supported media at all locations—at a substantially increased cost.

Of course, as is always the case in network design, the presence of legacy systems may alter your plans. If you have both Token Ring and Ethernet in your legacy systems, then you will have no choice but to support both. However, in these cases, try to choose one as your *preferred* medium, and plan all new installations around this preference, with the goal of retiring the non-preferred medium as your legacy systems retire.

Types of Network Media

You should not, however, feel constrained to select a single medium for all components of your network. This limits your ability to provide robust services to your network users. Consider what happens if your core network is provided by the same medium as your access networks. When the access networks grow to sufficient size, the core network becomes a bottleneck to performance. Clearly this is not desirable. Give serious thought to how each type of medium best fits the requirements of each network component.

But before we talk about which media should be considered for each job, let's review some of the characteristics of the most common networking media available at the time of this writing.

Network media have traditionally been divided into two classes: *Wide Area Networking (WAN)* and *Local Area Networking (LAN)*. While there are no hard rules about what belongs in each group, or even which group might be appropriate for a given task, the general rule of thumb is that WAN media are typically point-to-point oriented, slower speed, and capable of spanning greater distance, while LAN media are typically multi-access, higher speed, and limited to short distance. WAN media are typically selected when you are trying to connect two groups together across longer distances, such as across a city, state, or country, or even across the oceans. LAN media, on the other hand, are typically used to interconnect a group of machines in a single department or building, or possibly on a single campus. Whether LAN or WAN media are selected for connecting buildings on a single campus is often decided by whether the organization can provide its own cable between the buildings or not. If the only possible data path between a set of buildings is that provided by the telephone company, then usually the only choice is to go with WAN media.

Media for Local Area Networks

As I said above, LAN media are typically high speed, and assume that the network spans a relatively small area. Here are the most common media you'll be dealing with:

Ethernet

Perhaps the most common LAN medium is the *Ethernet*. In its traditional form, it is a 10 Megabits per second (Mbps), shared-access network that may be run on either coaxial cable (one of two varieties) or unshielded twisted pairs of copper wire.* Its primary advantages are that it is widely available, inexpensive, and very flexible—to add a new connection, you need only connect a cable between the workstation and the coaxial cable or twisted-pair hub. Its chief disadvantages are that two fast machines can monopolize the

---

* Except for FDDI, we usually think of LAN technologies in terms of traditional electrical cabling ("copper"). However, all the media described in this section have specified methods for transmission over fiber optic cables, usually at increased distances, allowing them to be used between buildings in a campus environment. In fact, use of copper connections between buildings should be discouraged due to their tendency to get struck by lightning.

network while communicating with each other, and it is difficult to provide security because any single machine can monitor all traffic on a segment.

Switched Ethernet

A variant of the traditional Ethernet that is gaining in popularity is *Switched Ethernet*. Switched Ethernet provides a dedicated 10 Mbps connection to each machine, or to a small group of machines. The latter case is called *micro-segmentation* and helps to mitigate the chief disadvantage of switched Ethernet—its cost. Switched Ethernet's advantages include all of the advantages of the traditional shared Ethernet, and increases the available network bandwidth to each machine on the network. Because it uses traditional twisted pair copper as its physical medium and standard Ethernet signaling and cables, it is possible to replace a shared Ethernet hub with an Ethernet switch without having to change the cable or the computer interfaces. Further, because it limits the traffic visible to any single computer, it provides increased security to data on the network.

Fast Ethernet

Competing with FDDI and CDDI for the high-speed LAN market is a newer LAN technology that has probably already surpassed in deployed base, even though it is many years younger. This technology is *Fast Ethernet*. This is simply the traditional 10 Mbps Ethernet running at 100 Mbps. All the frame formats and media access protocols are the same as for 10 Mbps Ethernet, and, like 10 Mbps Ethernet, Fast Ethernet may be either shared or switched. In fact, when switched, it may be seamlessly joined with 10 Mbps Ethernet. The changes in Fast Ethernet occur in the network adapter card, the cabling, and the hub or switch. All of these components must be capable of supporting the faster communications speeds of Fast Ethernet.

Fast Ethernet is popular in part because its 10 Mbps counterpart is well understood, and there isn't much difference between it and Fast Ethernet. However, where the differences do occur is important. Because Fast Ethernet runs at a higher speed, it is much less tolerant of violations of its cabling standards than Ethernet is. Individual copper cable runs must be limited to 100 meters total, as is specified for Ethernet, but additionally, there may be only two class II repeaters between devices in a Fast Ethernet network, and those repeaters may be separated by a distance no greater than 5 meters. This means that the maximum length between any pair of devices in a Fast Ethernet network is only 205 meters. Compare this to 10 Mbps Ethernet where each cable may be 100 meters, and up to four repeaters are permitted for a total length of 500 meters between any pair of stations.

This is not the only disadvantage that Fast Ethernet has. There are several incompatible types of Fast Ethernet on the market. The most common, and the one that looks as if it will become the final standard, is called 100BaseTX. There are also a 100BaseT4 and a 100 VG AnyLAN. While these other standards work well, they are simply not achieving the same level of deployment, and are probably not going to become major networking technologies.

Gigabit Ethernet

Finally, research is currently proceeding toward a formal standard for Gigabit Ethernet. While the exact form this technology will take has not been pinned down yet, it is expected to use the same kind of framing as Ethernet and Fast Ethernet, but it is not clear what the maximum cable lengths will be, or whether a shared version will be specified. Keep your eye on this technology. Over the next few years, it may well explode into popular use.

Token Ring

After Ethernet in its various forms, the next most common LAN medium is the *Token Ring*. While called a ring, in practice the stations in a Token Ring network are connected at one end of a spoke, with the other end connected to a device called a *MAU (medium access unit)*. Then, the MAUs are connected to each other to form a pair of rings. The primary ring is used for communications, and the secondary ring is there for redundancy. This dual-ring structure is one of Token Ring's greatest strengths—if the primary ring should fail, perhaps because of a cable break or because of failing electronics, the second ring can be used as a built-in redundant path automatically.

The second major strength of Token Ring is its resistance to being monopolized by a pair of fast machines. Because of the token-passing design, every machine on the Token Ring that wishes to transmit is guaranteed a fair share of the available network bandwidth, traditionally 4 Mbps, but 16 Mbps is becoming increasingly common.

Token Ring is not without its disadvantages, however. Its chief disadvantage is its limited availability. While many machines on the market come with an Ethernet interface, or one can be readily purchased, Token Ring interfaces are not as widely available, and when they are, they are often more expensive than an equivalent Ethernet interface. They only really seem to have caught on for PCs and for IBM mainframe equipment. Still, you should not rule out support for the Token Ring, especially if interfaces are available for all the machines you must connect.

FDDI

Another LAN medium you should be aware of and consider is *FDDI*, which stands for *Fiber Distributed Data Interconnect*. This high-speed LAN technology is based on the dual-ring topology of the Token Ring, but operates at

100 Mbps over fiber optic cables. While termed a LAN medium, it is possible to build an FDDI ring that spans several kilometers.

Traditionally, FDDI is thought of solely as a core technology, primarily because of the limited availability of interfaces and the expense of both the interfaces and the fiber optic cables. However, these constraints are changing rapidly. It is now estimated that fiber optic cable costs little more per installed foot than high-quality twisted copper, and interfaces are becoming more widely available and cheaper. When you add to this the development and availability of *CDDI (Copper Distributed Data Interconnect)*, or FDDI over copper, FDDI becomes a viable option for any component of your network, from the core to the distribution, and even to the desktop.

Media for Wide Area Networks

WAN media tend to be more similar to each other than LAN media, and also less familiar. In general, they may be broken into two broad categories, based on the duration of an individual connection. WAN media may be dial-on-demand connections, where a connection is brought into existence, data is transmitted, and the connection is terminated, or they may be permanent, dedicated connections that always exist, whether data is present or not.

The greatest advantage to a dial-on-demand connection is cost. Because the connection only exists for as long as there is data to be transmitted, costs can be less than for an equivalent sized permanent connection. Additionally, it is possible for multiple destinations to be dialed as needed, with only a single network attachment, which calls each in turn, as needed.

There are disadvantages as well. Because there is not a connection present all the time, the initial data is delayed, however slightly, while a connection is established. Further, if multiple dialed connections share a single network attachment, it may be that the connection is already busy, either on the local end or the remote end, and communication is not possible until the previous exchange concludes. Still, for network traffic patterns that are transitory in nature, a dial-on-demand connection may be a reasonable trade-off between cost and availability.

Analog Modem

So what kinds of dial-on-demand connections are common? The most common dial-on-demand connection, and probably the most common WAN connection in use today, is an analog modem. While primarily useful as an access technology, simplicity and cost make it attractive for any low-volume connections. All that is required is a serial port, a modem, a voice telephone line at each end, and software that knows how to establish the connection and when to tear it down.

A dialed connection by itself isn't sufficient to carry data; you also need a framing protocol. Two framing protocols are in common use. The older of these is *SLIP (Serial Line IP)*. SLIP has the advantage of simplicity, but it can only pass IP traffic across the line, and has little error detection or recovery capability. The second is *PPP (Point to Point Protocol)*. PPP is more complex, but can handle non-IP traffic, dial-back security, encryption, error detection, and other features. It is also the protocol most often implemented in networking equipment such as routers. If you have a choice, use PPP. Legacy networks may force you to use SLIP.

Using an analog modem has two big drawbacks. A voice line is tied up during the call, and a modem can't provide the speed you get with other technologies. Tying up a phone line may be important when the site is a home office with a single voice telephone line. While the data connection is in place, customers or co-workers trying to call will get a busy signal. As for speed, current technology for analog modems is limited to 56 kbps, and while this may not be the highest capacity, there will ultimately come a limit beyond which the analog phone circuits simply cannot carry more data. Furthermore, you only achieve 56 kbps if the quality of the voice connection is extremely good.

ISDN

The solution to the problems of analog modems is a technology that has been around for several years, but is just now becoming popular. *Integrated Services Digital Network (ISDN)* is a digital transmission scheme developed by the phone companies in an effort to create a network capable of handling voice, data, video, and other services, all at a reasonable price, and using the existing copper subscriber lines. As with analog modems, an ISDN device establishes a connection to another ISDN device by placing a call, which may be answered or rejected (busy). However, unlike analog modems, transmission speeds are higher (64 kbps per "call"), and the phone line is not monopolized during the data exchange—other calls are still possible concurrently. These additional calls may be to the same destination, to increase bandwidth, or to different destinations. There may even be a mix of voice and data calls simultaneously on the same line.

How many simultaneous calls may be placed depends on the type of service, of which there are two. A *Basic Rate Interface (BRI)* provides two B channels, which can each carry a voice call or a data call, and a single D channel used for control and signaling. By combining the two B channels, a total of 128 kbps of data exchange can occur between two sites. Alternatively, two separate 64 kbps calls can be placed to two different sites. Further, it is possible for a voice call to be accepted while a two-channel data call is in progress, by dropping one channel out of the data stream to accept the voice call. This reduces the number of busy signals that a customer or co-worker will get.

The second type of ISDN service is called *Primary Rate Interface (PRI)*. PRI provides 23 B channels for data and one D channel for control and signaling in North America, or 30 B channels and one D channel elsewhere. Again, each B channel may be used independently for data or voice calls, or multiple B channels may be aggregated into one higher bandwidth data connection by placing multiple calls to the same destination. Typically, BRI service is used at a branch office, or in a home office, where the data needs are limited, and PRI service is used at a central site to receive remote office calls. However, there is no requirement that it be used this way. Two smaller sites might each subscribe to a BRI service to call each other, or two larger sites might use PRI services to have on-demand bandwidth to each other.

To connect to an ISDN service, you need an ISDN *Terminal Adapter (TA)*, often incorrectly called an ISDN "modem." The TA may take the form of a card plugged into a PC, or a separate device with a LAN attachment that either routes or bridges network traffic. In either case, it may also provide a place to plug in ordinary telephones, FAX machines, or analog modems for access to voice services. Providing network services over ISDN requires a framing protocol; PPP is almost always used.

ISDN service is probably most appropriate for access from a home office to the corporate or university LAN, or between a branch office and the main office, especially when data transmission needs are transitory. It handles moderate amounts of data well, and has the advantage that you only have to pay for the actual use.

Leased Lines

The other type of WAN connections mentioned above were permanent, dedicated lines. In their simplest form, these take the form of lines leased from the telephone company between two sites that wish to exchange data. At each end of the line is a modem-like device called a *DSU/CSU (Data Service Unit/Control Service Unit)*. It is best to buy the DSU/CSUs at each end of the line from the same vendor to ensure interoperability. The DSU takes data (usually synchronous) from a router, bridge, or computer and transmits it across the leased line to its partner, which decodes the data and gives it to its attached device.

On top of this data path, the devices again use a framing protocol, just as they do for the analog modems and ISDN services. Typical protocols used include PPP (described above) or *High-level Data Link Control (HDLC)*. Each has some minor advantages over the other, which we will not explore here. Which you use depends on which your network devices support. PPP is generally supported by all major router vendors, so is a good choice for interoperability. HDLC is slightly more efficient in its use of the available bandwidth, but not all vendors implement it.

Because leased lines use a digital signaling scheme, they are capable of much greater speeds than analog modems, and because they use high-quality copper or fiber optic media, they generally also beat ISDN service. A wide range of speeds are available, but the most common speeds are *Digital Signaling 0 (DS-0)*, or 56 kbps; *DS-1* (also called T-1), running at 1.544 Mbps; and *DS-3* (often mistakenly called T-3), running at 44.736 Mbps. It is also common to order *fractional* T-1 or T-3 service, when one of the above speeds is not a good fit to your needs.

Leased point-to-point lines have two distinct disadvantages, however. The first of these is cost. Typically you have times when data is not flowing between the sites, or is flowing at less than full capacity, but there is no credit for this time. You pay the same as when the line is running at full capacity. However, if data is flowing most of the time, you might well find that your dial-on-demand service is always connected, and the cost of that may well be greater than the permanent line.

The second disadvantage is scalability. Because each leased line is dedicated to a single remote site, to support multiple connections requires multiple router ports, multiple DSUs, and multiple leased lines, all of which cost money. At a central site this may result in dozens or even hundreds of ports, DSUs, and lines, many of which will be idle for some amount of time. For this reason, point-to-point leased lines are generally best used when the number of remote sites is relatively low, or bandwidth needs to the sites are consistently high. In other cases, one of the technologies discussed next may be a better fit.

Frame Relay

If we could combine the ability of a dial-on-demand service to handle multiple connections with a single physical line, with the permanent availability of a leased line, we could alleviate both the scalability problem that point-to-point lines exhibit, as well as make better use of the line, since it is unlikely for all the connections sharing the line to be idle at the same time. One WAN technology that does just this is *Frame Relay*.

In Frame Relay, a subscriber site leases a permanent dedicated line, just as if it were a point-to-point line, except that the remote end terminates at a Frame Relay switch, often located in a telephone central office (CO). Then, by means of manual provisioning, logical connections are established to one or more remote Frame Relay subscriber sites. These logical connections, called *virtual circuits*, all share the same physical port on the router or bridge, the same DSU, and the same leased line. The software on the router or bridge then uses these virtual circuits just like real point-to-point circuits to transmit traffic to one or more destinations, which may be arranged in any number of topologies including stars, partial meshes, and full meshes, all of which will be described later.

Frame Relay often has a significant cost advantage over a leased line. The cost of a leased line is usually proportional to its length. The cost of Frame Relay service usually depends on the bandwidth you require, and not on the physical length of the connection.

The speed of a Frame Relay service is simply the speed of the underlying leased line, and does not have to be identical at all subscriber sites. A central site might provision a DS-3 circuit, with several branch offices using DS-1 or DS-0 circuits, depending on their needs. This gives Frame Relay an additional advantage over point-to-point lines, and makes it excellently suited for connecting branch offices of various sizes to a central site, or joining two or more peer sites together with a minimum of equipment required at each.

SMDS

Another technology that uses a single leased line from a subscriber site to a central location is *Switched Multi-megabit Data Service (SMDS)*. Like Frame Relay, SMDS circuits terminate at a switch usually operated by the telephone company, though it could be privately operated. Unlike Frame Relay, SMDS is not a circuit switching technology. No virtual circuits are created to connect destinations to each other. Instead of using virtual circuits, SMDS is a *datagram switching* technology. Like other datagram switching technologies, including IP, each frame contains a source and a destination address. In essence, an SMDS network becomes very much like a wide-area Ethernet. Any device may communicate with any other device by addressing a frame to it, unless prohibited by administrative control.

One of the goals of SMDS was to provide a high-speed data communications path for distributed processing. In support of that goal, SMDS defines access speeds of DS-1 and DS-3, with several different access classes available on the DS-3 service that correspond to 4, 10, 16, 25, and 34 Mbps. As in Frame Relay, different subscriber sites may use different access speeds to access the network, allowing for smaller lines to branch offices, and larger lines to a central site. This, combined with the lack of manually configured virtual circuits makes SMDS an attractive alternative for peer-to-peer or branch office to central site communications.

In the end, the difference in the customer equipment to use point-to-point lines, Frame Relay, or SMDS largely becomes one of quantity and software. The underlying physical connections are the same: a suitably fast port on a router or bridge, a DSU, and a leased circuit. The real differences are in the software that is running on the device, and what is on the other end of the line. Which is best for your network will partly depend on the number of connections you need to make, the tariffs applied by the carriers in your area, and the services available.

Asynchronous Transfer Mode (ATM)

Some readers will see that *Asynchronous Transfer Mode (ATM)* has a section of its own and say, "Looks like we have an ATM bigot." In truth, while I run ATM in my network, I am by no means an ATM bigot. Instead, ATM is being treated separately from the LAN and WAN technologies because it is both.

Developed originally by the telephone companies as a high-speed network technology for transmitting voice, ATM has been adapted by the data networking community to be a very high-speed networking technology (anywhere from 25 Mbps up to gigabits per second). It also offers the ability to unify an organization's voice, video, and data networks, traditionally three independent entities, into a single unit capable of providing for the specific needs of each type of traffic. But this is not its only strength. In addition to unifying voice, video, and data transmissions, ATM can seamlessly join the LAN and the WAN in ways never before possible.

Joining the LAN and WAN is accomplished by establishing a link between a local ATM switch, normally operated by an organization's networking staff, and a remote switch operated by another organization, such as the telephone company. Devices then attach to the local switch (or multiple interconnected switches), and communicate using the same protocols, methods, and physical connection. They do not need to know whether the device they are communicating with is attached to the local switch or some remote switch.

Like Frame Relay, ATM uses virtual circuits to establish these connections with other devices. Unlike Frame Relay, these circuits may either be manually established, as they often are in wide-area ATM, or created and removed on demand, as is often the case in local-area ATM. Also like Frame Relay, the links in an ATM network don't need to be the same speed. Local links might be a mix of speeds from 100 to 622 Mbps, while WAN links might be a mix of DS-1, DS-3, or 155 Mbps links.

The final advantage that ATM's proponents tout is its ability to provide quality of service guarantees. Most traditional networking technologies consider all data equal in priority. All data is handled on a first-come, first-served basis, and congestion of links is possible. With ATM, devices tell the network what kind of service they expect for each connection, and agree to keep their traffic within a set of bounds agreed to between the device and the network. This allows the network to avoid situations where links are oversubscribed, and also to selectively discard data when congestion does occur by identifying either lower-priority traffic, or traffic that has exceeded the agreed to contract. This means that a video stream, that might not tolerate loss or delay would get priority over a voice stream that might tolerate a little loss or delay and still be intelligible, and both would get priority over data that can be easily retransmitted by higher-level protocols, like email.

Unfortunately, as its detractors will quickly point out, ATM is a very complex system of cables and switches, with some standards that are only a few years old, and others still to be written. Given the newness of these standards, and the complexity of managing an ATM network, they will claim that ATM is not yet ready for prime time. Whether you agree or not, you should definitely familiarize yourself with this emerging technology, even if only in the lab or in a limited test network. You may find that it is ready for your network (or, perhaps your network is ready for it). If not, at least when the standards mature and products become more interoperable over the next couple of years, you will be ahead of the game.

Traffic Patterns

When selecting which media to use in each component of your network, the two most important things to keep in mind are the primary function of each of your network components, and what traffic patterns you have or expect to have in your network. You want to ensure that your most heavily used links are capable of handling the traffic presented to them.

For many years, there has been a rule of thumb in the network community about how much of a network's traffic stays local, and how much goes remote. This rule is variously presented as the 80/20 rule, the 70/30 rule, or even the 90/10 rule. The numbers in the rule are intended to express the ratio of local traffic to remote traffic. The exact numbers chosen don't really matter. Instead, this rule says that in any well-designed network (or subnetwork), the majority of the traffic should remain local. This means that it is not a good idea to locate all of your clients on one network, and place their file server on another network. Since the clients probably won't talk to each other as much as they talk to the file server, most of your traffic in this design will be remote. In a LAN environment, this may not be critical, but it can be a killer in a WAN environment where links are generally slower and more expensive.

So this means that you should concentrate all of your high-speed links in the access and distribution components, right? After all, this is where your clients (and presumably their servers) are located. Not really. While it is true that the majority of your network traffic should remain local to a network segment, your network core must handle the aggregate of all of the non-local traffic from the access networks. For example, assuming that your network with 10 Ethernets exhibits an

80/20 distribution of traffic, when you take that 20 percent from all 10 Ethernets and send it through your Ethernet core, you present it with 200 percent of the traffic you'd expect to see on any of the access networks. Clearly your core will be congested.

While it is not always possible to analyze your traffic patterns to determine exactly what traffic you are presenting to your distribution and core network components, a good guideline to follow is to ensure that at each layer of the network, the technology chosen for that layer is at least as fast as the technology used in the next lower component. This means that if your access networks are all Fast Ethernet, using shared Ethernet for your distribution component is likely to be a problem, even if you achieve a 95/5 traffic distribution in your network. Instead, you should be using a 100 Mbps technology, such as Fast Ethernet or FDDI, or some faster technology in your distribution and core.

Keep in mind, however, that it is almost always the case that the aggregate bandwidth in one layer will often exceed that of the next higher layer, even if the individual link speeds are slower. Take, for example, a network with 40 shared Ethernet segments in the access component. If the distribution component is composed of two routers connected by a 100 Mbps Fast Ethernet, each supporting 20 of these Ethernets, the aggregate bandwidth of the access, 400 Mbps, easily exceeds that of the distribution with only 100 Mbps. However, if this network exhibits even a 70/30 traffic pattern, the distribution component should be adequate for the load.

Examples of Media Selection

In this section, we will present a few networks and identify the network media used for each component of the network. Because our media selection depends partly on which component of the network we are looking at, it is important that we understand as well as possible where the components are—keeping in mind that not all networks have clearly defined lines between the various components. A small business might have three access segments connected to a router, with a dial-up line to the Internet. For example, in Figure 2-2, the core of the network consists of the router itself. The distribution component is also contained in the router, while the access component would be the network segments, station adapters, and the dial-up line to the Internet. For this kind of network, the access component can be whatever is most convenient—the router should easily keep up with the traffic from the access networks.

On the other hand, a large university with one campus might have hundreds of access networks, with routers located in various buildings on the campus. The distribution component in this network connects these routers to the routers in a central data processing center. The routers in the data processing center and the

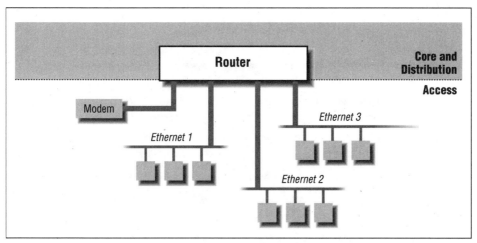

Figure 2-2. A small network with no distinguishable distribution component

network segment interconnecting them form the core, as shown in Figure 2-3. In this network, it's easy to identify the three components.

If we assume that the access networks are shared Ethernets (a common choice), then the distribution component might be shared or switched Ethernet, or a combination of the two. As long as traffic patterns adhere to some version of the 80/20 rule, our distribution should be adequate. The core interconnect of this network, though, should certainly have more capacity than a switched Ethernet. If you think about the aggregate traffic from the distribution networks, even with a 90/10 traffic pattern, the core is likely to be overwhelmed in short order. Instead, it should be something like the FDDI ring shown.

Look again at the technologies chosen for each of the components. The core is at least as fast as the distribution component, which is at least as fast as the access networks. However, each can be changed independently of the others, which is one of the strengths of a layered design. If the FDDI network should prove to be a performance problem, it can be upgraded to an ATM network without changing the other two components. Likewise, if the access networks receive an upgrade to switched Ethernet, neither the core nor the distribution must change. However, if you decided to take the access networks to FDDI, or to Fast Ethernet, you would want to give serious thought to upgrading the distribution networks so they are at least as fast as the access networks. Fortunately, you can upgrade parts of the distribution system to support its attached access networks without having to change it all.

For our next two examples, we'll look at what to do with WAN links connecting various parts of a large, multi-campus corporate or university network. As our first

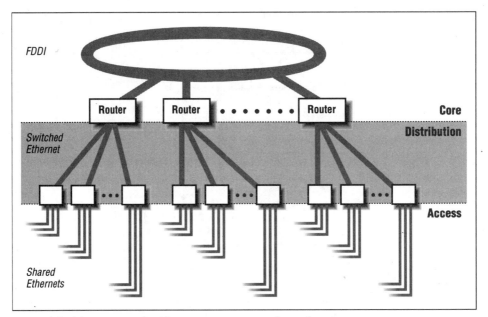

Figure 2-3. A large network with many access networks and routers

example, we consider a network with a main data processing center at a central site and satellite locations connected to the main site with WAN links. This network is shown in Figure 2-4. Let's assume that the central campus network is the same network we discussed above, with clearly definable components. Let's also assume that the satellite locations range from a single-access network to perhaps four or five networks with a router to connect them together and to the enterprise WAN. How do these satellite networks fit into our three-component structure?

The access networks at the remote sites clearly fit into the access component; it also seems clear that there are no core components at the remote sites. The question becomes whether we consider the WAN links and remote routers to be part of the access component, or the distribution component. There is no clear answer. I prefer to think of these WAN links and remote routers as part of the access component, though you can easily make the case that they are part of the distribution component. The important fact is that each of the branch networks needs to be more or less self-sufficient. In other words, make sure the remote offices have their own file servers, print servers, and other network services, and it won't matter much that the WAN link is slower than the access networks. In this case, the WAN links may be analog modems, ISDN, even low-speed permanent links of one of the other WAN technologies. It all depends on the volume of traffic between the various sites.

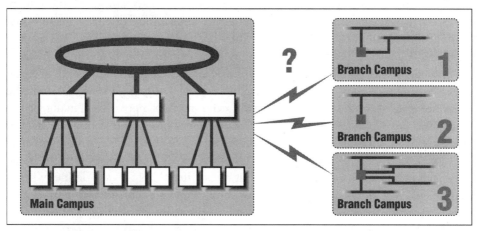

Figure 2-4. A main campus with satellites

For our second multi-campus network, let's consider the network shown in Figure 2-5. In this network, we have two or more large campuses, each with their own network structures in place, and interconnected by one or more WAN links. Clearly, it doesn't make sense to relegate the entirety of any one campus to the access component of our combined network. In fact, it makes a lot of sense to treat each campus network as an independent network, each with its own core, distribution, and access components. In our example, the core of the network on campus A is a small ATM network connecting routers in its main data center, while that for the network on campus B could be a large, multi-building complex of routers and FDDI interconnects.

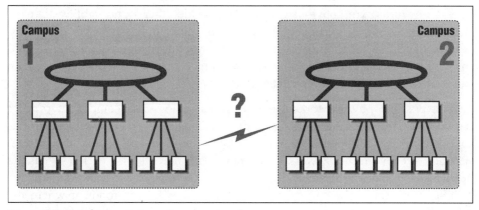

Figure 2-5. Two large campuses in one network

Structured this way, the WAN links connecting the campuses could fit into the access components of both campus networks, the distribution component of both campus networks, the core component, or they can simply be thought of as external to the campus networks. Which is appropriate depends on how the campuses interact with each other. If they are governed centrally, with a great deal of cooperation between the campus data centers, the WAN links are best thought of as part of the core or distribution components of the network. On the other hand, if they are largely autonomous, with separate network staff, the links are probably considered external to the campus networks. Finally, if the campuses have independent network staffs, but one of the campuses has an oversight role, thinking of the WAN links as part of the access component may be most appropriate. In any of these cases, the WAN links function in the same way, but deciding how to think about these links helps you define who is responsible for their operation and whether they are considered part of the local network environment, or are outside, especially for security concerns. As for which WAN technology to use, a dial-on-demand service is probably not going to be cost effective, since there is probably a near-continuous stream of data flowing between the campuses, but any of the permanent links will do, with speed being the main question.

Physical Topology

Once you have selected which media to use for the components of your network, you need to consider the physical topology of your network. While your network's logical topology is part of the definition of your chosen technology, and much of your physical topology will be influenced, if not dictated, by the media you have chosen to support, you still have a fair amount of leeway in how you build your network. For example, if you use FDDI in your access networks, you obviously have to provide fiber optic cabling to each network host. But do you really need to string fiber optics between each adjacent pair of hosts, or should you use a star-shaped topology with a hub located in a wiring closet? Likewise, how do you structure the interconnects between the routers and switches in your network?

Several possible physical topologies are available for each component of your network. Among these, the simplest conceptually is point-to-point cabling. In this topology, shown in Figure 2-6, you simply extend a cable from the nearest machine already on the network to the new machine you wish to add. It has the advantages of being extremely flexible and requiring little advanced planning. Point-to-point cabling is particularly common in a WAN environment where the cost of a leased line often depends on the distance. However, point-to-point cabling becomes rather chaotic after just a few additions. Eventually, it becomes nearly impossible to isolate the effects of a change in the network to a small, predictable set of machines, because the interdependencies are extensive.

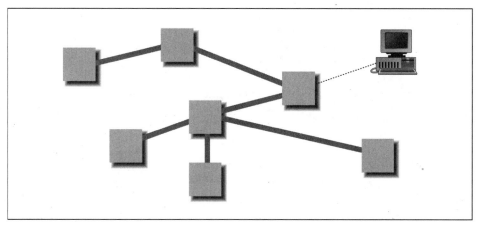

Figure 2-6. Adding a machine to a point-to-point network

A mesh topology gives a more ordered approach. In a mesh, links are established between each new machine and a number of existing machines in the network. At one extreme, you can establish a single link to each new machine, in which case you end up with a point-to-point network. At the other extreme, you can establish a link between every pair of machines in the network, resulting in a full mesh. A more likely choice, somewhere between these two extremes, is a partial mesh. In Figure 2-7, we have decided to establish between three and six links to each node in the network. Initially, when adding a new node, we establish just the minimal three links; these links would connect the new machine to some other node that doesn't yet have six links. As other nodes are added, some of them would connect to this node until it has six links. This approach is extremely flexible; it is also reliable because it is highly redundant, with many paths between any two nodes. However, a disadvantage is the cost of all of these redundant links. If taken to an extreme, a mesh also scales poorly. In a full mesh, each node must have connections to every other node. For a network of 4 nodes, this is not too bad—you have a total of six links to maintain. But with 10 nodes, you're responsible for 45 links; with 100, the number of links jumps to over 4,000! Still, for the core of a network, a mesh may not be unmanageable.

A third topology, shown in Figure 2-8, is a ring. Keep in mind that we are talking about physical topologies, and specifically about cable routing. In a ring topology, each node is connected to exactly two other nodes—the two nodes to either side of it. When a new node is to be added to the network, the link between two adjacent nodes is broken, and new links between the new node and each of these adjacent nodes are established. This structure has the flexibility of the point-to-point network, while supplying structure and manageability to the network. Its

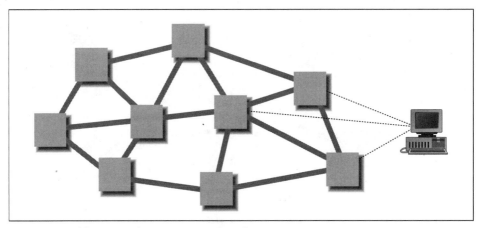

Figure 2-7. Adding a machine to a partial mesh

chief disadvantage lies in identifying which two nodes the new node belongs between, especially if no nodes are near the new node. However, it is a natural choice for ring-based networks such as Token Ring or FDDI, especially when the number of nodes involved is small and the nodes are close to each other.

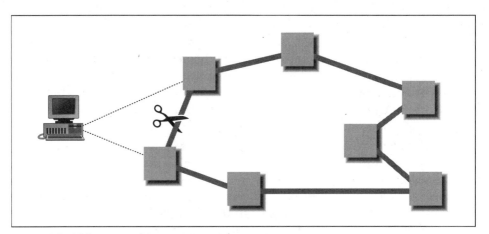

Figure 2-8. Adding a machine to a ring

The fourth physical topology, and one that is seldom seen today, is a bus topology, shown in Figure 2-9. In this topology, each host has exactly two neighbors, except the hosts at the ends of the bus, which have only one neighbor. While almost never seen in WAN environments, the bus is the natural topology for coaxial-based Ethernet networks, though as Ethernet has been replaced by twisted pair media, the bus topology has given way to the star topology discussed next. The biggest drawback to a bus topology is when a node must be added. If the node is to be added to one end or the other, it is simple to extend a cable from the new node to the end of the bus. However, if the new node is not near the end, the bus must be broken between two nearby nodes, and new cable extended from each to the new node. This is highly disruptive to the network and lends itself to sloppy maintenance practices, since it is tedious to remove a machine's connection when it is no longer needed.

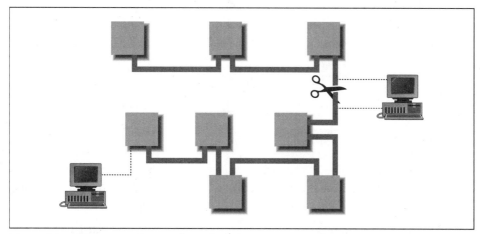

Figure 2-9. Adding a machine to the end of a bus is easy—in the middle it is harder

The fifth physical topology we will discuss is the star, shown in Figure 2-10. In this topology, all nodes are connected directly to a central hub site. In the access component of a local network, this would likely be a wiring closet, while in a WAN, it is likely to be the central data processing site. This topology has many advantages; among the strongest is its ability to scale indefinitely. Each new node added to the network gets a new, independent connection to the hub and has no direct impact on the existing connections. Further, because all of the cabling originates from a central site, you can move an existing connection at that central site without having to disturb other users, or even going out to the remote node. This topology also has the flexibility of the point-to-point network. New links can be established without having foreseen their need when the network was originally designed. Finally, you can make a star network emulate any of the other basic network types by adding cables between the nodes and the hub. A physical star configuration is frequently used for Ethernets and for any of the ring networks (Token Ring, FDDI, etc.); it's also a natural configuration for networks based on a central switch (switched Ethernet and ATM, for example).

Finally, hybrid topologies combine any or all of these basic network types. For example, we might decide to build a group of star-shaped networks interconnected by a ring. Or we might create a group of ring-shaped networks connected by a star. In fact, hybrid networks are more common than any of the basic

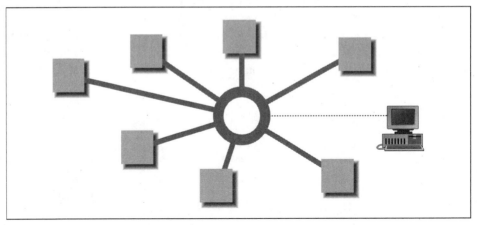

Figure 2-10. Adding a machine to a star network

network topologies. This is primarily because of the need to support different media in the various network components, because of physical constraints outside of the control of the network designer, or simply because of cost.

Probably the most common hybrid network topology, and one that I recommend for campus networks whether new or as a replacement for an existing plan, is a star of stars. In this hybrid topology, you would typically have either two or three layers of stars. Figure 2-11 shows both these options. At the center of the network, a star of fiber optic cables fans out from a central location to each building. Next, an optional second star of either fiber optics (preferred) or copper runs from the building *point of presence (POP)* to each wiring closet in a building. If you prefer only a two-layer star, you would extend the central star of fiber optics all the way to each wiring closet. Finally, a star of copper fans out of each wiring closet to the desktops. If possible, use the highest quality wiring available. For example, even though Category 5 wire is more than is necessary to run Ethernet or Token Ring connections, it is only moderately more expensive than Category 3 wire, and it will support future migration to CDDI, Fast Ethernet, or ATM. After all, you may have to live with this wiring for 10 years or more. Although wiring is the simplest component of a network, in practice it's the hardest to change. It's much harder to rewire a building than to upgrade a router.

This hybrid topology is one of the most common for a simple reason—flexibility. If you provide more than a single cable for each spoke of the star, you can build any of the basic topologies discussed above, and even most of the simpler hybrid topologies. For example, to create a ring from a star, you would have one cable that goes out to each node and one that comes back. Then, you would simply connect the inbound cable of each node to the outbound cable of the next node in the ring, as shown in Figure 2-12. When complete, you have a logical ring

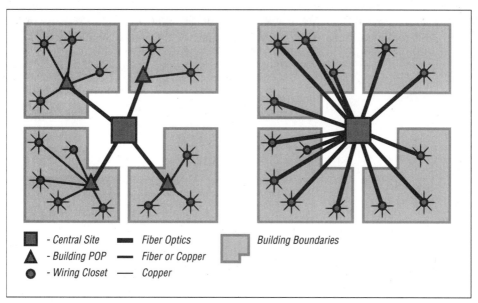

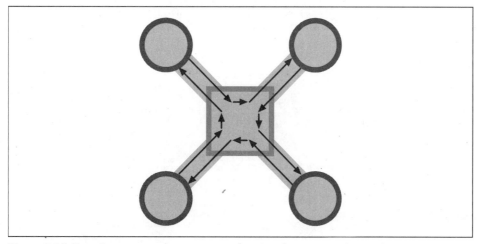

Figure 2-11. Three-layer (left) and two-layer (right) star topologies

topology built on a physical star topology. Similarly, you can create partial meshes and point-to-point networks by adding extra cables.

Figure 2-12. By using extra spokes, a star topology can be connected as a ring

Once you have the physical topology of your network in mind, the next step is to select where to place your routers. Some of this decision is made for you, based on your topology and media selections, but much is left up to you, and you have great leeway. This will be a topic of the next chapter, as will the selection and assignment of subnet masks, issues involved in supporting different sizes of subnet masks when you are using a classful dynamic routing protocol, proxy ARP, fault tolerance and redundancy, and some of the issues surrounding multi-protocol routing.

3

Network Design—
Part 2

In the previous chapter, we began our discussion of network design, covering such topics as stating your goals, network architecture, media selection, and physical topology. Those topics tend to be fairly abstract, and can be explored without referring to the physical realities of your network or organization. However, you should be working towards a physical design for your network. By now, you should have a good idea what physical topology or topologies you plan to use in your network, even if you don't have the specifics of exactly how the cable runs will be handled, or where your wiring closets are located.

This chapter continues the discussion of network design, beginning with where you need or want to place your routers. This task is far more concrete than thinking about what kinds of media you will use, or what physical topology your network wiring will assume. For this task, you need a fairly good idea of the physical realities of your network and organization layouts.

After discussing where to place your routers, we turn our attention to selecting and assigning subnet masks and numbers. We discuss fixed and variable subnet masks, how you might use variable subnet masks in the presence of a classful dynamic routing protocol, assignment of subnet numbers in a way that supports aggregation, and using proxy ARP to deal with hosts that cannot work with your subnet scheme. Finally, we consider fault tolerance and redundancy, and touch on issues surrounding multi-protocol routing.

Hubs, Bridges, Switches, and Routers

Before we discuss placement of routers in your network, let's consider whether you need routers at all. Can't you use devices like bridges or switches instead?

This is a valid question and one that salespeople you encounter may force you to answer. Each kind of device has its appropriate place in a network. It is important that you understand the different strengths each has, as well as its weaknesses.

The simplest network device is the hub, which will probably be the most common active component in your network. Hubs exist for most of the common LAN technologies, such as Ethernet, Token Ring, or FDDI, and are fairly simple to select, install, and maintain. We won't go into detail about selecting hubs since they are generally well understood. The medium you've chosen either requires a hub or it doesn't. Hubs from different vendors are likely to be similar, differing primarily in whether or not there's a management interface. Bridges, LAN switches, and routers, on the other hand, are a different matter entirely.

A few years ago, the hot topic in computer networking was whether networks should be built using bridges or routers. Bridge advocates claimed that routers were the major impediment to fast, efficient networking, and that they were too complicated to configure and maintain. Router advocates claimed that bridges did not provide enough control in the network, and that bridges would not allow networks to grow to the size they envisioned. Both groups were right, but as you no doubt know, the router advocates won out, most likely because of the scalability issue. Networks indeed did grow, and grew very large.

So why don't bridged networks scale well? The answer has to do with how bridges work. When a bridge receives a frame from the network, it examines the frame's destination address and consults a table of destinations that it knows about. If it finds a match, it decides whether to forward the frame, based on whether it came from the network segment where the destination is known to be. If it did not, the bridge forwards the frame to the segment leading to the destination. If the bridge knows that the frame came from the same segment as the destination, it ignores the frame, knowing that the destination machine will receive it without any intervention.

If the bridge does not know about the destination address, it forwards the frame under the assumption that the destination might be anywhere in the network. If the destination sends a response, the bridge will see that response and be able to add the response's source address to the table of addresses it knows about. Thus, a bridge learns about network topology by watching the source address on frames it receives.

This process works well, and is the heart of bridging. But there is a class of frames that the bridge must send everywhere. These are the hardware broadcast and multicast frames. Since every machine on the network must receive them, the frames must always be forwarded, or *flooded,* throughout the network.

Broadcast and multicast frames limit the scalability of bridged networks. As the number of machines on the network goes up, the number of broadcasts tends to increase proportionately. If, on the average, a single machine sends one broadcast every 10 seconds, then in a network of 1,000 machines, you will see an average of 100 broadcast packets every second. In a network of 10,000 machines, this number is now 1,000 broadcasts per second. In a network of 100,000, it becomes 10,000 broadcasts per second!

So what is wrong with all these broadcasts? Consider that every one of them must be heard by every machine, so must be forwarded by all bridges. This means that they appear on every segment of the network. Since the theoretical maximum for the number of packets per second, whether broadcast or not, on an Ethernet is 14,800, you see that in a network of 100,000 hosts, the majority of the traffic on the network would be broadcasts.

But network bandwidth is not the only problem with broadcasts. Because they must be examined by every machine to determine if the frame contains something of interest, every machine must interrupt its normal processing for every broadcast frame. Typically, this will result in one interrupt for every frame, or, in our 100,000 host network, 10,000 interrupts per second. This could bring a slower machine, or one with a less efficient network protocol stack, to a standstill.

Is it realistic to assume that machines send one broadcast every 10 seconds? Consider why broadcast and multicast packets are used. In the IP protocol suite, broadcasts are used for address resolution (the Address Resolution Protocol), routing updates, information for services such as rwho, and other applications. Multicasts may be used for some of these same functions, most notably routing updates and newer versions of some services, but to a bridged network, they aren't really any different from broadcasts—they still must be flooded. Some of these broadcast and multicast packets are sent on a periodic basis. For example, rwho and some routing protocols send out information every 30 seconds. While rwho may only send one packet at this frequency, some routing protocols, such as RIP, will send as many packets as it takes to carry the routing information. On a reasonably large network, this could be 10 or more packets.

Other protocols also have an effect on broadcast and multicast traffic. Protocol families such as AppleTalk use broadcasts and multicasts heavily for resource location, routing, and address assignment. Likewise, protocols such as Novell's IPX (used in Netware) also tend to use broadcasts and multicasts heavily for service announcements and resource location.

With all these broadcast and multicast uses in mind, it is not hard to believe that an average of one broadcast or multicast frame per machine every 10 seconds is, at best, conservative. It could well be that your mix of machines and protocols would produce far more.

So why does a routed network not suffer from the same problems? What is it about routers that allow a routed network to scale better than a bridged network? To answer this, you need to understand how routing differs from bridging.

Why Is Routing Different?

Earlier, I said that a bridge decides whether to forward a frame based on the destination hardware address. If the destination is unknown, or is known to be on a segment other than the segment on which the frame arrived, the bridge forwards it. A router makes a similar decision when it routes a packet. The difference is that the router looks at a network-layer address, not at the hardware address, to make its decision. But if that were the only difference, routing would scale no better than bridging.

The real difference is that network addresses are assigned by a human being with the topology of the network in mind. They are assigned so that all addresses with a given common prefix are in the same part of the network. In constrast, hardware addresses are assigned by manufacturers and generally have no relationship to where the device is in the network. Assigning addresses with topology in mind allows for greater information aggregation. Where a bridge on a 1,000-host network potentially must keep track of 1,000 destinations to make its decisions, a router for the same network might only need to keep track of 10 or fewer address prefixes.

Information aggregation is a large part of what makes routing scale better than bridging, but it is not the only aspect. A bridge must listen to every frame on its attached network segments because it never knows whether the frame needs to be forwarded until it has heard the frame's destination address. A router, on the other hand, does not need to listen to every packet, because part of the decision about whether to forward the packet to another network segment has already been handled by the packet's sender. If the sender determines that the destination is not local to the segment to which it is attached (by whatever mechanism the protocol specifies), it sends the packet directly to a router using the router's hardware address as the destination. Thus, the router really only needs to listen to packets addressed directly to it, greatly reducing the traffic that the router must process.

But this is not the greatest reason for routing's scalability. A bridge must forward any broadcast or multicast packet, since all devices in the network must be able to see it. Because a router understands network topology, it can be intelligent about forwarding broadcast and multicast packets. Routers establish *broadcast*

broadcast domains, which are portions of a network within which a broadcast is seen by all machines (a single IP network, in the case of TCP/IP). A router does not forward broadcasts unless specifically configured to do so, and then it typically is only configured to forward broadcasts and multicasts that meet a select set of criteria. For example, you might configure a router to forward BOOTP or DHCP broadcast requests to a remote server, and to forward IP multicast packets onto segments with registered listeners. By not forwarding other broadcasts and multicasts, a router conserves network bandwidth on other segments, and allows the network to grow to a larger size.

Finally, when a router receives a packet for a destination that it does not know how to deliver, it drops the packet, and may send a message back to the sender, informing it of this failure. In contrast, a bridge would forward the packet in the hopes of learning where the destination is. By not forwarding undeliverable packets, routers again conserve network bandwidth.

In a nutshell, then, routing allows for greater scaling for these reasons:

- It has a high degree of information aggregation, due to topologically assigned network addresses.

- It moves the decision about whether the assistance of a router is necessary to the sending host, rather than requiring the router to listen to all packets on all segments.

- It establishes broadcast domains to suppress broadcasts and multicasts in order to conserve bandwidth and avoid unnecessary interrupts on machines on other network segments.

- It drops packets for unknown destinations, rather than flooding them throughout the network, thereby saving bandwidth that would be wasted by transmitting packets to destinations that will never receive them.

Routers vs. Switches

It is not difficult to see why routing won out over bridging. However, the advantages bridging offers over routing, namely simpler configuration and better throughput, are not to be ignored. Additionally, as machines have gotten faster, they have become capable of monopolizing all of the bandwidth available on a local network segment, thus making contention for network bandwidth a problem for some networks. This is the drive behind the current popularity of network *switches*.

Network switches, most often Ethernet switches (though Token Ring and FDDI switches are becoming more common), increase the effective bandwidth of the network segment by reducing the contention for the bandwidth that is available. This is a simple concept. If you have a finite resource that is running short, you have two choices—you can increase the amount of the resource, or decrease the demand. In networking, you increase the amount of bandwidth available by changing network media. For example, if you replace all of your 4 Mbps Token Ring with 16 Mbps Token Ring, you increase the available bandwidth by a factor of four. Likewise, if you replace all of your 10 Mbps Ethernet with Fast Ethernet running at 100 Mbps, you increase the available bandwidth by a factor of 10. But replacing all of your network hub equipment *and* the adapters in all your network hosts is an expensive proposition. This is the problem that trying to increase the amount of bandwidth available presents. Instead, if you reduce the demand for the bandwidth, the remaining machines will see more bandwidth than they can use since there is less contention. One way to reduce demand is to remove machines from the network, but doing so is not really the best idea and is definitely a step backwards.

This is where network switches come into play. Every machine on a shared network segment is part of a single *collision domain,* so named because contention for bandwidth on an Ethernet results in a transmission collision. If we shrink the number of machines in a collision domain, we increase the effective bandwidth available to each machine on the network, since it is shared among fewer machines. In the extreme, each machine is in a collision domain by itself, though small groups are more common.

Reducing the size of a collision domain is possible with routers, but it can be rather expensive, and there is that nasty problem of the perceived slowness and complexity of routers. Consider that a very fast router with 24 Ethernet segments attached could easily cost more than $100,000. A 24-port Ethernet switch, on the other hand, could achieve the same level of segmentation for less than $8,000. That is a major cost savings, and the switch is likely to be easier to install and configure, and will probably be faster.

So why not throw away all your routers and convert your entire network to a switched network, as the switch vendors would like you to do? The answer is simple once you realize what a network switch really is. But rather than spoil it all by telling you, let's take a quick look at how a network switch does its job.

When a switch receives a network frame, it must determine where in the network the destination device is located. To do so, the switch examines the destination hardware address of the frame and checks a forwarding table. If it finds a match, it forwards the frame on the port indicated in the forwarding table. If it does not, it sends the frame out *every port except the one it came in on,* hoping that this will elicit a response frame that the switch can then use to update its forwarding table by noting the source address and port on which the frame was received. Broadcasts and multicasts are forwarded on all ports, or *flooded,* throughout the network.

But wait! Isn't that the same approach that a bridge uses? The answer is "Yes!" All a network switch is in reality is a multi-port bridge. It may be a very flexible multi-port bridge, supporting multiple media types and with the ability to group different ports into common broadcast domains, but it is still just a bridge. As such, a switch suffers from the same scaling problems that plague bridges. For example, consider a network consisting of 100 segments, or broadcast domains, each of which contains around 150 hosts. The network segments are connected by a half-dozen routers. Along comes a switch vendor, who convinces the network administrator (or his manager) that those routers are really the bottleneck that is keeping the network from performing smoothly. By replacing the routers with network switches, he could segment his network into 1,000 collision domains with 15 hosts each, and see a tremendous increase in productivity. Additionally, the switches are easier to configure than those routers, and cost less, too.

So what happens? Eventually, those 15,000 hosts start generating broadcast and multicast frames. But because there are no routers, all of these machines are in a single broadcast domain, and the network suffers a severe performance degradation. But never fear! These switches are intelligent switches and can be configured (relatively easily) to segment the network into 100 broadcast domains, each composed of 10 collision domains of 15 hosts each. This keeps the broadcasts to a manageable level, since they will not be propagated beyond a single broadcast domain.

Okay, the broadcast problem is solved, but how do we allow the hosts in one broadcast domain to talk to the hosts in another? Of course! We add routers to route between the broadcast domains. Oops! Now we not only have our routers back in the network (in the same way they always were), but we also have the switches to manage and configure. So much for getting rid of the routers!

The answer to this dilemma is to understand the strengths of each type of device and know when to use it. Network switches are a great way to reduce contention for bandwidth by shrinking the size of the collision domains in your network. I strongly recommend their use for this. Additionally, since many switches now are flexible enough to support multiple broadcast domains, it is possible to use one switch to support multiple subnets. Routers, on the other hand, link broadcast domains and provide information aggregation that allows the network to grow to great size. They do not do much to reduce contention for bandwidth within collision domains, except to keep broadcasts and multicasts where they belong.

So, it seems inevitable that you will need routers to help glue all but the smallest networks together. Unfortunately, routers do not have the extreme simplicity that bridges, switches, and hubs have, and must be configured, monitored, and tended with great care. It is this complexity that gives so many network administrators such a hard time, and is, of course, the reason for this book.

Router Placement

After you have decided on your physical cable topology, and that you will have to use some routers, you should think about where in your network you will place them. Placing all of your routers in a central location, easily accessible to your network staff, is a great advantage. By locating your routers in a common area, you can provide backup power, special air conditioning, and easy access for hardware and software maintenance. Of course, locating your routers in a common area may not be possible. Certainly it is difficult to achieve this goal in a network that spans multiple campuses and includes WAN links. It may also be difficult to achieve in a single campus network that is a mesh, a ring, or a hybrid with one of these components at its heart. In these circumstances, it still pays to minimize the number of different locations where routers are installed.

For example, in a campus network based on a ring, it may be possible to service multiple buildings from a single router or small cluster of routers located in one of those buildings, rather than placing a router in each building. Of course, any time you change from one network medium to another, you must provide some piece of equipment to handle the translation between the two media. One piece of equipment that can do this is a router, another is a bridge, and a third is a LAN switch, all of which were discussed earlier.

But router placement is more than identifying where you have to join two different media together. The placement of a router also defines the boundaries of your IP subnets (your broadcast domains). As you plan the placement of your routers, think about the communications paths within your organization. Some of these will be obvious: for example, people in a department typically talk to each other more than they talk to people in other departments, and it is likely that your billing department communicates frequently with your shipping department. However, some communications paths may be less clear. For example, your engineering department may communicate more frequently with marketing than with manufacturing.

Often, these human communications pathways are mirrored by computer communications pathways. This is only natural, and a successful network is one that has been designed with these paths in mind. Packets that pass through a router are always a little slower than packets that directly traverse a single LAN segment, no matter how fast the router is. Granted, the time difference for a single packet is minuscule (on the order of a millisecond or two), but when you consider the millions of packets that may flow on a busy network over a relatively short time, delays start adding up.

Recall that all machines on a single IP subnet can communicate directly with each other, without the assistance of a router. Since a router adds a non-zero delay to any packets it must handle, the fastest possible communications occur within a single subnet. What this means is something that seems trivially obvious when stated:

> Keep machines that communicate frequently with each other on the same subnet when possible.

Unfortunately, communications paths often aren't reflected by the physical locations of the groups involved. It is possible, and even likely, for two groups with a strong need to communicate with each other (perhaps engineering and technical writing) to be in entirely different buildings. This is where your topology planning comes into play. If you have chosen a two-layer star topology, it is fairly easy to group the two departments on a common subnet by interconnecting the spokes of the first-level star that provide connections to the groups, as shown in Figure 3-1.

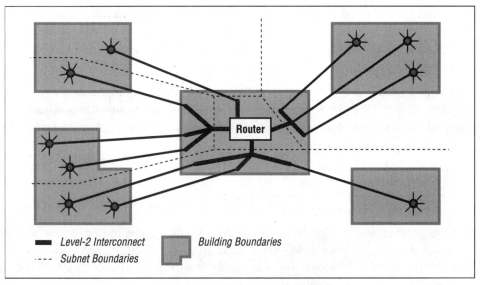

Figure 3-1. Putting groups in different buildings on one subnet

If the spokes of this first-level network have sufficient excess capacity, it is possible to isolate groups within a building from each other but provide a common subnet between each of these groups and other groups in other buildings. This may be necessary because one of the groups in a building might deal with sensitive information that needs to be handled more securely than the other groups. These kinds of needs must also be considered when planning your subnet boundaries and router locations.

In addition to communications paths, what else should you consider? If you want to route non-IP protocols (as discussed later in this chapter), you should consider the presence of these other protocols in your network. Other protocols often show up in departmental LAN environments; they may place constraints on which machines must be part of the same subnet, as well as which must not be together because the protocol does not provide adequate separation between different workgroups.

You must also consider the usage of broadcast-based IP protocols, such as BOOTP or DHCP. Remember, by default a router does not pass broadcast packets between interfaces. If you intend to place the clients for one of these protocols on a segment separate from the server for that protocol, you must configure the router to forward these protocols to the servers. This is as easy as:

```
interface Ethernet 2*
  ip address 172.16.1.1 255.255.255.0
  ip helper-address 172.16.23.17
```

The `helper-address` statement forwards all IP broadcasts for specific protocols received on this interface to the specified host address. Forwarding is done with a unicast packet, so none of the other routers need to be aware of this forwarding relationship. Different interfaces can have the same helper address or different addresses.

So which protocols get forwarded? Certain protocols are forwarded by default. Because the default list may change in future versions of the IOS software, you should consult your documentation. To control which protocols are and are not forwarded, add lines like these to your configuration:

```
! forward bootp and dhcp protocols†
ip forward-protocol udp bootp
! never forward the tftp protocol
no ip forward-protocol udp tftp
```

These commands affect all IP broadcast forwarding by the router. If you want to prevent a protocol from being forwarded from only one interface, you would need to construct an access list and apply it to the interface. This will not be covered here, since each situation is unique.

Subnet Assignment and Mask Selection

Once you have a general idea of where the routers, and thus the subnet boundaries, will be in your network, it is time to assign network or subnetwork numbers to each segment you have created. First, estimate how many machines

---

* Information about configuring common interfaces on a Cisco router is presented in Appendix A.

† BOOTP and DHCP use the same UDP port, and are in general upwardly compatible (a DHCP server can serve both DHCP and BOOTP clients). Thus, there is not a separate `ip forward-protocol udp dhcp` command.

that need IP addresses will be connected to each subnet. Don't forget to leave yourself some room for future growth of a group. While it is theoretically possible to have as large a subnet as you wish, the practical limits placed by either the network medium or available bandwidth put an upper limit of approximately 1,000 hosts on any subnet. This number, however, is impractical unless you're using an extremely fast network medium, or are building a subnet for machines that rarely use the network. A more realistic maximum is somewhere between 200 and 500, and only if these machines are light users of the network, are on a faster medium, or are on a switched or micro-segmented network segment.

After you have an idea of how many addresses you need to support on each subnet, you have a big decision to make: Should you use a common, fixed-length subnet mask on all subnets, or should you allow the subnet mask to vary between segments?

Fixed vs. Variable-Length Subnet Masks

If you expect each subnet to have nearly the same number of hosts, then the simplest solution is to select a fixed-length mask that allows you sufficient addresses on each segment from Table 3-1, replicated from Chapter 1. However, this is not the usual case...

Table 3-1. Number of Subnets and Hosts for Various Masks and Netblocks

# bits	Subnetwork Mask	Number of subnets if netblock is			Effective # of Hosts
		16 bits	20 bits	24 bits	
16	255.255.0.0	1	-	-	65534
17	255.255.128.0	-	-	-	32766
18	255.255.192.0	2	-	-	16382
19	255.255.224.0	6	-	-	8190
20	255.255.240.0	14	1	-	4094
21	255.255.248.0	30	-	-	2046
22	255.255.252.0	62	2	-	1022
23	255.255.254.0	126	6	-	510
24	255.255.255.0	254	14	1	254
25	255.255.255.128	510	30	-	126
26	255.255.255.192	1022	62	2	62
27	255.255.255.224	2046	126	6	30
28	255.255.255.240	4094	254	14	14
29	255.255.255.248	8190	510	30	6
30	255.255.255.252	16382	1022	62	2

Table 3-1. Number of Subnets and Hosts for Various Masks and Netblocks (continued)

# bits	Subnetwork Mask	Number of subnets if netblock is			Effective # of Hosts
		16 bits	20 bits	24 bits	
31	255.255.255.254	32766	2046	126	-
32	255.255.255.255	65534	4094	254	-

A more likely scenario is that you need one or two very large subnets (perhaps as many as 400 machines each), several mid-sized subnets (around 50 machines each), and a few very small subnets (less than 10 machines each) that might be server farms or WAN links. If you select a single subnet mask large enough for the largest of these subnets (which would allow for 510 machines), most of your subnets will consist largely of unused addresses. In fact, you will probably waste more than half of your address space! In this case, you have two choices. The first is to rearrange your subnets to make them all approximately equal in size. The second is to use *variable-length subnet masks (VLSM)*.

Using variable-length subnet masks means that each segment of your network may have a different subnet mask. You can therefore use a subnet mask appropriate for the number of hosts on the segment, and minimize wasted addresses. But using variable-length subnet masks is not a decision to be made lightly. If you use variable-length subnet masks, you will probably find it more difficult to remember the mask for a given subnet without resorting to lookup tables. Also, because of their relative newness, you may limit your choice of router equipment to those that fully support variable-length masks. This probably isn't a severe limitation, since most router vendors do support them, but you may find that other IP software on your hosts won't support a variable mask. If so, all is not lost. You can patch over host limitations with *proxy ARP*, discussed later in this chapter, or you may find that these hosts work just fine with a static default route, provided they are not multi-homed. Finally, if you use variable-length masks, you will be limited to static routing, or to a dynamic routing protocol that can properly handle variable masks, though limited use of variable-length masks can be supported by a classful routing protocol, if great care is taken during the network design. This will be discussed more fully later.

A fixed subnet mask has the advantage of simplicity. It will be easy for your network staff to remember the subnet mask for any given subnet (it is exactly the same as for all other subnets), and it will be easier for the system administrators who have to configure the subnet mask on various machines if it is consistent throughout the network. Its main disadvantages lie in the potential waste of address space and in the reduction of the flexibility of your network.

Selecting Variable-Length Subnet Masks

If you choose to use variable-length subnet masks, there are a few things you can do to minimize the problems associated with them. First, use as few different masks as possible. While this will increase your overall address waste, it may not be a significant loss, and it is far easier to remember three or four masks than a dozen or more. Besides, you should allow some room for growth in each subnet. Second, don't assign subnet masks haphazardly. If you do, you will have to resort to lookup tables to help you figure out the mask for a given subnet; if you aren't careful, you may end up with overlapping subnets. A more structured approach makes it easier to remember, or at least guess, what the mask is.

Consider a 20-bit address block such as `172.16.0.0/20`. Let's assume that we need 1 subnet for about 400 machines, 10 subnets for about 100 machines each, 12 subnets for about 45 machines each, and 6 subnets for 2 machines; these small subnets are for WAN links to connect remote offices. First, we need to take care of that large subnet.* We start by selecting a subnet mask that will give us at least 400 usable IP addresses on a subnet. By consulting Table 3-1, we find that a 23-bit mask will give us 510 usable host addresses per subnet. We then use this mask to divide our network into 8 subnets of equal size, and assign the first block to the subnet of 400 machines, as shown in Figure 3-2.

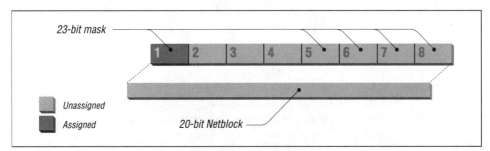

Figure 3-2. Divide the address space into blocks large enough for the largest subnet

If we were using fixed-length masks in our network, we'd be done. We'd also be out of addresses before we even finished assigning subnet numbers: we need a total of 29 subnets, but with our current mask, we only have 8! We need to continue dividing the address space to handle all of our subnets.

Next, we need to assign addresses and masks for the 100-machine subnets. Looking at our table, we find that we can use a 25-bit mask to get 126 usable host addresses per subnet. Using this mask, we start subdividing the unused blocks created by our original 23-bit mask. It turns out that we get four 25-bit subnets

---

* An alternative approach to assigning subnets with variable-length masks is documented in RFC 1219.

from each 23-bit block, so we use three of the 23-bit blocks to give us 10 subnets that can handle roughly 100 hosts each. The results are shown in Figure 3-3. We then have two unused 25-bit blocks left over. These two 25-bit blocks can either be reserved for use as new 25-bit subnets later, or they can be further subdivided with other masks.

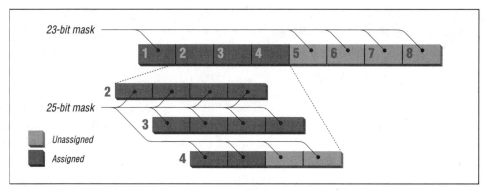

Figure 3-3. Step two divides three of our 23-bit blocks into twelve 25-bit blocks

To handle our 45-host subnets, we find that a 26-bit mask will give us 62 usable addresses per subnet. We could use 25-bit masks, but we would waste over half of a subnet for each segment. (Wasting these addresses might not be unreasonable if we expect a lot of growth in these subnets.) Again, we take as many of the 23-bit divisions as we need to give us 12 subnets. Since we get 8 subnets from each 23-bit block and we need 12, we will subdivide two of these blocks to get sixteen 26-bit subnets. Alternatively, we could use one of the 23-bit blocks to get eight of our subnets, and use the two unused 25-bit blocks for the other four. This would give us exactly the 12 subnets we needed, but doesn't leave room for our network to grow. Leaving some space unused is not a problem.

Finally, we need to handle the six WAN links. By consulting our table, we determine that we need a 30-bit mask to get two usable hosts. We could subdivide another of our largest blocks, but that would result in the creation of 128 two-host subnets! Instead, we should consider using one of the smaller blocks left over from the other masks we defined. If we select one of the four extra 26-bit subnets, we can further divide it with our 30-bit mask to get 16 two-host subnets. The final results are shown in Figure 3-4.

Using the subnet structure in Figure 3-4 for the netblock `172.16.0.0/20` yields the subnet numbers in Table 3-2. An asterisk denotes subnets that are not currently in use, and may be divided further, if needed. Note that the first address

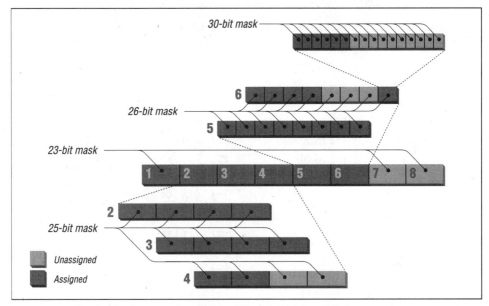

Figure 3-4. The final subnet mask assigment for our 20-bit netblock

and last address in each subnet cannot be used as host addresses. The first designates the subnet itself, and the last is the subnet's broadcast address.

Table 3-2. The Resulting Subnet Numbers and Addresses

Subnet	First Address	Last Address
172.16.0.0/23	172.16.0.0	172.16.1.255
172.16.2.0/25	172.16.2.0	172.16.2.127
172.16.2.128/25	172.16.2.128	172.16.2.255
172.16.3.0/25	172.16.3.0	172.16.3.127
172.16.3.128/25	172.16.3.128	172.16.3.255
172.16.4.0/25	172.16.4.0	172.16.4.127
172.16.4.128/25	172.16.4.128	172.16.4.255
172.16.5.0/25	172.16.5.0	172.16.5.127
172.16.5.128/25	172.16.5.128	172.16.5.255
172.16.6.0/25	172.16.6.0	172.16.6.127
172.16.6.128/25	172.16.6.128	172.16.6.255
*172.16.7.0/25	172.16.7.0	172.16.7.127
*172.16.7.128/25	172.16.7.128	172.16.7.255
172.16.8.0/26	172.16.8.0	172.16.8.63
172.16.8.64/26	172.16.8.64	172.16.8.127
172.16.8.128/26	172.16.8.128	172.16.8.191

Table 3-2. The Resulting Subnet Numbers and Addresses (continued)

Subnet	First Address	Last Address
172.16.8.192/26	172.16.8.192	172.16.8.255
172.16.9.0/26	172.16.9.0	172.16.9.63
172.16.9.64/26	172.16.9.64	172.16.9.127
172.16.9.128/26	172.16.9.128	172.16.9.191
172.16.9.192/26	172.16.9.192	172.16.9.255
172.16.10.0/26	172.16.10.0	172.16.10.63
172.16.10.64/26	172.16.10.64	172.16.10.127
172.16.10.128/26	172.16.10.128	172.16.10.191
172.16.10.192/26	172.16.10.192	172.16.10.255
*172.16.11.0/26	172.16.11.0	172.16.11.63
*172.16.11.64/26	172.16.11.64	172.16.11.127
*172.16.11.128/26	172.16.11.128	172.16.11.191
172.16.11.192/30	172.16.11.192	172.16.11.195
172.16.11.196/30	172.16.11.196	172.16.11.199
172.16.11.200/30	172.16.11.200	172.16.11.203
172.16.11.204/30	172.16.11.204	172.16.11.207
172.16.11.208/30	172.16.11.208	172.16.11.211
172.16.11.212/30	172.16.11.212	172.16.11.215
*172.16.11.216/30	172.16.11.216	172.16.11.219
*172.16.11.220/30	172.16.11.220	172.16.11.223
*172.16.11.224/30	172.16.11.224	172.16.11.227
*172.16.11.228/30	172.16.11.228	172.16.11.231
*172.16.11.232/30	172.16.11.232	172.16.11.235
*172.16.11.236/30	172.16.11.236	172.16.11.239
*172.16.11.240/30	172.16.11.240	172.16.11.243
*172.16.11.244/30	172.16.11.244	172.16.11.247
*172.16.11.248/30	172.16.11.248	172.16.11.251
*172.16.11.252/30	172.16.11.252	172.16.11.255
*172.16.12.0/23	172.16.12.0	172.16.13.255
*172.16.14.0/23	172.16.14.0	172.16.15.255

One possible problem with our assignment of subnet numbers is that we have used *subnet 0* in our largest blocks. Originally, subnet 0 was not allowed because it could be confused with the network number. Likewise, using the last subnet number was not allowed because it could be confused with the all-subnets broadcast address. According to the most recent standards, these problems no longer exist, and you are free to use these two subnets. However, keep in mind that the software in many of your hosts may not be able to handle these previously forbidden values. If you face this problem, you can address it in one of three ways. The first is to skip over the first and last subnets in your assignment. Unfortunately, this solution wastes address space whenever you have even a single large subnet. A better alternative is to assign your smallest subnets at the beginning and end of your address space. The only real drawback here is that you may end up with some of your smaller subnets separated by larger subnets. The final approach is to use *proxy ARP* on the subnets that include hosts that cannot handle the newer standard.

Assigning Subnet Numbers to Support Aggregation

While you are figuring out your variable subnet masks, or when assigning subnet numbers to network segments using a fixed mask, you should try to keep subnet numbers grouped topologically in your network to allow aggregation. In other words, keep 172.16.14.0/24 and 172.16.15.0/24 near each other so that other routers only need to carry a route for 172.16.14.0/23. This saves routing table space. Each network requires a separate entry in a router's routing tables. Within an organization, each subnet also requires a separate entry. By allowing for aggregation, you can shrink the size of the routing table in some of your routers. While this may not be important in a network with a few subnets, it may be the difference between success and failure for a large network with many subnets.

An example of how aggregation works is shown in Figure 3-5. In this network, Router1 must know in detail the subnet numbers attached to it. However, it doesn't need to tell Router2 about each individual subnet. Instead, it can send one aggregate route for four of them (172.16.0.0/24 through 172.16.3.0/24 are aggregated into 172.16.0.0/22), and one separate route for the fifth (172.16.66.0/24). Router2 can give Router3 even less detail, as it can aggre gate both of Router1's routes with some of its own to send two aggregates (172.16.0.0/22 and 172.16.64.0/22). Thus, even though the network consists of 10 network segments, Router3 only needs four entries in its routing table.

Unfortunately, efficient subnet mask assignment and topological assignment of subnet numbers are sometimes at odds with each other. When the conflict is minor (one or two subnets that are not topologically assigned) the conflict can be safely ignored. One or two (or even a dozen) subnets that cannot be aggregated with others are unlikely to bring your network down. It is nearly impossible to achieve 100 percent aggregation in any real network, and you are likely to make changes that will cause exceptions as the network grows and changes.

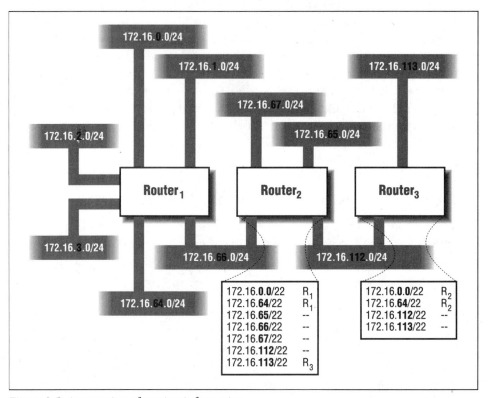

Figure 3-5. Aggregation of routing information

If you have a more significant conflict, you can rearrange your subnet mask division to accommodate the realities of your network. For example, in our hypothetical network, if it works better to take some of your 25-bit masks from the space after, instead of before, your 26-bit and 30-bit masks, go ahead and do so. The end result will be the same as far as the number of subnets you have and the amount of address space wasted, but you might achieve better aggregation in your network.

But what if you don't plan to run a classless dynamic routing protocol, or if you can't? It is still a good idea to assign your subnet numbers with aggregation in mind, even if you will use static routing exclusively. When you ultimately convert to a classless routing protocol (and you probably will), address aggregation will just happen or will require minimal network reconfiguration. Additionally, it may also help you and your staff to remember where a given subnet is if subnet numbers are assigned topologically.

Using Variable-Length Subnet Masks with a Classful Routing Protocol

Up till now, I have said that a classful routing protocol like RIP cannot use variable-length subnet masks. This is not entirely true. If you design your variable-length masks carefully, and place them in your network with care, you can get away with a *limited* number of variable-length masks. While the ideas in this section may get you out of a bind, mixing variable-length subnet masks with a classful routing protocol is a *very* bad idea. If you choose to do it, be absolutely sure that there is no better way to solve your problem, and then use extreme caution. Although all of my WAN links could be handled by this trick, I do not use it in my own network. Instead, I am actively working to migrate to a classless routing protocol, and *only then* will I consider using 30-bit masks on my WAN links.

The problem with using variable-length masks with a classful routing protocol is making sure that all the routers in your network unambiguously know how to route to all other destinations when the routing protocol does not carry mask information. The trick is to keep the number of routers that must know about subnet masks as small as possible (ideally, just one), and then get these routers to tell the others about a larger subnet that contains all of the links, as in Figure 3-6..

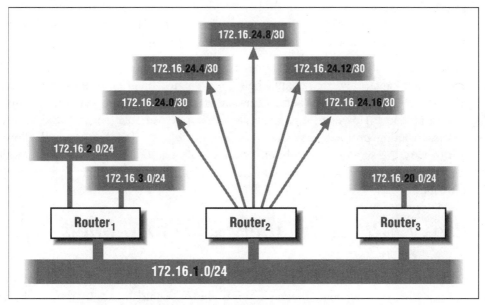

Figure 3-6. Variable-length masks with a classful protocol

Here we have three routers supporting a portion of a class B network using a classful dynamic routing protocol. This network uses a 24-bit subnet mask for all of its subnets, except the five point-to-point WAN links on Router2. These fivelinks use a 30-bit subnet mask to avoid wasting address space. The variable-length masks don't bother Router2 in the least because it is attached to these point-to-point links. It knows to use the longer 30-bit mask on the point-to-point destinations, but to use the shorter 24-bit mask for all others. This is absolutely the correct behavior. But what of the other two routers (and, presumably, the rest of the routers in the network)? How does Router2 tell these other routers about these subnets without being able to tell them about the odd-sized mask? Two ways are possible.

The first way for Router2 to tell the other routers about these five point-to-point links with the 30-bit masks is *not* to. Instead, the other routers can all be config-ured with static routes for these links containing the 30-bit masks. Then, each router can know which mask to use without difficulty. But static routing is painful to configure in a large network, and is subject to maintenance errors when networks move.

A better way to approach this problem is to have Router2 remain silent about the five subnets with 30-bit masks, and instead advertise a single route for the 24-bit subnet that contains them. For example, in Figure 3-7, we see that Router2 now advertises the subnet 172.16.24.0/24, which contains the five subnets used for the links (as well as many more not used). Since all of the 30-bit subnets are accessible from Router2, this kind of lying results in the correct behavior without requiring the other routers to know about the variable length mask. An example of this is shown in Chapter 6, *Routing Protocol Configuration.*

As long as all of the odd-sized subnet masks are contained within a single full-size subnet, and they are all attached to a single router, this kind of limited support for variable-length subnet masks is possible with a classful dynamic routing protocol. However, it is far easier to support variable-length masks with a classless routing protocol; use one if at all possible. A classless protocol allows you to vary the size of your subnet masks at will, without having to worry about confining knowledge of these variable-length masks to a small part of your network.

Proxy ARP as an Alternative to Subnets

When a host prepares to send an IP datagram, it first determines whether the destination is on the same network segment or a different one. If the destination is on a different segment, the host sends the datagram to an IP router. If the sending host and destination are on the same segment, then the packet is sent directly.

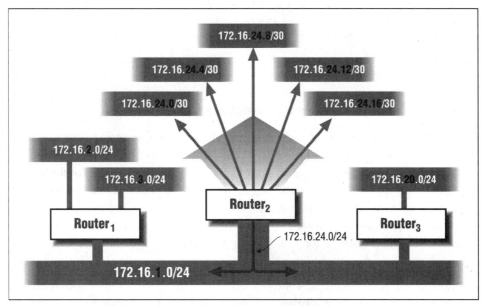

Figure 3-7. Advertising one full-size subnet instead of smaller subnets

However, the data link layer has no knowledge of IP addresses. Each machine usually has a unique hardware address with no relationship to its IP address. Hardware addresses are assigned to machines (or interface cards) by the manufacturer, without regard to where the device will ultimately be used. IP addresses are assigned by a local administrator and have a structure that is locally controlled and contains a lot of information about where the device is located. When an IP host wishes to send a datagram on the local segment, it must somehow map the destination's IP address to its hardware address.

There are three basic methods for mapping an IP address to a hardware address. The first is a lookup table. Each machine has a fixed list of mappings from IP address to hardware address for each machine on the local network segment. While this approach is simple, maintaining the table is error prone, and updating the tables when a single hardware address changes is a nightmare for more than about a dozen machines.

The second method is to provide an algorithmic mapping between the IP address and the hardware address. One example would be a data link layer with 8-bit hardware addresses. A host could then map an IP address into a hardware address by using the low-order octet of the IP address as the hardware address. This works fine if the administrator can set the hardware address, and if such a simple mapping exists.

The third method, and the most common choice in the IP protocol suite, is to use a network database that a host queries when it wishes to know the hardware address for a given IP address. This database can be located on a single server, or it can be distributed, with each host responsible for answering inquiries for its own hardware address.

ARP—The Address Resolution Protocol

On most common LAN media, the standard method used to provide this mapping is the *Address Resolution Protocol (ARP)*. Using this protocol, a sending host sends a message using the hardware's broadcast facilities, if possible, asking for the machine at a given IP address to respond with its hardware address. When the appropriate machine answers, the original machine sends IP datagrams for this machine using this hardware address. Because it is likely to send more datagrams in the near future, the sender stores a copy of this mapping in a cache for future use.

Normally, each machine only answers inquiries regarding its own IP address. However, there is no restriction in the protocol preventing a machine from answering for other IP addresses for which it would normally be the next hop router. In these cases, the router answers with its own hardware address; the sending machine accepts this address as a valid mapping, and therefore sends the IP datagram to this machine. This is known as *proxy ARP*, or the *ARP hack*.

Proxy ARP was conceived as a way to smooth the transition to IP subnetting. Many machines had IP software that did not understand subnet masks. These machines believed that all hosts on a classful network were directly reachable via the data link layer and would ARP for machines on other subnets. By providing proxy ARP services, an IP router could allow these machines to function in a subnetted IP network without requiring them to be upgraded to new software. Today, machines that don't understand IP subnets are rare. However, many people believe that proxy ARP is a useful alternative to configuring proper subnet masks (and sometimes even routing) in the hosts on a network. Often, they don't understand until too late the disadvantages of using proxy ARP indiscriminately.

Problems with Proxy ARP

Enabling proxy ARP everywhere has some appealing advantages to the over-worked network administrator. He no longer needs to tell LAN administrators and users what their subnet mask is, nor does he need to explain what a subnet mask is. Taken to extremes, it may even be possible for the hosts on leaf networks to be completely ignorant of IP routing issues and ARP for *everything*, even IP addresses at remote sites, and have the routers do all the work.

One of the problems with using proxy ARP this way is that the load on routers, which may already be high, increases greatly. A properly configured IP host that is communicating with four machines on other network segments will know that the datagrams for these sessions must be sent to the IP router. When the first packet is to be sent, the host may have to ARP for the hardware address of the router, and will store it in its ARP cache for future use. The other three sessions will also route to the same router, but the host already has the router's hardware address in its ARP cache, so it does not need to ask again. In contrast, a machine relying on proxy ARP must ARP for the hardware address of each machine with which it is conversing. In our example, this increases the ARP handling load by a factor of four. When you multiply this by all the machines, connected to all the router's interfaces, the additional load on the router can be excessive. Further, since ARP requests are broadcast to all machines on a local link, every machine on the segment must interrupt its normal processing to check the incoming ARP request to see if it is for its IP address. So, not only does the load on the routers increase, but the load on your other hosts also increases.

Another drawback to widespread proxy ARP is that it hides configuration errors. I recently dealt with a set of machines on the local campus network that had their default route pointing at an IP address that was unassigned, but which will eventually be used for a router on a future subnet. However, the router on the local subnet had been configured for proxy ARP many years ago, and time has not permitted verifying whether proxy ARP was still needed, so the misconfigured machines on this subnet were happily sending packets successfully. Had this problem continued to go undetected, a future change to the network might have rendered them mysteriously unable to communicate. The nightmare of any administrator is making a change and having something unrelated fail.

Unfortunately, some router vendors enable proxy ARP by default on all interfaces. Apparently, they believe that proxy ARP helps to make IP networking as *plug-and-play* as possible for small sites without a great deal of expertise. While they may be correct for some sites, it is still my opinion that proxy ARP generally does more harm than good. Fortunately, it is usually simple to disable proxy ARP. The code below shows part of the configuration for a pair of Ethernet interfaces on a Cisco router. The first has proxy ARP enabled on it, as is the default, and the second has had it disabled because it is unneeded.

```
! proxy ARP enabled explicitly (it is on by default)
interface Ethernet 0/0
 ip address 172.16.1.1 255.255.255.0
 ip proxy-arp
! proxy ARP disabled on this interface
interface Ethernet 0/1
 ip address 172.16.2.1 255.255.255.0
 no ip proxy-arp
```

When Is Proxy ARP Necessary?

Even with its drawbacks, you sometimes need proxy ARP to work around a problem. Rare as it may be, you may still find one or two hosts on your network that cannot handle IP subnets. Unless you can eliminate these hosts, you will have no choice but to support proxy ARP on the segment or segments where they are located. Another possibility, and one that is still rather likely, is that you have hosts that cannot communicate properly with hosts belonging to subnet 0 and the all-1s subnets. (Remember that these subnets were formerly reserved.) When you find one of these hosts, you may have no choice but to lie to it about its subnet mask so that it doesn't think that these addresses are in one of these problem subnets, and enable proxy ARP on your routers.

Regardless of why you find proxy ARP necessary, it is important to control its use carefully, and not spread it throughout your network. Try to keep the machines that really need it on as few segments as possible. It may even be possible to group them all together on a single segment; if you can, you only need to enable proxy ARP on a single router interface.

Redundancy and Fault Tolerance

At this point, you are almost through with your network design. But there is one major tool left to you to achieve your network design goals. This tool is redundancy.

Redundancy, in all its forms, is a great way to increase your network's reliability and availability. Properly designed redundant components can make the difference between a network failure that brings your organization to a halt, and one that goes unnoticed by the users. Redundancy is also a great way to increase the cost of your network. At one extreme, you have no redundancy, and no increase in cost. At the other, you have full redundancy, and have at least doubled your costs. Ideally, you find something in between.

Where Do I Need Redundancy?

Only you can decide where your network needs to be redundant. However, several guidelines can help you determine what is right for your network.

First, look over your entire network design and identify what can go wrong with it. Start by thinking in general terms such as a router failure or a cable break. Your goal is not to identify every last failure scenario, an impossible task, but rather to identify general classes of failure. Don't forget to include "failures" that are planned, as well. Redundancy may be able to keep portions of your network functioning while you are making changes that require equipment to be powered down or cables to be moved. For example, the redundant ring built into FDDI allows you to break the ring to add a new machine without actually taking the ring down. This kind of *planned* outage is often overlooked.

When identifying potential failures, look carefully at everything. One of the most commonly missed causes for network failures is the action of your own personnel. For example, when the cleaning crews wax the floors, they may overload an electrical circuit and bring down a critical piece of your network. If such a failure has happened recently, you will quickly think of it. However, if it has been nearly a year since the floors were waxed, you might have forgotten about it.

Once you have identified the general classes of failure, you next need to estimate how likely such a failure is, and how much impact it will have on your network and your organization. This is often the most difficult part of your task. Most of us have a difficult time being realistic about both the probability of a specific failure and the impact on the organization. We usually underestimate the probability and overestimate the effect. It is important to get these reasonably correct.

Next you should rank your failure modes from most probable and damaging to least probable and damaging. This ranking will probably be rather subjective, but don't let that bother you. Your goal is to identify where your efforts will have the greatest payoffs, not to produce a formal reliability study.

What Should My Response Be to a Potential Failure?

With this ordered list in hand, start thinking about how to address each failure mode. Start with the most likely and damaging, and assess how you might deal with this failure. Be careful not to go overboard with your solution. For example, one of the most likely network failure modes is a general power failure. The obvious solution is to put as much of the network as possible on uninterruptible power systems. But stop a moment and think about this. In a general power failure, will any of the network hosts be up and running? If not, how critical is it that the network itself be powered? Perhaps what you really need is to keep your key routers and hubs functioning, and allow the other devices to come back on with the power.

You should also be realistic with your solutions. If you spend enough, you may be able to prevent some failure from taking down the network, but should you really spend more money to prevent a failure that may never happen than the failure itself would cost? For example, the chance of an entire router failing is not extremely high. However, such a failure will have a pretty major impact on the operation of your network. Your first response may be to make your router installation fully redundant. However, routers aren't cheap, and you may well spend more trying to prevent the failure than it could ever cost your organization. A more reasoned approach is to have one full set of spare parts, so that you can replace any single router or router component that fails, and take the small, hopefully localized, down time necessary for you to swap in the spare parts when a router does fail.

What About Redundant Links?

One failure mode you are likely to consider is a cable failure. Someone digging a trench may cut through a fiber bundle, or a construction crew in a remote building may cut a copper cable, or someone may trip over a drop cable and damage a data outlet in the wall. All of these are potentially disruptive to your network operation, and the natural response is to consider putting in redundant links. You may also be tempted to put in redundant links to deal with the possibility of router failure or a power failure in a remote building.

However, before you simply start drawing redundant links on your brand new network design, stop and think carefully about what effect the link will have. In many cases, adding a redundant link may have the opposite effect from what you intended. Each new link means a new way things can go wrong, especially in the complex decisions involved in IP routing. For example, if you have redundant paths between two routers, you must be running a dynamic routing protocol, or your routers won't be able to detect a failure and take advantage of an alternate path. Routing protocols can be extremely complex. If a link fails, it takes a finite amount of time for the routers to detect the failure and agree on a new set of routes to bypass the failure. This is known as *convergence time* and will be discussed more in Chapter 5, *Routing Protocol Selection*. In some cases, the convergence time can be several minutes. When the failed link returns to service, the routers must again detect this and recompute the optimal paths through the network.

So what happens if the link is failing solely because it has too much traffic on it? When the routers detect the failure, they will begin routing traffic around the failed link. This reduces the traffic on the link, causing it to return to service. The routers will detect this, and begin sending traffic out the link again, increasing its load, and causing it to fail yet again. If this happens consistently, and especially if it happens faster than the router convergence time, the routers will always be in an inconsistent state and will spend increasing amounts of their CPU time computing and recomputing routes. This is known as *route flap*. If the redundant link had never been there, the rest of the network would have noticed the main link go away, and would have simply started eliminating traffic for that link.

This is not to say that redundant links are bad. On the contrary, they can be the lifeline of a network faced with a catastrophic failure. However, they need to be placed carefully, and you need to monitor the main link so that you know when it has failed. I have, from time to time, been surprised to find that an FDDI ring has been in *wrap* state, meaning that one of the primary links had failed and a backup was in use. The ring continued to function, hiding the fact that the main link had failed.

Where Do Redundant Links Belong?

If your network design followed the methods I have described, it has three identifiable components: the core, the distribution, and the access networks. One of the most tempting places to put a redundant link is between nearby access networks. The rationale is that these networks are near each other, and can heal a breach in the distribution or the core components.

A common result of this approach, especially if the basic network topology is a star or a star hybrid, is to connect more and more access networks to nearby networks until you end up with something that resembles a giant wagon wheel. When you consider how many links you have put in, you suddenly realize that the cost of such redundancy is quite high, and the increased complexity of the network has not only decreased its overall reliability, but has also decreased the network's flexibility. Remember, we chose to use a star topology because we could move things around with relative ease.

A more productive place to put redundant links is in your core or in your distribution networks. In these components, redundant links provide backup for several access networks, so you won't need as many for the same level of redundancy. But even here, resist the urge to haphazardly place redundant links between distribution networks. A few carefully placed links will increase overall reliability, and allow the network to survive a major failure in the core; but too many results in decreased reliability and flexibility, and increased complexity.

One of the best ways to provide redundant links, especially in a WAN environment, is to backup your permanent links with on-demand links. For example, for the additional cost of a pair of analog modems and a pair of telephone lines, you could provide a low-speed backup path for your high-speed WAN link between your main office and a branch office. While the backup path might not be able to handle the full load of the primary link, with appropriate filters it can allow the most critical traffic to flow while the WAN link is being repaired. It may be your only way to reach the router at the remote site to fix a configuration error that caused the failure in the first place. An example showing how to provide a dial backup link is included in Chapter 6.

When identifying your redundant components, whether links, routers, or uninterruptible power, think carefully about whether you are really providing redundancy. Often, redundant links share a common path for some, if not all, of their length. If your backup link and main link are in the same cable bundle, the backup won't help in the slightest when a backhoe cuts through the bundle. Likewise, dual power supplies connected to the same UPS system gains nothing if the UPS itself fails.

Finally, some of the best defenses against network failure are good management practices. The majority of network failures are caused not by forces from the outside, but by the normal, day-to-day changes that network personnel carry out. A hardware installer adding a new link in a wiring closet may accidentally disconnect an adjacent drop, or may move the wrong connection. Network operators may change a router configuration in a way that turns out to be wrong and that causes a ripple of failure throughout the network. Cables being pulled under the floor or routed into equipment racks can accidentally disconnect power to an entire rack of equipment. All of these are preventable by careful, methodical, and thoughtful planning, training, and actions.

For hardware failures, the two best defenses are still a set of spare parts and a selection of equipment chosen with a careful consideration of its reliability and repairability. In essence, if the equipment doesn't fail, then that is a network failure you don't need to worry about. This is one of the basic criteria we will talk about in Chapter 4, *Selecting Network Equipment.*

What About Multi-Protocol Networking?

While generally beyond the scope of this book, multi-protocol networking is far to common to ignore entirely. While we cannot delve into the details of how to make multiple protocols coexist happily, we can present some of the issues surrounding multi-protocol networking so that you can consider them, especially since multi-protocol networking can have an impact on your network design.

Few networks have the luxury of using only one protocol family or another. Most have some mix of protocols such as IP, IPX (used by Novell Netware), AppleTalk, DECNet, and possibly many others. Each protocol family presents its own set of challenges, and each follows its own rules about addressing, routing, naming, and so forth, and often these rules come into conflict.

So how should you handle non-IP protocols on your network? You have three options:

- Forbid non-IP protocols entirely.
- Allow non-IP protocols, but do not route them between network segments.
- Route non-IP protocols, putting them on an equal footing with IP.

Each of these options has its good and bad points, just like with everything else in computer networking. For example, it is difficult to forbid the use of non-IP protocols unless you want to dedicate one or more staff persons to constant policing to find and stop violations. Fortunately, this option is seldom necessary.

The second option has the benefit of allowing departmental LAN usage of non-IP protocols, which is often where these other protocol families shine. But because you don't route them between segments, any problems that they may cause are confined to single segment of the network. This isn't to say that they can't gray your hair or aggravate your ulcer, but the scope of potential problems is much smaller.

But there is a severe drawback to this position. If you allow non-IP protocols but do not route them, your decisions about how to assign machines to IP subnets will be constrained by whether they need to use one of these protocols, and with which group. For example, if a computer in the accounting department, which uses AppleTalk extensively, is to be connected to the network, it must be connected to the same IP subnet as the rest of the accounting department in order to allow the AppleTalk services to work. This may be difficult, expensive, or even impossible.

The Benefits and Costs of Multi-Protocol Routing

So why not turn on routing for non-IP protocols? After all, the benefits to routing non-IP protocols are non-trivial:

- Most network protocols are more similar than different. A router that can route one efficiently can generally route another efficiently.

- Routing non-IP protocols in a network's IP routers means that the protocols are administered by the same staff that administers the IP protocol family, reducing duplication of effort and equipment.

- Many non-IP protocols are the most efficient way for a LAN to operate. For example, Novell Netware (IPX) and Banyan Vines provide more efficient file and print services for a PC than IP's Network File System.

- Routing non-IP protocols increases the flexibility of your network to meet the needs of your users.

These considerations indicate that multi-protocol routing is a *Good Thing*, at least in the abstract. But there are equally good reasons to consider which, if any, non-IP protocols to route. These are some of the best reasons not to route non-IP protocols:

- Additional knowledge requirements. No one can be expert at everything, but you need an expert in each protocol that you route to understand its needs and diagnose its failures.

- Additional load on router equipment Each routed protocol requires its own routing table, and possibly also its own dynamic routing protocol, which take memory and processing power.

- Increased complexity. A multi-protocol router is a far more complex piece of software and hardware than a single protocol router, so weaknesses in the implementation of one protocol may affect the stability of the other protocols.

- More difficult design. Since each protocol family has its own rules for routing, address assignment, and so on, and these rules often conflict with each other, you must put more care and thought into creating a design that handles all the protocols you need properly.

• Decreased scalability. Some protocol families do not scale as well as others, or may not work well in a WAN environment, thereby decreasing the size to which you can scale your network.

Tunneling as an Alternative to Multi-Protocol Routing

An intermediate position that you might find useful, or that might happen on its own if you allow non-IP protocols but don't route them, is the creation of *tunnels* between isolated LANs that use these protocols. A tunnel is a means to pass a non-routed protocol between two hosts using the protocol by encapsulating it in another protocol (in our case, IP) that is routed. The machine at one end of the tunnel places the complete packet inside the data portion of an IP packet and sends it through the network to the other end of the tunnel. The receiving machine removes the packet from the carrier protocol, and retransmits it as a native packet of whatever protocol family it is.

While simple in concept, the tradeoff is a slight decrease in efficiency. The originating machine sends the packet across the local network to the tunnel host as a native packet. The tunnel host wraps it in another protocol, and transmits it to the far end of the tunnel. This transmission may cross the same local network segment as the original packet, depending on the network structure. The far end of the tunnel receives the encapsulated packet across its local network segment, removes the packet from its carrier, and then retransmits it to its ultimate destination. So, in the worst case, each packet traversing the tunnel would be transmitted across the local network segments at the ends of the tunnel twice. In addition, there is the matter of the extra octets needed to encapsulate the packet while it is traversing the tunnel.

Don't take this tradeoff to mean that tunnels are always bad. On the contrary, tunnels can be the best method for letting a small number of isolated LANs communicate using their native protocols without having to support those protocols in your routers. You may even be able to push off the support for these tunnels to the coordinators of the departmental LANs that need them. Since they are handling the tunnels, it may give them an incentive to look at alternatives, or to push their vendors to adopt IP as their universal transport protocol, as many proprietary LAN protocol vendors are committed to do.

The benefits of multi-protocol routing are potentially great, as are its costs. When weighing the decision about which non-IP protocols to route, if any, my rule of thumb is to route as few as you can get away with. Keep the network as simple as possible—don't route a protocol simply because you can.

4

Selecting Network Equipment

In previous chapters, we discussed the design process for a network. If you carried out that process, you should have two designs. The first is your ideal network—what you would do if you had no existing network constraints to worry about. The second is a modification of your ideal network design taking into account your existing network.

As part of these designs, you should have identified where routers are needed. The number of routers is not important, since you may discover that supporting the number of network segments you need in an area may require more or fewer routers than you expected. Your designs will probably undergo frequent modifications as you build and operate your network, and discover constraints that you had not originally planned on. As a simple example, you may discover that it is impossible to provide network connections for an entire building from a single wiring closet; there may not be a cable route for some offices that stays within the limits imposed by your chosen media. You will have to choose between changing your medium and adding a second closet, either of which may change how you place routers.

The most important parts of your designs are your overall goals, and the number and type of network segments you need to support from each router location. The design goals will help you to decide which features you need when you are evaluating routers: redundant power supplies, time to boot, and serviceability. The number and type of network segments you need to support will guide you in selecting among the interface types and densities available. I will assume that the number and type of segments you need is straightforward. After all, if you have four Ethernet segments coming together where you plan to put a router, it is clear you need at least four Ethernet ports, whether on one router or several. Instead, this chapter concentrates on evaluating IP routers based on the overall goals of your network designs.

What Is an IP Router?

Before we begin, we should discuss exactly what an IP router is. While this question may seem pointlessly simple, it is surprising how many different answers you will receive, all of which may be correct. Strictly speaking, an IP router is any device that joins two or more IP networks (or subnetworks) and switches packets between them. While this definition is useful for a theoretical discussion, it is far too abstract for our purposes. It does, at least, get the ball rolling.

Three major categories of devices meet this definition. The first is traditional level two network devices, such as bridges, hubs, and switches, that have had routing functionality added to them. The second category includes general-purpose computers with multiple interfaces and IP routing code. A UNIX machine with two Ethernets is an example of these *host-based routers*. The third are the dedicated, special-purpose hardware and software systems whose primary (and possibly only) purpose is IP routing.

Of these three, the first group usually suffers from either limited performance or limited flexibility. They are often used when an organization first discovers that it has outgrown its bridged network, and needs to implement routing. Often, these devices only support a single dynamic routing protocol (most often *RIP*, the *Routing Information Protocol*). Many times, the routing capability in these devices comes about because someone observes that the IP code they added to support management functions like SNMP or Telnet is easily changed to support basic IP routing. Unfortunately, this routing code is often poorly optimized, and is only suitable for very small scale designs. In general, I prefer to call these devices *routing hubs* or *routing switches* and will not deal with them further.

The remaining two groups, the host-based routers and the dedicated routers, each have large followings among IP network administrators. However, while many prefer one over the other, few attempt to declare the two types of routers equivalent. Instead, each group focuses on the strengths of their favorite device to perform a specific task better than the other.

Host-Based vs. Dedicated Routers

In the early days of IP, there were no dedicated routers. Engineers took general-purpose computer hardware, and either embedded the routing code into a general-purpose operating system, or built a custom operating system with embedded routing code. The first group of these early routers evolved into host-based routers, and the second into dedicated routers.

Of the general-purpose systems with embedded routing code, one of the most popular was a variant of the UNIX operating system produced by the University of California at Berkeley and known as the *Berkeley Software Distribution (BSD)*. This system has been ported to many hardware platforms; its networking design forms the basis for most UNIX IP implementations, as well as those of other platforms. Historically, much of the Internet depended heavily on this software for routing. In addition, Windows NT now supports host-based routing.

Host-based routers have several advantages. They are typically cheaper; the computer can be used for other functions such as file services; and the systems staff is already familiar with them. Most organizations already have a general-purpose computer capable of routing, and adding an additional network interface is very inexpensive. Most advocates of dedicated routers wouldn't disagree with these advantages. But host-based routers also have some significant disadvantages, and should be used with caution. It is difficult to do many things well; file servers usually make poor number crunchers, and number crunchers make poor file servers. This is because of the tradeoffs made to optimize operating system code to support one function in preference to another. In the same way, file servers (or number crunchers) tend to make poor routers, and routers tend to make poor file servers (or number crunchers).

In contrast to host-based routers, dedicated routers are highly optimized for switching IP packets. Their buffer management, process control, and interrupt handling schemes are designed with this one task in mind. This, combined with the lack of need to handle multiple users, compilers, and complex file systems, allows them a performance advantage over their host-based counterparts. The second major advantage that dedicated routers usually enjoy is port density. Typically, a host-based router is limited to 10 or fewer network interfaces, either by its operating system software, or the physical constraints of the hardware. Often, they are limited to just two or three. A dedicated router may easily support 100 or more network interfaces at one time. Greater port density allows an IP network to scale more easily, and significantly narrows the cost advantage of host-based routers. If a host-based router costs only one-tenth of a dedicated router, but the dedicated router offers 10 times the port density, the cost difference effectively goes away.

The third major advantage of dedicated routers is flexibility. Flexibility comes in two forms. First, dedicated routers support more interfaces types. Depending on the host system, a host-based router may only support one or two types of interfaces, such as Ethernet and FDDI. Dedicated routers may support a dozen or more interface types in a single chassis, allowing you to connect many different network media without having to purchase a single host for each. Second, dedicated routers often support many different dynamic routing protocols, and may support routing of many non-IP protocols, too. Host-based routers are typically confined to a single dynamic routing protocol (generally RIP) unless additional software, such as *gated,** is added. Host-based routers seldom can be easily extended to support routing non-IP protocols, which may be a requirement of your network.

The disadvantages of host-based routers mean that they have trouble supporting a network as it grows. This has led many organizations that started with host-based routers to migrate to dedicated routers over time. Still, if you believe that host-based routers have a place in your network, by all means, use them. While I will not discuss their configuration and management in any detail, you should be able to adapt the techniques and practices discussed here without difficulty. Some discussion of configuring host-based routers can be found in Craig Hunt's book, *TCP/IP Network Administration,* available from O'Reilly & Associates.

Router Selection Criteria

When selecting routers, keep the goals that you set in your network design foremost in your mind. It is pointless to worry about any other criteria if your stated goals are not well understood. Once you understand your goals, you can evaluate various criteria for selecting a router in terms of those goals. For example, if your goals include high availability, you are likely to rate a router more on its reliability than on its flexibility. Every network administrator should consider potential router selections based on the criteria I discuss here, but every network administrator is likely to weight them differently.

Functionality

Simply put, functionality means how well the router fulfills the functions you need it to perform. Any IP router will route IP packets. Your concerns here are for other functions. For example, if you intend to run a dynamic routing protocol, you would obviously not want a router that did not have that capability. What kinds of functionality are you likely to need? The list will vary from network to network, but some basic features that are likely to be needed in any network include:

- One or more dynamic routing protocols (RIP, OSPF, IGRP, EIGRP, BGP, etc.)

- Logging—either via a network logging protocol, or some kind of online buffering

---

* Gated, the gateway daemon, was originally developed at Cornell University, but its maintenance has since been picked up by MERIT, the Michigan state research and education network.

- A network-accessible configuration and management interface (Telnet, WWW, or SNMP)

A dynamic routing protocol is essential to building a large network. However, a dynamic routing protocol can also make it easier to manage a small network of routers, primarily by reducing the number of configuration changes necessary to support a change in your network. Having a choice of routing protocols is better still, especially if you have multiple vendors' equipment in your network. Hopefully, there will be a routing protocol that is common to all of the equipment.

Logging is probably one of the most useful diagnostic tools available to you. Because a network is a large and dynamic entity, it is often difficult to get a clue where to start looking when things break, or what might be the cause of a failure. Good, clear logging that does not overwhelm you with unnecessary detail can tell you not only where to start looking, but why a failure is occurring in your network. Better still is when the log messages are stamped with some kind of time value, whether absolute or relative to each other, to give you an idea when the event occurred.

Finally, a network-accessible configuration and management interface may save you many trips to remote routers, or dollars spent on modems and phone lines. Ideally, this interface to the router should be capable of doing at least as much as could be done by a terminal connected directly to the router. No matter how you plan, and no matter what your network looks like, you *will* have to configure and probe your routers from time to time. You should be able to use the network to do this.

In addition to these basic features, other desirable features include:

- BOOTP/DHCP forwarding
- SNMP manageability
- Some sort of time protocol, primarily to give the router an accurate view of the time
- Some kind of packet-filtering capability to allow you to protect a network segment from outside access or to confine users of a network segment to a select set of accessible destinations
- Support for variable-length subnet masks, even if not currently needed

If you are using, or plan to use, a dynamic address assignment protocol such as BOOTP or DHCP, you will want to consider whether your prospective routers will forward requests from one network segment to another. Many routers claim to, but some don't seem to get it quite right. Without this capability, you will be forced to abandon your plans to use these protocols, or to provide a server on each segment where they are used. This can be costly, is harder to maintain, and should not be necessary.

SNMP (the *Simple Network Management Protocol*) is often thought of as some-thing that only big, far-flung networks need. While it may be true that a large network can get more out of SNMP, and will also be more dependent on it, a small network should not ignore its potential. While your network is small, you can use some simple SNMP-based tools to probe your network for reachability and statistical information. However, if you don't consider SNMP from the begin-ning, you may have problems putting it in place as your network grows. If your earlier equipment can't be managed by SNMP, you will have to manage some of your network with SNMP, and the rest the old way.

There are two main reasons you might want your routers to implement a standard time protocol. The most obvious is that they can then provide a time base to the other machines in your network. However, if your routers do not implement a time protocol, it is certainly reasonable to use another server for that function. More important, routers need an accurate view of the time. Routers should give you a way to correlate log entries, or any other action that has a time stamp, to external events, logs maintained by other devices, etc. For example, one router may consistently log an event at 5:35 A.M. This information isn't terribly useful if 5:35 A.M. on one router occurs at 4:15 P.M. on another, and at 11:23 P.M. on another. If all your routers maintain time consistently and accurately, you might realize that backups always occur at 5:30 A.M.; this might be a clue about what is happening to your network.

Almost any router with a packet-filtering capability allows you to block traffic based on either a source or a destination IP address. This feature is so common that it is practically standard. However, there are times that you may need to delve deeper into a packet than the addresses. You might want to selectively allow some communications without allowing others. For example, you might want to permit a machine to send and receive electronic mail, but be unavailable for telnet access. A flexible packet-filtering mechanism should allow that granu-larity of control. Be warned, though, that when a router starts looking into packets at deeper and deeper levels, its performance will almost certainly suffer.

Finally, even if you don't currently need support for variable-length subnet masks, you should give serious consideration to ensuring that your routers support it fully. Like SNMP, you may not need it right away, but when you do decide that it has a place in your network, you don't want your older equipment to prevent you from using it. At a minimum, a router should be able to cope with subnet masks that are not on octet boundaries; preferably, it should correctly handle subnet masks that differ in different parts of the network, even if it doesn't have a dynamic routing protocol that can carry this information. You can always use static routes in a pinch.

Be cautious about getting caught up in a straight comparison of features, however. If a given feature has no use in your network, why do you care that one router supports it and another does not, unless you expect to use it in the future? Only compare features in areas that you will make use of, or can at least foresee a use for.

Interoperability

If you need to support an existing network, the need for interoperability is clear. Any equipment you add must be compatible with the equipment that's already there. However, even when starting from the ground up, you should consider how well your prospective routers interoperate with each other, as well as with your hosts and layer-two network devices such as Ethernet hubs or ATM switches. Don't assume that you will be able to settle on a single vendor for all time; make sure your prospects interoperate with each other. Although every vendor plans to be in business forever, vendors do go out of business, and you may find yourself having to change. If that happens, you will be more comfortable knowing that some of the vendors you rejected initially interoperate with the vendor you chose. Finding that you need to replace all of your existing routers to expand is a catastrophe too painful to discuss.

Don't assume that your equipment will work together properly just because your vendors quote standards compliance. Standards are often subject to some interpretation, and varying interpretations occasionally result in compatibility problems. If you are picky in only one part of your equipment evaluation, this is the one. Insist on *strict* adherence to standards on the part of your vendors.

Be cautious of a vendor's claims to exceed standard requirements, especially for physical issues like cable lengths. While it is certainly tempting to push the standards a bit and run a cable that is just 10 feet longer than the standard allows because a vendor permits it (and it makes your network topology fit), you are setting yourself up for trouble when you later have to replace that equipment with a vendor that was more strict in standards conformance. Just as you should insist that your vendors conform to standards, you, too, should adhere to network standards religiously, even if it costs you more. In the end, it *will* be worth it.

If possible, try to take the time to set up a small test network with as many different vendors' routers as you can. Try out the features that you expect to use to see how well they cooperate. Specifically, look first for the simple issues like whether basic packet sending and receiving work. Don't just send a few ICMP echo requests at the router and see that it responds. Instead, try to put some load on the router, perhaps by using your own staff as guinea pigs. This is the only sure way to generate not only a good traffic load, but something more typical to your network.

Second, look at how well the routers interoperate when using various dynamic routing protocols. Often, these protocols are complex, and may have specifications hundreds of pages long. It is easy for a vendor to slip up with one of these.

Finally, try simulating some failures in your test network, and see how well the routers detect and deal with these failures and the eventual recovery. Try to power up the routers and other equipment in different sequences; you may discover that some devices fail to initialize properly when others are not (or are) functioning. Turn on all the devices simultaneously, perhaps with a circuit breaker, to simulate an unattended recovery after a power failure. When you spot an incompatibility, don't immediately disqualify the router or routers in question. Instead, see if you can get the vendors to resolve the problem. This will also give you a handle on the quality of their customer support.

For example, in my network, we found ourselves investigating routers from a new vendor. Our backbone network was an FDDI ring connecting five routers together in a single room. When we added a router we were evaluating from a prospective vendor, the ring went into *wrap* state, indicating that one of the physical links was not coming up correctly. We isolated the link and discovered that it always occurred on the same side of the new vendor's router, no matter where in the ring we placed it. Rather than disqualify the new vendor's equipment, we turned both vendors loose on the problem and asked them for a resolution. Both had a vested interest in solving the problem. Our existing vendor wished to continue with us as a customer, so they would do well to please us, even if they were not at fault. Clearly, the new vendor had to prove to us how well they could deal with a problem, at least if they wanted to see our business.

In the end, both vendors came to the conclusion (not entirely willingly, I might add) that our original vendor was at fault. But, this was not sufficient for our prospective new vendor. They provided us a work-around in their router to allow us to interoperate. This clinched the deal, especially when our existing vendor informed us that they could do nothing to resolve the problem.

Reliability

Reliability is one of the hardest to quantify criteria in any equipment evaluation process. Vendors are quick to quote values for *mean time between failures (MTBF)* and *mean time to repair (MTR*)*, but these values are nothing more than

---

* Also known as MTTR in some literature.

averages. Generally, they only cover hardware problems and completely ignore software failure. Still, they can be interesting reading.

With this lack of easy quantification, how should you best evaluate a router's reliability? This is especially important, as reliability is one of the key factors that will help or hinder you in achieving your network goals. My advice is to talk to other network administrators. Ask your prospective vendors to provide a list of customers in your area, or with networks like yours. If a vendor tries to tell you that it is not their policy to divulge the names of their customers, be suspicious! While they may be legitimately trying to protect the privacy of their customers, they may also want to hide their problems from prospective customers.

When you do talk to their customers, make it clear that you are considering a purchase. You may want to describe in broad terms the type of network you are planning to build. Probe them for how often the hardware fails, what kind of repair response they get, how often the software fails, and their overall satisfaction with their choice. They may be willing to tell you what other vendors they considered and why they chose the vendor they did. Often, you will find that they considered some of the same vendors you are considering, and they may be able to tell you things you hadn't thought of.

In the end, though, a lot of the reliability question comes down to name recognition. You don't expect problems with reliability if the name on the router is Cisco, Bay, or Proteon, but Joe's Routers should make you pause for thought. Saving money up front often means you spend more in the long run, particularly if you have to replace failed equipment.

Serviceability

A router, whether dedicated or host-based, is one of the most complex pieces of hardware and software built. Regardless of how reliable the router or routers you select are, you will have both hardware and software failures. If anyone tries to tell you that their equipment *never* fails, *run*, don't walk, to another vendor! When a router fails, its most important quality is its serviceability. Among the things you want to look for are:

- Hot-swappable components
- Accessibility of these components to service personnel
- Self-diagnostic capabilities
- Ease of software upgrades

A few years ago, hot-swappable components were a rare item. But as our dependence on computer networks has grown, it has become unreasonable to have to turn off a router to replace a failed component. So, many vendors of modular computer and networking equipment worked to provide the ability to replace hardware components without powering down. Thus, it became possible to replace a failed Ethernet board in a router without having to disrupt any users who were not connected to that board. The ability to replace components while the router is running can be crucial as the size of routers and networks increases.

Routers that do not have hot-swappable components can make up for this lack by having easily accessible components. As an example, the DEC Rainbow PC could be completely stripped down to components and its mother board replaced in about 15 minutes with no tools. Even though the components may not be swappable with the power on, if the entire operation can be performed quickly, the disruption is minimal. Component accessibility is even more useful if hot swapping is possible. Of course, hot-swappable components or not, if you cannot tell what is failing, it doesn't help you. This is where self-diagnostic capabilities come into play.

Sometimes, a failure will be so obvious that you can identify the failed component based solely on external observation. More often, the component has failed in a strange way, or is partially functional. For these, you need an extensive set of online diagnostic capabilities. The router should be able to report how much traffic it is sending and receiving on each interface, how many errors of various kinds it is seeing, and maybe even the air temperature inside or the power supply voltage. With this information, it is possible to examine a router in great detail and determine what the problem may be without even touching the router physically. Diagnostic capabilities can easily pay for themselves by reducing the number of trips you make to repair the router, since you know what you should bring with you the first time.

For example, recently an FDDI interface failed in one of our routers. The failure was unusual in that the router containing the card could tell very little about the failure; more important, the card failed in such a way that the entire FDDI ring stopped functioning. By examining the information provided by the failing router and its neighbors on the ring, we were able to isolate the failure to one physical link between two adjacent routers; with a few cable swaps, we had determined which of the two routers was failing. Had the routers not provided low-level diagnostic information, such a failure could only have been isolated by trial and error testing of every link in the ring.

Finally, if a router's software is failing, you need some way to upgrade that software when your vendor provides a fix. In some instances, software can be upgraded on the fly—the new software is copied across the network to the router, and the router then reloads, starting this new software. During this time, the router continues switching packets, only disrupting service for the brief interval while the router reboots. I'll show an example of such an upgrade of a

Cisco router in Chapter 8, *The Technical Side of Network Management.* On the other hand, it is possible that a software upgrade may require replacing a set of ROM chips on one or more boards in the router. These upgrades are typically very disruptive and require special procedures and tools. Avoid any kind of upgrade process like this!

In addition to the issues of how you fix the router when it fails, two other issues should be considered part of your serviceability criteria:

- Environmental requirements
- Mounting requirements

If you're not used to dealing with large computers, you may be surprised that routers often require carefully regulated environments. While a small personal computer might be quite comfortable in an office environment, or even a home office, a larger computer often needs a carefully controlled temperature (i.e., air conditioning), humidity, and even power. Often, the conditions in an office that are sufficient for a personal computer are woefully inadequate for a larger machine. A large router may require an environment more like a data center's machine room than a back office or a closet. It is, after all, a large and powerful computer. Take environmental requirements into account when planning where you will put your routers and when selecting the equipment you will use. If you have no choice but to use a back office or a closet for a router in a specific location, don't choose a router that expects a more tightly regulated environment. Keep in mind also that a wiring closet typically has poorer ventilation than any office, and quite probably has a large amount of equipment (hubs, switches, and routers) generating heat. If anything, overestimate how warm your wiring closets may get if you are considering installing a lot of electronics in them.

You should also review mounting requirements carefully *before* you place an order. Among the things you should consider are whether the router can (or must) be mounted in an equipment rack, or whether it can (or must) be placed on a table or shelf. How much clearance should be maintained around the router? If necessary, can it be mounted flush to the wall? Will it fit in an existing rack? How much does it weigh?

While these issues probably don't have the importance of your other criteria, it is, to say the least, annoying to discover that you have no way to mount your brand new router, or that the great deal you got on your router means that you have to spend more to provide the air conditioning or power that it needs.

Support from the Vendor

In addition to considering how easy it is to service your routers when they fail, give careful thought to the kinds and level of support you can expect from your vendor, both when your router is failing and during normal operation. Support can take many forms. Here are some questions to ask:

- Do they provide a help desk that can answer routine questions, in addition to assisting you when you have problems?

- What kind of training courses do they offer?

- What kind of installation support do they offer?

- Is the equipment maintained completely by the vendor, completely by the owner, or some combination?

- What about software upgrades, will they be available, how often, and in what form?

Help desk support

A help desk can be your lifeline during a network failure. No matter how well documented a router's software is, when your network is failing, you may not have the time to wade through a few thousand pages of documentation. Often, someone at a help desk can either get you the answer you need directly, or route your call to a technician who can identify the problem, and then work to correct it. And because they deal with thousands of customers in situations like yours, they may be able to suggest a solution quickly because they have seen the problem before.

The help desk is also a good channel for giving the vendor information about bugs. Router software is extremely complex, and is almost certain to contain bugs ranging from minor nuisances to major problems. No matter how much the vendor tests the router, they cannot duplicate the conditions that exist in even a small fraction of the networks where their equipment may be used. Vendors must therefore depend on the users to find and report bugs.

When reporting a bug, do not disturb the state of the router if at all possible. If you have a bug that is only a minor nuisance, rather than a network-crashing monster, leave the router in the error state until you have talked to the vendor's support personnel. Often, they will ask you to provide them with the output of some diagnostic commands. This allows them to collect information and provide you with a permanent fix. On the other hand, if your network is severely affected, do whatever is necessary to restore operation, even if that means destroying state in the router by rebooting it. But, if possible, try to preserve as much information as you can.

Later, when we talk about diagnosing problems in your network, we'll discuss some of the information that a vendor is likely to request when you report a problem. Typically, this information takes just a few minutes to collect. Even if the failure is catastrophic, it's worth taking the time to collect any information the vendor is likely to need. After all, if you don't help the vendor fix the problem, the problem will just come back, and it may come back just as you sit down to a nice dinner.

Finally, find out whether the vendor's help desk is solely to help you resolve a network failure, or if it is also intended as a means for you to ask questions about new features you are thinking of deploying, or for clarification of a part of the vendor's documentation that is unclear. A good help desk will answer these questions to avoid future problems.

Training

No matter how much you know about network administration, and no matter how much time you spend reading the vendor's documentation, you should consider what the vendor offers in training courses. Documentation only goes so far. You cannot ask a piece of documentation to answer a question that the author did not anticipate. It also is seldom capable of helping you to understand the subtle interactions between features of the router and your network needs. For questions like these, you need to deal with a person, and a help desk can only go so far. We've said it before: an IP router is an incredibly complex piece of hardware and software. Who better understands this complexity than the people who made it? A well-designed training course can save you weeks of head-scratching exploration, and may be able to help you avoid an expensive network failure. In short, training courses are generally money well spent.

If your vendor does not provide training, find out if they endorse any third-party training services. Your vendor may have found it more cost-effective to train a few professional trainers and refer customers to them, rather than try to maintain their own training staff. If the vendor endorses a training group, consider them roughly equivalent to direct vendor training.

Installation support

Depending on your staff's skills, you may find that having the vendor assist you in installing your routers, at least the first one or two, is a useful way to get your network jump-started. If your vendor has good installation support, they can help you avoid many of the pitfalls that new customers wander into. By being familiar with their own equipment, vendors can help you concentrate on establishing your new network, or in adding their equipment to your existing network. If you are adding a new vendor's equipment to your existing network, it is even more important to seek your new vendor's assistance. This allows you to concentrate on making sure that your existing network doesn't come crashing down around you. It also helps you to identify what is at fault when things don't go quite the way you planned.

While most vendors offer some level of installation support, especially for new customers, it isn't always without cost. While charges for installation support should certainly be considered in your overall evaluation, give serious consideration to taking advantage of any resources the vendor offers. Once you become more familiar with their product, you will find that you can setup, upgrade, reconfigure, or reboot their equipment with confidence, sometimes while sitting at home in your robe and sipping a cup of coffee. Until then, seek help.

Who maintains the equipment?

This question is far more critical than many people think, at least until they are sitting in front of a dead router trying to get their network functioning, possibly with their boss standing right behind them. Vendor support contracts can range from total vendor maintenance to total self-maintenance. The level of support you need depends a lot on your staff's skills, and how serviceable the vendor has made their product.

On one extreme, the vendor may do everything for you, including configuring your routers, and making the changes you need as your network changes. This is generally expensive, and unless the vendor is ready to make changes on short notice, it can also result in delays when you need to reconfigure a router. If you and your staff lack the skills necessary to carry out the maintenance tasks, you should consider choosing vendor maintenance. For an additional charge, you can often negotiate a higher level of support, even if the vendor's standard contract assumes self maintenance.

At the other extreme, the vendor does nothing but replace failed components and provide software patches. In these cases, you need some additional skills in your staff. For example, if a router component fails, you first need to identify what has failed. This is often no trivial matter. Is it software? Is it hardware? If it is hardware, which piece? Once you have identified the failed component, you need to obtain a replacement. When that arrives, you need to remove the failed component and replace it with the spare part. As long as your staff has the skills to perform these tasks, there is certainly an advantage to self-maintained equipment. Vendor maintenance typically occurs only during clearly defined hours and days that may not match your business needs. A vendor may not be willing to do maintenance after your company's business hours. Self maintenance can be scheduled when it is convenient for you and your users.

Software updates

It is important to ask your vendor how software updates are handled. If you have a maintenance contract, some number of software updates (maybe all) are usually included in the contract. Software updates to add features may cost additional money, while bug fixes are free. In any case, you need to find out what the vendor's policy is *before* you decide on your routers. Otherwise, you may find that adding a feature that you later find necessary will cost more money than you saved.

Besides understanding what software updates you can expect to obtain and what they will cost, it is also useful to ask your vendor how often they update their software to add features. Over time, all vendors add new features to their software. The IP standards are an ever-evolving system. As new features are defined, or old features are found to be lacking, the standards change. Ideally, you want your vendor to offer you the new features you want or need, just as you want or need them.

It's worth putting some effort into figuring out how much effort your prospective vendors are expending to keep current with the evolving Internet standards. Sadly, some vendors seem to be so far out of touch that they really don't understand what the Internet is. The RFCs are a constantly changing array of interacting standards, proposed standards, and sometimes even half-baked ideas. While your vendor may have once had a thorough understanding of the Internet protocol suite, unless they are staying on top of things, they are likely to be implementing obsolete standards. The best possible way for a prospective vendor to keep on top of the latest standards efforts is to actively participate in them. Find out if your vendor has representatives in any of the *Internet Engineering Task Force (IETF)* working groups. Better yet, see if they have people who are chairing any of these working groups. The working groups work out the evolution of protocols in the IP suite, and those who are participating in writing the standards are much more likely to understand how to implement them correctly.

If your vendor frequently adds features of limited utility, you may find that you are paying for these features in hidden ways. One of these ways is increased complexity, resulting in more bugs. Another way is in slightly higher prices overall. In short, try to find a vendor with a good balance between release frequency and the quality of the features they add.

Another question to ask is how quickly your vendor can provide a patch for any bugs that affect your network. I am currently dealing with two different router vendors. One vendor seems to fix bugs 18 to 24 months after they are reported, if ever. The other vendor has often fixed bugs in less than a week, and sometimes has provided custom-built software images to fix a problem. Needless to say, the first vendor is no longer my vendor of choice. When you get the answer to this question, remember to be reasonable. The answer may depend on the severity of the bug. Something that has a severe impact on your network should be fixed in a matter of days, if not less. On the other hand, minor nuisances or bugs that are difficult to identify may linger for a month or more before being fixed.

Finally, ask your vendor how long they are willing to support older versions of their software. While no vendor supports old software forever, you don't want your vendor pushing you to upgrade to their latest version, complete with all its new bugs, just to get a fix to a bug in your otherwise stable older software.

Hardware upgrade options

When you are purchasing new hardware, one of the last things on your mind is replacing it. But all hardware eventually exceeds its useful life and must be replaced with newer, faster, and perhaps bigger hardware. When that happens, an important question is how much value your older hardware still retains, either on the second-hand market, or as trade-in credit with your vendor. A good vendor recognizes that your continued satisfaction means that you will be a repeat customer. Therefore, they may give you quite liberal trade-in options on your old equipment. One vendor I know of has even offered me trade-in credit on another vendor's equipment.

A related issue is how your vendor handles hardware upgrades that are necessary for the continued operation of your equipment. For example, we purchased several large LAN switches from a vendor when the devices were very new (we ran software version 1.1 on them). Within a year, the vendor discovered that they had been a bit too stingy in their initial allocation of memory, and announced that the next version of the software would not run without a memory upgrade. Rather than charge their loyal customers for what can be described as an engineering mistake, they offered to upgrade all of the switches to the new memory size at no cost. Needless to say, that made points with my management!

This isn't to say that all vendors should continually offer free upgrades to your hardware. If they did, they would surely go out of business and you'd be left with a bunch of orphan equipment. But a vendor who really wants to keep you as a customer *will* find ways to help you protect your investment in what can be very expensive equipment. Perhaps they do this through trade-in credits, free hardware upgrades to correct their own misjudgment, or by designing the newer hardware to allow you to carry forward some portion of your old hardware, such as interface boards. Whatever method they use, this kind of investment protection can be worth a lot of money down the road, so don't ignore this issue when you evaluate your vendors.

Finally, your vendor should be up front with you about their plans to phase out some models or options, and what support you can expect once your equipment has been discontinued. Clearly you should not expect full support for your older equipment. The amount of support you receive will most certainly decline as the equipment becomes older, but there is nothing more frustrating than buying a top-of-the-line router, only to find that the vendor discontinues it in six months and drops all support. Other customers can give you interesting information about how the vendor has handled obsolescence in the past.

Performance

In any network, the router can easily become a performance bottleneck. IP networks and IP routers are no different. Examining an IP datagram's destination address, looking up the destination in a routing table, and forwarding the datagram to another network segment clearly aren't instantaneous. The act traditionally called *routing* is actually composed of multiple, separable actions. In general, these activities can be described as *switching* datagrams from one network segment to another, and the *overhead* of maintaining routing tables, memory buffers, and so on. Because switching IP datagrams is the activity of most concern to the network's users, a well-designed router should take steps to minimize the impact of any overhead activities. If possible, these activities should be performed by a separate processor.

Regardless of how well the router handles its overhead activities, overhead will have some impact on packet-switching performance. Part of the impact comes from the need to update the routing tables that the switching engine uses to make decisions. While a table entry is being updated, it is unavailable to the switching engine. Other impacts come from the other overhead activities the router performs. For example, processing a dynamic routing protocol, providing a time base to the network, and even responding to network management requests all have some impact on the router's performance.

Because of the number of things a router may do that can impact its performance, and because no two router vendors implement the same architecture in either their hardware or software, it is not possible to compare meaningfully the performance of two different routers using direct measures of the impact of overhead activities on switching. Instead, vendors typically provide performance measurements that demonstrate in quantifiable and comparable terms how quickly their router can perform its assigned tasks. These measurements typically are composed of two principle values. The first of these is called the router's *throughput*, and the second is called its *latency*.

Throughput

The first important measure of a router's performance is its *throughput*. Throughput measures how much data the router can forward in a given time interval. Most often, the throughput of a router is measured in *packets per second (pps)*. Ideally a router that has a throughput of 1,000 pps would clearly be faster than a router that has a throughput of 900 pps. Unfortunately, throughput numbers by themselves are not terribly useful, nor even comparable.

To understand why throughput numbers may be hard to compare, consider the effect of a different packet size on the performance of a router. The minimum size for an Ethernet frame is 64 octets. The maximum size is 1,518 octets. Clearly, it takes longer to transmit a long frame than a short frame. If it takes longer to transmit a long frame, then the router sees fewer packets in the measurement interval and has more time to recover from each frame before the next arrives. For this reason, most router vendors test their equipment with the smallest possible frame sizes to obtain higher throughput ratings. So the first question to ask when reviewing throughput values is: *How big were the test frames?*

Even if two router vendors use the same frame sizes, other factors can affect the numbers dramatically. Consider different ways of testing a router with four Ethernet interfaces. The throughput numbers for this router will differ radically depending on how the traffic flows. For example, if you use two receiving devices, called *sinks*, one on each of two of the Ethernets, and two sending devices, called *sources*, on the remaining Ethernets, your results will depend on whether you set one source to send packets to one sink and the other source to send to the other, or you set both sources to send packets randomly to both sinks.

Finally, be sure to ask what else the router is doing while under test. Vendors are likely to quote test results when the router is not doing anything else. After all, they want the numbers to be the best possible, even if they are not realistic. For example, one current vendor quotes an impressive 250,000 pps throughput on one of their high-end routers. However, if you do something as simple as enable a packet filter on this router, you can cut that maximum performance from 250,000 pps to something closer to 28,000 pps. If you require IP fragmentation to occur, the numbers drop to around 2,000 pps!

But what is a reasonable value for throughput? The answer depends a lot on the number and type of interfaces present in the router and on the mix of traffic on your network. With a little work, you can get a figure that tells you whether your prospective router is in the ballpark. The first factor to consider is the mix of media you will be putting in a router. As the speed of the medium varies, and as the size of the packets varies, the number of packets arriving at the router changes. To figure out the largest number of packets per second that can arrive at the router from a given medium, you need to account for the time it takes to receive the smallest possible frame, and how much time is required between frames by the medium's specification. Theoretical values for the maximum packets per second for four typical media are presented in Table 4-1.

Table 4-1. Theoretical Maximum Packets Per Second for Common Network Media

Medium	Bandwidth		Min Packet Size	Max PPS
Ethernet	10	Mbps	64 octets	14,880
Token Ring	16	Mbps	64 octets	24,691
FDDI	100	Mbps	64 octets	152,439
T1	1.544	Mbps	64 octets	3,300

But these values are theoretical maximums, not real values. They assume that every packet on the network segment is bound for the router, that there is no traffic from the router (presumably from other network segments), and that all packets are of this minimal size. Analysis of real network traffic will show dramatically different values for the load a typical medium will present to a router. One such analysis presented by Bill Kelly of Cisco Systems[*] showed that a typical Ethernet under heavy load (30 percent of bandwidth) only presents about 300 pps of real load to a router. While his analysis did not present figures for other media, it is reasonable to assume that they would be proportional to the bandwidth of the media involved. If this is true, then a typical FDDI network under 30 percent bandwidth utilization with similar traffic characteristics to the analyzed Ethernet would result in a load of approximately 3,000 pps. While this isn't necessarily a heavy load for an FDDI ring, it is probably not atypical. Still, if you feel more comfortable working with a 60 percent bandwidth figure, double the packet count to 6,000 pps.

Consider a router with two FDDI interfaces, and 18 Ethernets. In theory, the maximum number of packets this router might have to deal with is the sum of packets on all interfaces divided by two (the packets have to leave the router somewhere) or:

$$\frac{18 \times 14,880 + 2 \times 152,439}{2} = 286,359 \text{ pps}$$

which exceeds the throughput ratings for most routers on the market. But this is a theoretical maximum, consisting entirely of minimum-length packets always going between network segments. No real network will exhibit these characteristics. If

---

[*] Bill Kelly is Director of Enterprise Technical Marketing at Cisco Systems. The analysis cited was presented as part of a presentation titled "Cisco Router and Switch Performance Characteristics" at Cisco's Networkers '95 in Stanford, CA.

we accept Bill Kelly's analysis of a more typical traffic load, we get a much more reasonable value:

$$\frac{18 \times 300 + 2 \times 3,000}{2} = 5,700 \text{ pps}$$

So should you just ignore throughput ratings? Certainly not! While it is true that an average load for our example router will be more like 5,700 pps than 286,359 pps, the bursty characteristics of real network traffic may well cause times when the instantaneous load approaches the theoretical maximum for short intervals, and your router should deal with these times as well as possible. However, this analysis does mean that you need to keep throughput numbers in perspective. If a router with only eight Ethernets is touted as having a throughput rating of 100,000 pps, it is not necessarily better than a different router with eight Ethernets that only claims a 75,000 pps throughput. Both exceed the maximum load that the eight Ethernets can provide by a comfortable margin.

Latency

Another important aspect of a router's performance is *latency*, also called *delay*. Most vendors quote latency statistics; examining them should be part of your selection process. Latency is simply the amount of time a packet spends inside a router. No matter how many packets per second the router is theoretically capable of switching, if it takes a long time to handle any one packet, users of the network will perceive that the network is slow. Studies have shown that from the time a user strikes a key on a keyboard until the time the character is echoed on the screen should be less than half a second, or the user perceives an unacceptable delay. Because most Telnet sessions are set up so that the remote host echoes the keystrokes back to the user's computer, delay in the routers must be kept minimal to go unnoticed.

As with router throughput, the way latency is measured affects the results. For example, when should timing start and end? You can get smaller latency measurements by starting your measurement when the last octet of the packet is received, and stopping when the first octet is transmitted. Ideally, the clock should start ticking when the first octet is received and stop when the first octet is transmitted, or it should start when the last octet is received and stop when the last octet is transmitted. Likewise, packet size can make some difference to latency measurements. If the router must copy a packet's data within its own memory, a longer packet will clearly take longer to copy than a shorter packet.

If you know how the measurements were obtained (when the clock started and stopped) and how long the packets were, you can convert two different measurements to a common basis for comparison, as shown in Table 4-2.

Table 4-2. As Quoted, Router 1 Appears to Have the Smaller Latency

	Router 1	Router 2
Quoted latency	1 ms	1.5 ms
Packet size	1,500 octets	1,000 octets
Measurement period	Last octet in to first octet out	First octet in to first octet out

In Table 4-2, Router 1 appears to have lower latency. However, this vendor has elected to use the most favorable measurement period available. If the packet sizes were the same, we could either correct the latency figure for Router 1 by adding the time it takes to receive the packet from the network (we will assume an Ethernet), or we could correct the latency figure for Router 2 by subtracting the time it takes to receive the packet from the network.

Because the packet sizes are different, we must correct both routers' latency values. For Router 1, we simply need to add the time to receive 1,500 octets from the network. For Router 2, we need to subtract the time that it took to receive the 1,000 octets from the network, and then add the time it would need to receive the 1,500 octets, just as we did for Router 1. The results are shown in Table 4-3.

Table 4-3. Correcting Latencies for Both Routers

Ethernet speed:	10 Mbps
Bits per octet:	8
Time per bit:	$\dfrac{1}{10 \text{ Mbps}} = 0.1 \mu s$
Time per octet:	$8 \times 0.1 \mu s = 0.8 \mu s$
Time to receive 1,500 octets:	$1500 \times 0.8 \mu s = 1.2 ms$
Time to receive 1,000 octets:	$1000 \times 0.8 \mu s = 0.8 ms$
Router 1 corrected latency:	$1 ms + 1.2 ms = 2.2 ms$
Router 2 corrected latency:	$1.5 ms - 0.8 ms + 1.2 ms = 1.9 ms$

When we correct the latencies to show comparable values, Router 2 actually has the smaller latency. Unfortunately, these corrections cannot take into account any differences in latency in Router 2 that may be due to copying the longer packet because that value is unavailable to us, but they do at least give us a more accurate comparison.

All this should tell you that figures for throughput and latency should be taken with a grain of salt. At a minimum, you need to understand under what conditions the figures were obtained before you can even begin to compare figures from different vendors. Even then, those conditions are likely to be nearly ideal, and unlikely to exist in any real network.

Flexibility

Some may argue that a dedicated router is not programmable. In one sense, they are right. However, in an abstract way, all programming languages are just a highly sophisticated way of configuring a computer to carry out a task. In this sense, the configuration languages of many of today's dedicated IP routers are highly task-specific programming languages.

Whether you call it programmability or configurability, it all boils down to how much control you have over how the router behaves. On one end of the spectrum, you have almost no control. Your options include little more than the assignment of IP addresses to interfaces, the definition of subnet masks, and the creation of static routes. On the other end of the spectrum, you may have so much control, that you can cause the router to violate one or more standards, or even not to function at all.

When you assess the *flexibility* of a prospective router, consider carefully the tradeoffs involved. A router that has few configuration options may well suit the needs of a large percentage of your network segments. After all, the options that aren't configurable will probably default to reasonable settings established by the vendor. However, your network probably has a few unusual segments where additional flexibility is necessary. You are most likely to need a flexible router if it needs to connect to an existing legacy network. The legacy equipment may not conform to standards, or the standards may have evolved since the equipment was installed, and its vendor has not kept up with the changes. The legacy vendor may even be out of business, which is the reason you are considering a new vendor in the first place.

To make matters worse, the network segments where you need additional flexibility may not yet exist in your network plan. Because no network design can foresee the future with perfect accuracy, you cannot be sure that the configuration options you need today will be all that you ever need. For this reason, it is a good idea to look for routers with more flexibility than you currently need.

Unfortunately, flexibility isn't without its drawbacks. Consider the difference between a portable radio and a component stereo system. Both can be tuned to receive a given radio station, and both can have the volume set to a comfortable listening level. But the component stereo system will probably have adjustments for bass, treble, balance, fade, and possibly a graphic equalizer. It may have a set of special controls that let you dub tapes, change settings depending on the source of music, and so on. Clearly, anyone who has been confronted with such a stereo system knows that the sheer number of buttons, knobs, and sliders presents a challenge to the average user who just wants to listen to the radio. The same is true for IP routers. As the number of configuration options goes up, the complexity of a typical configuration also goes up, and the sophistication of the person configuring the router must increase.

Fortunately, most routers with many configuration options also have reasonable default values. This helps, but it does not completely eliminate the need to understand the options available. While it is possible, and even likely, that most of the options will default to values correct for your network segments, you can't tell if the default settings are correct if you don't understand what the options mean.

What is a reasonable degree of flexibility? This depends on your network, but at a minimum, you really want to have the following options:

- Setting of IP addresses, netmasks, and broadcast addresses on each interface

- The ability to set multiple IP addresses on the same interface

- Enabling and disabling of proxy ARP on a per-interface basis

- The ability to configure static routes

- The ability to configure one or more dynamic routing protocols

- The ability to suppress dynamic routing protocol updates on a per-interface basis

- The ability to pass routing information between two routing protocols, should the need arise

- The ability to selectively block packets from going out or coming in an interface

- The ability to restrict Telnet or SNMP access to the router to a selected set of machines on your network

- The ability to control some or all of the aspects of the operation of your dynamic routing protocols, such as timers, preference of one route over another, and with whom the protocol is spoken

- The handling of source routed IP packets

- The generation of ICMP packets of various types

- The ability to control some interface-specific parameters

The last of these is perhaps the most unusual and the most dangerous. But when you need the ability, you *really* need it! As an example, recall the earlier example involving adding a new vendor's router to an existing FDDI ring. No matter what we tried, the ring would not come up fully. It always wrapped on one connection between the new router and the existing routers. In the end, we determined that the existing routers were not capable of keeping up with the new router when initializating the FDDI connection. Both vendors were technically in compliance with the standards; the new vendor was just faster. The solution was to configure the new vendor's router to perform one critical step just a few tens of milliseconds slower to give the older routers a chance to keep up. Had that option not been available, it is likely that the ring would have never been fully operational.

So when assessing the flexibility of a prospective router's configuration, you want to ensure that the router will be flexible enough to meet your current needs and needs you haven't anticipated, but not so complex that you get lost in the details. You also want to ensure that the options default to a set of reasonable values, and that you understand what these options do.

Methods of configuration

One final aspect of flexibility is the method you use to configure the router. Several different possibilities exist. Among them are a simple command line interface, an online menu-based system, a web-based configuration system using your existing WWW browser, the *Simple Network Management Protocol (SNMP)*, or a proprietary software package designed to run under some kind of windowing system on a workstation. Which you prefer is largely a matter of taste, but there are some general things to consider about each.

In a command line interface, you usually have access to the full range of flexibility that the router's configuration allows. Using this interface, you are free to select from a wide array of possible configurations, and you have the advantage that you can access the router using a simple terminal or terminal emulator program on a workstation. You can probably access this interface from the network via a remote login protocol such as Telnet. This makes it possible to configure a router or work on a problem without having to go to the router. Perhaps the biggest advantage of a command line interface is the ability to modify your configuration or debug your router with a minimum of hardware and software. You can easily use anything from a dumb terminal that lacks even full-screen addressability, all the way up to a fancy terminal emulator that is part of a workstation window system. You can also work with a wide range of connection speeds—anything from a low-speed dial-up line to a fast network connection. Try that with a graphical interface and see how frustrating it becomes on slower links!

Additionally, a simple command line interface can be scripted using tools like TCL Expect, described in *Exploring Expect*, by Don Libes (O'Reilly). While it is possible to script other styles of interfaces, such as text-based menus, getting them right is much harder than a simple command line—believe me, I've worked with both. Moreover, because a command line requires little special formatting, it is easier to show examples in training manuals for your staff, debugging notes, or email messages, whether to your staff or to your vendor's tech support staff.

One of the drawbacks to a command line interface is that it is often hard to know which options are appropriate at various points in the configuration process. In a well-designed interface, there will be context-sensitive help (the help topics presented only apply to your current task), but well-designed interfaces are not always the rule. Additionally, depending on your skills with a keyboard and the assistance provided by the router's configuration editor, typing the appropriate commands to cause a desired configuration change may be a problem. Again, a well-designed interface and editor make this less of a problem, but the truly well-designed interface is rare. Still, this is the interface I prefer.

With an online menu-based system, the router vendor attempts to provide you with a nicely-structured process to achieve a desired configuration. The advantage of a menu system is that you do not get lost in the details that are not immediately important to your task. It is also possible for the vendor to change the menus dynamically, to reflect your previous choices and thereby avoid many common mistakes. A menu based interface may be available via a remote login protocol, just as is the case for a command line interface.

One drawback of menu-based configuration is that it requires an intelligent terminal or terminal emulator. A common requirement is that your terminal or terminal program must be capable of emulating a DEC VT100. While this is certainly a common case, it does present some limitation to your choices of terminal equipment or programs. The second major drawback to a menu-based system is that it typically does not present you with all the options you may need; if it does, it can be hard to hunt for the appropriate option on all the menus and sub-menus. It is also somewhat difficult to view your entire current configuration in a convenient way, unless the system has such an option built-in.

A recent interesting combination of the command line interface and a menu system is a web-based configuration system. Using your standard web browser you access a server built in to the router to query its status or configure it. The one example of this that I am directly familiar with is the HTTP server built into recent versions of the Cisco IOS. By adding this command to your configuration:

```
ip http server
```

you enable access to your router from any browser, even a text-only browser such as lynx.*

Once connected to the router this way, you have access to some of the most common commands via hyperlinks, including full access to configure the router. But you also have access to some of the more common diagnostic commands without actually logging in to the router. This can be a useful intermediate position between the CLI and a menu-based system. The resulting router home page is shown in Figure 4-1. It's not pretty, but it is reasonably functional.

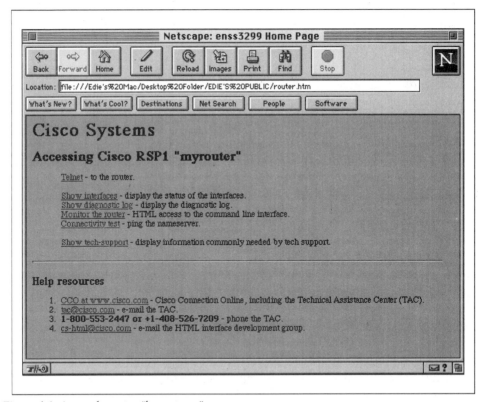

Figure 4-1. A sample router "home page"

---

* Like any interface to your router, this interface should be secured and limited to access by your network staff. How this can be accomplished will be discussed in Chapter 10, *Network Security*.

The problems I see with this kind of interface, though, are largely the same as with the menu-based system, and with the graphical interface system described below. Namely, you can't always access this interface from the simplest hardware. Additionally, as it is currently presented, the web-based interface is rather cumbersome and incomplete—accessing even a simple *traceroute* command requires multiple levels of links, but could be accomplished in just a few keystrokes on the router's CLI. Still, keep an eye on this evolving method of configuration and monitoring. It may improve and become an important tool for your help desk staff (with appropriate security safeguards).

Increasingly, network equipment is becoming configurable using SNMP. This protocol was designed for configuring and monitoring devices on a network. It defines a database of variables, known as a *Management Information Base (MIB)*, and carries out its tasks by reading or writing the values of these variables under the control of a piece of software running on a remote computer. SNMP usually does not replace other configuration options. Instead, it is provided as an alternative or as an enhancement to them.

Standardization is SNMP's big advantage. Because it uses a non-proprietary protocol and a well-defined MIB, it is possible to use the same software to configure equipment of many different types from several different vendors. Combined with its ability to monitor the state of this equipment, SNMP is gaining favor among network managers.

The main disadvantage of SNMP is that it requires management software running on another computer. Some vendors provide software capable of managing their own equipment, and at least monitoring that of other vendors, while others leave the user to his or her own devices. Fortunately, generalized SNMP-based network management software is available for a variety of host systems from a variety of vendors, such as HP's OpenView, Sun's Sun Net Manager, and IBM's Netview 6000, so the user is not completely out in the cold. Another disadvantage of SNMP is its complexity. In my opinion, the "simple" in the protocol name refers only to the simplicity of the mechanism for doing all tasks by reading and writing variables in a management database. To perform a configuration task using the protocol without special software provided by a router vendor is anything but simple. It may involve the correct setting of a dozen or more variables spread throughout the MIB.

A final disadvantage to SNMP is the difficulty of providing security in your configuration process. Each SNMP request and response carries a community string that is similar to a conventional password. If this community string is known or discovered, there is no security intrinsic in SNMP to prevent a malicious user from taking control of your router or other network device. While the same holds true for a password on a telnet session to the router, the password of a telnet session is only present on the network once, when the session is established, making it harder to retrieve by snooping since you have to be looking at the right time. Further, software is available that can prevent the password from traversing the network in clear text, such as Kerberos, TACACS, and RADIUS; these will be discussed in Chapter 10 when we talk about securing your routers.

SNMP version 2 addresses these security concerns, and provides a much stronger security model. However, finding vendors that fully support the security aspects of SNMPv2 is a daunting task. Further, you still need to find management software that takes advantage of these features, and then configure them all correctly. This adds enormously to the complexity of SNMP management. However, as a monitoring and troubleshooting tool, SNMP has some nice features, and should not be ignored.

Reject any router vendor whose sole means of configuration is a proprietary program running on a host computer. While these interfaces are often wonderfully intuitive, and may make excellent use of the graphics capabilities of whatever window system they run under, they suffer from some of the most extreme disadvantages of any of the configuration interfaces we have discussed. Chief among these disadvantages is that you are tied to a specific piece of software that the vendor provides, and the choice of platforms that the vendor wishes to support. How much use is that software to you if it only runs on a Windows-based PC when all of your machines are Apple Macintoshes? Another major disadvantage that such systems suffer is that they make it difficult to access the router's configuration from different locations. Rest assured that you will be called at 3:00 A.M. someday with a problem in one of your routers. If your only means of accessing that router is the machine on your desk at work, you will have no option but to get dressed and go to your office, unless the problem can wait until morning. If you have any kind of ASCII-based interface (command line or menus), you may be able to use a terminal or terminal program and a modem to dial-in to your router and fix the problem.

Finally, graphical-only configuration systems often make it difficult to understand what the resulting configuration of your routers will be until you have finished performing a task. Even then, it may be difficult to get a clear understanding of how things are configured, unless the vendor did a *very* good job with the interface. Again, stay away from any router vendor whose only means of configuration is through a flashy graphical interface.

Expandability

The final criterion you should consider when evaluating routers is *expandability*. Seldom will you accurately predict the correct number and type of interfaces that any specific router will ultimately need. When you underestimate your needs, you don't want to be faced with replacing the router you have outgrown, nor do you want to add an additional router to support one or two more network segments. Ideally, the router you bought initially had some excess capacity to handle this natural growth.

But you really don't want to have too much capacity sitting idle, unless you are absolutely sure you will need it. Consider a site where you expect you will ultimately need 10 or 11 Ethernet segments, but you currently only need 5. You could deploy a router with enough interfaces so that you don't have to replace it when your network grows. However, if you only have a choice between 6 interfaces and 12 interfaces, you might have a hard time convincing yourself that the money spent on the 7 idle interfaces was well spent. On the other hand, while 6 interfaces is a better fit for your current needs, it doesn't allow you much growth before you have to replace the router with the 12-port model.

This is where expandability comes into play. If the router allows you add interfaces incrementally, you can grow the router as your network grows. In other words, your ideal router might be one that has 6 interfaces initially, but that allows you to add more interfaces to keep up with growth. At the extreme, it may be possible to add interfaces one at a time, but this is often more costly than being able to install new interfaces in groups. When thinking about expandability, spend some time rethinking the serviceability issues discussed earlier. Ideally, you'd like the ability to add new interfaces without taking the router down and disrupting the users on the existing network segments. This is where hot-swappable components really stand out.

Adding more interfaces to a router isn't very useful if the processing power of the router is overly limited. While it would be nice to assume that router vendors would never sell a router that can be configured with more interfaces than the processing power of the router can support, this is not always the case. Often, it is not even an issue of the vendor trying to be deceptive, as much as it is that each network is unique and presents a unique processing load. In short, make sure that the router has enough processing power for its ultimate configuration, or be sure that there is a reasonable way to increase the power of the router, perhaps with an upgrade, when the time comes.

Special-purpose interfaces

In some cases, you may need to look at a prospective router's support for special-purpose interfaces. Nearly all router vendors support the common network technologies like Ethernet, Token Ring, FDDI, and serial interfaces, but what about your special needs? Three special-purpose interfaces that you might need to consider are:

- Direct attachment to a mainframe channel

- Asynchronous Transfer Mode (ATM)

- High Performance Parallel Interconnect (HiPPI)

If your network has one or more mainframe computers, you may find it advantageous to have a direct attachment to the mainframe's channel. This type of high-speed link to the mainframe may reduce the processing load on the system's central processor, and may eliminate the need to purchase other types of network hardware. Furthermore, this connection will probably provide faster access to your mainframe than LAN technologies like Ethernet or Token Ring for far less money. However, not all router vendors support such attachments, nor do those that do necessarily support them in all models of their routers. Similarly, if you believe that your network may eventually migrate in whole or in part to an ATM network, or if you have (or plan to acquire) a supercomputer with a HiPPI interface, the ability to support such a network in at least one of your routers will be crucial to integrating it with your existing network.

Unfortunately, it may not be possible to find a router or a router vendor that can support all of the special-purpose interfaces your network needs, and is capable of handling your network's more mundane requirements. You may be forced to buy routers from two or more vendors. If at all possible, try to keep the number of vendors to a minimum. Whenever you have multiple vendors' routers in your network, you increase the time needed to train network personnel in their operation, you increase the likelihood of interoperability problems and mistakes, and you limit your ability to exploit the features of your routers to those that all support. As a result, you often fail to achieve one or more of your network goals, and the gains are questionable.

5

Routing Protocol Selection

In previous chapters, I have focused the discussion on network design and router selection. While these topics are important if you are building a new network or planning whole or partial replacement of an existing network, they're only of theoretical interest if you already have a network in place. In this case, which is far more common, you don't get to choose your topology, media, or router vendors. You're stuck with the decisions you and your predecessors have made. At best, you can design your ideal network, and think about how to migrate to that design over the coming years.

This chapter shifts from the theoretical aspects of network design to the more practical aspects of network management. While there will certainly be some theoretical discussion, especially in the first few sections, theory will be balanced with a more practical discussion of configuration issues, whether for a new network or an existing network.

Static vs. Dynamic Routing

Before exploring the issues surrounding the selection and configuration of dynamic IP routing protocols, it is appropriate to discuss static routing as an alternative. In Chapter 1, *The Basics of IP Networking*, we saw that each machine in an IP network makes decisions about how to reach a destination by consulting its own private routing table. Rather than computing the entire path to a destination, it merely selects the next hop leading to that destination, and relies on the next hop machine to select a further hop that gets the packet closer to its destination. Independent hop-by-hop routing requires that all machines have a consistent view of how to reach all destinations in the network. If consistency is lost, two or more machines (presumably routers) can form a routing loop, and the packet never makes it to its destination.

To achieve consistency, a network administrator can either manually configure each machine with a precomputed set of routes that he or she knows to be consistent, or the machines can communicate routing information to each other through some kind of protocol. The first approach is known as *static routing*, and the second as *dynamic routing*.

Advantages of Static Routing

Static routing has some enormous advantages over dynamic routing. Chief among these advantages is predictability. Because the network administrator computes the routing table in advance, the path a packet takes between two destinations is always known precisely, and can be controlled exactly. With dynamic routing, the path taken depends on which devices and links are functioning, and how the routers have interpreted the updates from other routers.

Additionally, because no dynamic routing protocol is needed, static routing doesn't impose any overhead on the routers or the network links. While this overhead may be minimal on an FDDI ring, or even on an Ethernet segment, it could be a significant portion of network bandwidth on a low-speed dial-up link. Consider a network with 200 network segments. Every 30 seconds, as required by the RIP specification, the routers all send an update containing reachability information for all 200 of these segments. With each route taking 16 octets of space, plus a small amount of overhead, the minimum size for an update in this network is over three kilobytes. Each router must therefore send a 3 Kb update on each of its interfaces every 30 seconds. As you can see, for a large network, the bandwidth devoted to routing updates can add up quickly.

Finally, static routing is easy to configure on a small network. The network administrator simply tells each router how to reach every network segment to which it is not directly attached. Consider the network shown in Figure 5-1. This network has three routers connecting five network segments together. Clearly, the only path from Router1 to a host on `172.16.3.0/24` goes through Router2. Likewise, the only path to hosts on subnet `172.16.4.0/24` goes through Router3.

Here are the relevant fragments of the configurations of these three routers using static routing. Note that each router configuration must contain a static route for the networks attached to the other routers, but not those directly attached to the router itself.

Configuration for Router1:

```
hostname router1
!
interface ethernet 0
    ip address 172.16.1.1 255.255.255.0
!
interface ethernet 1
```

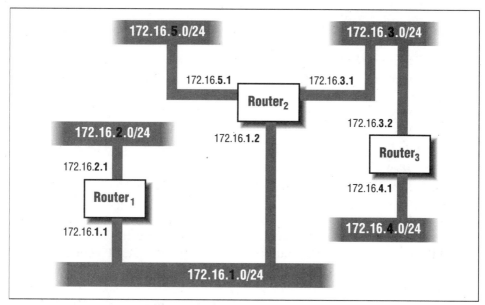

Figure 5-1. A small network using static routing

```
        ip address 172.16.2.1 255.255.255.0
    !
ip route 172.16.3.0 255.255.255.0 172.16.1.2
ip route 172.16.4.0 255.255.255.0 172.16.1.2
ip route 172.16.5.0 255.255.255.0 172.16.1.2
```

Configuration for Router2:

```
hostname router2
!
interface ethernet 0
    ip address 172.16.1.2 255.255.255.0
!
interface ethernet 1
    ip address 172.16.3.1 255.255.255.0
!
interface ethernet 2
    ip address 172.16.5.1 255.255.255.0
!
ip route 172.16.2.0 255.255.255.0 172.16.1.1
ip route 172.16.4.0 255.255.255.0 172.16.3.2
```

Configuration for Router3:

```
hostname router3
!
interface ethernet 0
    ip address 172.16.3.2 255.255.255.0
!
interface ethernet 1
```

```
     ip address 172.16.4.1 255.255.255.0
  !
  ip route 172.16.1.0 255.255.255.0 172.16.3.1
  ip route 172.16.2.0 255.255.255.0 172.16.3.1
  ip route 172.16.5.0 255.255.255.0 172.16.3.1
```

Each configuration starts by giving the router a name, and then defines an IP address and subnet mask for each of the router's interfaces. For example, on Router2, the second Ethernet interface (ethernet 1) is assigned the IP address 172.16.3.1, and the netmask 255.255.255.0. Similar commands defining addresses and netmasks for local interfaces will appear in all router configurations, regardless of whether a router is participating in a dynamic routing protocol. If the configurations stopped here, each router would have entries in its routing table for the networks attached to its own interfaces, and no others. But the configurations go on to define static routes showing how to reach networks attached to the other routers. Each ip route statement defines a static route to the destination indicated by the network number and mask by way of the router IP address listed. For example, the first ip route statement in Router3's configuration defines a route to 172.16.1.0, with a mask of 255.255.255.0 (172.16.1.0/24) via the router at 172.16.3.1. The static routes, together with the the local interfaces, let each router populate its routing table with information about each destination and the next hop to reach it.

While this small network doesn't require many static routes to achieve complete connectivity, and Router1 and Router3 could get by with static default routes pointing to Router2, it is easy to see that the configurations for a large network with hundreds of network segments and routers would be very complex.

And the Disadvantages of Static Routing

While static routing has advantages over dynamic routing, it is not without its disadvantages. The price of its simplicity is a lack of scalability. For five network segments on three routers, computing an appropriate route from every router to every destination is not difficult. However, many networks are much larger. Consider what the routing might look like for a network with 200 network segments interconnected by more than a dozen routers. To implement static routing, you would need to compute the next hop for each network segment for each router, or more than 2,400 routes! As you can see, the task of precomputing routing tables quickly becomes a burden, and is prone to errors.

Of course, you could argue that this computation need only occur once, when the network is first built. But what happens when a network segment moves, or is added? While the computation may be relatively easy, to implement the change, you would have to update the configuration for *every* router on the network. If you miss one, in the best case, segments attached to that router will be unable to reach the moved or added segment. In the worst case, you'll create a routing loop that affects many routers.

Finally, because static routing is, by definition, *static*, it cannot use redundant network links to adapt to a failure in the network. Consider what would happen to our network if we add an additional interface to Router3 and connected it to `172.16.2.0/24`, but left routing unchanged. If Router2 fails, Router3 would be unable to adapt to the change in the network topology and would still be unable to reach hosts on `172.16.1.0/24`. This inability to adapt to network failures, even when redundant paths are available, and the problems associated with scaling, are the primary motivations behind dynamic routing.

Advantages of Dynamic Routing

The chief advantages of dynamic routing over static routing are scalability and adaptability. A dynamically routed network can grow more quickly and larger, and is able to adapt to changes in the network topology brought about by this growth or by the failure of one or more network components.

With a dynamic routing protocol, routers learn about the network topology by communicating with other routers. Each router announces its presence, and the routes it has available, to the other routers on the network. Therefore, if you add a new router, or add an additional segment to an existing router, the other routers will hear about the addition and adjust their routing tables accordingly. You don't have to reconfigure the routers to tell them that the network has changed. Similarly, if you move a network segment, the other routers will hear about the change. You only need to change the configuration of the router (or routers) that connect the segment that moved. This reduces the chance that errors will occur.

The ability to learn about changes to the network's configuration has implications beyond adding new segments or moving old ones. It also means that the network can adjust to failures. If a network has redundant paths, then a partial network failure appears to the routers as if some segments got moved (they are now reached via alternate paths), and some segments have been removed from the network (they are now unreachable). In short, there's no real difference between a network failure and a configuration change. Dynamic routing allows the network to continue functioning, perhaps in a degraded fashion, when a partial failure occurs.

And the Disadvantages of Dynamic Routing

I would be a liar if I told you that dynamic routing has no disadvantages. Chief among the disadvantages is an increase in complexity. Communicating information about network topology is not as simple as saying, "Hey, I can reach the following destinations..." Each router participating in the dynamic routing protocol must decide exactly what information to send to other routers; more important, it must attempt to select the best route for reaching other destinations from the candidates it learns about from other routers. In addition, if a router is going to adapt to changes in the network, it must be prepared to remove old or unusable information from its routing table. How it determines what is old or unusable adds to the complexity of the routing protocol. Unfortunately, the better a protocol handles the various different situations in a network, the more complex it is likely to be. This complexity tends to lead to errors in the protocol's implementation, or differences in how vendors interpret the protocol.

In order to communicate information about the topology of the network, routers must periodically send messages to each other using a dynamic routing protocol. These messages must be sent across network segments just like any other packets. But unlike other packets in the network, these packets do not contain any information to or from a user. Instead, they contain information that is only useful to the routers. Thus, from the users' point of view, these packets are pure overhead. On a low-speed link, these messages can consume much of the available bandwidth, especially if the network is large or unstable.

Finally, some or all of the machines in a network may be unable to speak any dynamic routing protocol, or they may not speak a common protocol. If that is the case, static routing may be your only option.

With all the disadvantages listed of both static and dynamic routing, you may be wondering what the best choice is. Only you can say for sure what is best for your network, but there is a reasonable middle ground that limits the complexity of dynamic routing without sacrificing its scalability. This middle ground is a *hybrid* scheme, in which part of the network uses static routing and part uses dynamic routing.

Hybrid Routing Schemes

In a hybrid routing scheme, some parts of the network use static routing, and some parts use dynamic routing. Which parts use static or dynamic routing is not important, and many options are possible. One of the most common hybrid schemes is to use static routing on the fringes of the network (what I have called the access networks) and to use dynamic routing in the core and distribution networks. The advantage of using static routing in the access networks is that these networks are where your user machines are typically located; these machines often have little or no support for dynamic routing. Additionally, access networks often have only one or two router attachments, so the burden of configuring static routing is limited. It may even be possible to define nothing more than a default route on these *stub networks*. Because of the limited connections to these networks, you usually don't need to reconfigure routing on a stub network when it gets moved to a new place in the network.

On the other hand, distribution and core networks often have many router connections, and therefore many different routes to maintain. Therefore, routers in these components of the network usually can't get by with a default route. Routers (and hosts) in the central parts of the network need complete routing information for the entire network. Furthermore, routers in the core and distribution networks usually need to be informed of changes in the connectivity of access networks. While it is certainly possible to inform each router manually when an change occurs, it is usually easier and more practical to allow a dynamic routing protocol to propagate the changes.

Another advantage of using static routes in your access networks is control. Depending on the structure of your network administration, you might not be able to control what happens in access networks. These may be handled by departmental LAN coordinators that do not report to you. When this is the case, it is often simpler to configure static routing with the access networks, and only run the dynamic routing protocol between routers and machines over which you have direct control. Because a dynamic routing protocol implies a certain level of trust, it is often safer not to use a dynamic routing protocol with such departmentally controlled access networks. In short, when dealing with routers not under your direct control, it is best to use static routing where you *can*, and to use dynamic routing only where you *must*.

Another type of hybrid routing structure to consider is based on network bandwidth issues rather than on administrative control. In this type of hybrid structure, you would run dynamic routing protocols on your high-speed LAN and WAN links, and use static routing for connections that cross lower-speed links. As an example, consider a multi-campus network at a university. Within each campus, there may be multiple routers, interconnected by Ethernets, FDDI, and other high-speed links. However, the link between the campuses may well be a 56 kbps WAN link. If the two campuses have separate network address spaces, it is unlikely that the routes between the campuses will change. In this case, the only advantage to using dynamic routing between the campuses is that packets that cannot be delivered to a machine on the other campus because of an internal network failure can be stopped before they traverse the low-speed link. However, this is the exceptional case. The normal case is that internal network operation is stable.

With this in mind, it is reasonable to ask how much bandwidth the dynamic routing protocol is taking on the low-speed link. While most routing protocols are designed to minimize the impact of the routing updates on the link, the overhead is non-zero. It may be better to use dynamic routing within each campus, but to use static routing for the inter-campus link, where bandwidth is at a premium.

Static routing between campuses connected by a slow link may even be worthwhile if the campuses share a common address space (perhaps a single class B-sized network aggregate). However, more work may be necessary. The problem with a common address space is that changes on one campus typically need to be visible to the dynamic routing protocol on the other campus. One solution to this problem is to divide the address space between the two (or more) campuses so that each is its own smaller aggregate, as shown in Figure 5-2. If you can divide the address space, you can simplify static routing between the campuses by working with the aggregates.

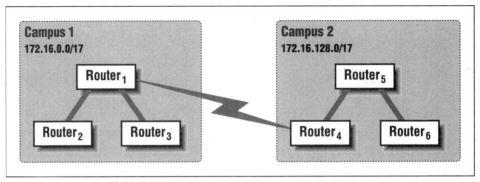

Figure 5-2. Two campuses sharing a common address space

In the figure, Router1 only needs a static route for the aggregate `172.16.128.0/17`. Likewise, Router5 only needs a static route for the aggregate `172.16.0.0/17`. This allows each campus to allocate subnets in their portion of the common address space independently, and yet keep static routing between the campuses simple.

A final problem with our multi-campus hybrid routing scheme occurs when the inter-campus link moves between routers. For example, what happens if the link is moved from Router1 to Router3? Router configurations on Campus 2 are unaffected, since the same IP addresses for the serial link can continue to be used, and the changes necessary on Campus 1 need not be extensive. Clearly, Router1 and Router3 must know of the change. After all, even without routing to deal with, they need to have interface configuration changes made. But does Router2 need to be reconfigured to know that the link to Campus 2 has moved? Not if the routers are all configured to include information about their static routes in the dynamic routing protocol.

Most routers have some ability to propagate information from one routing source to another. We usually think in terms of exchanging routing information between two dynamic routing protocols, but passing information about static routes into a dynamic routing protocol is really just a special case. We won't go into the details here of how this is done because it will be easier to explain once we have talked about the dynamic routing protocols and how to configure them, but you should be aware that including static routes in your dynamic routing protocol updates is an easy way to confine configuration of static routes to a minimum of routers.

Now that we have covered static, dynamic, and hybrid routing schemes, you should have a plan for where you would like to use dynamic routing, and where you will use static routing. The next step is to think more about dynamic routing protocols, and decide which are appropriate to use.

Classification of Dynamic Routing Protocols

Dynamic routing protocols can be classified in several different ways. I will discuss two classifications: exterior protocols versus interior protocols, and distance-vector versus link-state protocols. The first classification is based on where a protocol is intended to be used: between your network and another's network, or within your network. The second classification has to do with the kind of information the protocol carries and the way each router makes its decision about how to fill in its routing table.

Exterior vs. Interior Protocols

Dynamic routing protocols are generally classified as an *exterior gateway* protocol *(EGP†)* or an *interior gateway protocol (IGP)*. An exterior protocol carries routing information between two independent administrative entities, such as two corporations or two universities. Each of these entities maintains an independent network infrastructure and uses an EGP to communicate routing information to the other. Today, the most common exterior protocol is the *Border Gateway Protocol (BGP)*. It is the primary exterior protocol used between networks connected to the Internet, and was designed specifically for such purposes.

In contrast, an interior protocol is used within a single administrative domain, or among closely cooperating groups. In contrast to the exterior protocols, IGPs tend to be simpler and to require less overhead in a router. Their primary drawback is that they can't scale to extremely large networks. The most common interior protocols in IP networks are the *Routing Information Protocol (RIP), Open Shortest Path*

---

* The Internet Protocols originally called routers *gateways*. This usage is no longer common, but it still appears in routing protocol discussions.

† Not to be confused with the *Exterior Gateway Protocol version 2* (also known as *EGP*), which is one of many exterior gateway protocols.

First (OSPF), and the *Enhanced Interior Gateway Routing Protocol (EIGRP).** The first two are open standards adopted or developed by the Internet community, while the third is a proprietary protocol designed by Cisco Systems for use on their routers.

While it is possible to use an interior protocol as an exterior protocol, and vice versa, it is seldom a good idea. Exterior protocols are designed to scale to the largest of networks, but their inherent complexity and overhead can quickly overwhelm a small or medium-sized network. On the other hand, while interior protocols are fairly simple and have little inherent overhead, they don't scale well to larger networks. Because of the difference in focus between interior and exterior protocols, I will not discuss exterior protocols in this chapter. Instead, I will reserve our discussion of exterior protocols to later chapters where we will be discussing connections to the world outside of your organization.

Distance-Vector vs. Link-State Protocols

Another way to classify dynamic routing protocols is by what the routers tell each other, and how they use the information to form their routing tables. Most protocols fit into one of two categories.

The first of these categories is *distance-vector* protocols. In a distance-vector protocol, a router periodically sends all of its neighbors two pieces of information about the destinations it knows how to reach. First, the router tells its neighbors how far away it thinks the destination is; second, it tells its neighbors what direction (or vector) to use to get to the destination.† This direction indicates the next hop that a listener should use to reach the destination, and typically takes the form "send it to me, I know how to get there." For example, RIP route updates simply list a set of destinations that the announcing router knows how to reach, and how far away it thinks each destination is. The receiver infers that the next hop to use is the announcing router. However, an update can also take the form "send it to this other router who knows how to get there." This second form is usually used only when the router that should be used to reach the destination cannot (or will not) speak the routing protocol being used by the other routers. Not all routing protocols support this form of third-party route update.

---

* EIGRP has largely supplanted IGRP, its predecessor, because EIGRP has all the advantages of flexibility and simple configuration while improving on speed and resource consumption. It is also capable of being a unified routing protocol both for IP and some non-IP protocols, eliminating the need to run multiple routing protocols in a multi-protocol network. I will point out any significant differences between the two.

† The mathematical definition of a *vector* is direction and length. Unfortunately, when network engineers refer to a distance-vector protocol, they refer to the direction only. To avoid confusion, we will try to limit the use of the term.

The other part of the protocol, the distance, is where distance-vector protocols differ. In each case, the protocol uses some *metric* to tell the receiving routers how far away the destination is. This metric may be a true attempt at measuring distance (perhaps using a periodic measure of the round trip time to the destination), something that approximates distance (such as hop count), or it may not measure distance at all. Instead, it may attempt to measure the cost of the path to the destination. It may even involve a complex computation that takes into account factors like network load, link bandwidth, link delay, or any other measure of the desirability of a route. Finally, it may include an administrative weight that is set by a network administrator to try to cause one path to be preferred over another.

In any case, the metric allows a router that hears about a destination from multiple routers to select the best path by comparing the "distance" of the various alternatives. How the comparison is made depends heavily upon how metric is computed. For example, the metric in RIP route updates is defined to be a hop count, in which one hop is supposed to represent handling by one router. A destination with a hop count of 16 is considered unreachable. When a router receives RIP updates from different routers referring to the same destination network, it selects the router that is announcing the lowest metric. If this metric is lower than the metric for the route that is currently in its routing table, the router replaces its routing table entry with the new information from the other router.

In order to allow the information to propagate throughout the network, each router includes in its announcements all the destinations to which it is directly attached, as well as all destinations that it has heard about from other routers. When a router includes the information it has learned from other routers, the routing protocol requires it to adjust the metric to reflect the additional distance from itself to the router from which it learned the information. In the case of RIP, this means that before a router announces information that it has learned, it adds one hop to the metric for each of these destinations. In this way, the farther you get from the destination, the higher the metric will be.

In contrast, in a link-state protocol, a router doesn't provide information about destinations it knows how to reach. Instead, it provides information about the topology of the network in its immediate vicinity. This information consists of a list of the network segments, or *links*, to which it is attached, and the *state* of those links (functioning or not functioning). This information is then *flooded* throughout the network. By flooding the information throughout the network, every router can build its own picture of the current state of all of the links in the network. Because every router sees the same information, all of these pictures should be the same. From this picture, each router computes its best path to all destinations, and populates its routing table with this information. How a router determines which path is best is up to each protocol. In the simplest case, a router may simply compute the path with the least number of hops. In a more complex protocol, the link-state information may include additional information to help a router determine the best path. Such information may again include the bandwidth of the link, the current load on the link, administrative weights, or even policy information restricting which packets may traverse the link. For example, a given link might not be allowed to carry confidential information.

Distance-vector and link-state protocols have their own strengths and weaknesses. In a properly functioning and configured network, either type yields a correct determination of the best path between any two points. However, this is not to say that there are not tradeoffs involved in selecting one type of protocol over another.

The drawbacks of distance-vector protocols

In general, distance-vector protocols are simpler to configure and to understand than link-state protocols. They are also typically less processor intensive, freeing more of the router to other tasks, such as forwarding packets. Their major drawbacks, though, are often the result of their simplicity. One of the chief drawbacks is that there is typically no indication of how a router knows about a destination that it has included in an update. For example, consider the simple three-router network shown in Figure 5-3. Router1 tells Router2 about the network 192.168.100.0/24. Router2 will, of course, tell Router3 about it, but it may also tell Router1. Likewise, Router3 may tell Router2 that it knows how to get to the same network, even though its path to that network is through Router2.

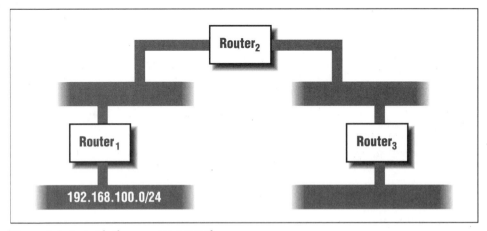

Figure 5-3. A simple three-router network

Normally, this is not a problem because each router compares the metric it is hearing to the metric in its routing table and selects the best path. But what if

Router1 loses its connection to 192.168.100.0/24 due to a hardware failure? It stops telling Router2 about it, and eventually Router2 removes the entry from its routing table (it will either time it out, or it will be told by Router1). However, it may then hear about the network from Router3, and think it should add this "new" path to its routing table and tell Router1. Of course, it also tells Router3, which discovers that the path through Router2 has gotten worse. No matter, it updates the metric in its routing table, and adjusts the metric it announces in its routing updates the next time it sends one to Router2. This now causes Router2 to update its metric, and announce a slightly worse route to Router3, which then re-announces it back to Router2 with an even higher metric. Eventually, they hit whatever value the protocol has declared to be "infinity." When this happens, both routers remove the route from their tables.

Depending on how high the protocol has set the infinity value, and depending on how often the routers send updates to each other, this period of unstable and inaccurate routing can last from fractions of a second to minutes. Clearly, you don't really want your routing tables to be unstable for minutes at a time every time a piece of your network fails! Most distance-vector protocols have added some additional complexity to help avoid these situations. The first thing they typically add is a concept called *split-horizon*. In split-horizon, when a router is building its routing update for a particular interface, it omits any reference to routes it has learned from routers reached by that interface. In our example, this means that Router2 tells Router3 about 192.168.100.0/24, which it learned from Router1, but it omits any reference to this network when it sends its update to Router1. Likewise, Router3 refrains from telling Router2 about this network, since it was Router2 that told it about it in the first place. A slight modification to split-horizon updates is *poison reverse*. In poison reverse processing, instead of omitting the route from its routing update, the router includes it, but flags it as unreachable. This causes any receiver that might be depending on the invalid route to remove the destination from its routing table.

The result is that simple network instability like the situation described above does not happen. However, neither split horizon nor poison reverse solves the whole problem. If there is a cycle in the network that connected Router3 to Router1, perhaps through Router4, as shown in Figure 5-4, a routing loop may occur even with poison reverse. In this network, Router1 tells Router2 and Router4 about its connection to 192.168.100.0/24, probably with the same metric value. They in turn tell Router3 about this network, again probably using the same metric. Router3 selects one of these paths (probably whichever it heard first) and enters it in its routing table.

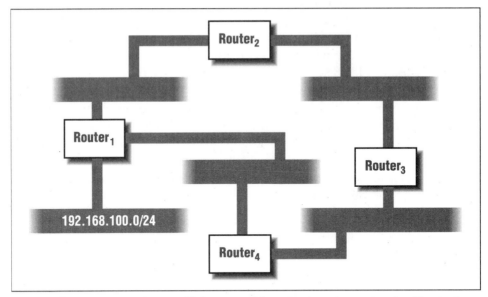

Figure 5-4. Poison reverse is not sufficient to avoid routing loops in a network with a cycle

Let's assume that Router3 selects the path through Router2. Because of poison reverse, it would send that route back to Router2 with an unreachable metric, as it is supposed to. However, because it chose not to use Router4's path, it will not perform poison reverse processing on that link, but instead includes the route to 192.168.100.0/24 through Router2 in its updates to Router4, which ignores the update and prefers the route through Router1.

All goes well until the link between Router1 and 192.168.100.0/24 fails. At that time, Router1 ceases advertising this route to Router2 and Router4. These routers, in turn, cease sending the route to Router3, but it is possible that Router4 will hear Router3's advertisement before the process is complete. Since it does not have this route, it installs it in its routing table, and informs Router1 of this apparently new information. Router1 then informs Router2, which continues sending the information to Router3.

The loop will eventually be broken, as each router will increase the metric as it passes routing information around the loop; eventually, the metric will reach the protocol's infinity value. How long it takes the routers to *count to infinity*, as this behavior is called, depends heavily on how often they update each other, what the protocol's infinity value is, and how many routers are involved in the loop. The solution to this new problem is to introduce a *hold-down* interval. When a router learns that a destination is no longer reachable along the path it was previously using, it starts a timer during which it ignores any other routing information it might hear about this destination. The idea is to allow other routers to learn about the failure before it starts depending on their routes. In our example, when Router1 determines that it can no longer reach 192.168.100.0/24, it begins a hold-down period for this destination. During that time it ignores the updates it hears from Router3. If the hold-down period is long enough, by the time Router1 starts listening again, Router3 will have learned that its path to the destination is invalid, and won't be advertising it.

The drawback to the hold-down interval is that it is hard to know how long the interval should be. After all, how long does it take for all of the routers that you might hear from to learn that a destination is not reachable? This is especially bad for a protocol like RIP. In its simplest form, RIP sends a routing update every 30 seconds. Because there is no acknowledgment of these updates, it is possible that one could get lost. Additionally, while an update includes information about what is reachable, it does not normally include information about what is no longer reachable, so there is no indication to a router that it should remove a route that is no longer valid.

To allow for lost updates, RIP sets a timer for each route that it learns. Every time it hears an update for a route, it resets the timer. If it doesn't hear an update for 180 seconds, it removes the route from the routing table and stops advertising it to its neighbors. In this way, if an update gets lost, the routes it would have contained do not immediately get removed from the routing table. Presumably, they will be in the next update, and their timers will be refreshed then.

In practice, this means that it can take a long time for a routing change to make it through a large network. Consider once again the network with three routers shown in Figure 5-3. When Router1 determines that it has lost its connection to 192.168.100.0/24, it simply ceases to advertise it in its updates to Router2. Router2, however, continues to believe that it has a route to this network for three minutes from the last time it heard about it from Router1, and continues to send updates containing this destination to Router3. After three minutes, Router2 determines that Router1 must have lost its route, so it removes the route for 192.168.100.0/24 from its routing table, and ceases informing Router3 about this destination. However, Router3 will continue to use the old information for up to three minutes more itself.

Now consider what happens if we keep adding to the network until we have dozens of routers. If each router has to wait three minutes from the time the router closer to a failed network stops advertising a route, it is conceivable that a route might not be completely gone from the network for as much as 45 minutes! It is clearly unreasonable that the hold-down interval for a network should be even a significant fraction of this time. To help reduce the time that a network has inconsistent routing information, distance-vector protocols often allow routers to include *negative reachability* information for routes that they have recently advertised, but can no longer reach. Negative reachability information allows routers to find out immediately that some route is no longer valid. For RIP, negative reachability information takes the form of a route with a metric of 16. Other protocols tag such information in whatever manner is appropriate.

Negative advertisement helps speed the propagation of route failure through the network, but it doesn't eliminate the delays. When Router1 discovers that its connection to 192.168.100.0/24 has been lost (or restored), its next update to Router2 will contain this information. In the case of RIP, if it just sent an update, it could be up to 30 seconds until this update occurs. Further, once Router2 hears from Router1, it may also have to wait up to 30 seconds before it can notify Router3, which will wait up to 30 seconds, and so on. Even though this information traverses a large network quickly, especially compared to the time it takes for a route to time out, it can still take a few minutes for all of the routers in the network to hear about the change and update their routing tables. This delay between the time a network change occurs and the time all of the routers have adjusted to it in a consistent manner is known as *convergence time.* A long convergence time is clearly a problem for any routing protocol.

To minimize convergence time, a distance-vector protocol may allow *flash or triggered updates.* A triggered update is sent whenever a router's routing tables change in a way that would affect its routing updates. If each router uses triggered updates, and includes negative reachability information, it is possible for information about the failure of Router1's connection to 192.168.100.0/24 to speed through the network to all routers in a matter of a few seconds, thereby shortening the convergence time and thus the time that routers need to be in a hold-down interval.

But, like everything else, it isn't that simple. If triggered updates aren't carefully controlled, an intermittent failure can ripple back and forth through the network, consuming the routers' time with processing routing updates rather than forwarding packets. A common solution is to lengthen the hold-down timer slightly, and to introduce a short interval timer that is set after every flash update. During this interval, the router suppresses new flash updates to help dampen the effects of the original failure.

The other major drawback to distance-vector protocols also stems from their simplicity. Because the network topology can change, either because of link failure or the addition or removal of network segments, all dynamic routing protocols must update routers about the changes. In a distance-vector protocol, updates are usually performed by periodically broadcasting (or multicasting) routing packets on some or all of a router's interfaces. Often, these routing updates contain complete routing information, as the sending router sees it. Periodic updates are useful for keeping the routers on a network segment informed, but they introduce additional network overhead during periods of network stability (the majority of the time, we hope). Some newer distance-vector protocols such as Cisco's EIGRP only announce changes to the routing tables, but these protocols still tend to be the exception, rather than the rule.

So, while a distance-vector protocol tends to be conceptually simple for humans to understand, and easy for a router's processor to work with, this simplicity can result in unusual behavior in response to a network failure, and often results in long convergence times between the failure of a network component and the re-establishment of consistent, stable routing in all routers. It may also result in the consumption of network bandwidth and router processing power even during periods of relative stability. While changes to the protocol can help lessen these problems, once you've added poison reverse, hold-down intervals, triggered updates, and so forth, the protocol is no longer simple, either to understand or to process.

The drawbacks of link-state protocols

Link-state protocols have some important advantages. Because a link-state protocol computes its routes based on the topology of the network as indicated by the link-state updates, it can't form a loop in response to a partial network failure, like a distance-vector protocol might. Further, because a change in link-state gets flooded throughout the network immediately and causes all routers to update their topology map and routing tables, convergence time is minimal. Finally, because most link-state protocols are designed to send link-state updates only when the state of a link changes, they tend to conserve network bandwidth and router processing power during periods of network stability.

While a link-state protocol avoids loop-forming behaviors, long convergence times, and stable-state resource consumption, they have their own drawbacks. Chief among these is complexity. Complexity is primarily an aspect of the protocol's implementation, but it often shows up in configuration as well. In fact, OSPF, an interior protocol, is a more complex protocol than even BGP, an exterior protocol. Fortunately, in a typical configuration, most of this complexity is hidden from the user.

Why are link-state protocols so complex? Consider what we have said about how the routers determine their routes. They collect all of the link-state updates from other routers and build a topology map of the network. Using this map, they compute the best path to each destination. The first complexity is generating the topology map. While a human being can easily draw pictures based on instructions about what is connected to what, a computer must have a way to represent the resulting picture in a way that allows it to carry out its processing. The standard way to do this is to use one of numerous types of graphs. Each type of graph has its own set of operations that it supports well, and another set that are nearly impossible to perform on it. A lot of research has been devoted to describing different types of graphs and the operations they support. Often, a protocol specification does not detail how the protocol should be implemented. It may not even specify what types of data are needed. However, even if the types of data are identified in the protocol specification, how the data are represented (i.e., which type of graph and how the graph is represented) is often left to the implementer. A poor selection can result in subtle failures in the resulting code on the router.

The second complexity in implementing a link-state protocol has to do with computing the best path to all destinations. While there are algorithms for computing the best path using a variety of graphs and metrics, it is again up to the implementer to select one and implement it correctly. Mistakes can also have interesting results in the finished product.

But implementation complexity shouldn't be a concern to the network administrator *if* the resulting code works correctly. However, even if the code is correct, a complex implementation usually requires more processing power and memory in the router. For example, the topology graph will take time to generate, and must be stored. In fact, it must be stored indefinitely, since link-state updates only contain information about changes in the network topology. The additional memory and processing requirements cause some network administrators to stay away from link-state protocols, but this is not their only concern. A greater concern is the complexity, or the perceived complexity, of configuring a link-state protocol.

Most link-state protocols are more complex to configure than most distance-vector protocols. However, if the configuration interface is implemented well, and if it includes a set of reasonable defaults, it is possible to configure a "no frills" link-state protocol with little more effort than a distance-vector protocol. The complexity of configuring a link-state protocol should only appear if you want to depart from the defaults.

Both link-state and distance-vector protocols will result in correct routing in a stable network, and should eventually converge on a new set of routes after a network failure. Therefore, which type of protocol you select for your network is a matter of personal preference. If the complexity of link-state protocols is not to your liking, or if you are concerned about the consumption of resources on your routers, try to select protocols that use a distance-vector algorithm. On the other hand, if you want the fast convergence and low bandwidth consumption of a link-state protocol, or don't want to deal with the odd loop-forming behavior of a distance-vector protocol, then select a protocol from the link-state family.

Selecting a Routing Protocol

Now that most of the background information about dynamic routing protocols is behind us, it is time to talk about what criteria you should consider when selecting a dynamic routing protocol. You may have a preference for either a link-state or a distance-vector protocol. But deciding what kind of protocol to use without considering other options can severely limit your choices, depending on what your router vendor supports. A more useful approach is to consider which protocol or protocols best suit your needs, and then use a preference for one type over another as a weighting factor later in the decision.

One of the most important criteria is how quickly the protocol adapts to changes in the network. Earlier, we identified this as convergence time and said that it was the amount of time between a change in the network and the reestablishment of consistent and correct routing tables. Ideally, you want this time to be small enough to be unnoticed by users.

Traditionally, the next most important criterion is resource consumption. However, with the current push for more efficient use of the IP address space, it is likely that you plan to use variable-length subnet masks. If this is the case, then support for variable-length masks is probably the most important feature your routing protocol must have. After all, if your routing protocol does not support your use of variable-length subnet masks, they won't do you much good.

The third criterion you should consider is how much of your network resources the routing protocol consumes. Consider not only the network bandwidth consumed by the protocol messages, but also how much processing power and memory is required in your routers. A link-state protocol will typically do better on the bandwidth consumption, and a distance-vector protocol will do better with processor and memory consumption, but this is not always the case.

Next, consider how well your prospective protocols deal with multiple paths to a destination. This may or may not be critical in your network, and how much weight you give it depends on your network design. If you have no redundant paths, you probably won't care about how well your protocol supports them. Still, while you may not have redundant paths today, you may add them in the future and you might need to change protocols to support them. Even if one of your prospective protocols does not normally support multiple paths, consider whether your router vendor's implementation does anyway. For example, RIP does not normally support multiple paths to a destination network, but the RIP implementation in a Cisco router does handle such redundancy, and will even do load sharing across multiple paths with equal costs (metrics).

You might also need to consider how well your network protocols will scale to the size you expect your network to achieve. Link-state protocols usually scale better, but some distance-vector protocols, such as Cisco's EIGRP, have proven themselves in networks with 1,000 or more routers.

Finally, you may have to consider whether a protocol is an open standard or a proprietary protocol. This may be because of policy constraints of your organization, or it may be because you must support multiple vendors' routers in your network. A protocol that is only spoken by half of your routers isn't terribly useful to the other half. Table 5-1 summarizes these criteria for the most common interior routing protocols you are likely to be considering.

Table 5-1. Summary of Common Routing Protocol Features

Protocol	RIP	OSPF	IGRP	EIGRP
Type	distance-vector	link-state	distance-vector	distance-vector
Convergence Time	slow	fast	slow	fast
VLSM	no	yes	no	yes
Bandwidth Consumption	high	low	high	low
Resource Consumption	low	high	low	low
Multi-path Support	no[a]	yes	yes	yes
Scales Well	no	yes	yes	yes
Proprietary	no	no	yes	yes
Routers Non-IP Protocols	no	no	no	yes

[a] Some vendors may support multiple paths in RIP.

From the table, it may seem that EIGRP is the ideal choice. It is fast, consumes little resources, supports VLSM, and scales well. But it is also proprietary, and unless you have a single vendor for all your routers, and that vendor happens to be Cisco Systems, you will immediately be faced with multiple routing protocols in your network. The complexity involved in running multiple routing protocols should not be taken lightly, so give careful thought to any proprietary routing protocol or solution before you make your decision.

Once you have selected a protocol, or have at least narrowed your choices down to one of two, it is time to start thinking about how you would configure your protocol to achieve your network goals and solve any problems that you may have in your network. The next chapter presents several common scenarios that are likely to arise, and shows how to use each of the protocols in Table 5-1 to solve that problem. While looking at these examples, you may discover that your chosen protocol may make it difficult for you to solve some specific problem in your network; or, if you have not chosen a specific protocol, seeing how each of your prospects works for or against your specific network situation may provide you with the remaining information you need to select between them.

6

Routing Protocol Configuration

Now that you have selected a routing protocol, or at least narrowed your choices, you need to be able to configure your routers to use the protocol. You will find that the default settings provided by your router vendor will be sufficient for most cases. Even so, you are likely to run into any number of cases where the defaults just aren't going to do what you want, or you need to solve a special problem. In this section, I present some of the most common scenarios you are likely to face, and show you ways to resolve them using RIP, OSPF, and EIGRP.* Although these examples are all based on the configuration language of a Cisco router, the concepts used should be adaptable to whatever router you have. Keep in mind that these examples only present one way to solve each problem. There are no promises that these will be exactly right for all situations, nor even for your network.

---

* I won't show IGRP configurations. EIGRP has largely supplanted IGRP because of its superior performance, and should be used in preference to IGRP wherever possible. It should be easy to adapt the EIGRP configurations for use with IGRP since the configuration differences are minor.

Basic Configurations

Before presenting configuration ideas for special-purpose needs or problems, I will establish some basic configurations that serve as a basis for the more advanced configurations. These simple configurations represent the bare minimum necessary to get each routing protocol functioning, and are inappropriate for all but the simplest networks, but they are easily understood.

RIP

For a basic RIP configuration, let's use the two networks `172.16.0.0/15` and `192.168.100.0/24`. The configuration below starts by telling the router to start a RIP process. It then tells the router the networks on which it should send and listen for RIP updates. Because RIP is a classful protocol, the configuration can't specify the aggregate `172.16.0.0/15` directly; instead, we supply a `network` statement for each of the class B networks that make up the aggregate (`172.16.0.0` and `172.17.0.0`). These statements do not restrict what routes can be carried to and from this router, only which of the router's directly attached networks will be configured for RIP processing.

```
! start a RIP process on my networks
router rip
 network 172.16.0.0
 network 172.17.0.0
 network 192.168.100.0
```

OSPF

Our OSPF network also consists of networks `172.16.0.0/15` and `192.168.100.0/24`. This configuration starts by telling the router to start an OSPF routing process. The number following the `router ospf` statement identifies which OSPF process this is; a router may have many OSPF processes. For consistency, it should be the same for all routers in your network.

```
! start an OSPF process and place all interfaces in area 0
router ospf 1
 network 0.0.0.0 255.255.255.255 area 0
```

The second line of this configuration declares that all network interfaces not otherwise attached to areas (explained below) should be assigned to area 0. The mask used in these `network` statements is different from the masks we have seen so far. Here, a `1` bit is a wildcard, and indicates that the corresponding bit of the address can be either a one or a zero. Thus, a mask of `255.255.255.255` matches *all* addresses, and our `network` statement puts all interfaces into area 0. Should additional areas be necessary, they will be defined with similar `network` statements, each listing a network and mask that defines a set of matching interfaces and assigns them to an area. Each interface can only be in one area; the list is evaluated in order, and each interface is assigned to the first area it matches.

OSPF areas

Unlike the other routing protocols I will talk about, OSPF has the concept of an area. An area is simply a contiguous portion of a network whose internal topology details are hidden to routers outside of the area.* They allow an additional level of hierarchy different from that provided by IP's network classes, and can be used to aggregate routing information and contain the knowledge of details. This ability to hide details and aggregate routing information is part of what makes OSPF scale to large networks.

Why are these features important? In Chapter 1, *The Basics of IP Networking*, I said that in most cases, every destination subnet or network requires an entry in the routing table of all routers. For a network with a few dozen network segments or subnets, this is not likely to be a problem. However, consider a large corporate network with hundreds or thousands of network segments. If each of these requires an entry in the routing tables of each router, the amount of memory taken can be significant. Furthermore, in Chapter 5, *Routing Protocol Selection*, I said that OSPF is a link-state protocol, and floods information about all of the network segments throughout the network. When this topology information is received by other routers, they then begin calculating the shortest path to each destination network segment. If there are thousands of network segments and hundreds of router attachments, this calculation will not be trivial. Worse, if a single link in the network changes state, all of the routers must recalculate the shortest path for *all* destinations.

An OSPF area can be used to confine knowledge about individual subnet routes and the internal topology of an area to those routers that are attached to the area. All other routers simply see an aggregate route covering multiple subnets, and an opaque blob whose internal structure they don't know or care about. For example, consider the network shown in Figure 6-1. In this network, the routers in area 1 must know about the details of the links connecting them to each other, and the Ethernet segments they connect to, as well as the details of the individual subnet routes. But routers outside area 1 only see the links between them and area 1, and the two aggregate routes, `172.16.48.0/22` and `192.168.0.0/24`, that cover the subnets contained in area 1. If a network link goes down in area 1, only the routers within area 1 need to recompute their shortest path calculations. The other routers never find out that the link state has changed.

---

* By using a concept called a virtual link, it is possible to have a discontiguous area in an OSPF network that is made contiguous by this virtual link. In most cases, virtual links are unnecessary, and their use is generally discouraged, so I will not explore them in this book. For those who wish to understand the concept better, RFC 1583 defines OSPF fully, and presents the topic of virtual links. Refer to your router's documentation for the details of how to establish such a link in your network.

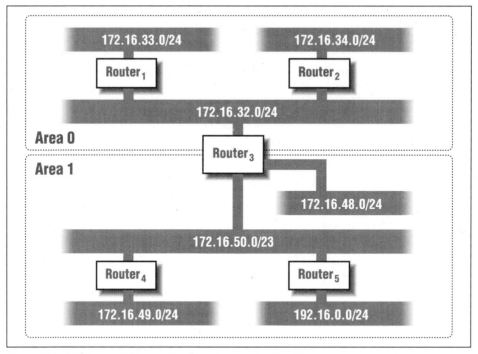

Figure 6-1. OSPF areas hide details of topology and subnetting

An OSPF area must be contiguous. In our example, the path between any pair of network segments within area 1 can be reached without traversing any segments outside of area 1. In addition, a network segment or link can only belong to one area. Thus, if I exclude Router4's connection to `172.16.50.0/23` from area 1, I must also exclude all other routers' connections, and the segment itself.

Although a router's interfaces are considered part of an area, the routers themselves usually aren't. Notice that Router3 straddles the line between area 1 and the rest of the network; some of its interfaces are part of area 1, and some are not. We only think of a router as part of an area if all of its interfaces are part of the area. Otherwise, the router is known as an *area border router*, which means that it straddles the border of an area and therefore provides summary information for the routes and links contained within the area to the rest of the network.

OSPF does not allow an arbitrary connection of one area to another. While doing so would allow a great deal of flexibility in network design, it would also have increased the complexity of OSPF enormously, and might have doomed it to failure.* OSPF's designers settled on the restriction that all areas had to border

---

* OSPF was originally defined in 1989, when processing power in routers was extremely limited. Even with the restrictions on area interconnections required by the protocol, many felt that OSPF was far too processor-intensive to be feasible for network deployment.

directly on a special area called the *backbone* area. This area is given the identifier 0, and it must exist in any OSPF network. With this in mind, we are now ready to look at configuration fragments for some of the routers in our example. First, we'll take a look at the OSPF configuration of Router1. We'll assume that it doesn't connect to any areas other than area 0:

```
router ospf 1
  network 0.0.0.0 255.255.255.255 area 0
```

As you can see, this router's configuration is identical to our basic example. I simply define an OSPF routing process, and tell the router that all interfaces are part of area 0, and I am done. Router2 would have the same configuration, assuming all its interfaces are also in area 0. The configuration for both Router4 and Router5 will look similar, with one minor change:

```
router ospf 1
  network 0.0.0.0 255.255.255.255 area 1
```

The difference here is that the configuration tells these routers that all of their interfaces are part of area 1, rather than area 0. Notice that I did not have to tell Router5 anything special about `192.168.0.0/24`—it is already covered by the `network` statement. It is only Router3 that really looks different:

```
router ospf 1
  network 172.16.48.0 0.0.3.255      area 1
  network 0.0.0.0      255.255.255.255 area 0
```

This configuration starts an OSPF routing process and tells the router that any interface that is part of `172.16.48.0/22` belongs to area 1. Then, the configuration tells the router that all other interfaces are part of area 0. Notice that the configuration did not have to tell the router that `192.168.0.0/24` is part of area 1, even though this network doesn't match the first `network` statement, because it has no connection to this network. So far, this configuration for Router3 is sufficient to establish areas and confine link-state topology information to the areas. However, I will not automatically get route summarization because the router has not been told how much the summary route should cover, and can't determine this on its own. After all, it doesn't know what is behind Router4 and Router5, yet. To tell it how much to summarize, I include the following:

```
  area 1 range 172.16.48.0 255.255.252.0
```

This tells Router3 that it should generate a summary route for area 1 whenever it has a valid route to any part of the aggregate, and it should tell this summary to the rest of the network. Notice again that I did not tell the router about `192.168.0.0/24`, since this route is already as summarized as it can be; it can't be merged with any of the other networks in area 1.

So what should go in the different OSPF areas you are defining in your network? This is a hard question; the answer is unique to each OSPF network. Here are some guidelines for making these decisions.

- Each area of your OSPF network *must* be contiguous, and each area *must* connect to area 0 directly.

- Each network segment, and each router interface belongs to *exactly one* area. Together, these two rules will dictate some of your choices for you.

- A link-state advertisement is flooded throughout an area, but doesn't go beyond one area. Also, whenever a link changes state, every router in the area must recompute its shortest paths to all destinations. Keep your areas as stable as possible to minimize recalculation. This means it isn't a good idea to include a transitory link (such as an ISDN line or a dial-on-demand link) in area 0 or in a large area. Every time this link is brought up or dropped, all routers attached to the area containing this link must recalculate their shortest paths. Consider putting transitory links and dial-up IP services in a single area consisting only of transitory links. Better still, use static routing for these links and redistribute the static routes into your OSPF network (discussed later).

- Lay out your areas to maximize route aggregation. Since aggregation occurs only at the boundaries of areas, the ideal area layout generates a single summary route for each area. This guideline keeps your routing table size down.

- Keep the number of links and interfaces in an area to a reasonable value. One rule of thumb says that you don't want more than about 100 links in a single area, unless the links are *very* stable. This may be too large for your network, or it may be too small. The best answer is to pick a reasonable starting point, then adjust up or down as you see how your network performs.

- Another rule of thumb says a router should be in at most four areas. Again, this figure may be too large or too small for your network. If the areas are relatively stable and small, then a single router might easily handle a dozen. On the other hand, if your areas are even slightly unstable, or very large, the memory consumption and processing requirements might mean that a router should be part of no more than two. Experiment and be ready to adjust.

In the end, you'll probably decide on the areas in your network by iteration. Initially, you will probably place your entire network in area 0. As you identify links that are a bit too unstable, or you find that the OSPF link-state topology map is taking too much of your routers' memory, you'll segment off pieces of your network into one or more new areas. Therefore, it's important to assign subnet numbers that conform (at least to some extent) to your topology. Otherwise, you will find that your area border routers are unable to form reasonable summary routes when the time comes to create areas.

There are many commands for tuning and tweaking the behavior of OSPF. Some invoke authentication keys* for an area, some change the timers used for OSPF messages, and some change the default cost values assigned to different interface types. You will seldom need these features, and should ignore them unless you know exactly what you are doing and why.

EIGRP

For EIGRP, we'll build our configuration with the same two networks: `172.16.0.0/15` and `192.168.100.0/24`. Creating an EIGRP routing process requires an identifier; as with OSPF, the identifier can be arbitrary, but unlike OSPF, it must be the same on all the routers in your network. You can create multiple EIGRP routing processes on the same router by using different identifiers. With multiple EIGRP processes, the router treats each process as a separate routing protocol and doesn't automatically pass any information between the processes. Multiple processes may be useful in some special cases, but would not normally be the way you would want to configure your routers.

```
! start an EIGRP process on my networks
router eigrp 1
 network 172.16.0.0
 network 172.17.0.0
 network 192.168.100.0
```

Although EIGRP is a classless routing protocol, we must still break our aggregate into two classful networks when we tell the router where the routing process should be running. Hence, we use three `network` statements, as we did for RIP, even though we really only have two networks. This feature keeps EIGRP configuration similar to configuration for IGRP, its predecessor. In our example, the router sends and receives EIGRP on both networks.

Propagating Static Routes

One of the most common problems you'll face is how to propagate static routes. Static routes may exist because of legacy networking equipment that doesn't speak the dynamic routing protocol you've chosen, or because you don't wish to accept dynamic routing updates from another network administration. Or you may have a static default route pointing to your Internet connection. In these cases, you need a static route on the router or routers closest to these static routing needs. However, you don't want to install the static routes manually on all

---

* I'll discuss why you might want to use authentication keys, and how to do so in Chapter 10, *Network Security*, when I talk about network security.

the routers in your network, which would be time-consuming and error-prone. Instead, you'd like these edge routers to propagate any static routes using your dynamic routing protocol.

RIP

In the configuration below, I added a static default route through the host 192.168.100.250, presumably our Internet connection, and told the router to redistribute all static routes using the RIP protocol. This is the general form any route redistribution takes, but be warned: distributing routes from one protocol to another isn't simple. I'll cover it more later, but one of the most important tasks is specifying how to translate the metrics of one protocol to another. In the case of static routes and the RIP protocol, the software defines a default metric of 1, so this router sends the default route in its RIP updates with that metric.

```
router rip
 network 172.16.0.0
 network 172.17.0.0
 network 192.168.100.0
 ! redistribute my static routes with a default metric
 redistribute static
 !
ip route 0.0.0.0 0.0.0.0 192.168.100.250
```

OSPF

Again, I've added a static default route through 192.168.100.250, and I'd like to propagate this route to the other OSPF routers in the network. Unlike RIP, OSPF doesn't have a default metric for static routes. While I could have defined a default value to use for all metrics translated from other routing protocols, that limits my options, so I've chosen to state explicitly that all static routes should get an OSPF metric of 1. Unlike RIP's metric, the OSPF metric doesn't represent a hop-count. Instead, it's used to compare the relative cost of this default route to the cost of another route it might learn about.

```
router ospf 1
 network 0.0.0.0 255.255.255.255 area 0
 ! redistribute my static routes with a type-2 external metric of 1
 redistribute static metric 1
 ! originate a default route if I have one
 default-information originate
 !
ip route 0.0.0.0 0.0.0.0 192.168.100.250
```

I've chosen to use a type 2 metric in this example. A type 1 metric could be speci-fied by saying:

```
redistribute static metric 1 metric-type 1
```

OSPF defines three types of metrics. The first is used for a network internal to the OSPF routing domain. This type of metric is inappropriate for routes that are redistributed into an OSPF routing domain. Instead, we must use an external metric of either type 1 or type 2. The difference between these two metric types, and which you should use, is beyond the scope of this book. However, you do need to make sure that all external routes that may need to be compared to each other carry the same metric type. In the case of the above, the default is a type 2 metric.

Because I wished to propagate a default route into the OSPF routing domain, I had to include the `default-information` `originate` statement in the configuration. Unlike RIP, OSPF treats the default route as a special case in the IOS. Without this additional statement, the default route, regardless of its source, will not be injected into the OSPF routing domain. If you only wish to propagate non-default static routes, you do not need this statement.

EIGRP

Again, I have defined a static default route that I wish to redistribute. As is the case with RIP, EIGRP defines a default metric to use for static routes, so I don't need to do anything else special.

```
router eigrp 1
 network 172.16.0.0
 network 172.17.0.0
 network 192.168.100
! redistribute my static routes with a default metric
 redistribute static
!
ip route 0.0.0.0 0.0.0.0 192.168.100.250
```

Using Variable-Length Subnet Masks with a Classful Protocol

In Chapter 3, *Network Design—Part 2*, I said that it is possible, in limited circumstances, to use a variable-length subnet mask with a classful routing protocol. I also said that this is a *very* bad idea, and should only be used when there is no other choice. If you are using a classful routing protocol, you should use the same subnet mask everywhere in any single IP network, whether class A, B, or C. You can still use different masks in different networks. If you're forced to use variable-length masks within one network, you must strictly follow these rules:

- The odd-sized mask must be longer (smaller subnets) than your normal mask

- A group of subnets using the odd-sized mask must belong to a single subnet using your normal mask

- Each group of subnets using the odd-sized mask (and that are part of a single normal subnet) must be attached to the same router

Figure 6-2 demonstrates these rules. The normal subnet mask is 24 bits long
(255.255.255.0), and I have chosen to use a 30-bit mask for the point-to-point
links. This satisfies the first rule since my 30-bit mask is longer than my normal 24-
bit mask. I have assigned subnet numbers to the first group of serial lines such
that they are all part of 172.16.100.0/24, which is a normal-sized subnet
using my standard 24-bit network mask, and all of these serial lines are attached
to Router1. Additionally, I have a second group of serial lines that also uses the 30-
bit mask; these are all part of 172.16.101/24 using my standard mask, and are
all attached to Router2. Both groups satisfy the second and third rules. Finally,
because the two groups are connected to two different routers, they must use
different normal-sized subnets, even though I don't fully use either.

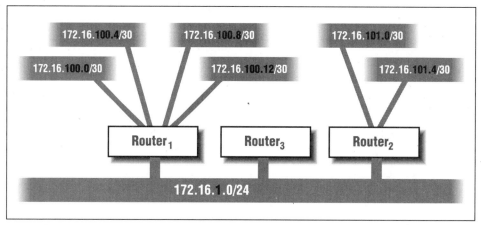

Figure 6-2. Variable-length subnet masks with a classful routing protocol

Since my dynamic routing protocol cannot carry information about the serial
links, I have two choices for telling the rest of the world about these links. The
first is to install static routes for the serial links on all the routers. This is both time
consuming and error-prone, especially if I have hundreds of routers to configure.
The second option is to lie to the other routers about the serial links. This is the
approach I will take. The goal is for Router1 to advertise a route for
172.16.100.0/24, and to remain silent about the individual serial links. Likewise, I want Router2 to advertise a route for 172.16.101.0/24, and to remain
silent about the more specific routes.

So how do I get Router1 to lie about the serial links? The secret is to configure a
static route on Router1 for 172.16.100.0/24, and then have it propagate this
static route to the other routers:

```
hostname router1
!
interface serial 0
```

```
  ip address 172.16.100.1 255.255.255.252
!
interface serial 1
  ip address 172.16.100.5 255.255.255.252
!
interface serial 2
  ip address 172.16.100.9 255.255.255.252
!
interface serial 3
  ip address 172.16.100.13 255.255.255.252
!
interface ethernet 0
  ip address 172.16.1.1 255.255.255.0
!
router rip
  network 172.16.0.0
  redistribute static
! define a null route for the subnet containing my serial lines
ip route 172.16.100.0 255.255.255.0 null 0
```

Notice that the static route points to the null 0 interface, rather than to a specific IP address. In the Cisco IOS, this route is considered present as long as the interface it points to is up. By definition, the null 0 interface is *always* up, so this route is always present. Because the route points to a null interface, the router won't use it itself, but will propagate the route to the other routers using RIP. Because they have a different subnet mask, the serial links will not be propagated, so there is no need to filter them out.

The configuration for Router2 would essentially be identical to this, except that addresses and interfaces would be changed to match its connections. Router3 needs no special configuration—it just has a normal RIP configuration for a router that only knows about a single subnet mask. Of course, EIGRP or OSPF would handle this situation without any extra help because they are classless protocols.

As you can see, it is possible to use a limited number of variable-length subnet masks if you are using a classful routing protocol. It is better not to stretch the ability of your classful routing protocol by doing this in more than a small number of cases, and then only with careful testing. Instead, you really should use a classless protocol that can correctly handle these variable-length masks.

Backup Static Routes

You may find it useful to have a static route that is in place as a backup to your dynamic routing protocol. For example, you might want such a route on a remote router (perhaps at a branch office) to which you do not have convenient access. This route would prevent you from losing contact with the router if you make a mistake while configuring it from your office. By having a backup static route, you can take advantage of dynamic routing, while knowing that the backup static route will allow you to fix mistakes without traveling to the router in person.

The trouble with a static route is that, on most routers, static routes normally supersede any route learned by a dynamic protocol. We only want the static route to take effect in an emergency—for example, because we've screwed up the dynamic protocol with a configuration error. In other words, we want the dynamic protocol to take precedence, but we don't want to be without a route when the dynamic protocol doesn't have one.

The way to allow a static route to be superseded by a dynamic routing protocol varies from router to router. In the case of Cisco IOS, you assign an *administrative distance* to the static route that makes it less preferable than your dynamic routing protocol. Other routers will probably have a similar mechanism that lets you select routes learned from one routing protocol over another; this mechanism will usually treat static routes as another routing protocol. To set the administrative distance for our backup static routes, we need to know a few of the many default administrative distances that Cisco has assigned. The important ones for our examples are listed in Table 6-1. For a complete list, see your Cisco documentation.

Table 6-1. Default Administrative Distances of Selected Routing Sources in the Cisco IOS

Routing Information Source	Default Distance
Connected Interface	0
Static Route	1
EIGRP Summary[a]	5
EIGRP Internal	90
IGRP	100
OSPF	110
RIP	120
EIGRP External	170
Unknown	255

[a] EIGRP defines three different route types—internal routes are the normal routes derived from attached network segments on the various routers, summary routes are routing aggregates manufactured by an EIGRP router somewhere in the network and covering multiple internal routes, and external routes are routes redistributed into EIGRP from another routing protocol.

A lower administrative distance is preferred over a higher distance, and a routing source with an administrative distance of 255 is never used. So, in each of our examples, I need only increase the administrative distance of the static route to the network management subnet to something higher than my dynamic protocol. To do so, I append the desired distances to the end of the static route statement. I could set the distance as high as 254 to deal with the possibility of changing my dynamic protocol, but it is generally better to be conservative about selecting distances. If you change routing protocols, you had better look over your entire configuration carefully and adjust your distances based on your new choices.

In each of the examples below, I have removed the redistribution of static routes into my dynamic routing protocol. This is important. We started with the premise that the dynamic protocol had somehow been misconfigured and therefore lost the dynamic route to the management station; we want the static route to take precedence in this situation. But a static route still depends on the next hop router toward the management station being in a usable state. This is only true if that router is not misconfigured or that router is misconfigured, but it also has a backup static route. In either case, if I allow my router to start advertising the backup static route, I will either override the next-hop router's backup static route with the dynamic advertisement, or I will advertise a possibly better metric in my dynamic routing update and cause it to assume my first router is the better route. In either case, I will have a routing loop and will lose control of the router. You should not propagate backup static routes in your dynamic protocol. If several routers need a backup static route, install one on each router individually.

If you need both to propagate non-backup static routes and to have backup static routes in a router, you will need to do some filtering. I'll describe route filtering shortly.

RIP

```
router rip
 network 172.16.0.0
 network 172.17.0.0
 network 192.168.100.0
 ! set the administrative distance on my static route to be higher than
 ! RIP
 ip route 172.16.10.0 255.255.255.0 172.16.1.5 130
```

OSPF

```
router ospf 1
 network 0.0.0.0 255.255.255.255 area 0
 ! set the administrative distance on my static route to be higher than
 ! OSPF
 ip route 172.16.10.0 255.255.255.0 172.16.1.5 120
```

EIGRP

```
router eigrp 1
 network 172.16.0.0
 network 172.17.0.0
 network 192.168.100
```

```
! set the administrative distance on my static route to be higher than
! EIGRP
ip route 172.16.10.0 255.255.255.0 172.16.1.5 100
```

Using Backup Static Routes to Provide Dial-on-Demand Backup Links

One popular use for backup static routes is to provide a dial-on-demand backup link that automatically starts when a primary link fails, and then is removed from service when the primary link comes back up. The Cisco IOS provides a built-in mechanism for providing an on-demand backup link on the same router as the primary link. For Cisco users, this is the preferred solution because it results in minimal routing changes for your network and is relatively simple to set up. It is also well documented in the IOS documentation, so I will not discuss it here. But it is not always possible to provide the dial-on-demand backup link on the same router as the primary, especially if you have dozens of primary links spread throughout your network and would like to back them up with a smaller number of on-demand links. For these purposes, a backup static route can help.

Let's consider a network that has several permanent WAN links attached to different routers. As the network administrator, you want to ensure that if any of these links fail, you can still pass critical business traffic to the affected site, even though normal communications are not available. You also want to make sure that you can reach the remote router across the network during one of these failures. Finally, in order to limit the cost of backup service, you are willing to accept that only one backup link can be provided at a time (in other words, if two links fail concurrently, one of the sites will be cut-off and the other will be connected by an on-demand link). When the current budget crunch ends, you expect to be able to add more backup links, but it isn't going to happen this year. This is shown in Figure 6-3. Normally you want the permanent WAN link to each site to be used, but in the event of a failure, you'd like Router3 to dial the remote site to allow some communications to continue.

So how do you proceed? First you need to provision each remote router that needs a backup with some sort of on-demand WAN link. Whether this link is an asynchronous serial interface and analog modem, an ISDN interface, or a switched synchronous serial interface isn't important. We'll assume that it is easiest to use analog modems and the auxiliary asynchronous port on each of these routers. Likewise, you need to provide an analog modem attached to an asynchronous serial port on one router at your main site. Any router will do.

Now you are ready to configure your routers to provide this dial backup. Since the only real differences between the configurations at each of the remote sites is

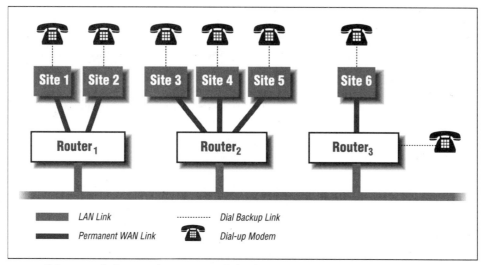

Figure 6-3. Using dial-up modems to provide backup to WAN links

the specific IP address used by the router, I'll only present one example of the remote site configuration:

```
! this dial-up link will be used as a backup only
interface async 1
 ip address 172.16.200.2 255.255.255.0
! limit traffic on this link to avoid swamping it with our normal load
 ip access-group 101
 dialer in-band
 dialer-group 1
! map the central site IP address to its phone number
 dialer map ip 172.16.200.1 5551000
!
! allow traffic to the network management station and to the order
! entry subnet so that business can continue
access-list 101 permit ip 0.0.0.0 255.255.255.255 172.16.100.97  0.0.0.0
access-list 101 permit ip 0.0.0.0 255.255.255.255 172.16.131.0    0.0.0.255
!
dialer-list 1 list 101
!
! make sure this route to the central site has a high administrative
! distance so it is only used as a backup
ip route 0.0.0.0 0.0.0.0 172.15.200.1 250
```

In this configuration, I have told the router that it has an asynchronous interface called `async 1`, whose IP address is `172.16.200.2` and which uses a 24-bit subnet mask. Your first reaction may well be "24 bits for a point-to-point link! What a waste!" Trust me on this. It will become clearer why we want such a large subnet mask when we look at the central site shortly.

Next I told the router that it should apply an access control list to this interface to limit the traffic that flows through it. The `ip access-group` statement associates an access control list with the interface. The number following this statement indicates which access control list to use; the lists themselves are defined by the `access-list` statements further down in the configuration. The `access-list` statements define a series of permit and deny conditions based on the source and destination IP addresses. These conditions are expressed in terms of a base IP address and a mask of wildcard bits for the source address, followed by a base IP address and mask for the destination address. An implicit "deny everything else" is inserted at the end of the list by the software.

In the example, the first `access-list` statement indicates that we wish to permit packets with any source address to the specific host `172.16.100.97`. This is the network management station—I want any packets sent to the management station to be permitted so it can get error reports and so I can log in to the router. The second `access-list` statement specifies that I want packets from any host going to subnet `172.16.131.0/24` to be passed. This subnet is where the company's order entry machines are located, and I want to ensure that those packets are carried by the backup link as well.

So why do I want to control access in the first place? Why not just let all packets flow from the remote site to the central site? An analog modem line is almost always going to have less bandwidth than a permanent leased circuit. If I allowed the entire load of the primary line onto this backup line, I'd probably swamp it and little useful traffic would get through. It rarely makes sense to have a backup without some restriction on the traffic the backup will carry.

In addition to controlling the traffic that is permitted to pass, I have also specified what traffic should be considered "interesting" enough to cause the link to be dialed, and to keep it up once it is connected. To do so, I associate a dialer group with the interface using the `dialer-group` statement, which specifies dialer group 1. I then associate one or more access lists with the dialer group. The second task is achieved by the `dialer-list` statement further down in the configuration. It associates access control list 101 with dialer group 1. While I could have chosen a different access control list with different selection criteria, I reasoned that the traffic I wished to permit on the interface should also be considered interesting enough to bring it up and keep it up, so I reused the existing list.

I also told the router that this interface was a dial-on-demand link, and that dialing would take place using in-band controls of the attached modem. The details of the in-band communication with the modem and for logging in to the remote router are controlled by chat scripts that are not shown. Because chat scripts are specific to the modem used, you should consult the Cisco IOS documentation and your modem documentation to build one for your site.

Finally, I included a static default route pointing at `172.16.200.1`, my central site router, and told the router what phone number to use to dial this router. I gave the static route a high administrative distance so that any dynamic routing protocol I run will supersede it. And speaking of dynamic routing protocols, you should be sure to mark this on-demand backup interface as passive, as described later, to prevent your routers from bringing it up while trying to exchange routes over it.

The central site router has a similar configuration. The main differences are that there are several `dialer map` statements, and that the access control list is defined differently. Access control lists are applied to packets being sent on an interface. Because we are at the other end of the link, the packets the access control list applies to are flowing in the opposite direction, so the source and destination addresses need to be reversed.

```
! this dial-up link will be used as a backup only
interface async 1
 ip address 172.16.200.1 255.255.255.0
! limit traffic on this link to avoid swamping it with our normal load
 ip access-group 101
 dialer in-band
 dialer-group 1
! map each site's backup IP address to its phone number
 dialer map ip 172.16.200.2 5551212
 dialer map ip 172.16.200.3 5552889
!
! allow traffic from the network management station and from the order
! entry subnet so that business can continue
access-list 101 permit ip 172.16.100.97 0.0.0.0   0.0.0.0 255.255.255.255
access-list 101 permit ip 172.16.131.0   0.0.0.255 0.0.0.0 255.255.255.255
!
dialer-list 1 list 101
!
! make sure these routes to the remote sites have a high administrative
! distance so they are only used as backups
ip route 172.16.95.0 255.255.255.0 172.16.200.2 250
ip route 172.16.64.0 255.255.252.0 172.16.200.3 250
```

The `dialer map` statements tell the router the phone numbers it should use for each remote site. You would need one of these for each of your remote routers; in our example configuration, we're only showing two remote sites. For each remote router, you also need a backup static route that sends traffic for the site's networks to the remote router.

It should now be clear why I defined a 24-bit mask for these dial-up links. In order to keep the routing and the calling as simple as possible, we want all of the backup interfaces to be on a common subnet. I could use a longer mask, but it must allow enough addresses for all of the routers that can use this backup line. If I were defining separate on-demand links for each site, rather than having them all share this one, I would have used a 30-bit mask, which would be adequate for these links.

Using Backup Static Routes to Limit Route Flaps

Another use for backup static routes is to limit the scope of route flaps. A route is said to flap when it goes through several transitions between being reachable and unreachable in a short time. While this is normally an error condition, and should not be tolerated for long, in reality, you may have to live with a route flap for days, or even weeks. It can take a long time to get a bad link repaired. It's even possible that the problem route is in your neighbor's network, and he is unwilling or unable to repair it, and you want to limit the effect of the flap on your network. In either case, a backup static route could be your answer.

Consider what happens if you install a backup static route in the router that connects to the faulty link or the neighbor with the problem. When the route disappears from the dynamic routing exchange, your router would normally prop-agate this information throughout your network, only to have it change again in a few seconds when the route comes back. By installing a backup static route, you can confine the knowledge of the flapping network to this one router. When the route disappears, your router installs the backup in its routing tables, and has no reason to notify any other router in your network of the change; it is still the best route to use to get there (even if it ends up pitching the packet because the link is down).

Where you point the backup static route depends on why the route is flapping, and what works best. If the route is flapping because your neighbor's network is propagating his internal flaps to you (not very nice, to say the least), then you probably want to point your backup route at one of his or her routers. While that router may not be the best path to the problem network, it might have a way there through other links that you haven't yet been told about. When the correct route is up, your router will replace this backup route with something more appropriate. On the other hand, if the flap is caused by the link between your router and the remote router, and the link cannot be repaired for several days, it might be appropriate to point the backup route at another valid path (perhaps a dial-on-demand link) or to the router's null interface (called `null 0` on a Cisco router). The null interface discards any packets sent to it, but is always up—some-thing that your faulty link might not be able to claim. When the faulty link is repaired, dynamic routing takes over, the route stops flapping, and the backup static route is no longer in use. However, you don't need to remove it immedi-ately (such as if the link is repaired at 2:00 A.M.). Just remove it when it is convenient.

The same idea applies to containing your own route flaps within your network, and not propagating them to your neighbors. It is often less disruptive to all networks involved (especially the Internet) to throw away packets than to have your routes flapping and causing excessive load on far-away routers.

Suppressing Advertisements

Your network may have one or more links to which you do not want dynamic routing updates sent. One reason might be that you have a low bandwidth link between two sites on which you have chosen to do static routing. Or there might not be any device on the link to listen to your updates, such as a stub network using a static default route. In this case, there is no reason to consume bandwidth with messages that no one cares about.

The interfaces to such links are known as *passive interfaces*. Most routers and routing protocols allow you to specify that some or all interfaces on a router are passive. The mechanism varies, but it typically takes one of two forms. The first is to use the name that the configuration language of the router uses, such as serial 2. The other is to use the interface's configured IP address. In either case, all interfaces are typically considered active until the router is told that they are passive. On a router running multiple protocols, each protocol usually maintains its own view of which interfaces are active and which are passive, so you must tell each protocol about passive interfaces separately.

In each of our examples, one Ethernet and one serial interface are listed as passive, so the router will not send protocol updates on them. The network or subnet number of the attached link will be included in the routing updates sent to other interfaces, if it would otherwise be included.

Declaring an interface to be passive does not mean you won't listen to routing updates that arrive on that interface. If a machine is sending updates on such a link, the router will listen to and process them, whether or not the interface is passive. This can lead to all kinds of routing problems. Consider that the router is using information it learns from the remote router, but it has no way to inform the remote router of its routes. We'll discuss how to prevent the router from listening to routes it might hear in the next section.

RIP

```
router rip
 network 172.16.0.0
 network 172.17.0.0
 network 192.168.100.0
! suppress advertisements on these interfaces
 passive-interface ethernet 1
 passive-interface serial 0
```

OSPF

```
router ospf 1
 network 0.0.0.0 255.255.255.255 area 0
 ! suppress advertisements on these interfaces
 passive-interface ethernet 1
 passive-interface serial 0
```

EIGRP

```
router eigrp 1
 network 172.16.0.0
 network 172.17.0.0
 network 192.168.100
 ! suppress advertisements on these interfaces
 passive-interface ethernet 1
 passive-interface serial 0
```

Restricting Sources of Routing Information

In the previous example, I discussed suppressing routing updates on a given link. However, this is only half the story. Often, when you have suppressed updates on an interface, you also want to avoid learning any routes that another router might be sending. Why it is sending them is a good question, and the answers vary from matters of policy to configuration errors. You may wish to avoid hearing updates on a specific interface because the source of the updates is not trusted. Perhaps another administrative domain is connected to the link, and you would rather not have your routing disrupted by their mistakes. Or you may need to filter the source of updates more finely. Perhaps you need to hear some routing updates on a shared link, possibly from other routers under your control, but you wish to ensure that some of the routing updates, perhaps those coming from a misbehaving machine, are not heard by your router.

Restricting the routing information you receive has obvious consequences. At worst, the routers you aren't listening to may have the only routes to some destinations; these destinations will be unreachable. Less drastic, the routers you're not listening to may have the best routes to some destinations. In this case, you'll have to put up with less than optimal routing. Of course, a few unreachable destinations and suboptimal routes are usually preferable to having your routing screwed up by an unreliable router that's not under your control—but you should be aware that there's a tradeoff.

Administrative distances are one possible way to restrict what your routers hear. The next section discusses how to gain even more control over routes you hear, perhaps allowing some routes from a set of routers but disallowing others.

RIP

```
router rip
 network 172.16.0.0
 network 172.17.0.0
 network 192.168.100.0
 passive-interface ethernet 1
 passive-interface serial 0
 ! set the default administrative distance to ignore routing updates
 distance 255
 ! set the administrative distance for these sources back to normal
 distance 120 172.16.1.0 0.0.0.255
 distance 120 172.16.2.0 0.0.0.255
 distance 120 172.16.8.0 0.0.0.255
```

In this example, I have taken one of two approaches to preventing incoming routing updates from being considered. Recall that an administrative distance of 255 is considered unusable by Cisco's software. I configured the router to use that distance by default for all sources of RIP updates. I then included a list of RIP sources that should be restored to the default RIP distance of 120. The address-mask pairs in these statements are different from most others, but they are exactly like the masks used in OSPF's network statements. Instead of 1-bits in the mask indicating that a bit in the address is significant, they indicate that the bit is a wild card. So the first statement following the default distance indicates that any RIP update coming from a router with an address on `172.16.1.0/24` should be given an administrative distance of 120.

This approach is useful if you only want to listen for routes from a few routers, and ignore updates from most routers. If you want to listen to most routing sources, excluding only a few specific sources, you would take an approach like the one I demonstrate in the EIGRP example.

OSPF

Using administrative distances to filter routing updates in an OSPF routing domain is an extremely dangerous proposition, and is not recommended. For OSPF to function properly, each router needs a consistent view of the network topology, and this is frustrated by attempts to suppress routing updates. Therefore, I will not present an example for OSPF. You can achieve a similar effect by declaring an OSPF interface passive. If an OSPF interface is passive, the routing process will not form an adjacency with any router on that link, and will treat it as a stub network. This has nearly the same effect, and tends to be safer.

EIGRP

In this example, I assume that I want the router to hear updates from most routers, except those on specific subnets. To do this, I allow the default administrative distance for EIGRP to prevail, but I selectively tell the router that some sources, those that match the address-mask pairs shown, should be considered unusable. If I want to ignore updates on all subnets except those that I specifically enable, I would follow the RIP example shown previously.

```
router eigrp 1
 network 172.16.0.0
 network 172.17.0.0
 network 192.168.100
 passive-interface ethernet 1
 passive-interface serial 0
 ! set the administrative distance for these sources to ignore them
 distance 255 172.16.1.0 0.0.0.255
 distance 255 172.16.2.0 0.0.0.255
 distance 255 172.16.8.0 0.0.0.255
```

I might want my restrictions to have even finer granularity, disallowing some routers while allowing others to be heard. To achieve either goal, I need only adjust the address-mask pairs on our `distance` statements to select the appropriate distances to assign to each routing source. For example, I might have decided that the routers on `172.16.8.0/24` are generally pretty good, but that the one router at `172.16.8.24` is prone to error. In this case, the filtering statements would become:

```
distance 255 172.16.1.0  0.0.0.255
distance 255 172.16.2.0  0.0.0.255
distance 255 172.16.8.24 0.0.0.0
```

To achieve the same effect in the RIP example, I'd need the following statements:

```
distance 255
distance 120 172.16.1.0  0.0.0.255
distance 120 172.16.2.0  0.0.0.255
distance 255 172.16.8.24 0.0.0.0
distance 120 172.16.8.0  0.0.0.255
```

In the RIP example, both of the last statements match the router at `172.16.8.24`. When several statements match the same router, the first match applies. So when the RIP process determines if it should process an update from `172.16.8.24`, it matches the fourth line and decides to ignore the router.

Finally, you can select administrative distances that aren't all or nothing. Perhaps the errant router at `172.16.8.24` is still better than nothing, if all of the other routers on the subnet are down. In this case, I might assign it an administrative distance that is higher than the dynamic protocol would normally receive, but still less than 255. However, if I do this, the router will ignore any route from

`172.16.8.24` that it also hears from another router, regardless of how bad its metric is. Meanwhile, the router will gladly use any route the suspect router tells us that another router does not. If this is not exactly what you want, consider some alternative to administrative distances.

Filtering Specific Routes from an Update

You may need more fine-grained filtering of routing updates than the previous examples allowed. For example, you may need to listen to the routes advertised by a router that is not under your control, but you want to make sure that you don't hear some specific routes that the router might be advertising.

Take this seriously! Years ago, my network lost its normal default route because of a break in its connection to the Internet. However, one of the departments on campus was accidentally sending a default route in its advertisements. This errant route was not filtered out by the routers that heard it, so they believed and used it, causing a routing loop and some interesting trouble reports. While this route should have eventually aged out of the network once the metric counted to infinity, a misconfiguration in one of the other department's routers caused this default route to get its metric *reconstituted*. No matter what metric it was told by its neighbors in routing updates, the router would reset the metric to a relatively small value before sending it on to other routers. This problem could have been prevented if the routers all filtered the routing updates that they heard from this departmental network and discarded anything unusual, as they do now. In short, practice safe routing, because when you do unsafe routing with someone, you do unsafe routing with everyone they do unsafe routing with.

As an alternative to blocking specific routes that you do not wish to hear from another router, you might choose to discard all routes *except* for a few specific routes that they should be sending you. Both of these alternatives are possible, and there are multiple different ways to achieve what you want. I will demonstrate two fairly common ones in our examples below. Our RIP example demonstrates how to achieve both forms of route filtering using administrative distances, while our EIGRP example uses distribution lists.

Again, since OSPF relies on all routers forming a common view of the network topology, it is not a good idea to attempt to filter the contents of the routing updates heard or sent to other routers. Instead, our OSPF example discusses a way to form OSPF adjacencies with foreign routers without losing control over what routes they inject into your own routing system.

RIP

For this example, I assume that I want to restrict who I hear routes from, but I am willing to trust the routers on `172.16.1.0/24` and `172.16.2.0/24` to tell me anything, probably because they are under my control. But the routers on `172.16.8.0/24` are not to be fully trusted. By appending an *access list* to the `distance` statement for that link, I can selectively allow routes from routers on that network.

```
router rip
 network 172.16.0.0
 network 172.17.0.0
 network 192.168.100.0
 passive-interface ethernet 1
 passive-interface serial 0
 distance 255
 distance 120 172.16.1.0 0.0.0.255
 distance 120 172.16.2.0 0.0.0.255
 ! set the administrative distance for these sources back to normal
 ! but only for routes that pass access list 1
 distance 120 172.16.8.0 0.0.0.255 1
 !
access-list 1 permit 172.16.9.0  0.0.0.255
access-list 1 permit 172.16.20.0 0.0.0.255
access-list 1 permit 172.17.0.0  0.0.255.255
access-list 1 deny  0.0.0.0      255.255.255.255
```

Access lists are a general feature of Cisco's IOS. When first encountered, most people expect them to be used as an access control facility, preventing packets from selected IP addresses from being sent on an interface. I'll discuss this use of access lists in Chapter 10. But access lists are far more general. Cisco uses them as a general way to represent any selection criteria that is based on IP addresses.[*] Other routers have their own mechanisms, perhaps several, to accomplish the same tasks.

In the example, the access list defines which routes I will permit my router to hear from `172.16.8.0/24`. The `access-list` statements allow these foreign routers to tell my router about `172.16.9.0/24`, `172.16.20.0/24`, and `172.17.0.0/16`, and no others. Evaluating an access list is straightforward. Each prospective address is compared with the address-mask pairs in order. When a match occurs, the accompanying action (permit or deny) is immediately applied, and the access list ends. Should the access list be completely evaluated without a match, an implicit *deny all* action (which I explicitly show above) is selected, and the address is rejected. Note that the routes my router actually hears

---

[*] There are also equivalent access list structures for each of the other protocols that the Cisco IOS routes.

do not have to match these three networks exactly. Subnets of `172.17.0.0/16` will pass the access list and will be dealt with normally by the routing protocol.

The access list's dependence on order makes it easy for the router to process, but it makes it difficult to edit. You cannot simply append a new entry to the end (the only operation allowed by the IOS configuration process other than deleting an entry) and have the correct effect, unless the new entry really belongs at the end. In Chapter 8, I present some tips to work around this limitation.

In this example, I assume that I do not want to hear about routes from most routers. If I want my router to listen to all routers except those I deem to be problematic, I would achieve the same level of control over the routers on `172.16.8.0/24` by using these `distance` statements and the same access list:

```
distance 120 172.16.8.0 0.0.0.255 1
distance 255 172.16.8.0 0.0.0.255
```

In these statements, by default I accept all routes with the normal administrative distance for RIP (120). I then declare that all routes from routers on `172.16.8.0/24` that pass access list 1 should also be accepted with a distance of 120. Finally, I declare that all other routes from all routers on `172.16.8.0/24` should be ignored by giving them a distance of 255.

OSPF

The need for all routers in an OSPF routing domain to have the same view of the network topology makes any kind of route filtering within the OSPF domain problematic. As a rule, you only want routers under a single administrative authority participating in an OSPF routing domain.

But there are times when you need to allow a foreign router (or routers) to exchange routing information with your routers. One way to accomplish this is to run two OSPF routing processes in the router (or routers) that must exchange information with the foreign routers. The first OSPF process would be the one that you use to exchange information with the routers under your control. This process can be configured without special restrictions on routing information because you can trust your other routers to provide the correct information (we hope!). The other OSPF process would be configured to exchange routing information with the foreign routers. Then, to allow information from the foreign routers to be propagated through your network, you would set up a controlled redistribution between the OSPF processes that only passes the routes you wish to allow into your network. The details of redistribution can get messy quickly. Here's a simple example that allows all routes from the foreign routers in except the default route:

```
! start an OSPF process for my routers
router ospf 1
```

```
  network 172.16.0.0 0.0.255.255 area 0
  redistribute ospf 2 route-map nodefault metric 1
  !
  ! start a second OSPF process for the foreign routers
  router ospf 2
   network 192.168.128.0 0.0.0.255 area 0
   !
  ! define route maps to block the default route from the foreign routers
  route-map nodefault deny
   match ip address 1
  !
  route-map nodefault permit
   match ip address 2
  !
  access-list 1 permit 0.0.0.0 0.0.0.0
  !
  access-list 2 permit 0.0.0.0 255.255.255.255
```

I have started two OSPF processes. The first one (our routers) runs on all interfaces on 172.16.0.0/16. The second (for the foreign routers) runs on all interfaces (probably only one) on 192.168.128.0/24. The tricky part comes in defining how routes should be controlled between the two OSPF domains. Under Cisco IOS, you define a *route map* to describe the processing you want. Each route map is given a name, and multiple route maps may share the same name. When multiple maps share a name, they are processed in the order they are encountered in the configuration.

Each route map defines a set of *match* conditions that cause that route map to apply. They may also have one or more set actions that allow fine tuning of information specific to the routing protocols; our example doesn't use them. Finally, each route map defines the disposition of routes that match this map.

In our example, I have two route maps named nodefault. The first states that any route (address) that matches access list 1 matches this map, and will be denied. Once a match occurs, no further route maps are considered, so this prevents routes matching access list 1 from being propagated. In our example, access list 1 matches the default route. The second route map states that any route that matches access list 2 matches this map, and will be permitted. In our example, access list 2 matches all routes. Taken together, the two route maps state that the default route will be filtered out, and all other routes will be propagated.

All that remains is to apply this route map to the routes from the second OSPF process, and redistribute them into the main OSPF process. This is accomplished by the redistribute command. Our redistribute command tells the router that OSPF process 1 (the one for our routers) should receive all routes from OSPF process 2 (the one for the foreign routers) that pass the route map named nodefault, and that they should be given a metric of 1. These routes will be distributed among our routers as type 2 external routes, by default.

As you can see, running OSPF among a set of routers that are not entirely under your control can rapidly become a configuration nightmare. The example was about as simple as it can get, and it is still rather complex. If you wanted even more control, or wanted to fine tune any of the various OSPF parameters, the complexity could quickly become unmanageable.

EIGRP

In this example, I use a distribution list to control what routes I allow the router to hear and to advertise on various interfaces. Note that this is the first example that selectively announces routes, in addition to selectively listening for routes.

```
router eigrp 1
 network 172.16.0.0
 network 172.17.0.0
 network 192.168.100
 ! filter EIGRP from ethernet 2 through access list 12, and EIGRP to be
 ! sent on serial 1 through access list 22
 distribute-list 12 in  ethernet 2
 distribute-list 22 out serial 1
 !
access-list 12 permit 172.17.0.0 0.0.255.255
access-list 12 deny   0.0.0.0     255.255.255.255
 !
access-list 22 deny   192.168.128.0 0.0.0.255
access-list 22 permit 0.0.0.0       255.255.255.255
```

The distribute-list in statement controls which routes the router hears. This statement tells the router that it should process all routing updates from the named interface (ethernet 2) by filtering them through access list 12, and only allow those that pass the access list. This means that I will only allow routes matching access list 12 to be heard on ethernet 2. Note that this mechanism does not let us apply different rules based on the source router. To do that, I must use administrative distances.

In a similar way, I use the distribute-list out statement to control what the router will announce on an interface. I have told the router that I only want to announce destinations matching access list 22 on interface serial 1. Since access list 22 permits all routes except 192.168.128.0/24, it prevents the router from announcing that network and its subnets over the interface serial 1. As with distribute-list in, it is not possible to apply different rules to our outbound announcements based on anything finer than an interface. However, if you recall that routing updates are generally either broadcasts or multicasts, it really doesn't make any sense to try.

Dynamic Routing with Multiple Paths

One of the most useful and interesting tasks you will need to perform is supporting dynamic routing in the presence of multiple paths between various points. Clearly, if you designed a network with redundant paths, you would like these paths to be used in the event of a network failure. You may also want them to be used to do some form of load-balancing.

Controlling the selection of routes in a multi-path network is no easy task. Since each router makes its own decisions about how it should route packets, it is possible, and even likely, that routers in different parts of your network may select different paths. Packets from host A to host B may take one path, while packets from host B to host A may take another path. This is known as *asymmetric routing*. Some network managers feel that asymmetric routing is to be avoided. While there is a certain merit to having the path from A to B be the exact reverse of the path from B to A, this is often difficult to achieve and may not be worth the effort. When all is working, the primary advantage of symmetry is that you can put monitoring equipment on any segment along the path and see both sides of a conversation. However, when it comes right down to it, you could put monitoring equipment on either the ultimate source or destination segment and see both sides of a conversation anyway.

Far more important than symmetric routing is *stable and predictable* routing. The routes selected by your routers should not be a crap shoot. If you know which routers and links are functioning, you should be able to compute manually which path packets between two hosts will take. This is critical for your ability to determine where to start looking for problems when the packets do not flow correctly. For example, if you have three network segments connected by two routers, as shown in Figure 6-4, it is clear that packets from host A to host B must traverse the three segments from left to right. If the packets should fail to reach their destination, you have a clearly defined set of places to look for failures.

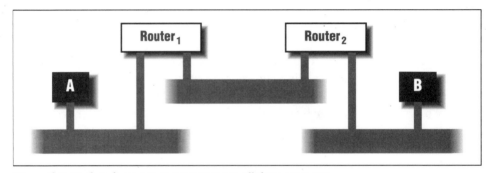

Figure 6-4. Packets from A to B must traverse all three segments

If you add a redundant link between the two routers (say, an FDDI ring), packets from A to B may flow across either the upper or the lower link. If they fail to make it, which link do you probe? If you have predictable routing, you know which link to probe, and you can cut your troubleshooting time significantly, especially when your network contains dozens of routers and hundreds of segments.

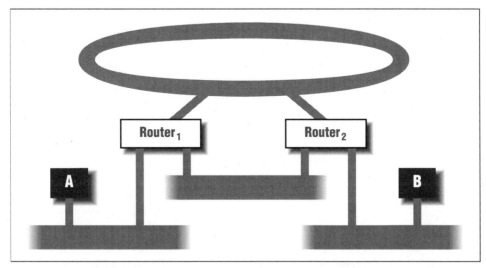

Figure 6-5. With a second link, the path from A to B becomes harder to predict

How you achieve predictable routing is specific to each network and routing protocol. Several criteria can enter into the router's decision; each protocol gives you different ways to affect this decision. In general, the primary control you have over this decision is the protocol's route metric. Recall that the route metric is how a routing protocol communicates the cost of using a specific route. For RIP, the metric is simply a hop count, while OSPF computes an administratively defined link cost based on the speed of the link by default, and IGRP and EIGRP use a complex metric consisting, in part, of link bandwidth, load, and reliability. In our examples, I will explore a few of the ways that metrics can be adjusted to achieve predictability. For our examples, I'll use the network shown in Figure 6-5.

RIP

By default, RIP has no knowledge of the relative bandwidths or load of the links in your network. The router makes its routing decisions based solely on the RIP metric, which is a simple count of hops to a destination. In our example, the hop across the Ethernet is considered equivalent to the hop across the FDDI ring. Furthermore, a router using RIP will not take advantage of multiple paths. Instead, it latches onto the first path that it hears, and only abandons this path in favor of one with a lower metric, or when the original path fails. In the case of two equal cost paths, only the first heard will be used.*

Because you cannot predict which path a router will hear first, to achieve predictable routing you must adjust the metrics along one path to be better or worse than along the other. One simple way is with the `offset-list in` and `offset-list out` statements. Proceed with caution! Applying offsets to metrics without careful thought can easily result in routing loops and black holes.

```
router rip
 network 172.16.0.0
 network 172.17.0.0
 network 192.168.100.0
 ! increase the metric for all routes learned or sent over ethernet 4
 offset-list 32 in  1 ethernet 4
 offset-list 32 out 1 ethernet 4
 !
 access-list 32 permit 0.0.0.0 255.255.255.255
```

In this example, the `offset-list in` statement tells the router that all updates arriving on `ethernet 4` that match access list 32 will have their metrics increased by one (in addition to the one they would normally be increased to account for the added hop). Since access list 32 matches all routes, anything the router hears on `ethernet 4` will have a metric one higher than that heard on `fddi 1`, so `fddi 1` will be preferred whenever it is functional. In the same way, the `offset-list out` statement tells the router that it should add one to all metrics (in addition to any normal adjustments) for routes matching access list 32 (all routes) before it sends them out on `ethernet 4`. This causes the other router to prefer the FDDI ring as a return path; the Ethernet becomes a backup path.

In general, however, it is better to apply metric offsets only on inbound routing updates or on outbound updates, not both. To understand why, consider what happens if the other router in our picture were to apply its inbound and outbound offsets in the opposite direction:

```
offset-list 32 in  1 fddi 2
offset-list 32 out 1 fddi 2
```

Ignore for the moment that it is unlikely that you would want to favor the Ethernet over the FDDI ring. The result of this configuration is that the first router is trying to favor the FDDI ring, and cause the other router to do the same, while the second router is trying to favor the Ethernet, and cause the first to do the

---

* The Cisco IOS will use multiple equal cost paths, even when learned from RIP. It does a form of load-balancing across the paths that depend on other factors in the router's configuration that we will not discuss here.

same. The result is that they cancel each others' efforts: neither favors either network, and we use whichever route is heard first.

OSPF

Unlike RIP, OSPF is aware of the bandwidth of the links in the network, but only in an indirect way. Each link in a network is given a cost by the OSPF protocol. By default, the cost of a link is determined to be:

$$\frac{10^8}{\text{bandwidth}}$$

The resulting costs for various networks is shown in Table 6-2.

Table 6-2. Default OSPF Costs for Various Link Bandwidth Values

Link Bandwidth	Default OSPF Cost
56kbps serial link	1785
64kbps serial link	1562
T1 (1.544Mbps) serial link	65
E1 (2.048Mbps) serial link	48
4Mbps Token Ring	25
Ethernet	10
16Mbps Token Ring	6
FDDI or Fast Ethernet	1

Because of these default costs, an OSPF router will automatically prefer a single hop over a FDDI ring to a single hop over an Ethernet. In fact, barring any adjustments of costs for administrative reasons, an OSPF router would prefer to take nine hops across nine FDDI rings to a single hop across an Ethernet. For this reason, I altered our example to assume that the redundant links are both Ethernets so that they will default to equal costs.

OSPF is unlike RIP in another important way. When OSPF has multiple paths of equal cost to a destination, it will use both paths and attempt to do some form of load balancing. This is normally what you want, but if it is not, you need to adjust the costs of the links. You might want to do this for security reasons, or perhaps because you are doing some real-time processing that cannot tolerate the chance that some packets may arrive out of order or with varying delays. I have adjusted the costs to demonstrate this in the example.

```
interface ethernet 1
 ip address 172.16.1.1 255.255.255.0
 ! change the cost of this interface to make it less preferred
 ip ospf cost 11
```

```
!
interface ethernet 2
 ip address 172.16.2.1 255.255.255.0
 ! explicitly set the default cost as a reminder that it is what we want
 ip ospf cost 10
!
router ospf 1
 network 0.0.0.0 255.255.255.255 area 0
```

I have set the cost of ethernet 1 to 11, and that of ethernet 2 to 10 (the default). This makes ethernet 2 the preferred route. I could have allowed the cost of ethernet 2 to default to 10, but the cost is clearer if I explicitly configure it. Any time that you depart from the default in one case, it is useful to configure the default explicitly in all the others, both as a reminder of what the default is, and that you meant to use the default value.

EIGRP

RIP normally uses only one path, even if multiple equal cost paths are available. A router implementation may use multiple equal cost paths, but that is implementation-specific, not part of the protocol. OSPF uses equal cost paths concurrently, but all paths of a higher cost will be unused. EIGRP is unlike either of these protocols in that it not only uses multiple equal cost paths, but it can also use multiple unequal cost paths. Further, it uses each path in inverse proportion to its cost to distribute the load.

In our example, I have returned to our original multi-path network where one path is an Ethernet, and the other is an FDDI ring. By using the variance statement, I can tell the router that it should accept up to four alternate paths that are worse than the best path (this is defined by Cisco's implementation), and it should use them in inverse proportion to their metrics. Thus, a path that is three times worse than the best path will be used only one third as much as the best path.

```
router eigrp 1
 network 172.16.0.0
 network 172.17.0.0
 network 192.168.100
 ! allow unequal cost paths to be considered for use
 variance 10
```

It may take some experimentation to find the best value for the variance. By increasing the variance, you allow the router to consider worse paths. However, if you set the variance too high, a path that you may not want to include at all may be used. A good strategy is to set up your network initially with a variance value of 1 (the default), and then slowly increase it until the less desirable routes you want get included in your routing table, but stopping before routes you do not want to use get included.

Using Multiple Routing Protocols at the Same Time

If you can, you should select one IGP and stick with it throughout your network. Each protocol works differently, and there are seldom valid translations between the metrics of one protocol and another. For example, consider EIGRP and RIP. Both are distance-vector protocols, and thus behave in somewhat similar manners. However, how do you translate the RIP metric, involving only hop counts, to the complex EIGRP metric involving bandwidth, delay, load, etc.? Now consider what happens if one of your protocols is OSPF, a link-state protocol. Translating one metric to another has even less meaning.

However, you often have little choice about running multiple dynamic routing protocols in your network. Two common reasons are that you have to perform dynamic routing with routers under another administration's control, and that you are migrating from one protocol to the other. Regardless of your reasons for running multiple protocols, it is best to have a clearly-defined demarcation between the two protocols (you weren't *seriously* planning to run *three*, were you?). If at all possible, have the demarcation between the two routing domains exist in only one or two routers. This limits the complexity of handling multiple protocols in the same router to only a few routers.

For our multi-protocol example, I assume that you are running a campus-sized network and have chosen to use EIGRP for your routing protocol. However, you have a department on campus that has its own network, and wants to attach to yours. The only problem is that they have chosen to use RIP, perhaps because it is easy, or perhaps because it is all that their routers can support. You have three basic choices:

- Convert their network to use EIGRP

- Convert your network to use RIP

- Run multiple routing protocols on the router connecting them to you

If the first option is possible, it is probably the best, since you can avoid multi-protocol problems entirely. However, if they can't or won't switch, this option is unavailable. The second option is just plain ludicrous. Why should you give up the benefits you have configured into your network just to connect to another group? Besides, what happens when you bump into another department that is running yet another routing protocol? You can't keep changing your routing protocol to match the groups you attach to.

Okay, so you decide to do multiple routing protocols on the router connecting to this other department. First, you must define your goals clearly. Your first goal should be protecting your own routing stability. If that is not even on your list, you are making a big mistake. While it is unlikely that the network administrator for the other department will intentionally cause you problems, mistakes happen. Besides, he should be just as cautious about you messing up his routing, and will probably be taking steps to protect against your mistakes. One of the best ways to protect your routing stability is to list explicitly which routes you will accept from these foreign routers. If you do not want to change your configuration every time the other department adds a new network, you might want to list the routes you simply refuse to accept from them. This list will probably include routes to your own network, and other networks that you know you should never hear from the foreign routers. You also don't want to accept the other network's default route if you are otherwise connected to the outside world.

Your second goal should be to provide information about these foreign routes to the other routers in your network as concisely as possible, while still maintaining correct routing. For example, you do not want to propagate subnet routes you might hear from your neighbor to your own routers if you are on different IP networks.

Your third goal should be to optimize the way your network selects paths into your neighbor's network, especially if you connect to it in two or more locations. To do so, select a consistent translation between your neighbor's routing protocol metrics and yours. If you only connect in a single place, then you can easily default all of your neighbor's metrics to the same value for your routing protocol.

Fortunately, more modern routing protocols such as EIGRP and OSPF provide for multiple types of routes. In both these protocols, routes that come in from the outside are tagged as external routes, and are processed specially by the receiving routers. RIP has no such concept, so routes that arrive from the outside are indistinguishable from internal routes.

Finally, after you have determined how to deal with the information your neighbor will be sending you, you need to decide what to tell him about your network. If you are the only outside connection for your neighbor, the simplest solution is to send a default route to his routers. This is also the most common case. On the other hand, if your neighbor has multiple connections to various groups, a default route may not be the best choice. In this case, you need to be sure that what you send him provides his routers with enough information, in a form that they can use, to compute reasonably optimal routes to your network, without filling up their routing tables unnecessarily.

```
router eigrp 71
  network 172.16.0.0
```

```
! pass my neighbor's routes into my network via EIGRP with a default
! metric
 redistribute rip
 default-metric 10000 250 255 1 1500
 !
router rip
 network 172.30.0.0
! pass my routes to my neighbor via RIP with a metric of 1
 redistribute eigrp 71
 default-metric 1
! limit what I hear from my neighbor, and only send him the default
! route
 distribute-list 11 in
 distribute-list 12 out eigrp 71
 !
access-list 11 permit 172.30.0.0 0.0.255.255
access-list 11 permit 192.168.15.0 0.0.0.255
access-list 11 deny 0.0.0.0 255.255.255.255
 !
access-list 12 permit 0.0.0.0 0.0.0.0
```

In this example, I have started an EIGRP process to communicate with my internal routers. I have also started a RIP process to communicate with my neighbor's routers. For each routing protocol, I have told the router to redistribute the routes of the other, and to assign them appropriate default metrics. For RIP, this default metric is just a hop count of 1. The metric for EIGRP is complex, so I have to set values for all of its components. The components and the values I set are:

link bandwidth (in kbps):	10000
route delay (x 10 µ sec):	250
reliability (0-255):	255
loading (0-255):	1
path MTU:	1500

These values are reasonable for a lightly loaded, highly reliable Ethernet. If the load is higher, increase the loading value. If the link is less reliable, decrease the reliability value. The exact values aren't important unless the routes from your neighbor might be heard from alternate paths.

In the RIP routing process, I have gone further than redistributing the routes. Here I have told the router that it should pass all routes learned from EIGRP process 71 through access list 12; only routes that match should be sent via RIP. In our example, only the default route matches access list 12. By not including a source interface or routing protocol on the distribute-list in statement, I have also told the router that it should pass *all* inbound RIP updates through access list 11 to filter out any advertisements I do not want to hear. In this case, access list

11 specifies two networks, presumably owned by the department I am connecting to, that I will accept from them. All other routes will be ignored.

Instead of using an inbound distribution list on the RIP process, I could have put an outbound distribution list on the EIGRP process, and filtered the RIP routes there. While that would have protected our other routers from hearing undesirable routes from our neighbor, it would have done nothing to protect the router itself. By putting the filter on the inbound RIP processing, I stop the routes before they ever get to the routing table.

As you can see, running multiple routing protocols in a single router can be confusing. It's even worse when you try to run them in parallel across links of your network. Avoid this at all costs; only do it during the (hopefully) short time it takes to change routing protocols. In these cases, make liberal use of administrative distances, or whatever mechanism your router provides, to select one protocol over another so that you favor your existing routing protocol. Then, when you are convinced that your new routing protocol is correctly configured, you can change the administrative distances to allow the new protocol to control routing decisions before turning off your old routing protocol for good.

7

The Non-Technical Side of Network Management

The real work begins once you have your network operational. Keeping that network running smoothly, fixing it when it doesn't, and expanding and improving it are a whole different game. Fortunately, a well-designed network will have fewer problems and will allow more time for you and your staff to work on expansion and improvement, which are much more fun. ·

When most people think about network management, several things come to mind. These are likely to include routing protocols and tables, SNMP management stations, cables, and so forth. Often, though, they fail to consider some of the more intangible or non-technical components of network management. Some of these are every bit as important as the more technical components, and often even more important. This chapter and the next focus on aspects of managing and maintaining your network, and explore some of the tasks and tools that help you avoid problems, troubleshoot the network when it has problems, and control its growth to keep it manageable. Chapter 8, *The Technical Side of Network Management*, focuses on techniques and tools, hands-on kinds of things, while this chapter focuses on the more abstract and intangible parts of network management.

How You View Your Network

Perhaps the most important aspect of network management is how you view your network. In my experience, successful network administrators seem to share a common way of looking at their network that their less successful counterparts have missed. The concept is simple (though not always simple to adhere to):

> The network is more than the sum of its parts. It is a complex, interacting system and must be treated as such.

Consider how you think of your body. Most of the time, you probably think of your body as a unit, rather than thinking about its individual parts. Even when you do think of its individual parts, you rarely think about the individual tissues, or even cells, that make up that part. Have you ever really thought of your body as a loose collection of cells that happen to be moving in a common direction?

Your network is the same. If you think in terms of a router here, a file server there, a few cables, and dozens of hosts, you are not thinking of your network as a system. On the other hand, if you think in terms of data flowing smoothly between clients and servers, where the routers, hubs and cables are just incidental background that keeps the whole thing humming along, then you are getting the right idea. In other words, *notice* the trees, but *see* the forest. If it helps, think of your network as a living entity. As with most living things, any change to one part of the system has effects on other, more distant parts of the system. If you injure your foot, you may get a queasy feeling in your stomach, even if there is no blood to make you squeamish. The injury may also make you light-headed, or even trigger sympathy pains in parts of your body that are uninjured. In the same way, a problem with one part of your network may be felt most acutely in another distant area.

Recently, a failing board in one router in my network took nearly three weeks to locate. This difficulty arose because the symptoms that were most noticeable appeared to be hardware problems in *four* other routers (though not simultaneously). The truly sick router was largely unaffected. It was only after other minor problems were correlated that this router was identified as having problems. You must look for the effect of your actions beyond the confines of the single router or switch you are currently configuring. You must be constantly asking, "What will this change do to the stability and efficiency of my network?" not "What will this change do to this router or switch?" Once you start looking at the network as a system, you have a much better chance of understanding the consequences and the tradeoffs involved in your decisions and actions.

Defining the Boundaries of Your Network

Closely related to understanding the network as a system is understanding the network's boundaries. Often, these boundaries are defined by the structure of your organization. These boundaries are, of course, arbitrary and artificial, but if they are imposed by means outside your control, they are nonetheless real. In some cases, you may be able to define these boundaries yourself. Perhaps you are building a new network and have been given a great deal of freedom, or you are reorganizing an older network and your employer has given you great leeway in defining the result. Regardless of your situation, it is important to know where these boundaries are, or that you clearly define them if it is within your power to do so. By knowing where these boundaries are, or by defining them yourself, you help yourself and your staff to understand the limits of their responsibilities and authority. Just as important, you help to confine the scope of network problems and to define which problems truly belong to the network.

The question of where to place these boundaries is harder to answer than you might think. Consider several possibilities for a multi-building campus network:

- The boundary of your network is at the end of the fiber optic cable in each remote building.

- The boundary of your network is at the connection between your router and a department's LAN.

- The boundary of your network is in the wiring closet.

- The boundary of your network is at the wall plug.

- The boundary of your network is at the back of a machine connected to it.

- The boundary of your network is at the interface card in the machine.

- The boundary of your network includes the host systems.

As you move through the list, the boundary of the network moves further and further out, until, finally, it includes the machines attached to the network. The network has also gotten more complex and more interdependent. Which boundary is correct? They are all correct. The answer depends on several factors that are unique to your organization and its structure, and may be outside of your control. But if you are setting the boundaries yourself, keep a few things in mind:

- If you set the network boundary too close to the core, you limit your ability to provide quality service, and reliable network access to your customers. For example, if your network boundary is at the end of the fiber cable to a remote building, it may be difficult or impossible for you to provide redundant links between buildings.

- On the other hand, the further out you put the boundary, the more problems you are responsible for solving. Consider the difference between having your boundary at the wall plug and having it at the back of the machine. On the surface, this would appear to be nothing more than responsibility for another few feet of cable. But what happens when the occupant of an office rearranges the furniture? It may now be your responsibility to disconnect the cable from their machine before they start, and then to reattach it, perhaps using a different length cable, when they are done.

As an example, consider where your boundaries might be if you have a small company with two Ethernets, a router, a file server, and twenty PCs. You may be the only computer support person in the entire company, and your network is likely to include all of the system administration tasks for the server and the client machines. If your organization is a large multi-national corporation spanning three continents, the boundary of your network may be set by your corporate headquarters and may be at the end of the WAN link to each site.

Again, where you put the boundary may depend on the external structure of your organization, but some of the better choices are:

- The connection between your router and a department's LAN. This allows for a clean break between equipment that you own and maintain and equipment that a department owns and maintains.

- The wiring closet. This allows for a distinction between the electronics in the network (hubs, routers, etc.) and the wiring in the walls, and is especially useful if your organization assigns responsibility for these components to different groups.

- The wall plug. This provides a convenient demarcation between equipment that the user can and cannot touch, thereby helping to eliminate problems caused by user actions.

The important thing is not what boundary is best for your network, especially since they are artificial, but rather that you know where that boundary is and keep it in mind. This not only saves you quite a bit of troubleshooting time, but it may be required by strict policy. Consider what it means if your network boundary is defined to be the wall plug. When a user calls and indicates that his workstation is no longer working on the network, you (or your staff) quickly examine the state of your routers and hubs and determine that all appear to be working well. You next grab a laptop computer, or other test device, and head for the user's office.

Once there, you disconnect the computer *at the wall plug* and plug in your laptop using your own cable. If the laptop works, you inform the user that the problem is either in his cable or his computer, and that he should seek further assistance from whomever is responsible for these components. You might, if you are in a good mood or he was the best man at your wedding, quickly try connecting your laptop to the network using his cable, just to eliminate an obvious possibility, but even this may be seen as a transgression by the people responsible for the machine and its cables. While I may seem overly bureaucratic, that is not my intent. The idea is to have a clearly defined line where your responsibility (and authority) end, not only to keep your staff from running afoul of someone else's territorialism, but also to keep them from getting swamped with problems that they can do nothing about. If you bend the rules once, it is harder to hold firm the next time around.*

Another part of understanding the network's boundary is that you know how to segregate broken equipment from the rest of the network. If the boundary is at the wall plug, you can disconnect the offending machine at that wall plug. If your network boundary is at a building connection, you would need to disconnect an entire building if its problems were disrupting the remainder of your network.

Staff Skills

One of the hardest and least tangible components of network management is assessing the skills that your staff possesses or needs. It is also one of the most easily overlooked, possibly because it is so difficult to deal with. Nevertheless, you must strive to understand the skills of your staff, if for no other reason than to know who is most appropriate for handling a task.

Regardless of whether you are a manager looking for a set of skills in a potential employee, or an employee looking for ways to improve your own worth, the problem is the same. Before you can assess whether a person has skills valuable to your organization, you must first understand what skills are essential to managing a network. What these skills are is not a simple question, and the list that I discuss is certainly not exhaustive. You undoubtedly have others that you think are more important and appropriate for your network and organization, and may think that some of the ones listed are unnecessary for your situation. Think carefully before you change the list around, but in the end, it is your network, and your judgment should prevail.

If the network is truly a single system, then many of the skills needed to manage it will be the same as those necessary to managing a large computer system. Among these skills are:

- Good organization
- Attention to detail
- Good record keeping
- Good problem solving skills
- Good team abilities
- Good communications skills

---

* If your organization is overly political, it also avoids accusations of favoritism that can occur when you help one person, but not another. Given today's extremely litigious society, adhering to your own policies religiously can avoid all kinds of hassles.

There are also, of course, skills that are valuable in any employee. But there is also a set of skills that is more specialized to the technical aspects of computer networks:

- The ability to understand and implement wiring and cabling standards, and to adhere to them strictly

- The ability to troubleshoot and diagnose failures in electronic components

- The ability to troubleshoot and diagnose failures in software components

- The ability to plan and carry out an installation on scales varying from a small LAN to a large, multi-building or multi-campus network

- An ability to recognize relationships between components of the system

Certainly, everyone on your staff doesn't need all of these skills, but everyone should have a good measure of most of them, and all of the skills should be present in your technician-level staff. Fortunately, unlike the first list of skills, the skills in this second list can be learned.

This leads us to the most important quality for everyone of your staff. In the computer network arena, it is absolutely essential that every person on your staff should be self-motivated to improve, to learn, and to keep current with the trends in the industry. A lecturer recently stated approximately 20 percent of a person's technical networking knowledge becomes obsolete each year. What this means is that if you and your staff are standing still, you will be left completely behind in just five years! Unfortunately, few corporations can afford to keep all of their staff current in the latest technologies, and very few seem even to try. This may be because they believe that training their staff will enable them to seek higher-paying jobs elsewhere, but the result is that employees are left to themselves to learn new technologies and keep up with changes made to the old.

Another invaluable skill is the ability to understand the technology on an intuitive level. A person with this ability does not necessarily need to understand what every bit in the header of an IP datagram means, nor does he need to understand the physics of signal propagation in a cable. Instead, this person understands the big picture—how all of the pieces fit together and what the interactions are. For example, a person with this skill will understand that checksum errors on an Ethernet cable will cause retransmissions of TCP segments. But more important, he or she will understand the implications of these retransmissions: throughput on the network drops both because of the need to send the same data across the wires again, and because of the back-off behavior that TCP exhibits when it needs to retransmit.

Fortunately, while this ability is rare, and a person with this ability and extensive experience with TCP/IP is rarer still, network protocol suites are rather like programming languages. For example, a competent programmer who understands all aspects of software development and is able to work in any facet of it, does not need to be fluent in every programming language. After the first one or two, others are learned quickly and easily. It's the same with network protocols. Once the basic concepts have become second nature, a person who understands the network as a system can easily pick up the details of protocols that he hasn't already worked with. In other words, if a person can see the big picture, and has little or no experience with TCP/IP, but extensive experience with a protocol such as IPX or AppleTalk, the TCP/IP experience will come easily. As rare as this ability to intuitively grasp the big picture is, it is worth allowing some leeway when a prospect possessing this skill lacks direct experience with IP networking.

One reason that you might add skills to my lists, and possibly even delete skills, is your defininition of the network boundary. If your network includes all of the machines attached to the network, then you are likely to add such skills as application programming, user support, and traditional operating system support to your list. You may have to provide these skills in your staff even if your network boundary is elsewhere because you need to support some of your own hosts, perhaps to provide services like the Domain Name System. Another reason for adding specialized skills is that your organization does not have a group to install cables or fiber optics. In this case, you may need personnel who can install and terminate copper cables or fiber optic links, or even to provide additional power to an area to support electronics.

Aside from these special skills, every network group needs at least one person who can establish, maintain, and preach a coherent network vision to the other staff. Many networks with problems, especially with uncontrolled growth, are in trouble because they do not have anyone to maintain the vision. The symptoms are easy to identify: There seems to be no clear pattern of growth, nor any rhyme or reason for how things are done. Network personnel drift from task to task, and even technology to technology, with no overriding sense of purpose. Similar problems appear when several people have competing visions, or, worst of all, the person charged with the vision is ham strung by management.

The role of vision-keeper is not one that anyone can play—that's why I think of it as a skill. The vision-keeper must be convinced that the network is a living being. He must be able to keep the big picture in mind, rather than being distracted by focusing on a single component. He must be trusted and liked by other employees. The vision-keeper must seek out new technologies, as well as remain firmly grounded in the present; it's impossible to decide what's appropriate for a network without understanding the present reality in addition to long-term goals. Finally, the vision-keeper must truly understand the vision and not lose sight of it; and he must be able to articulate it so others can understand it.

Sometimes, the person responsible for the vision is the group manager (perhaps you), but it doesn't really matter who it is, provided that he has the management's trust. The worst problems arise when management feels threatened by the freedom and responsibility the vision keeper has. It is easiest if the person with the vision manages the group. If he isn't the manager, management must trust him with the vision, and back him with the authority to carry it out. This is a particular problem when it comes to selecting new technologies; it's easy for management, often unconsciously, to sabotage the vision-keeper's efforts.

Costs

Most network administrators don't spend enough time exploring the costs of maintaining their network. Perhaps this is because the people who manage networks are usually technical, and tend to get glassy-eyed at any discussion of business issues. But ignoring cost is the surest way to doom your network, and perhaps your business, to failure. Another common mistake is to underestimate the cost of running your network. Let's face it, building a network is expensive. Running a network is more expensive.

Most network administrators have little problem understanding the cost of building their networks. They figure out what kinds of equipment and cable they need and compute these capital costs. Then they estimate the amount of labor necessary to install the cable and equipment, and add up these costs to arrive at a pretty good idea of how much money they need. But estimating the costs of maintaining the network seems a mystery. It doesn't need to be. If you think about what you will need to spend money on, you can come up with reasonably accurate estimates of your recurring costs.

The easiest costs to calculate are those that can be known up front. If you have a leased line in your WAN, you know the cost of this line on either a monthly or annual basis for at least a year into the future. After that, it is not likely to change dramatically, so you can easily project out several years. Likewise, the cost of salaries and benefits for your employees are readily estimated, provided you can assess how many of each type of employee you need. Remember that you will need more employees as your network grows, and your employees will expect some increase in compensation as time goes by.

Where costs get harder to estimate are in the areas of growth and replacement. Unless you planned your network so you won't need any new equipment to support growth, you will have to purchase new equipment—routers, hubs, switches, modems, and so forth—to support this growth. And, by the way, if you *did* manage to plan your network so that all of the growth was covered by the initial installation, you probably wasted some money in that process.

How to estimate growth is beyond the scope of a book on network management. However, to give you a few rules of thumb, the Internet is currently *doubling* in size every 9 to 12 months! While you probably won't see this kind of growth in your network, you may be surprised how quickly things grow. My network is currently sustaining a 6 percent growth rate every six months. In the past six years, it has more than tripled in size, and is on the brink of a major growth period brought on by a new telecommunications initiative. So take your best shot at how quickly you think your network might grow, then double it. It is better to overestimate and have money left over than to underestimate and go broke! After the first year, you will have better figures to work with, and you will see just how quickly your network grows. With this information, you can revise your estimates and more accurately estimate how much new equipment you will need to purchase.

Growth is not the only reason you will need new equipment. From time to time, you will need to replace older equipment—either because of failure, or to gain new features. If you have a good maintenance contract, it should cover failure replacements. Still, this contract is an expense that you must budget. Fortunately, it is generally known in advance. If you don't have a maintenance contract, you can still use the cost of one as a guideline for your replacement costs. A typical maintenance contract for something like a router will cost approximately 10 percent of the router's list price annually. Since the provider of the contract has to cover expenses to maintain your router, this is a good starting point for estimating your own expenses.

Keep in mind that a maintenance contract often covers more than hardware failures. Typically, they also provide you software updates on some reasonable schedule, access to technical assistance, and possibly access to special training from your vendor. Without a maintenance contract, these costs must be made up somewhere. You *will* upgrade software from time to time, you *will* occasionally need technical assistance, and you *will* occasionally need training. Furthermore, there is a hidden cost in going without a maintenance contract. If you run into a problem, you and your staff will have to figure it out on your own without the vendor's help. This is time that could be spent doing other tasks. Since these tasks need to be done regardless, you may find that over time, you need to hire a new person to take up the load. Don't underestimate the value of that maintenance contract!

Purchases to gain new features are also a reality that cannot be ignored. It is currently estimated that CPU power is doubling every 12 to 18 months. If you assume that newer, faster machines require (or, at least, their users desire) faster network connections, then you could need to upgrade the speed of your network on a daunting schedule. Fortunately, many network components can last longer than the typical PC lifetime of three years. However, you should still plan on upgrading your existing router equipment in as little as five to eight years! This is where open discussion with your vendor can help. They should be up front with you about their plans for newer and faster devices, and willing to work with you to protect your investment in their products.

Finally, when you are considering the costs of maintaining your network, keep in mind all of the opportunity costs that you may incur. These are the things that you might have been able to do, had you had more time, more money, or better equipment. Buying cheaper equipment does not always save you money, especially if you sink a lot more time into maintaining it. The same is true for dealing with many different vendors. Don't ignore the cost of learning multiple configuration and user interfaces, integrating these devices in your network, and troubleshooting problems.

Establishing a Help Desk

Regardless of where you have placed the boundary of your network, your user community will, from time to time, have problems that require your assistance. When a user's machine cannot connect to a file server, the user needs someone's help, whether your network boundary is the wall plug, or includes the user's machine itself. If you don't set up a help desk, however informally, the users will either get frustrated because they have no one to call for help, or they will start calling your staff directly. Once they get a problem resolved by calling one of your staff directly, they will continue to call that same person again and again, no matter what the problem is. When this person can't handle the problem, he or she must then refer the call to someone else, a process that takes time and keeps them from their regularly assigned tasks. Worse still, when this person is on vacation, the user again has no one to call.

By establishing a help desk, you do several important things:

- You present a consistent point of contact. Users can always contact someone for help. Since users always call the same number, or send email to the same address, they feel comfortable reporting a problem or seeking assistance.

- You free your overworked technical staff from dealing with the most common and trivial problems. Experience indicates that well over half of the problems reported to network staff fall into a few easily resolved categories. These are ideal problems for a non-technical help desk staff person to resolve.

  This is not to say that your help desk must be able to solve every problem; this is not a reasonable goal. However, the help desk should be able to handle common and trivial problems (such as making sure the machine is plugged into the network) and eliminate a few possible causes (a power failure in the building where the file server is located). After eliminating the most common and trivial problems, they should then be able to refer the problem to the correct staff person or persons accurately.

- You eliminate redundant problem reporting. When a router fails, many people are affected by the problem, and many of them will report it to you. Don't get me wrong, it is a good thing that people report problems. But you don't want dozens of people calling your technical staff to report the same problem. Answering all the phone calls will prevent anyone from actually solving the problem. A help desk allows phone calls to be answered by people who are not trying to fix the problem.

Having decided to establish a help desk, how should you proceed? First, ask yourself how formal the help desk should be. If your network is relatively small, perhaps a half-dozen Ethernets connected to two routers in a single building, your help desk can be fairly informal. It could be as simple as a cordless or cellular phone that is passed among your staff on a rotating schedule, where each person spends a week receiving help desk calls. On the other hand, if your network is large or complex, perhaps spanning many buildings and hundreds of network segments, you may find that you need some full-time employees who do nothing more than answer help desk calls.

In either case, establish a clear point of contact. The phone number people use to report problems must be constant; it should not depend on the person assigned to help desk duty. This is why I suggested using a cordless phone or a cell phone; it's easy to move from one employee to another. It's also a good idea to have a special email alias that the help desk person or persons receive. However, email shouldn't be the only means of contact; if the network is broken, email probably won't get through.

Your help desk people should have a complete list of the most common questions and problems they are likely to be called on to resolve. This can be a printed book, but since it will need to be updated frequently, it is likely to be out of date quickly. A better idea is to provide an online list. One good format for this could be a set of pages on a special-purpose web server. These pages can be updated easily, and can show diagrams, contain multiple fonts, use hyperlinks to allow your help desk to navigate the list based on what the user reports, and even change based on the minute-by-minute state of the network.

Finally, your help desk should have a clear set of procedures for logging incoming calls, and dispatching problems to technical staff that they cannot handle themselves. One excellent way to achieve this is to establish a trouble ticket system.

Regardless of how formal your help desk is, the concept should be clearly established in your mind, your staff's minds, and your users' minds, and it must be responsive to the users during a well-established set of hours. If users contact you or your staff directly, politely remind them that the help desk is the proper place for such calls. Whether the problem is then resolved, or the phone call is transferred to the help desk, is a matter of policy.

Establish a Trouble Ticket System

Perhaps the greatest benefit of establishing a help desk is that you gain the ability to track your problems with as much detail as you wish. This information is invaluable when you're estimating the cost of maintaining your network, or when you're trying to analyze long-term problem patterns. One highly effective way to gather this data is to establish a trouble ticket system.

In case you're not familiar with a trouble ticket system, here's a brief description. Whenever a user reports a problem to the help desk, a ticket is opened and a case number assigned. This ticket should document what the problem is, who the user is, when the problem occurred, and who took the call. As people work on the problem, they should add information about further contact with the user, and work done to resolve the problem. Finally, when the problem is resolved, the ticket should be updated with the final resolution and the time the problem was resolved. The user should be informed of this resolution. The closed ticket is then filed for future reference, statistics, billing, or whatever. The sample trouble ticket below shows all of these items.

Ticket: A923 **Time-in**: 5/31/96 13.27 **Time-out**: **Taken-by**: Joe **Called-by**: Mary Jane Smith
Phone: 555-1893 x232 **Email**: mjs@marketing **Description**:
Mary Jane reports that her machine (rose.marketing) has been unable to access the Marketing file server since she got back from lunch. Confirmed that her network drop was connected and was functional (ping). Was unable to ping Marketing file server from help desk.
Status: Referred to Bob for investigation
Updates: 5/31/96 14:00 Investigation shows that the Marketing file server has a failed network adapter. Work in progress to replace it. Estimate repairs will be completed by 14:30.
Resolution:

Any problem, no matter how trivial, should have a trouble ticket opened. This allows you to generate statistics for analyzing trivial problems, just as you can for more complex problems. For example, if you can demonstrate that you have a large number of power failures in a certain location, you might be able to justify an uninterruptible power supply for some of the equipment there, or you might be able to spot an electrical circuit that is consistently overloaded and get a new one installed.

What you use to establish your trouble ticket system is largely a matter of what you want it to do, and there are several on the market, and even a few freely available on the Internet. When you look for a trouble ticket system, keep in mind a few things:.

- *Ease of use.* Your staff won't want to keep the tickets up to date if it is a burden to do so.

- *Permanent storage.* You will want to keep your trouble tickets not only as long as it takes to resolve each, but possibly for months or even years to establish long-term trends, or identify related problems.

- *Online handling.* The quickest way to lose a trouble ticket is to print it out on paper. Instead, consider having the ticket exist completely online. This allows for the use of email to distribute the ticket (keeping a copy in the system, of course), referring the ticket, and even updating the ticket. This is also the only viable way to extract usable statistics about your tickets.

- *Statistics gathering.* You will likely want to be able to ask questions about what percentage of problems are handled directly by the help desk, how many tickets are referred to which technicians, and how long a ticket is open on average. You may also want to ask what percentage of problems are of a given type.

- *Cross-referencing.* Several tickets are often related to each other. In our example, it is unlikely that Mary Jane is the only person reporting a problem with the file server. These other calls can generate tickets that cross-reference this ticket and exist only for statistics gathering. Cross-referencing helps you diagnose whether you are simply treating symptoms rather than the underlying problem. By tracking tickets, you might spot trends that can help you to find the real problem.

Even if you do nothing more than use a standard ticket format similar to the one above and email the tickets around, you will be ahead of the game. But be careful not to get caught in the pitfalls that sometimes plague a trouble ticket system.

Perhaps the biggest pitfall is the tendency to misuse statistics gathered from the tickets to assess the productivity of your employees. Your goal should be for problems to get resolved, not for tickets to get closed. If you start trying to compare employees based on the number of tickets handled, two things happen. First, your employees start trying to select the simpler tickets because they know they can be handled quickly. In the process, they avoid the harder problems, which are often the ones most detrimental to your network and therefore most in need of a solution. Second, your employees start feeling pushed to close a ticket even if the problem isn't completely resolved, just to make their quota.

Both these problems can be avoided if you are careful about how statistics are generated and used. Perhaps Joe is closing fewer tickets than Bob because the tickets that get assigned to him are typically harder to diagnose or fix. You might also find that Mary has far more open tickets than any of your other staff. This could be because she is not handling them efficiently, but it could also be that she is the only person on your staff with the skills to solve many of the problems your network is experiencing. If this is the case, the right answer is to get Mary some help either by training another employee, or hiring someone with the right skills. The safest way to use trouble ticket statistics is to look for network trends, rather than employee trends. There are far better and fairer ways to evaluate employees.

The technical aspects of network management are often easier to understand and identify. Briefly, these aspects of network management include monitoring the network, detecting problems; troubleshooting, identifying and fixing the problems detected; and managing changes. These are discussed in the next chapter.

8

The Technical Side of Network Management

In the last chapter, we explored the non-technical side of network management, including topics like costs, staff skills, help desks, and so on. But more important, I presented the idea that a network is a living, breathing entity. This concept is crucial because the topics I discuss in this chapter—monitoring the networks, troubleshooting, and change management—tend to be more hands-on and will have an affect on your network. If you don't understand how your network will react, or you don't consider the effect of your activities on the entire network, you will find tasks like troubleshooting to be a nightmare.

Fortunately, for many network administrators the technical side of network management is often more enjoyable than projecting costs or interviewing candidates for staff. Perhaps this is because it does tend to be more hands-on, and it has a tangible quality to it that the tasks in the preceding chapter do not.

Monitoring the Network

In an ideal world, once you establish your network and have it working, nothing would ever go wrong. Unfortunately, computer networking is far from an ideal world. Besides the unpredictable failures due to hardware failure, power failure, cable cuts, and software bugs, there are many ways that everyday operations can cause problems. Sometimes something as simple as adding a new application to your network software can cause traffic patterns to shift in unpredicted ways that lead to disaster. This is where monitoring your network comes into play.

Regardless of the size of your network, whether a dozen nodes or thousands, you *must* establish a way to monitor the status of your network to see where it is working and where it is not. If you do not, you will be in the dark about what is going on, and you will constantly be fighting fires that could have been avoided.

Fortunately, monitoring your network does not have to be complicated or expensive. Depending on the type of monitoring you want to achieve, you may be able to get away with little more than some homemade software running on a machine already on your network. At the other extreme, you may need to purchase special-purpose hardware to assist you.

Reachability Monitoring

Reachability monitoring is where many networks start out. All you care about is whether two machines connected to the network can reach each other. However, testing reachability between all pairs of machines on your network can be an impossible task, especially in any network larger than a few dozen hosts.

Of course, some will point out that the users of your network will be practicing a form of reachability monitoring every time they attempt to use the network, so why bother? While it is certainly true that your users will often discover a problem for you, many will not bother to report it, especially if they aren't happy with the way your staff responds to problems. Besides, it reflects badly on you and your staff if your first response to a report that the network is not functioning is "Really? I didn't know that!"

So, if monitoring every pair of potential communicators is not feasible, yet you need to monitor your network so that you detect reachability problems before your users do, how should you proceed? While not perfect, a reasonable approach is to establish one (or a few) points in your network that probe network reachability to all other points in the network. If machine A (your monitoring machine) is able to reach machine B *and* machine C, there is a reasonable probability that machine B can reach machine C. However, there are situations in which this is not true, even if the network is functioning correctly. One such situation is when you have a firewall or packet filters in your network. It may well be that your monitor point can reach a machine protected by a firewall, but another machine, equally reachable from your monitor point, cannot. Such administratively caused discontinuities are normal, and can only be dealt with by documenting their existence. You can also run into situations where simple reachability tests fail when your dynamic routing protocol is malfunctioning or misconfigured. Think about what would happen if the router that your monitoring point connects to has routes to the networks where host B and host C reside, but the routers connected to these networks do not have routes to each other. More often than not, these situations are caused by misconfigured protocols, but the misconfiguration may be subtle and only show up when a primary link fails.

Still, even though not perfect, simple reachability monitoring can be enormously helpful in providing you with information about the status of your network.

However, you and your staff must be careful in interpreting what your monitor (or monitors) is telling you. For example, when the network segment that your monitor is connected to fails (perhaps because someone spilled a drink into an Ethernet hub*), your monitor is likely to report that the entire network is down. In fact, it isn't. By looking carefully at the pattern of what has failed, you should be able to rule out several possibilities. You can make diagnoses easier by using several monitoring machines connected to different parts of your network. This way, even though one may be taken out of service by a failed network segment, they don't all fail. This works best if the monitoring machines can be set up near each other, such as in a central machine room, because this allows you to see them all at the same time. When this isn't possible, such as in a multi-campus environment, you want trained people at the remote sites who can be your eyes, or you need another means to retrieve the status of the monitor without relying on your network, since the part of your network that might have failed is the link between your campuses.

So what should you monitor to get the most information possible? Clearly there are problems with monitoring every machine on your network. For one thing, if you have thousands of machines, it is likely that your monitor will spend all of its time monitoring, possibly at the expense of the network to which it is attached. Another problem is that many desktop workstations in your network may get rebooted or turned off regularly. If you monitor connectivity to each of these, your monitor will be sounding so many alarms that you will soon begin to ignore it.

As you think about what to monitor, ask yourself what you are trying to achieve. When you consider adding a new host to monitor, you should be asking yourself what information monitoring this host gives you that you don't already have. If the only reason is to answer the question, "Is this specific machine reachable?" then you should be sure that the machine is essential. A good candidate for this might be your main DNS server. Let's consider the network shown in Figure 8-1.

We'll assume that each network segment has several other machines connected, but they are primarily user workstations. The monitor machine is on segment 1 at M. The first candidate for monitoring is the router attached to M's network segment. But that router has many IP addresses, so which should we monitor? Depending on your router's manufacturer, the answer is probably all of them. If your router reports that one of its directly attached networks is unreachable when that network segment fails (like the Cisco IOS), monitoring all of your routers' interfaces goes a long way to establishing what failed when your reachability monitor sounds the alarm. On the other hand, if the router answers for all of its

---

* This really happened! Fortunately, they confessed quickly and service was restored in a few minutes.

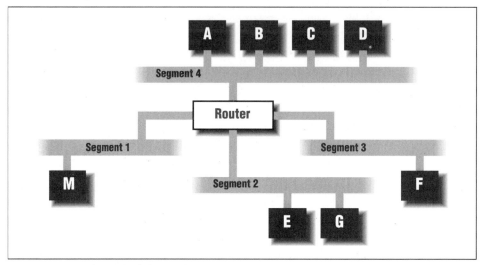

Figure 8-1. Deciding which hosts to monitor

interfaces, regardless of the status of each, then testing reachability to a dozen interfaces on a single router does nothing but consume processing power in the router, and bandwidth in your network. You would do better to probe reachability to a single interface on the router, perhaps its connection to your backbone, and check the individual segments in another way.

While you could stop with monitoring your routers' interfaces, this probably isn't enough. Beyond your router, your network segments are made up of various combinations of cables, hubs, switches, and so forth. These can fail and yet leave the router believing that the attached network segment is operational. Additionally, your router vendor may have put responding to network probes from a monitor station at a lower priority than switching packets (we hope!). If this is the case, it is possible that under heavy loads, your router may not respond to some of your reachability probes but otherwise be switching packets without a problem. Therefore, you should consider monitoring a few hosts that are beyond your router, even if these hosts are otherwise unimportant to your overall network operations. It is a good idea to monitor two hosts per network segment, preferably in different rooms or buildings to avoid common power problems. Of course, these hosts should be reasonably stable (multi-user hosts or file servers, rather than user machines).

In Figure 8-1, there are only two candidates on segment 2, so you'd add both of them to the list. On segment 3, you have only a single viable choice, the file server at F, so you add that to the list. On segment 4, you have four good choices, so you need to make some decisions. Certainly, you could add all four, but you want to keep your monitoring traffic reasonable, and also provide good information. Since host D is also your main DNS server, it should be stable, and it is critical that it be reachable, so you should include it. The other three hosts, A, B, and C, are all just multi-user machines with nothing special about them, so select one at random to add to your list. Table 8-1 shows which addresses we have decided to monitor.

Table 8-1. Monitored Addresses on Each Segment of Our Sample Network

Segment	Monitored Addresses
1	R1 (Router Interface 1)
2	R2, E, G
3	R3, F
4	R4, A, D

Let's consider what combinations of unreachable alarms tell us about our network. If R1, R2, R3, and R4 are all reachable, but host D is not, you can assume that your router is working well, and concentrate your efforts on determining whether host D itself has failed, or whether part of the network that D is attached to has failed. If host A is also unreachable, the most likely suspect is a hub or cable in network segment 4. If host A is reachable, then host D is most suspect, but it could still be a hub or cable. Regardless, you can focus your attentions on that portion of the network. What if hosts D and A are not reachable, and R4 is also unreachable? This indicates a failure with the hub or cable that the router attaches to on segment 4, or a failure in the router interface itself. Again, direct inspection will be necessary to determine which.

Finally, what if all of the hosts are reachable, but none of the router interfaces are responding reliably? In this situation, it is most likely that the router is relatively busy and has deferred answering your reachability probes in favor of switching packets. While not a failure, you should investigate why the router is so busy. This may indicate a misconfiguration, or there may have been a momentary surge of activity that will not recur frequently. Again, direct investigation is warranted, but your network has not yet failed.

Okay, what kind of tools should you use to monitor reachability in your network? The answer is that it really depends. But rather than look at some examples of reachability monitoring tools here, let's explore other kinds of monitoring you might want to pursue and discuss common tools later.

Route Monitoring: A More Sophisticated Form of Monitoring

One of the problems with simple reachability monitoring is that it's not always true that just because host A can reach host B, and host B can reach host C, that host A can reach host C. While carefully selecting which hosts to monitor can help mitigate this problem, it cannot eliminate it entirely. To solve this problem you need to go beyond simple reachability and monitor the contents of routing tables in various places in your network.

If your network is well designed, your routing is predictable and stable. It should only change when the topology of your network changes, and this should only happen when you are actively making changes to the network. If it happens at any other time, it is most likely because a portion of your network has failed. But monitoring the topology of your network is not always possible. To do so accurately, you would have to monitor physically each cable, hub, and interconnection to identify what is connected where. It is more important to monitor the network's view of the topology: its routing tables. When they change, it is a safe bet that your network topology changed.

One of the problems with route monitoring is that it requires much more sophisticated monitoring software. Consider what the software to do reachability monitoring must look like. It would need to take as input a list of destinations to monitor, and would then have to probe them periodically for reachability information. This probe could be as simple as an ICMP echo request (ping), or a datagram sent to the UDP echo service, or anything else that determines the destination is reachable without putting much load on the network. The software would then collect the results of the probes and alert an operator that a destination did not answer. If it was a little more sophisticated, it might keep some statistics about how rapidly it received each response, which might help you form a rough idea of what traffic patterns are like. A programmer familiar with network programming might be able to put together a useful monitor in a few days.

Now consider what the software to do route monitoring might have to do. Again, it would take a list of destinations (presumably routers) from which it should solicit routing tables. It must then take these routing tables and analyze them to form a view of the current topology of the network. What it does with this view depends on what the programmer wants. One option would be to alert an operator if the topology changed. A more sophisticated option would be to display the topology graphically. Whichever display option was chosen, writing this software would be much harder than writing a simple reachability monitor.

Another problem with route monitoring is that it assumes that there are devices that can be queried for their route tables. Typically, this implies that the routers can respond to the Simple Network Management Protocol (SNMP), that the dynamic routing protocol used in the network has a method for soliciting routes, or that routing information can be deduced by eavesdropping on the routing protocol.

None of these is guaranteed to be true, though SNMP accessibility is coming close to being universal.

The final problem with route monitoring is that it is not a substitute for reachability monitoring, unless routing tables are solicited from machines other than the routers. To understand why, consider our sample network. Soliciting routing tables from the router only tells us the status of the router's attachments to the network segments. In other words, if the router's attachment to network segment 1 is functional, its routing table will contain an entry for segment 1. But this tells us nothing about whether host D is able to reach network segment 1.

Still, even with its complications and drawbacks, route monitoring can form an important piece of your network management scheme, since it gives a better picture of remote parts of the network than simple reachability monitoring permits.

Traffic Monitoring: The Most Detailed Picture

To get the most complete and detailed picture of your network's status, you need to consider the traffic on each segment. In addition to telling you when your network is not working because some component has failed, traffic monitoring warns you that you may be approaching failure because of traffic overload. It may even show you where your network, though functional, is performing poorly because of improper traffic patterns, such as when a pair of load-balancing links is not well balanced.

The most difficult part of traffic monitoring is that you can't do it by observing the network from one central point. Again referring to Figure 8-1, the monitor at M cannot tell anything about the traffic on segment 3, or between segments 2 and 4, simply by observing the traffic on segment 1. Instead, you need devices spread throughout the network that collect information from their point of view, which can then be analyzed by a central collection point to build a view of the network's traffic.

This doesn't mean that you need to place a special-purpose device on each segment of your network. Nearly all routers, switches, and hubs maintain traffic statistics as part of their operations. For example, most routers maintain counters for packets and octets that come in and go out each interface, and may even break these down by different categories such as protocol type. Likewise, a switch or a hub is likely to maintain similar statistics for each of its ports. The questions are how to collect all this information and what do you do with that information?

The first question, how to collect the information, is often addressed by using SNMP. SNMP does not define what information should be collected by a network device, but it does require that there be a Management Information Base (MIB) in a standard format. When SNMP was designed, its designers wanted the MIB to be extensible for new devices and for new protocols. So, even though it was designed before many of the devices now on the market were in common use (and even before some were invented), MIB extensions have been defined that describe what kinds of information should be available from nearly every class of network device imaginable. One relatively recent extension specifically designed for remote monitoring is the *RMON* MIB (RFC 1757). While the RFC talks in terms of a dedicated monitoring device, many vendors have begun including some or all of the RMON monitoring groups in their hubs, switches, and routers. The objects defined in the RMON MIB are grouped into 10 distinct categories, each of which is optional in an implementation, though if a group is implemented, all its defined objects must be implemented. These are the groups and a brief description of their intended purposes:

The Ethernet Statistics Group

Contains statistics measured by the probe for each monitored Ethernet interface.

The History Control Group

Controls the periodic statistical sampling of data from various types of networks.

The Ethernet History Group

Records periodic statistical samples from an Ethernet network and stores them for later retrieval.

The Alarm Group

Periodically takes statistical samples from variables in the probe and compares them to previously configured thresholds. If the monitored variable crosses a threshold, an event is generated.

The Host Group

Contains statistics associated with each host discovered on the network.

The HostTopN Group

Used to prepare reports that describe the hosts that top a list ordered by one of their statistics.

The Matrix Group

Stores statistics for conversations between sets of two addresses.

The Filter Group

Allows packets to be matched by a filter equation to form a data stream that may be captured or may generate events.

The Packet Capture Group

Allows packets to be captured after they flow through a filter equation described by the filter group.

The Event Group

Controls the generation and notification of events.

Most embedded RMON agents don't implement all of these groups because several (such as the packet capture group) can consume a lot of memory and other resources. But those groups that are implemented often provide a better set of monitoring variables than the standard MIB variables. You'll want to investigate what RMON groups your devices do implement, or consider purchasing some dedicated RMON probe devices to collect the data at various points in your network.

The second question, what to do with the information once you have it, is harder to answer. If we assume that you are using SNMP to collect the data, then your network management station software may provide several ways to manipulate and analyze your network's data. But these generally operate on historical data, and work over larger samples gathered over an interval to show trends, rather than minute-by-minute traffic loads.

In the simplest form, your analysis can simply compare the current traffic values to a set of thresholds and raise an alarm if any item should go above (or below, when appropriate) its threshold. This won't give you the historical trend data that the fancier analysis can give you, but it can still provide a useful picture of the current state of your network. Once traffic data is available, it isn't long before you want to see historical trends for making projections into the future. This is where careful consideration of what to collect, and how often to collect it, becomes important. For a large network of a hundred routers, collecting too many samples can easily generate *terabytes* of data each day! Since most machines still have disk capacities measured in a few tens of gigabytes, it is easy to see that you either need to be highly selective in what you monitor, settle for less frequent samples, or not maintain any information for historical analysis. Of course, if you cut historical information back too far, traffic analysis can't happen, and network monitoring rapidly degrades to little more than reachability testing.

So, given the various types of monitoring you can do, what *should* you do? This depends on how large your network is, how expensive downtime is, and what resources you have available to you. Because of its simplicity and low resource consumption—it only requires a host machine and some relatively simple software—reachability monitoring is often the first choice for smaller networks, or those that lack resources to establish other types of monitoring. Even larger networks can benefit from simple reachability monitoring, and there is no reason to stop using it when other monitoring techniques are implemented.

Route monitoring, combined with reachability monitoring, works well for medium-sized networks, but is often far more than smaller networks need. In a larger network, software to analyze the routing tables extracted from various equipment can become excessively complex unless confined to smaller sections of your network—perhaps those most prone to trouble or most costly when down.

Traffic monitoring is the most resource-intensive form of monitoring. It typically requires a dedicated management station to collect, store, and analyze traffic statistics, and then present them to network staff. It also requires some method for extracting traffic data from all devices, or at least a significant sample of devices, in the network. Because of the resources needed, most smaller networks will not benefit enough from traffic monitoring to make it worthwhile. Still, if downtime on your network is very expensive, traffic monitoring is the only way to identify problems before they occur, when they are least costly to repair. As such, it may be appropriate in limited forms for the parts of your network that are most costly when down.

Troubleshooting

No matter how much monitoring, analyzing, and predicting you do, and no matter how reliable your equipment is, and no matter how well you design your network, problems will occur. When this happens, you are likely to be under extreme pressure to isolate the problem (or problems) and fix it. Given that few people think clearly under pressure, you should carefully look at your network and identify what is most likely to go wrong, and then figure out how you would identify and correct each problem.

The two most likely failures in your network are equipment failures, whether hardware or software, and human error. Hardware failure is difficult to avoid, since few devices warn you that they are about to fail, and every device will fail eventually. Fortunately, hardware failures are easiest to detect and fix.

Later, I'll discuss how you identify the failed component. Once you have, you replace it with a new component and have the original one repaired, if possible. This requires that you maintain a stock of some spare equipment. How much spare stock to keep depends on the size of your network and how expensive downtime is, but as a minimum, you should keep one of each of the most likely devices to fail, and have a means to get the more expensive and less likely to fail devices replaced quickly. Keeping spares is one of the reasons for limiting the number of different devices in your network. For example, if you use four different brands of Ethernet hubs, you may need to keep four spare hubs in stock. This may not be that difficult or expensive, but consider now what happens if you have four different brands of routers, and you'll see that this can be a very expensive proposition.

Software failure is much more difficult to identify, and far harder to repair once it is identified. However, it is easier to avoid than hardware failures. One of the easiest ways to avoid software failures is *not* to insist on running the latest software from your vendors. If you do, don't upgrade to it the first day it is released. Let other people take the initial risks, and let them report bugs and problems. Recently, a major network vendor had a new release of software that they withdrew within two days because they discovered a fatal flaw that had not been identified during testing. While this is relatively rare, delaying installation of new software for two weeks would spare you the trouble of finding this flaw yourself.

But no matter how careful you are about new software, there will be times that you must move forward—either to gain a new feature or fix a problem. I recently spent two days dealing with a catastrophic failure in four-week-old software in my network. Even though four weeks is relatively old for router software these days, it still had a hidden defect that only showed up in specific configurations, of which mine was one. What can you do when this happens? First, consider why you upgraded to this newer software. Was it just to be reasonably current? To gain access to a new feature? To fix a major problem in a previous version? If the reason you upgraded was one of the first two, you should consider reinstalling the older software. If you upgraded to fix a problem, you have to decide which problem is worse and act accordingly. Of course, going back to the previous version isn't the only possibility. You might be able to upgrade to an even newer version that fixes your problem; if your problem is not totally debilitating, your vendor may be able to supply you with a patched version in a matter of days that fixes your specific problem.

Regardless of what you do, don't forget to inform your vendor of the problems you experienced, and what the circumstances were. You may have found a known problem and the vendor has a fix, or you may be the first to identify the problem, and the vendor will need to know of it to fix it in the future. When you report a problem to your vendor, be prepared to give detailed information about your network, your current configuration, software and hardware revisions, and especially what you did or observed that triggered the problem. If your vendor cannot reproduce the problem, it is difficult for them to repair it. What each vendor wants or needs to know is unique, and often depends on the particular device. Try to find out what your vendor wants to know before you have a problem, and collect that information prior to calling for tech support. If you can't find out what the vendor is likely to need, this is a good general list:

- The specific model and configuration of the router or other device that is having problems. This should include the interface cards installed, and may need to include the hardware revisions of these cards.

- The exact version of software installed on all components of the failing device, especially if different boards run their own versions of software different from the main system software.

- The running configuration that the device has or had when it failed.

- Any crash dump or log information that the device produced when it died, or when it rebooted.

- If your actions triggered the failure, *exactly* what you did to trigger it, especially if you can reproduce this bug at will.

- A description of the network topology in the vicinity of the failed device. Include such items as the number, type, and model of other routers or switches, and whether any of those devices recently got upgraded software or hardware. Make a drawing if necessary.

The commands to get some of this information from a Cisco router are:

show diag

Shows the current hardware revision of all boards installed in the router, and which slots they are in; only available on some router models. Check your documentation to be sure if your routers provide this command, or just try it. If it isn't implemented, no harm done.

show version

Shows the current version of software running on the system, including its compilation date and who built it.

write term

Shows the currently running configuration. If this is not the configuration that was running when the router failed, you'll need to obtain that from wherever you can. This command is different from the others for historical reasons. The equivalent modern command is `show running-config`, but if that command is available, you probably also have the `show tech-support` command, which is even better.

show stack

Shows stack dump information for the last crash.

show log

Shows the log information for the current run of the software, if the logging is buffered. Details on how you might configure your router's logging, as well as information about how to interpret the messages in your routers' logs will be discussed later in this chapter.

show tech-support

Shows all the information that technical support needs. Only available on the newest releases of Cisco's IOS software.

You might also consider giving your vendor access to your network. If you're experiencing a particularly difficult problem, letting them look around at how things are configured and operating may give them clues.

By far the best way to deal with a software failure is to avoid it. If you can test the software in a controlled environment before deploying it in your network, you can often identify problems before they take your network down. To do this, you will need some place to run this software, such as a test network. In order to be reasonably sure that your tests are valid, this test network should have the same types of components as your main network. This is another good reason to limit the number of different devices you use. For each type and brand of device in your main network, you need a duplicate in your test network. One excellent way to achieve this is to build your test network from your spare parts, but be sure that you don't violate your software license or maintenance contracts by using hardware that was meant to be spare parts. However you provision your test network, it should use the same brands and models as much as possible. It does little good to have a Cisco 2501 router in your test network if your main network uses Cisco 7000 routers; each of these devices uses a different binary system image, and these images may have different failure modes. True, different models of one vendor's routers probably share a lot of code, especially in the protocol processing sections of the system, but they will also have different code for different memory architectures, different interface drivers, and so on. Additionally, if they use a different CPU, the compilers used to produce the binary system image will be different, and compilers *can* have subtle bugs in them. Still, any testing is better than none.

No test network can exactly simulate your production network, and generating realistic traffic patterns on a test network is not easy. For this reason, consider connecting your test network to your main network at a controlled point, and then putting your network staff on the test network. Let them run on it as if it were a production network for a few weeks. If you don't find any problems, you can deploy the newer software in your production network. If problems occur, it is your network staff who are affected, and they are the people who can respond to the problem appropriately, perhaps by disconnecting from the main network.

Finally, the most likely cause of network failures is human error. This can be error on the part of your staff, a botched configuration or a wiring closet mistake, or on the part of your users, deleting network configuration files from their PC. There is little you can do about the user errors, but your staff errors can be avoided, for the most part. I'll discuss techniques for avoiding staff errors later. When they occur, the best way to troubleshoot them is to have a clear record of what the staff has been doing. If you have no idea which of your staff may have been in which wiring closets, or what configurations were changed recently, finding where a problem is becomes much more difficult. On the other hand, if you know that Joe was just in the fourth floor wiring closet adding a new network drop, and a user calls from the fourth floor claiming that her network connection mysteriously failed, you have a good idea where to start looking. Perhaps Joe accidentally pulled a wire loose, or cross-connected the new network drop over the user's. Either way, by knowing where Joe was and what he was doing, you can begin backtracking to figure out what happened.

Troubleshooting Techniques

While it is useful to discuss the sources of network failure in terms of hardware, software, and human error, when you are faced with a network outage, you rarely know what kind of failure you are looking at, or where the failure is. This is where having a set of techniques available for troubleshooting is a must.

Take notes

There is nothing more frustrating while troubleshooting a problem than discovering that you have been moving a bad component around believing that it was good. The best way to avoid this problem is to take notes about what you have tried, what the effect was, and what you moved where. These notes may take many forms, including the more mundane pen and paper type, and can be as extensive as you want. At a minimum, you should record all equipment moves, cable changes, board swaps, and configuration changes. For equipment moves, be sure to record the serial numbers of the devices you moved; this is the only way to know which of a dozen Ethernet hubs you had in each location. If nothing else, these notes will help when you fix the problem and need to put the network back in order. If you end up calling your vendor for help, detailed notes will give your vendor a head start on diagnosing your problem. They may even get you connected with a technical engineer more quickly because they will show that you are not some totally clueless user who doesn't have any idea what is happening.

Label everything

Related to taking good notes is labeling *everything* before you have a problem. At a minimum, this includes every device and *both* ends of every cable. Device labels should clearly indicate exactly which device this is; a typical network often has many identical devices. Each end of a cable should be labeled with which port of which device (be explicit) this end of the cable plugs into. It should also include where the other end of the cable is, though not necessarily with the same degree of detail. The reason you want to label your devices should be obvious— if you have six identical Ethernet hubs in a rack, you need to know which one you are trying to repair. These labels will also augment your notes (they should *not* replace them) about equipment moves. Just remember to update your labels when you are done moving equipment around. Don't delay or you will be working with useless labels the next time something breaks.

It's also obvious why you want to label the ends of the cables with where they connect. In most troubleshooting situations, you have to disconnect several cables from a failed device or interface card; the last thing you want to do is waste time figuring out which cable goes in which port. It's not so obvious why you should label each end of the cable with where the other end goes. After all, if you only disconnect one end of the cable, why do you care where the other end is? You may need to replace the cable itself, or you may discover that the device you thought was failing was just fine—the device at the other end is the problem. A label that gets you to the right device, if not the exact port, can save you lots of time locating that other end.

Physically labeling the cables and devices should not be the end of it. Many devices include the ability to label ports in software, so you can ask the router, switch, or hub what is attached to the port. We use this capability extensively with our Ethernet switches. Each port has a label that identifies where the next termination point is. If it is an Ethernet hub, the label contains the name of the hub. If it is a port in an office, then the label shows the room number and port identifier. This serves as a cross-check for changes, as well as a means to track problems within the network. On a router, labels may include information about which groups or buildings are serviced by an interface in a LAN, or they might include the remote device name, or the circuit number for a WAN link. For example, to label the router port connected to your WAN link to Chicago including its circuit ID, include the following command in the interface's configuration:

```
description WAN link to Chicago - 1ZB33489-997F
```

This information is displayed by the show interface command. While this information is also available in your wiring records, sorting through a mountain of documentation when your network has failed wastes precious time. It is much easier to ask your devices what is connected to them, or to look at cables and see where the next device is. Of course, labeling only works if you keep the labels current.

Define the problem

The first thing you want to do when your network fails is to take a deep breath and relax. Then, take another deep breath, and relax again. This may sound corny, but it really is important. You are about to call on your mind and body to work hard, and a couple of deep breaths gets some extra oxygen into your system, preparing it to work for you.

Now that you are ready, but before you go rushing off to fix your network, define exactly what the problem is. This may involve calling the user who reported the problem for more details, or it may involve trying to replicate the problem from your workstation. If the problem is centered around a specific group of machines, or a specific server, don't jump to the conclusion that the problem is within that group or server. This is likely, but it is not guaranteed. If the problem seems to be related to reachability, make some quick tests from a few different places in your network to see if the problem is localized or global.

In other words, stop and take a few moments to think about the problem, and the cause may become apparent. The worst thing you can do is rush in and start replacing components shotgun style. Once you have clearly identified the problem, you are prepared to fix it and get your network functioning again.

Process of elimination

The next technique that you may need to use is the process of elimination. Some-times, the problem defies a clear definition. For example, you have a user who is unable to connect to a file server, but your preliminary examination shows that both the user's machine and the file server are functioning normally. What now?

If you can identify what parts of your network cannot possibly be involved, you may be able to eliminate most of your network from consideration. For example, most of the devices located in buildings other than the user and the file server are probably not your problem. Examining what is left may make it obvious where the problem is. If not, at least you have a smaller set of equipment to examine. Sometimes, just considering which devices are unlikely causes will give you an idea about a possible cause. For example, while ruling out devices in other build-ings, your attention turns to your DNS server, and you realize that if the user's machine cannot talk to the DNS server, or perhaps the file server cannot, then connection between the two may be impaired. Or perhaps the DNS records for the user's machine were accidentally deleted, so the file server is refusing to connect.

Be cautious about ruling out things that don't, at first glance, appear to be the problem. Sometimes, a failure in one component can have widespread or unre-lated symptoms that can distract you into looking at the wrong part of the network.

Divide and conquer

Finally, if the problem is so overwhelming or stubborn that these techniques are of little use, you may have little choice but to use a technique called "divide and conquer." The premise behind this technique is straightforward; most people use it for everyday tasks without even thinking about it. When a problem is too big, or too complex to solve as a unit, you should break it into smaller tasks and solve each of them separately, then put the whole thing back together again.

For example, think about how you find someone's name in the phone book. You open the book at random, and see if the person's name is alphabetically before or after the spot where you opened. You then flip pages through the letter containing their name until you are close. You next search one page at a time, until you find the page containing the name, and then scan the page for the final answer. Had you instead decided to scan the phone book line-by-line from the beginning, you might take hours, or even days to find the entry. By dividing the task into smaller portions, you can complete it in a minute or two. This same kind of technique can help you with problems in your network, especially the catastrophic failures.

For catastrophic failures, the first step is to partition your network into as many pieces as it takes to restore function to some portion of the network. This may mean that you disconnect major portions of your backbone network, perhaps all the way down to a single router. After you have some portion of the network working, your next step is to get other portions working, and then recombine them with the first piece and test the results carefully. Continue with each piece of your network, until you either get a piece that you cannot recombine into the network, or your network is once again functioning. Should you find a piece that you cannot reconnect successfully, you may need to break it apart further and work with these smaller pieces, adding each to the functional network until you trigger a failure.

For example, if you have a router with many Ethernets, and an FDDI connection to the backbone that works well by itself but takes the network down when you reconnect the FDDI backbone connection, try disconnecting all of the Ethernets, and then reconnecting the router. If the resulting network functions correctly, you know that the FDDI connection on the router is probably not your problem, and you can begin examining the individual Ethernets, reconnecting them one at a time. The one that causes your network to fail again is the one you need to break apart to the next level, and keep going. Eventually, you may find that a machine on the network is spinning in a tight loop trying to access a device on another router, and the traffic is causing your routers to fail.

If instead your problem is of the stubborn but non-catastrophic variety, try dividing your network into two pieces, perhaps equally, perhaps unequally, and noting which side of the division the problem is on. Then subdivide the failing portion and add the functional piece back into the main network, if possible. Continue dividing the failing network into two pieces until you can isolate the problem and repair it. Then put any remaining pieces back into the network, and verify that the problem has gone away.

Tools for Monitoring and Troubleshooting

Regardless of the type of monitoring you choose, and there is no requirement that you use only one type of monitoring, or even use one consistently throughout your network or over time, you will need tools to help you to monitor your network effectively. Likewise, when you have a problem and have to troubleshoot it, a useful set of tools can make an impossibly complex job more manageable. Often, your troubleshooting tools and your monitoring tools are the same.

You can, of course, purchase tools from a wide selection on the market. For SNMP-based management, this is probably the only way to obtain your tools. However, there are many freely available tools that can help you with network monitoring and troubleshooting. In this section, I will talk briefly about a few of them. A more extensive list of both easily-available and proprietary tools is documented as a service to the Internet community in RFC 1470.

Out-of-Band Access

Most network devices now have an in-band mechanism for monitoring and configuration. The device may be accessed using Telnet or SNMP or both. But when your network has failed, you may not be able to reach your devices using such in-band mechanisms. At these times, providing out-of-band access can save time, and may be your only way to access a device that is far away without physically going to it.

The most natural way to provide out-of-band access to your network devices is using a dial-up modem attached to the device's management port. Then, when you cannot reach the device across the network, you can still dial in to it using a modem attached to your PC or terminal. Of course, you need to secure these dial-up lines with password-protected modems, callbacks, passwords on your management ports, or a combination. But the biggest problem with using modems is that it can get expensive to attach a modem to each device, especially if you include your hubs and switches. The expense is especially difficult to justify when you consider how often you are really likely to use it.

Using a terminal server is an alternative to providing modems for each device. This alternative works well when you need to access many devices that are close to each other—for example, the devices in a wiring closet or machine room. Instead of connecting terminals to each of the server's ports, you connect the management ports of the devices you need to access. To access the server, you can attach a terminal or a single modem, depending on whether the terminal server is in a remote location. You can now use this modem or terminal to access any of the devices attached to the server. If the terminal server is in your data center, you might not even need to attach a terminal directly; you may be able to place the terminal server on the same segment as your network management station. This connection would work unless the network segment containing your terminal server and your management station was itself failing. Fortunately, that segment is likely to be local and easily accessed for repairs.

The other advantage of using a terminal server is that you can configure a workstation to remain logically connected to the terminal server ports, and thus to the network devices' management ports, to capture any log messages that these devices might emit. Sometimes, these messages may be your only clues about why some device is failing. For example, even if your router has a log buffer, and even if it preserves some crash status information when it crashes and reboots, what happens if your router simply locks up and stops responding, but doesn't crash? It hasn't crashed, so it hasn't provided any crash dump information. It may have logged something in its buffer, but you can't get it to respond to let you look at that buffer, and if you power it off to regain control, this buffer will likely be lost. But if you have something watching the management console, it may well have said something just before it died that will give you a hint.

Ping

Ping is a program that is included with most basic TCP/IP software. It is available on platforms ranging from low-end personal workstations to high-powered supercomputers. Most routers, hubs, and switches include *ping* as part of their command interface. *Ping* works by sending ICMP echo request messages to a specified host. Each device that implements IP is required to respond to ICMP echo requests with an echo reply message. *Ping* measures the time between sending the request and receiving the reply, and reports both simple reachability (it either hears an echo reply or not) as well as the round-trip time.

Ping is probably the most frequently-used network monitoring and troubleshooting tool because it is so widely available. However, the information it provides is limited, and may even be misleading. For one thing, the echo request and echo reply may use different paths; asymmetric routing is common in large redundant networks. With this in mind, a missing echo reply does not tell you which of many possible paths might be broken, only that you cannot reach the destination *and* get back. Furthermore, ICMP echo request packets may be dropped due to congestion, and they may even add to congestion, since they themselves are packets. Still, *ping* provides a quick test of reachability and, as such, can form the basis of an extensive yet simple reachability monitoring system. It is often the first tool used when troubleshooting, if only to define how extensive the problem is.

Traceroute

Ping is useful to establish whether a given destination is reachable. But if *Ping* fails, it doesn't tell you which of possibly dozens of routers between the two endpoints is failing to deliver the packet. *Traceroute* fixes this problem by allowing you to find out each intermediate router on the way from host A to host B. It does this by causing each router along the path to send back an ICMP error message. IP packets contain a *time-to-live (TTL)* value that each router decrements as it handles the packet. When this value drops to zero, the router discards the packet and sends an ICMP Time-to-live Exceeded message back to the sender. *Traceroute* sends its first packet with a TTL value of 1. The first router decrements this and sends back the ICMP error message, and *traceroute* has discovered the first hop router. It then sends a packet with a TTL value of 2, which the first router decrements and routes. But the second router decrements it to zero, which causes it to send an ICMP error message, and *traceroute* has learned the second hop. By continuing in this way, *traceroute* causes each router along the path to send an ICMP error message and identify itself. Ultimately, the TTL gets high enough for the packet to reach the destination host, and *traceroute* is done, or some maximum value (usually 30) is reached and *traceroute* ends the trace.

What can go wrong with this clever scheme? Plenty! Some devices, either because their IP implementation is not fully conformant with the IP standards, or because they have been configured so, will not generate an ICMP Time-to-live Exceeded message. But that usually isn't a big problem, because the next device will do so, and you simply have a hop in the middle that isn't identified. The real problems lie with the packet that *Traceroute* sends and the way some firewalls are configured. Most *traceroute* programs send a UDP datagram to a randomly selected high UDP port. Most of the time, firewalls do not filter these packets out because it is difficult to distinguish them from legitimate user traffic. But sometimes they are filtered, and the *traceroute* simply dies. Other *traceroute* programs, most notably Microsoft's *tracert*, use an ICMP echo request message (a ping packet). It is far more likely that these will be filtered by a firewall, even though TCP-based or UDP-based communication is possible with the devices behind the firewall. In these cases, you are just out of luck. Since each has its potential problems with firewalls or non-conformant routers, neither is necessarily superior. Just keep these differences in mind, and you may better understand why your trace results don't match those of your users.

In its simplest form, *traceroute* (or *tracert*) takes a single argument, the destination host to contact:

tracert www.ora.com

```
Tracing route to amber.ora.com [198.112.208.11]
over a maximum of 30 hops:

1    *      *        *        Request timed out.
2   187 ms 2743 ms 169  ms    laf-gw0.holli.com [204.95.254.1]
3   235 ms 154 ms  1745 ms    204.95.255.245
4   157 ms 155 ms  180  ms    204.95.255.241
5   167 ms 154 ms  149  ms    204.180.39.42
6   202 ms 157 ms  153  ms    noon.nap.net [206.54.224.142]
7   158 ms 165 ms  156  ms    aads.mci.net [198.32.130.12]
8   404 ms 282 ms  257  ms    core3-hssi1-0.WillowSprings.mci.net
                              [204.70.1.197]
9   221 ms 229 ms  181  ms    core-hssi-2.Boston.mci.net [204.70.1.45]
10 189 ms 176 ms  247  ms     border1-fddi-0.Boston.mci.net [204.70.2.34]
11 177 ms 170 ms  171  ms     nearnet.Boston.mci.net [204.70.20.6]
12 182 ms 185 ms  245  ms     cambridge2-cr2.bbnplanet.net [192.233.33.2]
13 495 ms 219 ms  242  ms     cambridge1-cr1.bbnplanet.net [192.233.149.201]
14 186 ms 196 ms  176  ms     cambridge1-cr4.bbnplanet.net [199.94.205.4]
15 209 ms 280 ms  209  ms     ora.bbnplanet.net [192.233.149.74]
16 221 ms 265 ms  193  ms     amber.ora.com [198.112.208.11]


Trace complete.
```

There is a lot we can learn from this output. The first line indicates that the first machine did not answer us at all. This does not necessarily mean an error; it just means that the machine was unable or unwilling to reply to our request. Since the trace continues successfully after this first hop, no problem exists.

As you can see, my home machine is 16 hops from www.ora.com, and all of the routers in between are listed, along with their IP addresses, and names, if available. If you don't want *traceroute* to resolve the addresses into names, include the option to disable name resolution (usually *-n* for Unix *traceroute*, and *-d* for Microsoft's *tracert*). You would use this option if you are having problems reaching your DNS server, or if your DNS server might be having problems reaching the Internet (for example, if your Internet link were failing). The output also lists how long it took for a packet to go (roundtrip) to each router. Since this time may vary, and since the packets may get lost, *traceroute* sends three requests per hop for reliability.

If the trace did not reach its destination, it would probably fail for one of two reasons; each produces its own style of output. The trace below indicates that the router at hop 12 sent us an ICMP host unreachable message, indicating that it has no route to the requested destination:

```
12  !H  !H  !H  cambridge2-cr2.bbnplanet.net [192.233.33.2]
```

If this router is under your control and is supposed to have a route, then start investigating at this router to determine why it does not. *Traceroute* may also fail with several lines like this:

```
10  189 ms  176 ms  247 ms  border1-fddi-0.Boston.mci.net [204.70.2.34]
11    *       *        *     Request timed out.
12    *       *        *     Request timed out.
13    *       *        *     Request timed out.
14    *       *        *     Request timed out.
```

If allowed to continue, this output will continue until the maximum number of hops (30 by default) are reported. It indicates that the router at hop 10 has forwarded the packet, either to another router or to the ultimate destination, and the next hop is not answering. This could be because it is down, or because it has no route back to us. Either way, your next step is to start at hop 10 and work your way through the routers between there and the destination. However, don't be misled. Because of asymmetric routing, the routers used to send a packet from host A to host B are not necessarily the same routers used to send from host B to host A. *Traceroute* only shows you the route taken in the forward direction, not the reverse. It may well be that hop 11 sees our packet and sends a message back, but the reply takes a different route that does not intersect with any of the first 10 hops, and the reply gets dropped. Likewise, it may be that hops 12, 13, and so on, also are seeing our message, but the replies are getting lost because of a break in the return path used by the router at hop 11.

The only way to get the whole picture is to *traceroute* from host B to host A. Unfortunately, this is not always possible. One potential fallback is to use a *source-routed* packet to trace the route through the network. An IP packet can contain an option to take a side trip through the network to an intermediate destination, before it gets sent to the ultimate destination. Some *traceroute* programs allow you to request such a side trip. By requesting that the first intermediate destination be host B, and the final destination host A, you can sometimes convince *traceroute* to show you the entire roundtrip route. For example, to see how the machine noon.nap.net (a remote host) reaches laf-gw0.holli.com (the last hop before my machine at home), we would ask *traceroute* to include noon.nap.net in the path before ultimately sending the packet to laf-gw0.holli.com:

```
tracert -j noon.nap.net laf-gw0.holli.com
```

```
Tracing route to laf-gw0.holli.com [204.95.254.1]
over a maximum of 30 hops:

   1    187 ms    146 ms    169  ms   laf-gw0.holli.com [204.95.254.1]
   2    235 ms    154 ms   1745  ms   204.95.255.245
   3    157 ms    155 ms    180  ms   204.95.255.241
   4    167 ms    154 ms    149  ms   204.180.39.42
   5    202 ms    157 ms    153  ms   noon.nap.net [206.54.224.142]
   6    161 ms    163 ms    154  ms   206.54.225.250
   7    169 ms    155 ms    180  ms   204.95.255.241
   8    201 ms    154 ms    154  ms   204.95.255.245
   9    155 ms    155 ms    169  ms   laf-gw0.holli.com [204.95.254.1]

Trace complete.
```

Don't be surprised if the hops in one direction do not perfectly match the hops in the other direction as far as name, or even address. In each case, you are seeing the device as it is named *from the direction the packet is coming*. If the addresses or names are reasonably close, it is likely that the paths are really symmetric, or nearly so.

How you specify a source route depends on the implementation, and you should look at your system's documentation. For the Unix *traceroute* command, it is often specified with the *-g* option. For Microsoft's *tracert* command, you request a source route with the *-j* option, as in the example above.

If you are using source routes outside your own network, you should be aware that many Internet providers have configured their routers to reject source routes. This is because they may be abused to bypass security or to steal bandwidth from a provider without paying for it. In these cases, you *may* get a response like:

```
   12   !S  !S  !S  cambridge2-cr2.bbnplanet.net [192.233.33.2]
```

This indicates that the router at hop 12 has rejected your attempted source route. The other problem you may run into is that some destination hosts don't handle source routes correctly. They are supposed to, but not everyone's implementation of TCP/IP is fully compliant. If you discover this, then try to use the destination's first-hop router (the last hop before your destination) as your intermediate goal. It isn't perfect, but it is at least a good approximation.

Keep in mind that a router's primary job, whether in your network or your neighbor's, is to route packets, and not to respond to your *traceroute* or *ping* probes. This doesn't mean that you shouldn't use these tools to troubleshoot or monitor your network, but you need to use them sparingly. When used without proper restraint, they can push a marginal network over the edge into failure.

Telnet

Many times, network administrators overlook the Telnet program as a trouble-shooting tool. As a monitoring tool, it is probably too detrimental to the network, but for troubleshooting, it can be more useful than you might think. When a user reports problems accessing a multi-user time-sharing host, your first response is often to ping the host. This is a good first step, but if it succeeds, does it tell you if the host is accessible?

Using Telnet to contact the host, you exercise a larger portion of your network than *ping* alone can. Telnet runs on top of the TCP protocol, so establishes a more reliable indication of accessibility than ICMP echo requests can. It also tests higher-level functions of the destination host system. A multi-user machine may answer pings, since those are often handled in the operating system kernel, but still be inaccessible. It may also accept the TCP connection used by Telnet, again often handled by the operating system kernel, but it may not present the user with a login prompt because of other problems.

In addition, most Telnet clients will let you Telnet to ports other than the default Telnet service. Two of the most useful for network debugging are the *echo* service, on port 7, and the *daytime* service on port 13. The first of these echoes back every line you send it, while the second presents you with a human-readable time and date value from the destination host. Sadly, these TCP small services, as they are called, have been used of late to perpetrate denial of service attacks. You need to weigh their utility as diagnostics against this possible attack. If you choose to disable them and their UDP counterparts on your routers, add the following commands to your configuration:

```
no service tcp-small-servers
no service udp-small-servers
```

If you do leave them enabled, consider using packet filtering to limit reachability of these small services to within your own network. Similarly, you can Telnet to other TCP ports on your hosts to test out other functions. For example, you can Telnet to port 25 to verify that your email server is answering, and to port 80 to verify your Web server is answering.

Hub, Switch, and Router Statistics

Most network hubs and switches maintain counters that indicate how much traffic (often in both packets and octets) has been received and sent on each port. There are also likely to be media-specific counters to indicate loss of carrier, loss of tokens, or other error conditions. If you don't have an SNMP management station, you may be able to collect these statistics via Telnet or an RS-232 serial connection. By periodically collecting and clearing these statistics (or by collecting them and maintaining some history to determine what has changed and by how much), you can form a picture of which devices are the heaviest users of the network, and which links are experiencing the most errors.

Routers often collect the same types of statistics as hubs and switches, but they also collect information about higher-layer information, such as packet and octet counts per network address. By collecting this information, in addition to what your hubs and switches tell you, you can begin to determine what paths the data travel in your network, rather than just where it is coming from and where it is going to.

Netstat

Every machine connected to an IP network has an IP routing table. How you display this table, or if you can, depends on the specific operating system running on the machine. UNIX machines, and many IP software stacks derived from UNIX implementations, usually have a command called *netstat* that lets you access various network-level data structures in the operating system. The most useful of these is the IP routing table.

If you are running a dynamic routing protocol on your leaf networks, or if you are using UNIX hosts as routers, accessing their routing tables is essential to understanding why they, or some machine that depends on them for routing, cannot reach a destination. You can access the routing table using the command:

%netstat -r

```
Routing tables
Destination      Gateway       Flags   Refcnt    Use        Interface
localhost        localhost     UH        10     10622800    lo0
172.16.2.0       myhost        U         12      5275781    le0
default          myrouter      UG        14     12265327    le0
```

The output from this command is not as readable as we might like, and if we are having network problems, resolving addresses into names can be a painfully slow process. Instead, routing tables are best looked at without the names. To do this, include the *-n* option to the *netstat* command:

%netstat -n -r

```
Routing tables
Destination      Gateway         Flags   Refcnt   Use        Interface
127.0.0.1        127.0.0.1       UH        10    10622800    lo0
172.16.2.0       172.16.2.127    U         12     5275781    le0
default          172.16.2.45     UG        14    12265327    le0
```

Each line of output tells about one route in the host's table. For example, there is a route to the loopback network (127.0.0.1) pointing at the loopback interface (lo0), and reached directly, since the gateway address is local (127.0.0.1 is always local to any host). We have a direct attachment to subnet 172.16.2.0, on interface le0, and our IP address is 172.16.2.127. Finally, our default route is also on interface le0, by way of the router at 172.16.2.45. If this machine were acting as an IP router, we should also see routes for each directly attached subnet, each pointing at the appropriate interface. For details about what the other fields in the above mean, you should consult your system's documentation, since each system will have slightly different fields and meanings.

Ripquery

Sometimes, you cannot get to a UNIX machine or a router to look at its routing tables, perhaps because you do not have an account there. In this case, you need to consider ways to get a host or router's routing table from across the network. Two tools that can do this for you are *ripquery* and SNMP. We'll discuss using SNMP to obtain routing tables, as well as other data, later.

Ripquery is a simple UNIX utility that was originally distributed with the *gated* routing daemon. It only works if RIP is your dynamic routing protocol, and the information presented is very dependent on the host or router's implementation of RIP, but it is still a useful tool for probing. Using *ripquery* is straightforward; you simply tell it which host or router you would like it to probe:

ripquery myrouter

```
from myrouter (172.16.245.2):
    ???(172.16.103.0), metric 4
    ???(172.16.100.0), metric 4
    ???(172.16.101.0), metric 5
    ???(192.168.1.0),  metric 2
    ???(10.0.0.0),     metric 3
    ???(192.168.40.0), metric 3
    ???(192.168.41.0), metric 3
    ???(192.168.42.0), metric 3
    ???(192.168.43.0), metric 3
    ???(192.168.44.0), metric 3
    ???(192.168.45.0), metric 3
    ???(192.168.46.0), metric 3
    ???(192.168.47.0), metric 3
    ???(192.168.32.0), metric 2
    ???(192.168.33.0), metric 3
    ???(192.168.35.0), metric 3
    ???(192.168.36.0), metric 3
    ???(192.168.37.0), metric 3
    ???(192.168.38.0), metric 3
    ???(192.168.39.0), metric 3
```

This tells you that myrouter has a route to 172.16.103.0 with a metric of 4. The problem in interpreting this output is that it is not clear if the metric of 4 is what is in the router's table (some implementations respond this way), or if the metric is what the router would send in a RIP update on the interface on which it responded to the *ripquery*. But this doesn't always matter, nor does the fact that there is no next hop information contained in this output. What it does tell us is that myrouter has a route to these destinations, which is more than we knew before!

The three question marks, by the way, indicate that the machine running *ripquery* does not know the names of the networks to which it has routes. If it did, *ripquery* would indicate these names with each entry.

SNMP Management Software

If you are not running RIP as your dynamic routing protocol, or if you are and your hosts and routers won't respond to *ripquery* (not all do), you need another method to get at the routing tables of remote machines. SNMP can do this for you. The Simple Network Management Protocol (SNMP) was designed to allow remote management of routers and other network devices using a simple query-response protocol. Management and monitoring of an SNMP-capable device occurs when a *manager*, running on a management station, sends a request to an *agent*, running in the device to be managed, to extract a piece of information or change the device's configuration.

Each SNMP device maintains a database, called a *Management Information Base*, or *MIB*, which contains all the information that a device maintains or uses to configure itself. To monitor a device, you retrieve one or more values from its MIB. For example, the MIB contains a count of octets received on each interface. By retrieving these values, you can get a total count of all octets received since the counters were initialized, typically when the device last rebooted. To manage an SNMP-capable device, the user stores values into the MIB that affect the operation of the device. For example, the IP address assigned to a router port is part of the MIB. By setting the MIB entry that stores this value, you can change the address of the corresponding router port.

SNMP management software can be as simple as a general-purpose query tool that a network administrator might use to retrieve a selected set of variables, or it might be a suite of software running on a dedicated management station doing automated monitoring. When set up as part of a management station, it may even be possible for configuration changes to be scheduled to happen unattended late at night.

The main drawback of SNMP is the sheer volume of information stored in the MIBs of the various devices, and RMON doesn't help here in the slightest! Some people feel that the *simple* in Simple Network Management Protocol refers to how simple it is to get overwhelmed by this data. There is some truth to this, but there is nothing provided by the SNMP MIBs that is not also available to the user looking at the command line interface output, and no one complains that there is too much information there.

The real trick to using SNMP is to understand what information is useful, and when it is useful. For example, if you are not using the AppleTalk features of your router, then all of the values related to AppleTalk are not worth looking at, and can be ignored. Likewise, when you are not trying to monitor the amount of traffic your device is dealing with, the interface counters are not of interest. SNMP also becomes easier to use when you have a network management station with a good suite of software tools. These tools may be able to explore your network and build a topological map that you can display, perhaps at many different levels of detail, complete with color changes to signal alarms. They are also likely to contain predefined procedures to collect a complete list of a device's interfaces, the associated IP addresses and interface counters, and present this information to you in an easily understood table. Such an inquiry using the raw SNMP capabilities might entail hundreds of queries and responses that must all be interpreted and displayed, and may overwhelm both the novice and the expert.

The real strength of an SNMP management station and software suite is its ability to manage diverse devices from multiple vendors, all using the same interface and tools. No longer do you have to remember a dozen different commands to retrieve the appropriate values from your network devices just to analyze a path between a host and a server for errors.

SNMP Traps

SNMP was designed as a polled system. The management software polls the various agents in devices on some periodic basis. While generally useful for monitoring purposes, and more than adequate for many management tasks, polling lacks a certain immediacy that some network problems need. To understand why, consider polling a router for the status of its interfaces at five-minute intervals. If the interface fails immediately after your management software polls the router, it will be nearly five minutes before your management software detects the failure! The second problem is worse still. What if the router interface returns to life before the next poll? You may not even know that the interface went down at all!

To deal with this, the SNMP standards define a trap operation, which allows a device to send a report of some significant event to the management station without first being polled. Using a trap, the router can report the failure as soon as it is detected. Depending on the sophistication of the SNMP software running on your management station, it could then poll the router for more details about the current state, while alerting you to the problem.

Which SNMP traps your devices know how to send varies from one device to the next, and from one vendor to the next. Typically, traps are available for a link or port going down, a link or port coming up, and a cold start (reboot). Your device may be able to send traps when it gets too hot, if the power supply voltage drops too low, if someone mistypes a login password, or some other security related event occurs.

If you have the software to receive these traps,* you should turn on any that are likely in your network. In fact, about the only traps I turn off completely are link/port up/down traps on Ethernet switch and hub ports that attach directly to user workstations. I don't really need to know that a user has turned off a machine for the night, but I *do* want to know when the link between a hub and a switch fails. To enable traps, you typically need to tell the system that you want the traps, and where to send them. On a Cisco router, this becomes:

```
snmp-server host 172.16.11.22 public
```

This tells your router that it should send SNMP trap messages to the specified host using the `public` community, which is what most trap receivers expect. You can list multiple recipients, and each will get a copy of all traps. This could be useful if you have a router at a remote site, and you want both the site's operation center and your central management station to receive the traps. The `snmp-server` statement above is enough to enable traps; by default, this usually enables link or port up/down traps, and cold start traps. To enable traps for authentication failures caused by SNMP access violations, you would add:

```
snmp-server trap-authentication
```

Finally, you could (and probably should) add traps for configuration changes and environmental monitor problems, if available. Do that with:

```
snmp-server enable traps config
snmp-server enable traps envmon
```

You can even have the router send different types of traps to different trap hosts. Perhaps you want environmental monitoring traps sent to every trap daemon, but configuration traps sent only to your personal workstation. You can do this by appending the specific trap types you want to the end of the `snmp-server host` statement:

```
snmp-server host 172.16.1.1 public envmon config
snmp-server host 172.16.1.2 public envmon
```

---

* A freely available SNMP API that includes a trap daemon that runs on many UNIX hosts is available via anonymous FTP from *ftp.net.cmu.edu* in the directory */pub/snmp-dist.* This is the one I use to receive traps in my network. It logs the traps using the UNIX syslog daemon. Along with the trap daemon you will get a useful, if somewhat primitive, set of command line SNMP tools that can be useful for limited SNMP management. One especially useful command is the *snmpnetstat* command that uses SNMP to retrieve information similar to the UNIX *netstat* command. Check it out.

Since the list of traps may change as newer software becomes available, or depending on your router model, you should also check your documentation and enable any other traps that are important to you.

The Domain Name System

While not technically a network troubleshooting or monitoring tool, the Domain Name System (DNS) still warrants mention in any discussion of network monitoring and management. Having a complete and accurate database of names and addresses in your network can save hours of troubleshooting time. The DNS is just such a database. The important part is to make sure that it is complete and accurate.

As we said in Chapter 1, *The Basics of IP Networking*, the DNS is a system for mapping host names to IP addresses, and for mapping IP addresses to host names. Most humans can remember anywhere from a few to a few dozen IP addresses, and associate them correctly with the machines involved. However, they can more easily remember and work with a few hundred host names, and most network administrators are human, after all.* Because humans have limited ability to work directly with IP addresses, it is vital that all machines in your network that are assigned IP addresses are given unique names. The names need not describe the machine's function, location, or owner. In fact, these are often some of the poorer name choices, since function, location, and owner can change, yet the machine goes on.

Names that reflect the type of the machine are also usually poor choices, especially if they are likely to be referenced by users or documentation. One historical example is the machine that used to be the distribution point for the Kermit protocol software. For nearly a decade, all documentation referred to this machine, named cu20b, until people far and wide knew the machine well. The problem was that this machine probably got this name because it was the second DEC 2020 machine at Columbia University (hence, cu20b). When the machine was retired and replaced with a new UNIX machine, the name no longer had the right significance, but it was so well known that an alias had to be maintained for years while documentation was updated and user habits changed.

A far better way to name machines is to select a class of names, be it colors, flowers, trees, and so on, and then assign machines names from this class. The names are completely abstract, yet we still can work with them better than the corresponding IP addresses. The exception to these rules about not naming

---

* Yes, we have all met network and system administrators that we didn't consider human. Some of them we probably didn't even consider subhuman.

machines based on type, location, or function is your network infrastructure devices. These are your hubs, switches, and routers, and not your file servers, name servers, or news servers. Since people outside of your networking staff shouldn't need to refer to these devices, and since their names are most likely to be used while troubleshooting, it is useful for these names to have meaning.

There are lots of ways that you can make these names meaningful. You will need to come up with a scheme that works for you, a scheme that helps you and your staff identify a device rather than hinders. So, rather than simply giving your devices names like `hub1`, `hub2`, `hub3`, which tell you nothing more than that they are hubs, consider calling them something more like `math-230-hub-01`, or `cs-b27-hub-01`, which tell you where the hub is and which of multiple hubs are in the same location. But remember that these names will only be useful if you keep the DNS up to date.

It is also a good idea to give a unique name to each router interface. These names can be elaborate or simple, but they should have some meaning so you can remember what they are, and they should be related. For example, you might name one of them `chicago-s2-3` for interface `serial 2/3` on the router known as `chicago` and `chicago-f1-0` for interface `fddi 1/0` on the same router. Why do you want these names? Why not just give all interfaces the same name? The advantage to giving each interface its own name is that you can ping a specific interface by name without having to remember its IP address. You may also find that having the different interface names show up in the output of a *traceroute* command helps you better visualize how packets are flowing between adjacent routers.

Along with these interface-specific names, you should have another more generic name for your router. This name should either resolve to a loopback interface used for management, or to a very reliable backbone interface. If it is a loopback interface, it has the advantage of always being available, even if individual interfaces are down, but a reliable backbone interface may be just as good. You would use this as your primary target for Telnet, SNMP, NTP, and so forth, but ideally you would also use it as the source address for unsolicited messages from the router, such as SNMP traps. This can make it easier to sort log messages to select those from a single router.

If your routers (and even your hubs and switches) can operate as DNS clients, you should configure them to do so. For example, let's say you have just tried to ping the machine `merlin` from your workstation. Your ping worked, but you need to check connectivity from other points in your network. Unfortunately, the most convenient places to run other pings from are your routers, but they have not been configured to use the DNS, so now you have to remember (or look up) merlin's IP address. If your routers were configured to use the DNS, you wouldn't need to go through this exercise.

How you configure your routers to use the DNS as a client is, of course, dependent on your routers. On a Cisco router, the configuration commands are simply:

```
ip name-server 172.16.1.5
ip name-server 172.16.203.197
ip name-server 192.168.0.1
!
ip domain-list my-corp.com
ip domain-list your-school.edu
```

The first three statements define a set of DNS servers. How many you should have is up to you, but you should have more than one in case your first choice is unreachable or down. The ip domain-list statements define a list of domains that will be appended to names you ask the router to resolve. This list can be as long as you need, but you should keep it short or it can take a long time for the router to decide that the name you typed in error was an error. Alternatively, you could use the ip domain-name statement if there is only a single domain you would like appended. One important difference between ip domain-name and ip domain-list is that the domain in ip domain-name will only be appended to a name that contains no dots. The domain name list in ip domain-list will be searched for any name, whether it contains dots or not, unless it ends with a dot.

Having your router's command line resolve host names using the DNS can be a lifesaver, especially in the heat of troubleshooting. But as I said in Chapter 1, you should *never* rely on the DNS to resolve names in the configuration process itself. If your DNS server was unresponsive or unreachable while your router was booting, its configuration would fail. You can get around this by statically defining mappings between host names and IP addresses in your configuration such as:

```
host merlin 172.16.105.98
```

But such mappings are a maintenance headache. If merlin ever changes its address, you'll have to reconfigure all your routers, in addition to changing the DNS. It is easier and better to use IP addresses exclusively in your router configurations.

The Network Time Protocol (NTP)

The Network Time Protocol (NTP) is another troubleshooting and monitoring tool that is often overlooked. While not itself a tool for troubleshooting, or for monitoring, it is a way to make your other tools more useful. Consider what happens when you are looking at the logs in your routers, and you spot an unexpected message that seems to indicate that you had a problem at 6:15 A.M. on Router A. You also spot the same message on Router B, but it has a timestamp that indicates that the message was logged at 4:37 P.M. Is this the same problem, or two different ones? The only way to know for sure is to know the relationship between the clocks on the two routers.

The Network Time Protocol allows a set of devices on a network to agree about what time it is. They do this by periodically exchanging information, figuring out how far off from the consensus time each device is, and then adjusting their time to be closer to this consensus time. If one of the devices in the network is connected to an external time source, such as a radio clock, then the time at which they are in sync is reasonably close to the real time. Using NTP and a good time source, it is possible to maintain a view of time on your network that is within a few milliseconds of the absolute time maintained by world standards bodies.

To establish a Cisco router as an NTP client (and a server for the rest of your network), you need do nothing more than:

```
clock timezone EST -5*
clock summer-time EDT recurring! if needed
ntp update-calendar          ! on a Cisco 7XXX or 4500/4700
ntp source Fddi 1/0          ! always use the same source address
ntp peer 192.168.100.1       ! stratum 1: foo.blech.bar
ntp peer 172.16.234.97       ! stratum 1: twiddle.dee.dum
```

Always get permission from someone to use their NTP servers as a time base for your network; most sites with clocks are more than willing to provide a time base to others on the Internet. Try to select sites near to you, and remember to get their permission.

But even if an external real time source like a radio clock is not available, it is possible to establish an NTP time base on your network that, while not perfectly accurate, is at least consistent. Further, if you set the master machine's clock to some known reference point, perhaps your wristwatch, the difference between network time and real time may be just a few seconds, which is usually enough for correlating logs with real events. When managing a network, consistent time is more important than accurate time.

If you have Cisco 7000 or 7500 routers in your network, they have highly accurate time-of-day clocks, and make very good time sources, if an external source is unavailable. To set up one (and *only* one) of these routers as an NTP master, you would use:

```
clock timezone EST -5
clock summer-time EDT recurring  ! if needed
```

---

* Be sure to use the correct time zone for your location.

```
clock calendar-valid              ! my clock is good - use it
ntp master                        ! be the NTP master for the network
ntp source Fddi 1/0               ! always use the same source address
```

Regardless of which method you choose, using a local time base as if it were accurate or a remote clock, you can then set other devices in your network to use your routers as NTP servers and get consistent time throughout your network with no additional hardware.

Of course, you need to be sure that any options to timestamp log messages are enabled. Having good time doesn't help if nothing references it. On a Cisco router this is as simple as:

```
service timestamps log datetime localtime
```

The last parameter is there to convert the timestamps to local time. If you do not include it, the timestamps will be in Universal Coordinated Time (UTC).

Router Logs

Many network devices, and especially routers, generate log messages on their console or management port whenever a significant event occurs. These log messages can provide a wealth of information about the operation or failure of your router. You may also be able to selectively enable debug messages to assist your vendor's technical support staff to diagnose your problem. Unfortunately, unless you have a device attached to the management port to capture these messages, they are lost. Since it is not always practical to have something attached to each and every console port of each and every router (let alone your switches and hubs), a means must be established to capture these log messages and allow you to review them either during or after a failure.

The Cisco IOS provides two ways to capture these log messages when you are not logged in to the router, and an additional way to get them delivered to your terminal session when you are. The first of these capture methods is a circular log buffer maintained by the router that can be reviewed using the show log command. The use of this log buffer is not the default, but it is easily added to your configuration. Simply add:

```
logging buffered
```

to your configuration, and any message that would have been sent to the router's management console will be put in the buffer. In fact, it will not even be sent to the console, which can help to keep the noise level on the management console down when you are trying to debug a problem that generates lots of log messages.

The drawback to buffered logging is that there is a limit to how much the router can buffer. In a circular buffer, when the buffer fills and more room is needed, the oldest messages are discarded. How long a message remains in the buffer then is dependent on how long the messages are and how often they arrive. Some messages in my routers' log buffers have lasted for weeks, while other routers that are generating more frequent messages might cycle out old messages in a matter of minutes. If you have a router that is generating a large amount of log messages, or longer messages, and this is the normal state for the router, you might consider increasing the size of the log buffer. You can do this by appending a size in bytes to the end of the `logging buffered` statement. The size may range from 4,096 to 4,294,967,295, but defaults to 4,096 bytes. Keep in mind that the more memory you allocate to your message buffer, the less your router has for other important tasks such as routing packets.

But no matter how large you make your buffer, for any reasonable size it will fill up and you may lose information you needed to see. The alternative to buffered logging is to have the router use the syslog facility to send the messages to a host running a syslog daemon. Most UNIX hosts, and some other hosts have this daemon. By doing this, your log buffer can now be as large as you have disk space on the host. You can also use host-based tools to process the logs, summarize them, scan for abnormal events, and so on. You would also gain the advantage of having the log messages from several routers in one place where correlations between different messages might appear. To enable your router to use the syslog facility to send messages to a host, add the following to your configuration:

```
logging 172.16.1.234
```

You can also repeat the command multiple times with different hosts, all of which will receive a copy of the message. This helps to guard against lost messages when a single server host is down or unreachable. Keep in mind, though, that no matter how many hosts you list, if they are all unreachable (perhaps because your backbone interface has gone down) you will not be able to log to any of them and the messages will be lost. Still, if you carefully select your log hosts, the odds of them all being unreachable can be made as low as you wish.

Sometimes you'd prefer that the log messages were sent to your terminal while you are connected to the router. Perhaps you are working with a technical support engineer and he is asking for some low volume debug output. If you are on the console, no problem—just disable the log buffer and let the message go to the console. But if you are Telnetted to the router, you'd really rather the message came to your Telnet session. If you add the statement:

```
logging monitor debug
```

to your configuration, then you can cause a copy of the messages to be sent to your login session by typing `terminal monitor` on the command line. Note that all terminals that are monitoring see the same messages—there is no way to selectively send some messages to one session and others to another. This can be a problem if multiple administrators are connected to the router at the same time, but that rarely happens.

Okay, so how do you interpret these messages? In the Cisco IOS, all of the systems debug and event messages take the form:

```
%FACILITY-SUBFACILITY-SEVERITY-MNEMONIC: Message-text
```

FACILITY is a code consisting of two or more uppercase letters that indicate the facility to which the message refers. A facility can be a hardware device, a protocol, or a system software module. *SUBFACILITY* is only relevant to selected facilities in the system software, and most messages will not contain one.

SEVERITY is an indication of how important this message is, or how serious the condition being reported is. The severity values range from 0 to 7, with lower numbers being more critical. The severities are listed in Table 8-2. In general, messages that are of severity 6 (information) or higher are safely ignored, unless you are actively debugging a problem. Even many severity 5 messages can be safely ignored, unless the message text indicates that the message is of concern. Messages below severity 5 (and even some at severity 5) should get your attention. These messages may indicate anything from an interface going down (usually at severity 5) to a memory fault condition (severity 3) to a fatal system hardware or software error (severity 0).

Table 8-2. Log Message Severity Levels

	Level	Description
0	emergency	System unusable
1	alert	Immediate action needed
2	critical	Critical condition
3	error	Error condition
4	warning	Warning condition
5	notification	Normal but significant condition
6	informational	Informational message only
7	debugging	Appears during debugging only

For example, the message:

```
%LINEPROTO-5-UPDOWN: Line protocol on Interface serial 0 changed state
to down
```

indicates that interface serial 0 just when down. Notice that this message is at a severity level of 5 (notification). While this is potentially a serious message for an Ethernet interface, it is probably normal for an on-demand serial link. The corresponding message:

```
%LINEPROTO-5-UPDOWN: Line protocol on Interface serial 0 changed state
to up
```

would indicate that service on the interface has returned to normal. Other messages, such as:

```
%RSP-2-STALL: partially inserted or removed IPs on cyBus0
```

or

```
%ALIGN-1-FATAL: Illegal access to low address [hex]
```

indicate more serious problems. The first message can be resolved by making sure that all of the interface processor boards are seated correctly, but the second should be copied exactly and provided to technical support. In fact, it would not be unusual for the second error message to immediately precede a system reboot.

There are hundreds of other messages that the IOS can generate. Exactly which ones you might see depends on the model of router you have, which interfaces are installed, and, most important, which version of software you are running. To list them all here would take many pages, and the list would be out of date with the next release of the IOS. Instead, get familiar with the messages that you see on a regular basis, and get used to assessing their relative importance based on the severity level. When in doubt, consult your documentation and see what it says about your message or ones like it.

Change Management

The best way to handle network problems is to avoid them. The problem that you don't have to fix is the least expensive. Most network problems are caused by human errors, often by networking staff. Such problems can be physical, such as removing a connection in error, or they can be caused by configuration errors. Fortunately, these are also the easiest problems to avoid.

Keep Good Records

If taking notes while troubleshooting helps you avoid simply moving the problem around, consider how many problems you could avoid by keeping detailed records. For example, if your wiring closets and hubs all have accurate and complete records of what is connected where, the odds of removing a connection in error are much smaller.

So what kind of records are necessary? First, you should have an accurate and complete record of all physical connections in your network. It should be possible using these records and these records alone to physically trace a connection from any machine in your network to any other machine without leaving your office! These records should be detailed enough so that you can identify exactly which pair of wires or fibers connect two devices together, and they should identify the ports on any intermediate devices.

The second kind of records that you should keep are detailed change logs for all of your configurations. Ideally, these logs should show all lines or values added, changed, and deleted for each configuration change, the date and time the change occurred, who made the changes, and a brief description of why the change was made. This information then gives you the opportunity to review changes, and can help you to determine whether the desired goal was met.

How long you should keep these records is a matter of taste, but the longer the better. I once was able to correlate a rather low-frequency intermittent network problem with a single Ethernet segment as it moved from one router to another over a period of two years, simply by reviewing the log of configuration changes for these routers. Fortunately, keeping such a change log need not be an involved task, and can be nearly automatic.

Plan and Review Changes

Too often, computer support people have come to believe that "plan" is a four-letter word. They think it is something that real computer people don't need to do, or they have been convinced that it is wasted effort. However, by carefully thinking through a change *before* it gets executed, many pitfalls can be identified, and, if not avoided, their impact can be lessened. This planning and review process need not be exhaustive, but it should be thorough. Nothing should be assumed, and the more involved the change, the more extensive and detailed the planning should be.

For example, if an important network segment is to be moved between two routers on Wednesday morning, the configuration changes should be prepared and, if possible, staged on Tuesday evening. Likewise, any cables that may need to be moved should be identified and clearly marked, and all people involved should know their role before Wednesday morning arrives. This preparation can probably take place as late as Tuesday afternoon. However, if you were about to change your routing protocol, or replace a major piece of equipment, you would probably want to prepare your configurations, and probably run many tests for days or even weeks before the time comes to make the change.

Reviewing changes also doesn't need to be a burdensome task. It can be nothing more than just having one other pair of knowledgeable eyes looking over what you propose to do. Preferably, this review should happen with as little direct prompting from the person proposing the change as possible. Instead, give a brief overview of the intended goal, and then leave the reviewer alone. Because each of you will make different assumptions about what is going on, your reviewer is more likely to spot problems if he is not prejudiced by your views.

Finally, before you make any change, be sure you have a clear idea of why you are making the change. If you don't know why the change is happening, don't make it! This is especially true of software upgrades. If you are not upgrading your software with a goal in mind, why take the chance? Your current software is working just fine.

Fault Tolerant Booting Strategies

One of the most dangerous times for your network is when you are actively changing things. A network that exists in a steady state has relatively few failures to deal with. But your network cannot always exist in a steady state. You will make changes to add new connections, or to provide new services. One of the most disruptive changes that you will make is upgrading the software controlling your routers and other network devices. Think carefully about why you are making the change and be sure that the potential benefits are great enough to warrant the risk.

The greatest risk when a router (or other network device) receives a software upgrade is that the new software might fail to initialize properly. This may be caused by a flaw in the router image that was not detected by your vendor's testing, but these undetected failures are rare and are easily avoided by delaying your own upgrade for a couple of weeks after the software is released. Another serious problem that can occur is that, while the image is good, the copy stored on the router contains a flaw that makes it useless. It may then be that the router will not boot, and the only way to regain control is to physically access the router. You may even need to remove some portion of the router to load a good image. This kind of failure is harder to avoid, but there are a few steps that may allow you to retain control of the router in these situations. But before you can take steps to prevent boot failure, you first need to understand what happens during the router's bootstrap processing and what can go wrong.

When a router is powered on, a small program stored in read-only memory (ROM) is executed. This program is fairly simple and does little more than transfer control to a smarter program after a small amount of initialization. This initialization typically includes some basic diagnostic tests and hardware detection. The tests performed may be extensive, or, more likely, they are the bare minimum necessary to ensure that the next stage of the boot process can execute, during which fuller testing will occur.

The smarter program that the ROM boot code executes may also be stored in ROM, on some attached storage device such as a floppy disk or flash memory, or it may even be loaded across the network. This code executes more extensive diagnostic routines and more fully initializes the hardware. It may be the final running system image, or it may repeat the process by loading yet another program from some storage location and transfer control to it. This process may be repeated, but most vendors use at most three to four stages, including the initial ROM boot code.

Okay, so what can go wrong in this process? Obviously, some diagnostic test may fail. There is not much to be done about this, and no fault-tolerant booting strategy can work around a diagnostic failure, so I won't talk about it further. What you can do something about is the other likely possibility—namely that one of the intermediate programs, or the final program, might be corrupted or might not even exist.

It is rare for an image copied to a router's storage device, whether a floppy or flash memory, to be corrupted without detection. The network protocols used to copy the image across the network catch many errors, and the Cisco IOS runs a checksum calculation on the received image, complaining about any mismatch it detects. You should *never* attempt to start a software image that the router has complained about! But it is possible for the image to be corrupted while it is stored. Flash memory may have a weak bit that gets changed sporadically, or an error in the running system may inadvertently overwrite a portion of the software image on storage. A floppy can fail in similar ways, either because of a flawed spot on the diskette, or because of software errors.

A more likely problem is that the image the router is supposed to load is not there. This may be an oversight on your part, such as failing to put a copy on a router, or because of mistyping the file name either on the storage media or in the router configuration. Regardless of the cause, a missing image file is as damaging as a corrupted one—in either case you can lose control of the router.

Fortunately, you can configure a Cisco router so that if the first image it attempts to load is unusable, either because of file corruption or a missing file, it tries a backup image.* Ideally this image is the one that was last running successfully on the router. To enable this backup strategy to work, you need to do a few things at various points in the upgrade process. First, you must ensure

---

* For the truly paranoid, you can repeat this with three, four, or even more images that are attempted. On some platforms, you can also fall back to an image in system ROMs.

that you have a working backup image. The easiest way to achieve this is to make sure that your router's storage medium has enough space to store multiple system images simultaneously. Since Cisco routers use flash memory, this means ordering or upgrading your routers so that they all contain at least twice the flash memory needed to store the current software. Better still, buy three or even four times as much memory as you currently need. This way, as the software image grows or you enable new features that require larger software images, you still have enough space to maintain two working images. With the extra flash memory, you would store your upgrade software in a file whose name is different from the currently running image, *leaving the current image in the flash memory, too.* Older images may be removed. This process is shown below for a Cisco 75XX router. Different Cisco routers refer to their flash devices by different names; consult your documentation to find the device name for your router.

```
router# cd slot0:
router# dir
-#- -length- -----date/time------ name
1   6732912   May 13 1997 13:56:56 rsp-jv-mz.111-10.bin

9650960 bytes available (6733040 bytes used)
router# copy tftp slot0:rsp-jv-mz.111-12.bin
Enter source file name: code/rsp-jv-mz.111-12.bin
9650832 bytes available on device slot0, proceed? [confirm]
Address or name of remote host [255.255.255.255]? 192.168.12.156
Accessing file "code/rsp-jv-mz.111-12.bin" on myhost.mycorp.com
...FOUND
Loading code/rsp-jv-mz.111-12.bin from 192.168.12.156 (via FDDI0/0):!!!!
!!!!!!!!!!!!!!!!!!!!!!!!!!!!!!!!!!!!!!!!!!!!!!!!!!!!!!!!!!!!!!!!!!!!!!!!!!!
!!!!!!!!!!!!!!!!!!!!!!!!!!!!!!!!!!!!!!!!!!!!!!!!!!!!!!!!!!!!!!!!!!!!!!!!!!!
!!!!!!!!!!!!!!!!!!!!!!!!!!!!!!!!!!!!!!!!!!!!!!!!!!!!!!!!!
[OK - 6762468/13523968 bytes]
CCCCCCCCCCCCCCCCCCCCCCCCCCCCCCCCCCCCCCCCCCCCCCCCCCCCCCCCCCCCCCCCCCCCCCCC
CCCCCCCCCCCCCCCCCCCCCCCCCCCCCCCCCCCCCCCCCCCCCCCCCCCCCCCCCCCCCCCCCCCCCCCC
CCCCCCCCCCCCCCCCCCCCCCCCCCCCCCCCCCCCCCCCCCCCCCCCCCCCCCCC
router# dir
-#- -length- -----date/time------ name
1   6732912   May 13 1997 13:56:56 rsp-jv-mz.111-10.bin
2   6762468   Jul  4 1997  8:01:18 rsp-jv-mz.111-12.bin

2888492 bytes available (13523968 bytes used)
```

I first set my current directory to the flash memory device called `slot0:` and listed its contents to ensure that I had enough space for the new image. If there wasn't enough space, I would have deleted older versions of the software to make space. After verifying I had sufficient space, I told the router to use TFTP to copy the file *code/rsp-jv-mz.111-12.bin* from the server at `192.168.12.156` to the local filename *rsp-jv-mz.111-12.bin* on device `slot0:`. Remember that each router names its flash memory devices differently. The exclamation points show the packets being received by the router, and the capital Cs are the router performing a checksum calculation over the received file to verify its integrity. Finally, I listed the contents of the flash memory again; the first file is my currently running image, and the second is the new image I want to run. Before I show how to configure the router to boot these images in a fault tolerant way, let's talk about what you can do if you do not have enough flash memory to store two images.

Many routers can load their software from across the network. While this is usually not a good idea for production systems, it can be a viable option for fault tolerant booting. In this case, you either have a copy of the current image available on your TFTP server (from your last upgrade), or you need to copy it there from your router. To copy it from your router, you go through the same basic steps as you would to copy an image from the TFTP server to your router.

```
router# cd slot0:
router# dir
-#- -length- -----date/time------ name
1   6732912  May 13 1997 13:56:56 rsp-jv-mz.111-10.bin

50960 bytes available (6733040 bytes used)
router# copy slot0:rsp-jv-mz.111-10.bin tftp
Enter destination file name: code/rsp-jv-mz.111-10.bin
CCCCCCCCCCCCCCCCCCCCCCCCCCCCCCCCCCCCCCCCCCCCCCCCCCCCCCCCCCCCCCCCCCCCC
CCCCCCCCCCCCCCCCCCCCCCCCCCCCCCCCCCCCCCCCCCCCCCCCCCCCCCCCCCCCCCCCCCCCC
CCCCCCCCCCCCCCCCCCCCCCCCCCCCCCCCCCCCCCCCCCCCCCCCCCCCC
Address or name of remote host []? 192.168.12.156
!
```

This time I listed the contents of my flash memory device to be sure of the filename I wanted to copy. I then issued the *copy* command telling the router to copy the file from *slot0:rsp-jv-mz.111-10.bin* to the TFTP server at 192.168.12.156 and give it the name *code/rsp-jv-mz.111-10.bin* there. This time, the router computed the checksum before beginning the copy. This helps avoid putting a bad copy of an image onto your TFTP server. If the checksum calculation failed, you'd want to get a copy of the image from another router, or forego the extra safety net this time. Regardless of whether the image in the router's flash memory was good or bad, you would erase it to make room for your new image and then copy the new upgraded image from the TFTP server to your router. Whatever you do, be sure to leave the old image on your TFTP server!

At this point, you have your new image on your router's flash memory device, and you have the currently running image either on your flash device or on a TFTP server. You now need to tell your router to boot the new image, and to fall back to the old image in the event of problems. If you have enough flash memory to store both images, add these lines to your router configuration:

```
boot system flash slot0:rsp-jv-mz.111-12.bin
boot system flash slot0:rsp-jv-mz.111-10.bin
```

If you don't have enough flash memory, you'll want to load the backup (if necessary) from your TFTP server. To do so, use the following two lines:

```
boot system flash slot0:rsp-jv-mz.111-12.bin
boot system tftp:code/rsp-jv-mz.111-10.bin 192.168.12.156
```

When you restart your router, the first image runs if it is found and loads successfully, which is what you want. If it is not found or is corrupted, the router tries to load the second image. This image should be good since it was what you last ran on the router, and you made sure it existed.

Once your router has rebooted, you then need to check which image loaded. If the new image loaded correctly, you can remove the backup image and backup boot system statement, since the new image should be fine until your next upgrade. On the other hand, you may want to leave the backup in place as a permanent safety net. While it is rare for an image to become corrupted once it is copied to flash memory, it can happen, and your fault tolerant bootstrap process may save you a trip to the router.

You should note that TFTP is often viewed as a security problem because it performs no user authentication and requires no password for access to the files on the server. Many TFTP servers have been modified to provide some level of security, and you should look for one that you feel comfortable with, or provide some restrictions on its access some other way.

Online vs. Off-line Configurations

Many network administrators never consider the possibility that the online configuration methods provided by their networking vendors may not be the best way to maintain a device's configuration. Instead, they use what the vendor provides, and sacrifice a wealth of opportunity, information, and tools that they can use to make their jobs easier.

Many network devices can copy their configurations from a file on a Trivial File Transfer Protocol (TFTP) server located elsewhere on the network, and some can use the more reliable (and some believe more secure) Remote Copy Protocol (RCP). While this is not the best choice for loading these configurations at boot, such a capability opens the door to maintaining a device's configuration offline, perhaps on a UNIX host or other workstation. Once the change is made, it is a simple matter to copy the configuration to the device. You can store the configuration file for use the next time the device boots, or force the device to reread its configuration immediately. In the Cisco IOS, this is as easy as:

```
router# copy tftp startup
Address of remote host [255.255.255.255]? 192.168.12.156
Name of configuration file [router-config]? router/config
```

```
Configure using router/config from 192.168.12.156? [confirm]
Loading router/config from 192.168.12.156 (via FDDI0/0): !!!!!!!!
[OK - 37344/128975 bytes]

Warning: distilled config is not generated
[OK]
```

This copies the configuration file named *router/config* from the TFTP server at
192.168.12.156 to the router's startup configuration file in non-volatile RAM.
The warning, "distilled config is not generated," reminds you that this configuration has not been copied to the running configuration. You accomplish that by
using the command *configure memory*, which then *merges* the startup configuration in non-volatile RAM with the running configuration in volatile RAM. Note
carefully that I said it *merges* the startup and running configurations, rather than
replaces the running configuration. This is important because it affects how you
put commands in your configuration file.

For example, access control lists (whether used for security, route selection, or
otherwise) are order dependent. The first entry that matches causes the access list
to end. This means that you can't just add an entry to the end of the access list;
you might need to insert it in the middle. But if you blindly do that in your configuration file, and then load it using the above procedure, you won't get the effect
you want. Consider this access list:

```
access-list 1 permit 172.16.1.0 0.0.0.255
access-list 1 deny   172.16.0.0 0.0.255.255
```

As it stands, it will permit (match) anything on 172.16.1.0/24, but deny all
other addresses on 172.16.0.0/16. This might be appropriate to select a single
subnet for security restrictions. Let's assume that you have this access list stored
offline in a file, and you edit it to read:

```
access-list 1 permit 172.16.1.0  0.0.0.255
access-list 1 permit 172.16.27.0 0.0.0.255
access-list 1 deny   172.16.0.0  0.0.255.255
```

In other words, you extend it to permit anything on 172.16.27.0/24. But if
you copy this configuration file to your router and merge it with the running
configuration, you end up with this:

```
access-list 1 permit 172.16.1.0  0.0.0.255
access-list 1 deny   172.16.0.0  0.0.255.255
access-list 1 permit 172.16.27.0 0.0.0.255
```

The second clause matches addresses on 172.16.27.0/24 before the third
clause is examined, and the access list ends. This isn't what you wanted at all.

So how do you work around this? There are two solutions. First, you could change
the access list number to make a new access list, and then update the places in
your configuration that reference the list to use the new number. This may be work-

able if the list is used in only one place and you don't mind having a constantly changing set of access list numbers. However, I don't recommend this. Changing all the places that reference the old access list is error prone, and you will certainly miss one some day. Furthermore, it is a good idea to have access lists that are used the same way, or that have the same definitions, have the same numbers on all your routers, if possible. This way, the access list number has some meaning to you and your staff.

Instead of copying the access list and changing its number before editing it, I use a different mechanism. Since the router will be merging the startup and running configurations together, why not preface the access list that you are changing with a command to clear it? In your configuration file, you would have:

```
no access-list 1
access-list 1 permit 172.16.1.0   0.0.0.255
access-list 1 permit 172.16.27.0  0.0.0.255
access-list 1 deny    172.16.0.0   0.0.255.255
```

This clears access list 1 and rebuilds it from scratch when the router merges the configurations. The only drawback to this scheme is that, while the router is clearing and rebuilding the access list, packets may get past a security filter, or routes may get selected unintentionally. While this may be a problem in theory, in practice it has never shown up. You can reduce the chance that something will get by while you're unprotected even further by deleting the `no access-list` statement from your offline configuration file after you have loaded it on the router. Then, the next time you upload a configuration to the router, the `no access-list` statement won't be in the startup configuration. Other order-dependent parts of your configuration can be handled similarly, though they probably change infrequently compared to access lists.

Other commands in your configuration files may not be order dependent, but you may need to remove them. For example, while you can easily change the IP address on an interface by using a different `ip address` statement in your configuration file, to remove an IP address from an interface that you are no longer using, you cannot just omit the command. Instead you need to issue a command to clear the address from the interface. In the Cisco IOS, this is usually done by prefacing the command with the word `no`. Hence, to remove an IP address from an Ethernet, you would have:

```
interface ethernet 0
 no ip address
```

Other commands behave similarly, and some may need more extensive unraveling. While you can remove your RIP routing process by simply including the command `no router rip` in your configuration, if you have an extensive RIP configuration section in your running configuration and do this, the IOS has been known to behave strangely (it shouldn't, but it sometimes does). In these instances, you might want to load an intermediate configuration that undoes the RIP configuration before removing the RIP routing process itself. In other words, you might load:

```
router rip
 no network 172.16.0.0
 no redistribute ospf 101
 ! include other configured RIP commands here
no router rip
```

once, and then remove all references to the RIP routing process from your off-line configuration and load it again. Alternatively, you can simply reboot your router and let it start with a clean copy of the startup configuration, though you probably don't want to do this in the middle of the day.

Offline configuration management has many benefits:

- You can use your favorite text editor for writing your configuration files. Your favorite editor probably has many features that the vendor's configuration editor doesn't have; in addition, it's familiar, so you're less likely to make mistakes.

- You can use the wealth of tools available on your host platform. These tools often include search programs, preprocessors, macro languages, and even the ability to print the configurations on paper to allow comparisons, notes, and so on. Seldom do the tools provided by a router vendor even begin to approach the tools provided by a host computer.

- You can add comments to your configuration files. I said earlier that the configuration for a router (or other device) is a highly specialized program written in a configuration language. In the same way that you should comment what you are doing in your programs, you should comment what you are doing in your configurations. Such comments allow you to include notes to yourself about an upcoming change, a workaround for a bug, or justification for why something is done the way it is. This way, when you or one of your staff look at the configuration in six months, you can figure out *why* something was done, rather than just *how*.

- You will be running some kind of backup software on the host machine, so your configurations are automatically backed up. Better still, if a device should die, or completely lose its configuration, you need only put enough configuration information back on it, or its replacement, to be able to reach your offline storage location. Then, you simply reload the configuration file from there, and reboot the device. This has saved me more than once.

- You can use a revision control system, such as *RCS*,* to keep track of your configuration files. A revision control system is a set of tools that keep a record of changes to a file. It identifies when changes were made, what changed, and who made the changes—exactly the set of items that should be recorded. Most also allow you to retrieve any previous version of a file, so that you can see what the file looked like before a specific change occurred. Revision control systems also provide a simple locking mechanism that prevents two people from changing a file at the same time. While not foolproof, revision locking should prevent the most common instances of two administrators accidentally applying incompatible changes to the same file.

The only major disadvantage to offline configuration is that some devices have special context-sensitive help and error checking built in to their online configuration tools. These can make it easier to ensure that an unfamiliar change is correct, and that simple spelling or syntax errors don't render a configuration unusable. Still, if you are careful with your offline changes, and are familiar with what you are doing, this disadvantage doesn't hurt much. All things considered, the advantages to offline configuration far outweigh this lone disadvantage. As part of a comprehensive change management process, it can save you hours or days of debugging and troubleshooting.

Configure for Manageability

Finally, take the time to configure your network to make it more manageable. You need to take advantage of features and commands in your routers, switches, hubs, and workstations that make them your partners in network management instead of your adversaries. I have already given two examples of this: configuring your routers to use the DNS services of your network, and configuring them to use remote NTP servers to acquire accurate time, and then provide that to your other network devices.

Another way to configure for manageability is using the `description` statement liberally. This statement allows you to attach a brief description to each interface to help you identify what the intended purpose of the interface is. This description is displayed whenever the status of an interface of the router is displayed. For example, you might include in your description what groups, buildings, or important functions are connected to this interface.

It is also worthwhile to specify default options explicitly in your configuration files. Obviously, you don't really need to. However, configuring defaults explicitly

---

* RCS, the Revision Control System, is freely available for a wide-range of platforms including most variants of UNIX, VMS, DOS, and the Macintosh. It can be retrieved via anonymous FTP from *prep.ai.mit.edu*. For more information about RCS, see *Applying RCS and SCCS*, by Don Bollinger and Tan Bronson (O'Reilly).

serves two important purposes. First, the defaults may change in a future release of the device's code, and you may not notice that change in the release notes until it causes you problems. Second, it's useful to document that the defaults are definitely in effect, what they are, and that you meant to use them, especially if you use non-default settings in some locations.

Take whatever steps are required to disable any ports or services that you are not using. This helps to avoid uncertainty about why an interface is down or whether a service is really needed. It also reduces potential conflicts as your network contacts other established networks. For example, a Cisco router reports that an interface is *administratively down* when it has been shut down by its configuration, as opposed to simply reporting that it is *down*, if nothing is connected. The first makes it clear that you want the interface to be down, rather than that something has failed.

Finally, if you have the ability to maintain your configurations offline, and your router configuration language allows for comments, include them liberally. Like any other program, a router configuration can be difficult to figure out months after you construct it. Comments allow you to remember why you did something the way you did it, and what you intended to do.

9

Connecting to the Outside World

Previous chapters have focused on designing, building, and managing the network within your organization. In this chapter, we will turn our attention outward and discuss issues related to connecting your network to the outside world, whether this is a connection to the Internet or a private connection to another organization's network.

When many network professionals think of connecting to the outside world, the first, if not the only, outside connection they think about is the Internet. This is especially true now that the Internet is part of pop culture: mainline magazines, newspapers, and television commercials, as well as shows, movies, and even books, are advertising their World Wide Web pages. But this is only one type of connection to the world outside of the organizational network, and it is not even the most common. It's actually more common to set up a private link between your network and some other organization's. Such links should be planned and executed as carefully as an Internet connection.

Regardless of the type of external connection, there are common issues and pitfalls you should explore before ordering the first circuit. I will discuss these issues from the point of view of an organization making its first attempt at connecting to the world beyond, but many apply to organizations that already have external connections. You may want to review any connections you inherited in light of this chapter, and possibly make some changes.

Planning Links to Other Organizations and the Internet

Conceptually, there's little difference between a link to the Internet and a link to another organization. The issues involved are the same, with one small exception.

If neither organization is connected to the Internet, then they can choose any IP network numbers they want. Ideally, these would be non-overlapping choices from the private IP network numbers reserved in RFC 1918. In the worst case, both organizations are using the same network numbers, and they must sort out their addressing prior to connecting to each other, or they must use Network Address Translation (NAT) technologies discussed below. Because these external connections are more similar than different, I will treat them as being the same, and I only point out the differences that matter.

Here are some questions you should ask before setting up a link to another organization. Make sure they are answered to your satisfaction!

- Who is responsible for ensuring operation of the link?
- Where does this responsibility end (i.e., where is the demarcation point)?
- What traffic is permissible over this link?
- Who may send traffic over the link?
- Where may traffic be sent over this link?

The first two questions establish clear boundaries between your network and the other network. This is a direct extension of knowing where your network boundaries are. The last three questions make sure that everyone agrees about the purpose of this link. For example, if you have a connection to the Internet, and are establishing a private link to another organization, do you intend to allow this other organization to access the Internet through you? Will your Internet provider allow this?

If you are creating a link to the Internet, the answers to these questions are probably spelled out clearly in the contract governing the service. You and your staff should understand what the answers are, because ignorance of your service agreement will not carry much weight in a contract dispute. A private link typically has no contract governing it, and probably doesn't need one. But that makes it all the more important that the answers to these questions are understood by all parties.

The answers to these questions usually depend on the relationship between the organizations. These relationships typically fall into two broad categories. If one organization is subordinate to the other, policy is often set unilaterally by the parent organization, and the subordinate organization must simply go along. For example, you may be setting up a link between a parent company and a subsidiary; the parent company probably makes the rules in this situation. In the extreme, this type of link becomes an internal WAN link of a corporate network whose staff runs the local networks in both organizations.

The other type of relationship is one of peers, or at least near-peers. Neither group has authority over the other, so setting policy for the network connection requires negotiation and cooperation. Often, however, the negotiation phase is skipped, or is given little real effort, with the result that neither group gets what they really want, but they don't know it until the first time things go awry. As I said, it's important to reach a clear understanding about the policies and agreements governing the connection.

Whether the link is private or a link to the Internet, there are several ways to define who is responsible for the link and where the responsibility ends, and the combinations are nearly endless. However, there are two combinations that work reasonably well, and they differ only slightly. First, each organization owns its own routers, and one of the organizations provides a leased circuit and DSU equipment for both ends, and takes responsibility for operating the link, up to and including the DSU at the remote organization. The advantage here is typically the cost, provided both organizations already have an appropriate router port to use. The disadvantage is that the organization that "owns" the connection can't monitor or manipulate the other group's router to help isolate problems.

This leads to the second possibility, which is less common, but favored by many. In this scenario, one of the organizations owns and operates the leased line and DSU equipment, plus they own and operate a router at the remote organization and connect this router to a segment of the network there. This approach gives the organization managing the link a completely functional IP subnet to manage, provides a remote device, for which they are responsible, to ping or Telnet to and frees them from some of the hassles of dealing with changes internal to the remote site. The clear disadvantage is, of course, the cost of the router, but routers aren't that expensive these days.

The questions about what is permitted on the link—who can send traffic and where it goes—can also have many answers, and *must* be clearly understood. For example, if organization A wants to provide a link to organization B to handle inter-organizational traffic, but nothing else, organization B must understand that they are not getting a link, or a backup link, to the Internet through organization A. Similarly, if the link is intended to facilitate confidential or secret communications, both groups should understand the level of security required. Is the link encrypted? If so, how strongly? If not, who might have access to it? These are the kinds of questions that must be answered.

Finally, you have to know who is paying for the link. At first, you might say that whichever group is maintaining the link and any equipment associated with it should pay. But this may not be true. In my network, there are three links to the university's regional campuses. Each leased line, DSU pair, and remote router is controlled by the central campus, but they are owned and paid for by the regional campuses, since they were established to facilitate access by the regional campuses to central resources. The same kind of arrangement could be made between two peer organizations or between an organization and its Internet provider. It's common for the paying organization to lack experience in handling such links and prefer allowing the other to act as manager, while assuming the responsibility of paying the bills.

How Do I Connect to the Internet?

One of the greatest differences between an Internet connection and a private link is how you get connected. For a private link, you simply agree with the other organization that you want the link, order the equipment and the data circuit, and connect. But with the Internet, because of its decentralized and almost anarchic structure, things aren't always so cut and dried.

NSPs and ISPs

So whom do you contact? Since spring of 1995, the Internet, at least in the United States, has been a commercial venture. Prior to this time, the government provided much of the backbone infrastructure through exclusive contracts with organizations that could provide the service. The last form this took was funding from the National Science Foundation (NSF) to IBM, MCI, and MERIT Networking to provide the backbone known as the NSFNet. This three-way partnership evolved until an independent corporation was formed for the sole purpose of managing the network backbone. They ran the NSFNet backbone under contract until its demise in 1995. Funding for the NSFNet backbone stopped because the NSF wanted to allow commercial entities to compete on a more even footing for the growing Internet business.

But the NSF did not want the Internet to fall apart and set communications between researchers back into the dark ages. They specified several conditions that must be met for different classes of service that would be provided by various corporations. They also made some rules governing the minimum mandatory level of interconnection among these groups, and where these interconnects would take place. Out of this, two classes of service providers came into being. The larger of these are called *National Service Providers* or *Network Service Providers (NSPs)*. These NSP organizations have large, high-capacity backbone networks that span the continental United States, and often extend into Canada, or across the oceans. As customers, these providers have regional networks of universities and research labs, and large companies. Their customers also include the second class of service providers, known as *ISPs*, or *Internet Service Providers*. ISPs are typically smaller regional or metropolitan network providers who deal directly with smaller companies, schools, and the public. They then purchase services from one or more of the NSPs to achieve full Internet connectivity.

Enough history and background. Should you contact an ISP or an NSP? As with so many questions in this book, the answer depends on many factors. If you are a large organization and wish to be able to hand your Internet connectivity needs off to another organization, an NSP may meet your needs. Typically, links to NSPs will be dedicated leased lines, but this is not a requirement. On the other hand, if you are a smaller organization, or if you want to save some money and do the work of handling your Internet connection yourself, an ISP may be more appropriate. Typical connections to an ISP will be dial-up or ISDN lines, though many ISPs now provide dedicated leased line services.

When selecting an ISP or an NSP, connectivity means a lot. If your traffic has to funnel through a common link with traffic from dozens of other organizations, you may find that the performance is not what you expect. Don't hesitate to shop around. Prices for different kinds of service vary dramatically. But remember, there is some truth to the saying that you get what you pay for!

Next, consider what kinds of service the provider offers. Some simply hand you a data circuit and expect you to handle your end of the connection without further assistance. Others provide all of the equipment necessary to touch your network (an Ethernet, for example), and manage the entire connection to that point. Some run your DNS for you; others leave it up to you. Some may even provide you with firewalls, web services, toll-free access numbers for when your personnel are traveling, or any number of other services. Each typically has an added cost, and these costs should be compared as well, even for services that you don't currently expect to use.

In the end, however, selecting an NSP or ISP is very much like selecting your network hardware vendor. You don't want to be jumping from one provider to another when the service isn't what you expected, so do your homework early and save yourself time and bother later. Ask around and get recommendations for or against service providers from other network administrators in your area.

Multiple Providers, Or Multiple Links?

Just as you considered redundancy in designing your own network, you should consider designing redundancy into your Internet connection. This is especially true if you rely on the Internet for your business to function. There are two ways to set up a redundant Internet connection. One way is to connect to multiple different providers who do not share a common failure point. For example, if you choose to work with two ISPs, be sure that they haven't pooled resources and decided to share a high-capacity data circuit to an NSP. This single data circuit eliminates a lot of your desired redundancy. The other option is to obtain multiple links to a single provider that has built redundancy into its own network. For example, if your ISP has a link running to NSP A that leaves the city to the south, and another to NSP B that leaves the city to the north, running two links to this ISP is probably cheaper, easier, and just as reliable as dealing with two different ISPs. Alternatively, if you are dealing directly with an NSP, consider running two links to geographically distinct points in the NSP's backbone network.

Which is better? It's debatable, but having multiple links to a single provider has some advantage over dealing with two providers. You don't have to worry about your providers pointing fingers at each other when things go wrong. Furthermore, it should be cheaper to obtain a second line from the same provider than to deal with a separate provider. Finally, it is usually easier to get your service configured the way you want it if you have only a single provider who understands that you are multiply connected.

Addresses

When your network is isolated from the outside world, you can use any addresses you choose. While it is advisable to use the addresses reserved for private use in RFC 1918, nothing will fail if you go against this advice. When you connect your network to the outside world, whether via a private link to another organization or a public link to the Internet, this all changes. IP addresses must be unique among a collection of interconnected IP networks. How you achieve uniqueness when you connect to the outside world depends on what kind of connection you are making.

In the case of a private link, you need only be sure that you and your neighbor are not using the same addresses. This kind of coordination is relatively easy when only two organizations are involved, but it can become difficult as more join in. A link to the Internet is different because all address assignments are centrally coordinated so that they remain unique throughout the world. You obtain these globally unique addresses from one of two sources.

Provider-Independent vs. Provider-Assigned Addresses

First, you can obtain a globally unique IP address from the central addressing authority for your region. There are central registries for Europe and the East Pacific (Asia and Australia), as well as the original registry in the United States.*
Addresses obtained directly from one of these organizations are known as *provider-independent* addresses. In theory, these addresses are portable as your organization moves from one service provider to another. In practice, however, the policies of the registries are strict enough about assigning these addresses that they are too

---

* Addresses and phone numbers for these registries can be found in Appendix D.

small to be of use to larger organizations, and may not be globally routed by some of the larger backbone providers.

The alternative to provider-independent addresses is *provider-assigned* addresses. These are addresses that are part of the address space assigned to your service provider. The advantages of letting your provider assign addresses are that you can often get far more address space from your provider than you could get from the central registries, and the address spaces held by the service providers are typically large enough that they are globally routable. The advantage to the Internet is that these addresses, because they come from a larger block held by your service provider, are more likely to aggregate into a single routing entry. This saves space in routers all over the Internet at a time when routing tables are dangerously large.

But provider-assigned addresses are not without their disadvantages. The biggest disadvantage shows up when your organization decides to switch service providers. Because the addresses you have been using are held by your former service provider, you may be forced to reassign addresses on all of your hosts. While protocols like DHCP and BOOTP can make the task easier, reassigning all your addresses is an undertaking that's worth avoiding. This is another reason to choose your service provider correctly the first time.

In the end, the competing interests of address portability and address routability must be weighed carefully. Selecting routable addresses (i.e., provider-assigned addresses) and implementing dynamic addressing protocols like DHCP and BOOTP puts your network in the best possible position to adapt.

Lest the thought of having to reassign addresses give you too much cause for concern, IP version 6 has mandated that all addresses will be *topologically assigned*, which is just a fancy way of saying that they will be provider-assigned. Because of this, work is proceeding rapidly on ways to assist organizations with their re-addressing efforts. Fortunately, work done to support IPv6 will probably be adaptable to IPv4.

Network Address Translators

One way to avoid re-addressing your network hosts each time you change Internet providers is to use private IP networks from RFC 1918 internally, and then install a device known as a *Network Address Translator (NAT)* between your network and your Internet connection. A NAT sits between an organization's network and the Internet, or between two organizations' networks, and translates IP addresses from private internal addresses to globally unique external addresses.

The idea behind a NAT is that few of your internal hosts are accessing the Internet at any given time, so they can share a small pool of dynamically allocated addresses. When a host needs to access the Internet, the NAT allocates an address for it. When packets from the host are sent to the Internet, the NAT replaces the internal address with this dynamically allocated external address. When packets come back for that address, the NAT reverses the substitution and replaces the external address with the corresponding internal address. When the host is done, the NAT releases the external address for use by another host. NATs are not without their problems, though. The biggest problem is that they can only replace addresses in the IP header and certain other well-known locations in the data portion of the packets. For example, in the FTP protocol, one machine tells the other the IP address and port on which it is listening for a data connection. This information must be corrected by the NAT or the file transfer will fail. A NAT can handle this situation for common protocols like FTP, but may not be able to handle newer protocols or protocols that aren't widely used.

Another problem with NATs is determining when a connection ends, so that the allocated IP address can be freed. For a TCP connection, this is relatively simple, since TCP has well-defined connection setup and tear-down stages. But UDP is a connectionless protocol, and a NAT cannot always determine what to do. Its only choice is to rely on inactivity as an indication that the connection has terminated, but this is inexact. Performance is yet another issue. IP has a header checksum that includes the source and destination addresses. The checksum must be updated when the addresses change; this isn't a problem in itself because every router needs to update the checksum when it updates other fields in the IP header. But TCP and UDP also define checksums that cover the packet's data and a pseudo-header that contains the source and destination IP addresses. When these addresses change, this checksum must also be updated. While the IP header checksum typically only has to cover 20 octets of header information, a TCP or UDP checksum covers all of the data in the packet. Recomputing this checksum requires a little more power. But if the connection being processed by the NAT is no more than a T1 line, achieving satisfactory performance may not be that difficult. You simply need to ensure that if you use a NAT, it will perform at a speed adequate to your needs.

The advantages of using a NAT for connecting to the Internet are substantial. First, you don't have to decide whether to use provider-assigned or provider-independent addresses for your internal network. You use private addresses for the internal network, and use provider-assigned addresses for the external address pool that the NAT controls. Since the chief disadvantage of using provider-assigned addresses is the hassle of renumbering your hosts, using a NAT simplifies this problem to updating the range of addresses it manages. This gives you the advantage of having your external addresses be part of a larger block that is more likely to be globally routed. Second, you can use an internal address space as large as you want. Most organizations today would be unable to get access to addresses for more than a few hundred or a thousand hosts. By using private addresses from RFC 1918, you can easily have addresses for several million hosts! This is far more than you would be able to get from either a registry or a provider. Finally, NAT technology gives an increased measure of security. Because your internal addresses are not available to the outside world, and because a host only has an externally accessible address when it is connecting to the outside through the NAT, it is more difficult for a would-be intruder to access your internal network machines. In a way, the NAT becomes a limited firewall.

NAT technology is fairly new, and may not be readily available in the performance or price you want. At this time, only a few commercial products exist, but more are likely to appear as address space becomes harder to obtain. By being aware of NAT technology, you can prepare your organization to take advantage of it as it becomes more widespread. As a result, your network will be more flexible and ready to adapt.

Address Assignment for External Links

One issue you should consider is whether to assign IP addresses to the endpoints of your external link. Many routers allow unnumbered point-to-point links, which saves you or your neighbor address space. However, there are a few disadvantages to unnumbered links that you should consider before using them. First, there is no safeguard against mixing up the cables of your unnumbered external links. Since the devices have no IP addresses associated with the serial interface hardware, a pair of unnumbered interfaces could be connected to the wrong cables, and thus to the wrong routers. Depending on how your routers are configured, you may not detect this problem until you disable the link that you *thought* was the right link, only to have some other link go down. Second, an unnumbered link won't let you ping the router interface of the remote router, since it has no IP address. This may not be a problem if you never have need to do so, but *ping* is a useful troubleshooting tool. While you may be able to ping some other interface of the remote router, you really don't know that your packets are traversing the unnumbered link that you are trying to test. They may be traveling on an alternate path in one direction or both. Finally, unnumbered links can present problems for your routing protocol. If your router vendor supports unnumbered links then their routing protocol implementations will as well, but it isn't necessarily so. The protocol you choose may not handle unnumbered links well, or using unnumbered links may complicate configuration.

One alternative to unnumbered links is dedicating a few subnets to links. These subnets should have masks resulting in two usable addresses. (I discussed this approach in Chapter 3, *Network Design—Part 2*.) This is exactly what you need for your point-to-point external or internal links, but unless you are running a classless IGP such as OSPF or EIGRP, you must be careful that you don't cause routing ambiguities by using subnet masks that vary from one part of your network to another. Another alternative is to use private network numbers from RFC 1918 for your point-to-point links. This works well if you and your neighbor are willing, and if there is no need to be able to reach the endpoints of the link itself from outside your network. Finally, you can waste some of your address space and use a full subnet for your external links. While this alternative may seem wasteful, if you have to use a classful IGP and choose not to use unnumbered IP interfaces, it may be your only option. Most organizations have relatively few external links, so they don't waste a significant part of their address space.

External Routing

In Chapter 6, *Routing Protocol Configuration*, which focused on interior gateway protocols (IGPs), we said that there was another class of dynamic routing protocols used for exterior routing. Why is there a difference between an IGP and an Exterior Gateway Protocol (EGP)? One of the reasons has to do with the detail of information handled. An IGP must deal with fine-grained details like host-specific routes and subnets. This detail is necessary so that routing within a traditional classful IP network can occur. But a typical organization has only one or two links to the outside world, so this detail can be summarized and removed from routing information propagated outside the network. Eliminating details helps keep routing tables smaller. Each router does not need to know about the internal subnet structure of remote networks. For this reason, an EGP typically does not deal with the same level of detail as an IGP, relying instead on aggregate information. By not dealing with the details of the internal structure of an organization's networks, an EGP can scale to a larger network than an IGP.

IGPs and EGPs also provide a different degree of control. Most IGPs are designed assuming a set of trusting routers administered by a common authority. In this model, information about routing flows freely through the network and is openly trusted. But this model breaks down when external links are involved. Now the routers are not administered by a common authority, and trust is not absolute. Using different protocols internally and externally breaks the trust structure between organizations. This break prevents erroneous information in one organization from spreading easily into another.

A third difference also results from the need to separate organizations from each other. This time, the issue is not trust, but scope: with whom do you have to coordinate any changes you make to a network? You don't want to contact your network neighbors or some central authority every time you want to add, move, or remove a network from your internal network. By aggregating information about your networks and keeping other organizations isolated from your IGP's activities, an EGP allows you the autonomy you need to manage your network efficiently.

Using an Interior Gateway Protocol for External Routing

All of this isn't to say that using an Interior Gateway Protocol is not possible. In fact, in some cases using an IGP is exactly the right idea. The catch is knowing when an IGP is most appropriate, and understanding the limits of the IGP you select. As an example, using an IGP to connect a large organization to the Internet is the wrong idea. Both networks need the isolation that an EGP will give them. But connecting two smaller organizations, or connecting a smaller organization to its parent, may not warrant the complexity of an EGP. In fact, the connection may be simple enough that static routing is a better choice, but sometimes static routing doesn't allow enough flexibility, just as it doesn't always meet the needs within a network.

One of the first things to consider when using an IGP to connect to another organization is whether to use the same IGP you use internally, or to use a different one. The advantages of using a different IGP from the one used in your network is that you achieve the same break of trust and establishment of scope that an EGP provides. For example, if you use OSPF on your internal networks, and RIP on an external link to your neighbor, you have a clear point of control over the level of detail and trust that passes between your internal network and your external link. This point is where you redistribute information between OSPF and RIP. The drawback of using a different IGP for your exterior links is that it may be almost as complex as using an EGP. You still have to run two routing protocols, both of which you must understand, and you need to control the flow of information between them. Simply extending your OSPF protocol processing to your neighbor's router is easier. Of course, if your neighbor is using a different IGP for his network, he may want to use his IGP for the external link for the same reasons. One of you will have to give in.

Whatever IGP you select for your external links, you need to understand its limitations. For example, RIP limits the *diameter* of your network—the distance between the two most-distant routers—to a maximum of 15 hops because 16 is used as the infinity value, and designates destinations that are unreachable. If your network has a diameter of 10, and your neighbor's network has a diameter of 11, using RIP between your networks probably won't work too well, since the combined diameter of your networks may be as high as 21 hops! While it is possible to work around these problems with metric reconstitution (setting the metric back to a lower value when a boundary is crossed), reconstitution can result in more complexity and problems. Using a different IGP is likely to work better.

If you elect to use the same IGP for your external and internal links, you will seldom have any special configuration issues to worry about. However, you may want to configure your IGP carefully to avoid problems in your neighbor's network from becoming problems in your network. At a minimum, you should ensure that your neighbor never tells you about routes in your own network. Even better, *only* accept routes from your neighbor that you expect to hear. Consider the configuration below. I am using RIP as the IGP, and I am also using RIP for communicating with my neighbor. I have carefully defined a list of the routes I expect from my neighbor, who is on `192.168.100.0/24` (I expect to hear routes to `10.0.0.0/8` and `192.168.101.0/255`), and will accept no other information from him. At the same time, I will accept any information that my own routers tell me.

```
router rip
 network 172.16.0.0
 network 172.17.0.0
 network 192.168.100.0
 distance 255
 distance 120 172.16.1.0      0.0.0.255
 distance 120 172.16.2.0      0.0.0.255
 distance 120 192.168.100.0 0.0.0.255 21
!
! define the networks I expect my neighbor to send to me
access-list 21 permit 10.0.0.0        0.255.255.255
access-list 21 permit 192.168.101.0 0.0.0.255
access-list 21 deny    0.0.0.0        255.255.255.255
```

I have made no effort to restrict what I tell my neighbor. While it is certainly possible for me to do so, it is not unreasonable to expect him to configure his routers to defend against information that he does not wish to hear. This may be especially important if other neighbors share the `192.168.100.0/24` network. Because of RIP's broadcast updates, it is not possible for me to tell these neighbors different things. They simply must filter out what they don't want.

If you choose a different IGP for your external and internal links, you will probably have to redistribute routing information from one IGP to the other, and possibly back. As in the previous example, it's best to accept only those routes that you expect to hear from your neighbor. Here's an example. This time I am running EIGRP internally, but my neighbor has requested that I use RIP for the external link because his routers do not speak EIGRP. My first task is to establish a link between my EIGRP and RIP routing processes so that I tell my neighbor about my networks. I also need to establish a link between RIP and EIGRP to tell my other routers about my neighbor's networks. I also define a default metric for each of my routing protocols. Since I am not running RIP internally, but only as a pseudo-EGP with my neighbor, it is easier to use these defaults rather than to select an appropriate metric for each router. Presumably, my neighbor only hears my routes from me, and I only hear my neighbor's from my neighbor.

```
router eigrp 71
 network 172.16.0.0
 network 172.17.0.0
 redistribute rip
 default-metric 10000 250 100 1 1500
 !
router rip
 network 192.168.100.0
 redistribute eigrp 71
 default-metric 1
 ! use access list 21 to restrict what my neighbor tells me
 distribute-list 21 in
 ! use access list 22 to restrict what I tell my neighbor
 distribute-list 22 out eigrp 71
 !
 ! define the routes I will accept from my neighbor
 access-list 21 permit 10.0.0.0      0.255.255.255
 access-list 21 permit 192.168.101.0 0.0.0.255
 access-list 21 deny   0.0.0.0       255.255.255.255
 !
 ! invert access list 21 so that I tell my neighbor about everything
 ! except his routes (avoid feedback loops)
 access-list 22 deny   10.0.0.0      0.255.255.255
 access-list 22 deny   192.168.101.0 0.0.0.255
 access-list 22 permit 0.0.0.0       255.255.255.255
```

If I stop with simply redistributing RIP routes into my EIGRP process, and redistributing my EIGRP routes into my RIP process, I have two problems. First, I run the risk that my neighbor will send me anything at all, which my router will believe and spread throughout my network. Second, I can get routes redistributed from my EIGRP process into RIP, which then redistributes them back into EIGRP. This kind of feedback loop should be avoided. In the example, I have solved both problems using access lists. Access list 21 filters the inbound RIP updates from my neighbor to ensure that they only contain his two networks, and nothing else. I also configured my RIP process to filter my EIGRP routes with access list 22, which simply inverts list 21. Filtering the outgoing routes ensures that my neighbor's routes are not among them, preventing a feedback loop. Alternatively, I could have explicitly listed what I wanted to advertise to my neighbor in access list 22. Which you choose may depend on which is easier to maintain.

Exterior Gateway Protocols

EGPs provide a breaking point between the information carried by the connecting organizations' IGPs. They also summarize information about internal networks so that the details are hidden from other organizations. Unfortunately, they tend to be more complex than IGPs primarily because of the scale they must handle.

Where a typical IGP might handle a network with a hundred routers and a few thousand networks, a typical EGP is designed to handle networks with thousands of routers and tens or hundreds of thousands of network segments. As an example of the difference in scale, my network consists of twenty routers connecting almost 300 network segments. This is easily handled by RIP or OSPF. But the full Internet routing table currently contains over 45,000* routes handled by a few thousand routers. For this purpose, RIP would fail outright, and OSPF would have to be carefully managed, if it even worked.

Autonomous systems

The two most common EGPs, the *Exterior Gateway Protocol (EGP)* and the *Border Gateway Protocol (BGP)*, employ the concept of the *Autonomous System*. An Autonomous System is a group of networks and routers under a common administrative authority. Typically, this would be the networks of a single organization, but it may be a group of cooperating organizations, or it may be an autonomous subset of an organization, such as a subsidiary. While this definition seems vague, the realities are that the boundaries of an autonomous system are well defined and strict. A given network or router belongs to *exactly one* autonomous system.

Regardless of what constitutes an autonomous system, from the EGP's point of view, the interior of an autonomous system is hidden. These details are presumed to be handled by one or more IGPs; the EGP assumes that a packet addressed to a network inside the autonomous system can be delivered to any router in the autonomous system. It is the autonomous system's responsibility to ensure that the packet is delivered.

Because a router participating in an EGP must be able to determine what autonomous system it is in, as well as the autonomous systems of its neighbors, each autonomous system is assigned a unique 16-bit number. These autonomous system (AS) numbers are assigned by the same central authority that assigns IP network numbers. If you need an AS number, you should work with your ISP to obtain one. They should have current information for your region, and can assist you in filling out the request form.

The Exterior Gateway Protocol (EGP)

The original EGP was simply called the *Exterior Gateway Protocol* or *EGP*. At the time, there was only one with clear meaning. Today there are several EGPs, and confusion arises about whether EGP refers to the general class of protocols or to

---

* This number keeps growing at a phenomenal rate. Between the time I wrote this paragraph and a subsequent review several months later, this number jumped by 20,000 routes. By the time this book is published, the number will again be out of date.

the specific protocol. In the discussion that follows, I use EGP to refer to the specific protocol unless otherwise clearly indicated.

EGP originally was defined as the protocol that an autonomous system used to communicate its network routes to the ARPANet core routers. These core routers provided the backbone of the original Internet. Among themselves, they spoke the *Gateway to Gateway Protocol (GGP)*. Because the core gateways were under a common administrative authority, they formed an autonomous system.

EGP is no longer in common use, and should be avoided if at all possible. It has many limitations that prevent it from scaling to the size and complexity of today's Internet. It should only be used if you find yourself connecting to an organization that cannot use a more modern protocol. (If you're considering an Internet connection through an ISP that would force you to run EGP, do some more shopping.) Although I won't present examples using EGP, it is worth understanding some of EGP's shortcomings and why newer protocols were needed. One of EGP's more severe limitations is the way it exchanged routing information. The protocol requires that each router send a *hello* message to each of its neighbors every 30 seconds. This message serves only as a keep-alive to ensure that routers detect when their neighbors go away. The hello message in itself wasn't a problem. However, EGP also requires the router to send its routing table to each neighbor every two minutes (120 seconds). When the size of the Internet routing tables was only a thousand routes or so, this wasn't an issue. These days, with routing tables exceeding 45,000 routes, it's a problem for a router to process an update from a single neighbor before the next update arrives two minutes later!*

To make matters worse, EGP runs directly on top of IP, not on top of any transport protocol. Because each update is a single IP packet, an update can contain at most 65,536 octets of information. While this limits the number of routes that can thus be handled, a more severe limitation comes from what happens to this giant packet. Packets are subject to fragmentation according to the requirements of the lower-level protocols. On an Ethernet segment, a 65,536 octet packet would be split into more than 40 separate packets. If even one is lost, the entire message is lost because packet reassembly is not possible, and the entire message must be resent.

The remaining problem is that EGP was designed when there was only a single Internet backbone network, and all autonomous systems connected directly to the backbone. As such, it was not designed to handle today's multi-backbone Internet.

---

* I ran into this problem when the Internet routing table exceeded approximately 5,000 routes. The router speaking EGP with the Internet was unable to process the request in less than the two-minute interval to the next request. A temporary fix was to put in an intermediary that worked until about 8,000 routes, by which time the routing protocol could be changed to BGP, which does not have this problem.

EGP forbids an autonomous system from advertising routes on behalf of another autonomous system, except in the case of the one (and only) backbone autonomous system If you consider that this is exactly what the backbones of today's Internet must do for each other, you will see why EGP is not heavily used anymore.

The Border Gateway Protocol (BGP)

In response to the various faults and limitations of EGP, the Internet research community developed a new exterior gateway protocol called the *Border Gateway Protocol (BGP)*. BGP fixes EGP's problems and allows the protocol to scale to a much larger network. For example, to fix the problem of processing time for EGP updates, BGP exchanges the full routing table only at initialization; afterwards, it simply exchanges information about what has changed in each update. To fix the problem of IP fragmentation, BGP uses a TCP connection, which guarantees in-order delivery without loss or duplication.

But these are largely mechanical changes that could have easily been adapted for use in EGP. One of the biggest changes in BGP was eliminating the concept of the Internet core. Because it was designed for use in a multi-backbone, multi-provider Internet, its designers decided to make BGP flexible enough to handle an arbitrary topology complete with multiple paths between destinations. It does this by maintaining a list of the autonomous systems that a route traverses. This allows routers to detect loops in the BGP routing structure (the same AS number appears twice), to compare two different BGP routes for which is shorter (the shorter AS path is preferred), and even to apply policy filtering to prevent traffic from traversing a distant autonomous system (reject all routes containing a given AS number in the AS path).

Finally, BGP version 4 (BGP4) handles Classless Interdomain Routing (CIDR). CIDR states that the old IP network classes are no longer necessary. Instead, network numbers are specified in terms of a base network number (a prefix) and a mask of contiguous bits. BGP carries exactly this information and makes no assumptions about the size of a network based on its class. As such, this means that a network like `172.16.0.0`, in the traditional class B space, must carry its mask with it. Support for CIDR enables the Internet to continue growing in the face of the imminent exhaustion of the IP address space and the explosive growth of the Internet routing tables. Without CIDR, the Internet backbone routers would have long since ceased to be able to keep up.

BGP is far more flexible than EGP. Unfortunately, when a protocol becomes more flexible, it also becomes more complex. BGP is no exception, but if the vendor provides reasonable defaults, you may find that most of the complexity goes away. We will present examples of some common BGP configurations, but a full discussion of all that is possible would be a book in itself.

The basic BGP configuration for a Cisco router with one local network and one neighbor is shown below. It is not really any more complex than the basic IGP configurations presented in Chapter 6. We have a `router` statement that starts a BGP routing process. The number on the `router bgp` statement is the router's autonomous system number. You *cannot* select an arbitrary number—as you did for the OSPF and EIGRP process numbers. Following the `router` statement are one or more `network` statements. But where the `network` statements for IGPs like EIGRP specified what networks would participate in the IGP, BGP's `network` statement specifies networks that BGP considers local to the autonomous system, and so will originate to its partners in the BGP exchange. Finally, we must tell the BGP process who its neighbors are, using a `neighbor` statement. The minimum that BGP needs to know is what autonomous system each neighbor belongs to.

```
! our AS number is 101, our provider's is 102
router bgp 101
 network 172.16.0.0
 neighbor 192.168.1.1 remote-as 102
```

I said that BGP4 (the most common version) can handle classless network routes. Notice, though, that I did not specify a mask on the `network` statement. If you don't specify a mask, the IOS assumes that you mean the natural mask for the old-style classful networks. This may be exactly what you want, and can be a nice shorthand in those cases. But if you need to specify a classless network, you must append the mask to the `network` statement:

```
network 192.168.2.0 mask 255.255.254.0
```

This specifies that the supernet `192.168.2.0/23` is to be included in BGP updates. It does not mean that BGP will aggregate the two networks `192.168.2.0/24` and `192.168.3.0/24` automatically. It only means that if your IGP carries the supernet route, BGP will send it out as well. To get automatic summarization, you need to use a more complex configuration:

```
! our AS number is 101, our provider's is 102
router bgp 101
 network 172.16.0.0
 aggregate-address 192.168.2.0 255.255.254.0    summary-only
 neighbor 192.168.1.1 remote-as 102
 redistribute rip route-map aggregate
!
! set the origin of any route matching access list 41 to IGP
route-map aggregate
 match ip address 41
 set origin igp
!
! select the component routes of 192.168.2.0/23 for aggregation
access-list 41 permit 192.168.2.0 0.0.1.255
```

With this configuration, BGP advertises `172.16.0.0/16` whenever it, or one of its subnets, appears in the router's main routing table. Additionally, when either or both of `192.168.2.0/24` and `192.168.3.0/24` appears in the router's table, BGP includes an advertisement for the CIDR aggregate `192.168.2.0/23`, and suppresses the advertisement of the two more specific routes. This is the job of the `summary-only` clause.

The `redistribute` statement, `route-map`, and `access-list` are all needed to get the routes for the two networks redistributed from your IGP (RIP in this example) to BGP. If you simply used a `network` statement for them, or for the aggregate, BGP would advertise exactly what was in the `network` statements without regard to the aggregate.* Of course, if your IGP handled classless routes and carried a route for `192.168.2.0/23`, none of this complexity would be necessary. Alternatively, you could also handle this with a static route to your router's null interface:

```
! our AS number is 101, our provider's is 102
router bgp 101
 network 172.16.0.0
 network 192.168.2.0 255.255.254.0
 neighbor 192.168.1.1 remote-as 102
 !
! create a nailed-up static route for 192.168.2.0/23
ip route 192.168.2.0 255.255.254.0 null0
```

This configuration allows your classful IGP to carry the aggregate's component routes, while allowing BGP to advertise the aggregate route instead. The only drawback to this approach is that your router will always advertise this *nailed-up* route, even if it has no information from your IGP about any of the component networks. While this is good for the Internet, since it reduces route flapping, it may not be what you need if you have multiple links to the outside world.

As you can see, BGP configurations that are more than plain vanilla can quickly become extremely complex. A good way to solve your specific configuration problem is to look over others' configurations and ask lots of questions before trying to do anything too odd. A pair of test routers can be invaluable in helping you get your configuration right before foisting it on the world. Set up one of the routers with a basic configuration, and then try your more complex BGP configuration on the other. By looking at both routers' BGP and routing tables, you can get a good idea of what effect your complex configuration attempts are having without disrupting your production network. However, complex configurations are not always necessary. If you were to configure a BGP process with multiple

---

* I learned this when I configured my first aggregate advertisement in late 1994. I couldn't get it quite right, and finally asked the author of Cisco's code what I was doing wrong, and he explained how this all worked. Sometimes it still amazes me what power email can give a user!

neighbors, some in the same autonomous system, and some in different autonomous systems, BGP will figure out which routers need to hear about which other routes with no special configuration.

Okay, so your IGP is carrying your internal routes to your border router, which is sending them out to the Internet (or your neighbor) using BGP. What about the other direction? How do you tell your internal routers about the paths that BGP has learned? If you simply redistribute your BGP routes into your IGP, you may overrun its ability to function, and you will certainly lose information if your IGP is classful. In these cases, you either need to filter the information you redistribute into your IGP, exactly as you would between two IGPs, or you need to generate a default route and inject *that* into your IGP instead. Which is the right course depends on whether your border router is your only path to the outside world, or just one of many. If it is the only one, a default route makes the most sense—all traffic must go to it anyway. If you do decide to redistribute all or part of your BGP routes into your IGP, be careful not to introduce a feedback loop when you later redistribute your IGP back into BGP.

There are a couple of ways to generate a default route to your IGP. One is to define a static default route that points to your null interface, and then redistribute it into your IGP. This route will not be used by the border router itself, but it will convince your other routers to send all externally bound traffic to the border router. The only drawback here is that your border router will advertise this default route even if its link to the outside world is unavailable. Packets bound for the outside world will always be sent to the border router, even if the connection to the outside world is down and the router just throws the packets away. If this is not acceptable, you can add commands to your configuration to make the default route a little more dynamic. Select a route that, when present, indicates that your BGP session is up and running. This route is probably one belonging to your network provider that is near to your site. A good example might be the network used on the WAN line, or the provider's backbone network. In my examples, I'll assume that this is network 10.0.0.0/8, which, while private now, used to be the ARPANet backbone network. If you add the command:

```
ip default-network 10.0.0.0
```

your router will generate a default route whenever this network appears in its routing tables. If the network is directly attached, the router will always generate the default route, unless the interface goes down. Choose your candidate network carefully. Since you are depending on something outside of your control, you need to ensure that the network won't disappear without warning, leaving you without a default route in your IGP. To guard against this, you can include multiple ip default-network statements referencing different networks. Furthermore, this generated default route will be used by your border router. If you don't want this, you either need to redistribute the candidate network into your IGP and use `ip default-network` statements on your internal routers, or you need to use the static null route described previously.

Finally, you may need to filter the routes that you learn from one or more of your BGP neighbors. You can filter the inbound updates on a network-by-network basis as I described for an IGP, but if your goal is to ensure that you do not use any routes that traverse a specific autonomous system, filtering by networks won't achieve your goal. For example, let's assume that you want to filter all paths that traverse your competitor's network to ensure he cannot spy on your communications, but you don't want to filter the routes that lead to his networks; you still may want to communicate with him.* You need to remove routes from consideration based on the AS path that BGP carries with the route. This AS path is a list of the autonomous systems that would be traversed when using this route. By carefully specifying the set of AS paths that you wish to filter, you can eliminate routes that would use certain paths. In this example, you want to remove all routes that traverse your competitor's networks, but not the routes leading to his network. Let's assume that his autonomous system number is 777. The AS paths that you want to filter from updates that your router hears would then be all AS paths with `777` in the middle of the path, but not those ending with `777`. It shouldn't be any surprise that, if you're using a Cisco router, you implement this restriction with an access list. Other vendors may have similar provisions; check your documentation. Here's a fairly simple filter for a Cisco router:

```
! our AS number is 101, our provider's is 102, and our competitor's is
! 777
router bgp 101
 network 172.16.0.0
 neighbor 192.168.1.1 remote-as 102
 neighbor 192.168.1.1 filter-list 61 in
!
! define an AS path access list that blocks routes traversing our
! competitor's AS, but not those originating there
ip as-path access-list 61 permit _777$
ip as-path access-list 61 deny   _777_
ip as-path access-list 61 permit .*
```

I have applied AS path access list 61, defined by the `ip as-path` statements, to the routing updates coming from my provider by using a `neighbor` statement that specifies an inbound `filter-list`. Any route from my provider with an AS path that contains autonomous system 777 in the middle, but not at the end, will

---

* Then again, *maybe* you do. After all, as we will see in Chapter 10, *Network Security*, malicious or careless employees leaking information out of your organization is a potential threat. Still, filtering out their routes *might* be a bit extreme.

fail to pass access list 61 and will not be processed.* Had I wished to eliminate routes for networks *in* autonomous system 777, rather than just those that traverse it, I would simply omit the first `ip as-path` statement, which matches all routes that *originate* in AS 777. These should be the networks belonging to your competitor. But if there are no alternate paths to these filtered networks, you will be unable to reach them at all. For this reason, you usually don't want to use AS path filters unless you have multiple neighbors. In that case, you could conceivably apply filters to your neighbors in various combinations to ensure that certain paths were used through certain neighbors, and others through other neighbors.

Filtering by AS path is fine if you want to have the filter apply to an entire autonomous system. But sometimes, you need to filter updates from your neighbors on a network-by-network basis. One situation in which you might want to filter what you hear from your neighbors by network is when you are dealing with one of your customers, if you are a network provider. In this case, it is just plain smart to ensure that no matter how badly they muck up their configuration, they can only tell you the routes that you expect to hear from them. In Chapter 6 we talked about doing this in your IGP; the same applies to your exterior protocol, and it can be much more important there since the damage done may be more widespread. To configure network-by-network filtering with your BGP neighbors, create an access list that describes the networks you expect to hear, and then apply them to your `neighbor` statements using the `distribute-list` in clause. A corresponding `distribute-list` out clause exists to let you be explicit about what you send to your neighbors. Its syntax is the same as for inbound filtering, so I won't present an example.

```
! our AS number is 101, our customer's is 102
router bgp 101
 network 172.16.0.0
 neighbor 192.168.1.1 remote-as 102
 neighbor 192.168.1.1 distribute-list 97 in
!
! define the list of routes we expect to hear from our customer
access-list 97 permit 192.168.2.0 255.255.254.0
access-list 97 permit 192.168.4.0 255.255.255.0
access-list 97 deny   0.0.0.0       0.0.0.0
```

---

* Cisco's AS path syntax is a bit cryptic. Remember that it is a pattern matching syntax based on UNIX regular expressions. You don't need to be a regular expression guru to understand it if you keep a few key ideas in mind. First, a "$" matches the end of the path, and a "^" matches the beginning of the path. Since an AS path describes the path from your network to a destination network, that means that your AS number (or your provider's) will normally be at the start of any path you see, and the destination AS number at the end. Second, a "." matches any one thing, and a "*" means "zero or more times." This means that the two-character sequence ".*" matches anything, or nothing, as appropriate. Finally, an "_" matches any break between two AS numbers, or between an AS number and the beginning *or* end of the path. Simple, right?

In this example, I defined access list 97 to allow the routes that my agreement with my customer states I will accept. In this case, I allow the two routes `192.168.2.0/23` and `192.168.4.0/24`. The final deny clause is not necessary, since an access list implicitly denies anything it doesn't permit, but I included it for clarity. With this configuration, no matter how badly my customer messes up his configuration, my router will ignore anything he tells me, other than these two routes. In contrast, had I used AS path filtering, my customer could have cheated by advertising some routes that used a different AS path that he manufactured on his router to bypass my filter list. Whether this was intentional or accidental doesn't matter, my router would still accept them as valid.

As a final example, let's assume that you are connected to two providers and want to use the shortest path to the destination for most cases. This is the normal behavior without any filtering. However, you also want to make sure that the traffic to your friend's networks always uses provider A, even if provider B has a better route, unless provider A's link is down. This means that you do not want to filter your friend's routes from provider B's updates, you just want to prefer those from A. Finally, you want to ensure that your providers do not inadvertently use your network for transit to each other. In other words, you want to ensure that routes learned from provider A are not advertised to provider B, and vice versa.

```
! our AS number is 101, provider A's is 102, provider B's is 103, and
! our friend's is 777
router bgp 101
 network 172.16.0.0
 neighbor 172.16.1.1 remote-as 102     ! provider A
 neighbor 172.16.1.1 filter-list 81 weight 100
 neighbor 172.16.1.1 filter-list 82 out
 neighbor 172.16.2.7 remote-as 103     ! provider B
 neighbor 172.16.2.7 filter-list 83 out
 !
 ! define an AS path access-list that selects our friend's routes
 ip as-path access-list 81 permit _777$
 !
 ! define an AS path access-list that blocks provider B's routes
 ip as-path access-list 82 deny    ^103_    ! B's routes
 ip as-path access-list 82 permit .*
 !
 ! define an AS path access-list that blocks provider A's routes
 ip as-path access-list 83 deny    ^102_    ! A's routes
 ip as-path access-list 83 permit .*
```

Parts of this configuration should be familiar. Your AS number is 101, there is one local network to advertise to your providers, and two neighbors, one for each provider. But we also have a set of three filters for AS paths. Filter lists 82 and 83 simply define the routes that each of our neighbors sent us. Those from neighbor A will have A's AS number (102) first in the AS path. Similarly, those from neighbor B will have B's AS number (103) first in the AS path. By blocking these routes from being sent to the other provider, we avoid being a transit connection between them. To achieve this, we apply these filters to the outbound announcements to each neighbor using `filter-list` clauses. Of course, they should be filtering what we send them, but it is still better to be safe.

Filter list 81 defines any network that originated in our friend's AS, AS 777. Since these are presumably his networks, we want to give them an administrative weight of 100 when they arrive from provider A. Since the default weight for BGP paths learned from outside is 0, and higher weights are preferred, we will prefer any path to our friend through provider A, so long as there is one, even if B's path is shorter. Notice that we didn't filter these routes out of B's updates to us. If we had, then when the path through provider A went down, we would not be able to reach our friend at all.

As you can see, the options are nearly endless. Each BGP configuration is unique in some way, and there really is no *typical* BGP configuration. The best way to figure out how to achieve a particular goal is to talk with people more experienced than you, look over lots of configurations, and then experiment. If you are working with an Internet provider, the provider should be able to give the help you need.

Impact On Other Public and Private Links

There is one final aspect of configuring external routing that you must consider carefully. If you have multiple external links, whether public or private, each new external link may have an impact on the configuration you have in place for the others. For example, if you have a public link to the Internet, and have configured it to redistribute the contents of your IGP without filtering, what happens when you add a private link to a neighboring organization and redistribute their routes into your IGP? You may inadvertently be providing transit service for your neighbor to the Internet. This may violate your service agreement; it may also cause your neighbor routing problems or unnecessarily congest your own link. This is one of the strongest reasons for explicitly configuring the exchanges between your routing protocols to include only that information that should be there. If your Internet connection is configured to redistribute only your own networks from your IGP to your EGP, then the redistribution of routes from your private link into your IGP would have no impact; they would be filtered out. Likewise, configuring your private link with appropriate route filters prevents a new neighbor or public link from adversely impacting it.

Of course, there is nothing you can do to require your neighbors to adhere to the same policies, unless you have authority over them. All you can do is work with them to make sure that appropriate safeguards are in effect, so that your routes do not get propagated to their neighbors, and then watch carefully. If your routes do leak to the outside world through your neighbor, you might find that inbound traffic to your site could prefer your low-speed line to your neighbor over your nice new T1 line to the Internet. In cases like these, be prepared to sever communications with your neighbor until things can be resolved.

Finally, don't assume that just because you and your neighbors have it right at present that it won't be wrong later. Mistakes happen, personnel change, and networks grow. What may have been correct last week may not be correct this week when you or your neighbor add links, change providers, or upgrade routers. Be constantly on the lookout for routing problems with your external peers.

Permanent or On-Demand?

Many people assume that there is only one way to establish an external, long-lived connection with a neighboring organization or the Internet. They immediately assume that a permanent leased line is the right answer for all cases. While it is true that this is probably the most common external connection type, it is certainly not the only option. Before you skip this question and assume that a permanent service is right for your organization, do a little homework and consider the tradeoffs involved in permanent vs. dial-on-demand service. Dial-on-demand service may be ISDN, and does not always imply analog modems.

Whether you choose to use a permanent or dial-on-demand service to establish your external links will in part depend on what is available to you. If you are connecting to the Internet and your service provider does not support dial-on-demand, you may be forced to use a permanent connection. You may also have to deal with what your local telephone company can provide, or what your private link neighbor wishes to use.

One of the advantages of a dial-on-demand link is cost. Typically, a dial-on-demand service will cost less than a permanent connection with the same bandwidth, provided your access to the link is not sufficient to keep it connected all the time. If you do tend to keep the connection up most of the time, dial-on-demand service will probably cost as much or more than the permanent line. You need to consider this carefully. If you are setting up an Internet link, you should understand what your service provider will do if he receives traffic for your site when the connection is down. Some will dial the connection, possibly with an automated callback so that you pay any call charges, but most will refuse to establish the connection and drop the traffic. If you expect otherwise, be sure that is what you are getting.

Permanent services typically have the advantages of speed and simplicity. Often, the fastest dial-on-demand service you can find is 64 kbps or 128 kbps.

Permanent connections typically start at 56 kbps and can easily go as fast as 45 Mbps, four and a half times faster than an Ethernet in each direction! In some locations, you can even obtain faster service, such as 155 Mbps. It all depends on where you are, and where you need to go. However, some forms of dial-on-demand service let you place additional calls to the same destination when your bandwidth needs go up, and then disconnect the calls when bandwidth drops. This could be advantageous if your traffic needs exhibit short, high-bandwidth periods separated by longer periods of lower traffic rates.

A permanent connection has other clear advantages. Permanent connections are simple because you don't have to worry about setting up rules for when you connect, how long you stay connected when idle, and how soon after disconnecting you attempt to reconnect. In addition, packets in transit don't have to wait while the connection is being established. Still, the cost may be beyond the means of a small organization. One option that is gaining popularity is to maintain a lower-bandwidth leased line, and also to obtain dial-on-demand service to the same endpoint. The dial-on-demand service can provide a backup link or additional bandwidth at a relatively low cost. Creatively examining your options can result in significant cost and performance savings.

If you opt to use a dial-on-demand service, take extra care with the configuration of your routing protocol. Many people have discovered the hard way that their dial-on-demand links were being kept connected exclusively to allow their dynamic routing protocol to operate. This is wasteful and expensive. While your router vendor may provide fancier options, one solution that always works is to use static routing across the dial-on-demand link. For example, if your dial-on-demand link is to the Internet, then you would have your provider maintain static routes for each of your networks on his end, and advertise them to the Internet on your behalf, while you would maintain a static default route on your end. In this configuration, any traffic deemed interesting between you and the Internet will cause the link to come up, the traffic will flow, and then the link will close down. Besides reducing your connect time, it also reduces instability of your routes in the Internet. This is very important because each route assertion or withdrawal can cause routers all over the Internet to spend a fair amount of time dealing with the change.

Whether you are connecting to the Internet or to another organization, and whether it is a permanent connection or on-demand, any connection to the world outside your network should be carefully thought out, planned, and executed. After all, if the network is a living organism, then the impact of an external link should be given at least as much consideration as a new internal link. This is especially true for security, one of the greatest pitfalls of any external network connection. This is the topic of the next chapter.

10

Network Security

When discussing computer networks, the topic most likely to generate disagreement and confusion is network security. Some claim that it is the network's responsibility to provide as secure an environment for a host system as it had before it connected to the network. Others laugh at this and claim that the network has no business being involved in security at all. Most are somewhere in between. Regardless of your opinion, you are bound to feel a fair amount of trepidation and confusion whenever you think about the security of your network and the hosts on it. Even if you believe that the network has no responsibility for security, it is unlikely that you claim that your network-connected hosts are as secure as they should be.

This chapter discusses several network security topics, including some ways that the network can assist hosts to be more secure, as well as defend itself against attack. It may not answer all your questions, but it should give you a good start.

What Is Security?

If you ask a group of networking experts what security means, you will probably get as many answers as there are people in your group. Most will focus on some aspect of preventing unauthorized access to your network or hosts, but few will give you an inclusive, balanced answer, and all will certainly have differing opinions.

Security is not an absolute. It is a matter of degrees. It is not correct to say that a given machine or network is secure and that another is not. Rather, we should talk about how secure a machine or network is relative to some perceived threat. The higher the perceived threat, the more secure a machine needs to be made. But as is the case with most topics in computing, security has its tradeoffs. Consider the security of a host or network as a spectrum. On one end, label the scale *secure*, and on the other, label it *usable*. As we move a machine or network toward a more secure state, it usually becomes less usable. As we make it more usable, it becomes less secure.

If you doubt this, consider carefully the extremes. What is the most secure machine in any environment? The answer is the machine that is never turned on and is locked in a room with an armed guard. This machine is certainly quite secure. No malicious act can be performed against it without extreme effort. However, the machine is not very usable. On the other extreme is the machine that is out in the open and has no password protection. Any person can walk up to it and make it do anything they want without restriction. Most people would find this machine especially usable, but it has little or no security. Similar examples can be made for networks; secure networks are harder to use, while usable networks don't have the restrictions that make them secure. With this spectrum in mind, you must ask how much security you are willing to trade off against usability. The more usable you make your network, the less secure it is likely to become. On the other hand, the more secure you make it, the harder it will be for your users to get legitimate work done.

Aspects of Security

Security, as it applies to computer networks, means different things to different people. Most of the time, security means controlling access to machines and resources within the network. For example, people worry about unauthorized users breaking into their machines. This is one aspect of security that is heavily affected by external links in your network, but it is by no means the only aspect you should explore.

A second aspect of security, and one that is often overlooked, is data security. You need to consider how important it is to prevent eavesdropping. Unfortunately, preventing all eavesdropping is often an impossible goal. On an Ethernet segment, or any multi-access broadcast network, it is difficult or impossible to tell that a machine is attached to the network illicitly, or if the attachment is authorized, to detect it snooping on other conversations. But there are things you can do to limit the extent of eavesdropping and the effect that eavesdropping has on data security.

Data integrity is a third aspect of network security. What proof do you have that the data sent are the same as the data received? Network protocols guard against accidental changes caused by failing hardware or other events, but there is no such safeguard for the data while it is temporarily stored on some intermediate host, such as an email message on a mail server. And even if the data is not changed, how do we ensure that the sender really sent it, and that the message isn't a clever forgery? Forging email is trivial; most junior high school students could master it in an hour, yet we all blindly assume that the email we receive from Mary really came from Mary.

A final aspect of network security has nothing to do with preventing illegitimate access to either the systems on the network nor the data traversing it. Instead, it has to do with using the network to deny service to legitimate users of the network and its connected systems. Denial of service attacks, while possible on isolated systems, become relatively easy when a machine is connected to a network. They are also relatively effective. Unfortunately, they are becoming increasingly popular because they are easy and effective, and because it can be difficult to trace the attack to its source.

Each aspect of security must be handled in its own way, keeping the others in mind. Security is a holistic practice, and not something that can be done piecemeal. The methods you use to prevent unauthorized access are not going to do much about your eavesdropping problem, nor will dealing with your eavesdroppers do much to prevent unauthorized access. However, working together, measures designed to address each aspect can help the others. For example, some of the most sensitive data on your network are users' passwords. By preventing an eavesdropper from collecting this information, you reduce opportunity for unauthorized access. Likewise, since eavesdropping requires access to a network segment, preventing unauthorized access to machines on your network will help to contain eavesdroppers. In the next few sections, I will discuss some of the things you can do to deal with each of these aspects of security.

Assessing Your Security Needs

Before taking steps to deal with security problems, you should first assess what your security needs really are. Most computer and network administrators never stop to think about this. They immediately start hacking security into their networks without stopping to figure out what is most needed. While an in depth security assessment may be beyond your skills or responsibilities, even a cursory assessment will point out the areas that need most attention. For example, if your organization is involved in banking or finance, confidentiality of customer data may be the most important security concern. This isn't to say that access controls aren't important. We're discussing *relative* importance rather than absolutes. A public university, on the other hand, probably cares less about someone snooping financial records because they are likely to be public record by law. But preventing a student from changing his grades, or obtaining access to a copy of a final exam in advance, would be a top priority. We're looking at the broad picture, not the details.

Once you have decided what the most serious security concerns are in your network, you need to assess realistically the impact of a security breach in each area. In some cases, the result may be little more than an annoyance; in others, a breach could mean the end of the organization. The operative word here, however, is *realistic*. Don't declare a potential threat non-catastrophic because it is hard to address. Likewise, don't get fixated on a mere annoyance that may cost you a lot of time, and perhaps some sleep, and declare it a catastrophe in the making. For example, concern about sensitive data on machines in the administrative data center at a university led to installing an ad hoc firewall to shield these machines from intrusion from the campus network. However, no effort was made to address the security of that data as it traveled through the campus network to its legitimate users. Likewise, the security measures put in place were poorly thought out and had little real effect, other than to convince a few overly cautious people that their data was secure when, in fact, it wasn't.

Finally, for each type of security lapse that you consider, estimate how likely you think such a security lapse could be. In many ways, this process is much like assessing the cost and likelihood of failure scenarios in your network design (See Chapter 3, *Network Design—Part 2*). This time, however, you are assessing the likelihood of human action rather than equipment failure, so your estimates are much more subjective in nature. Once you have an idea of the relative costs and probabilities of security violations, you are better prepared to focus your attention and resources on preventing any lapses, or dealing with the lapses that do occur. You want to expend more effort on the most likely or costly problems before you worry too much about the least likely or least expensive ones.

Controlling Access

Controlling access to the network and its resources is the first, and often only, security concern that most network and host administrators are concerned with. The cause may be that they can easily envision the goals they are trying to achieve, or the publicity that surrounds break-in attempts, or simply that they equate access control with parallels in the non-computer world. It is usually easy to sell management on the need for access control. You can easily draw parallels between keeping an unwelcome visitor from entering your computers and keeping them from entering your home. Few people have trouble accepting this as a necessity. But it often gets undue attention when you consider the larger picture. We keep people from entering our homes not simply to keep them from being there, but because of what they do, or may do, once they are inside. We are concerned about our possessions, our privacy, and even our lives.

With a computer intruder, we don't have the same concerns. Someone who invades our computer or network is unlikely to endanger our lives, and while the intruder may endanger the safety of our data, he or she probably can't physically steal our memory, disks, keyboards, or other computer components simply by accessing them. While data theft is a real concern, most computer break-ins aren't attempts to steal data, or even to steal software. Intruders are usually trying to prove they can do it (thrill seeking), or to be destructive. With this in mind, the truth is that most of the concern about unwelcome visitors to our computers and networks is not what they might do while they are there, but rather the simple fact that they are there without our permission. While this is a valid justification for keeping them out, and there is the real threat of damage to data and privacy, a little perspective on the situation can help keep computer and network administrators from blowing the threat out of proportion. Be diligent, but realistic.

Firewalls

If you surveyed ten network administrators about how to prevent unauthorized access to hosts and other network resources, every one of them would immediately mention installing firewalls. So what is a firewall? The idea draws on the concept of putting a barrier between something dangerous, a powerful machine for example, and something to be protected, such as an office. As it applies to networking, a firewall is a device placed between the dangerous outside world and an internal network. This device follows a set of rules to determine what is and is not allowed to cross from the outside to the inside, and from the inside to the outside.

Partially because firewalls are so popular, it's easy to forget that they have disadvantages. The biggest is that a firewall is often a bottleneck. While this may be acceptable if the security needs warrant the loss in performance, it may be more than you are willing to allow. Examining every single packet before passing it in either direction requires a fairly hefty processor. While a router must do a similar examination, it typically does not need to delve any more deeply into the packet than to determine its destination address. A firewall processor must consider more. A second problem is that firewalls can be misconfigured, and may leave a wide-open path that an intruder can exploit. This would be like putting deadbolts, bars, and armed guards at all of your doors, and then leaving the windows wide open. Of course, any device is susceptible to misconfiguration, but the impact of misconfiguration on your primary means of network security can be devastating— particularly if it gives you a false sense of security. Any firewall you install must be as simple to maintain, configure, and verify as possible, while still retaining the flexibility that you need. Third, firewalls may be overly restrictive. Depending on how flexible the configuration options are, it may not be possible to allow one class of access while denying another similar class. If the firewall is overly restrictive, you and your users will look for ways to circumvent these restrictions, probably with the goal of getting more work done, but at the expense of your security. Examine any potential firewall system carefully to ensure that it is flexible enough to allow fine-grained access control policies.

These disadvantages may lead you to believe that firewalls are a bad idea. Not at all. If they are well thought out and understood, they can be a valuable tool in the network administrator's security arsenal. You simply must understand what their problems are so as to avoid them, or limit their affect.

Figure 10-1 shows a typical firewall configuration.* Starting from the left, you see the physical connection to the outside world attached to a border router. This border router may be under the control of the local network administrator, or it may be maintained by another organization such as an ISP. Communications through this border router are usually not restricted.

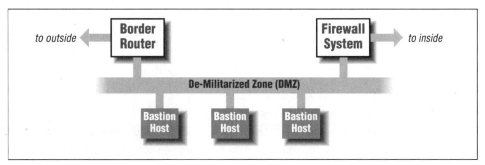

Figure 10-1. A typical firewall setup

A traditional LAN network, such as an Ethernet, is attached to the border router. This network is known as the dirty net or the *de-militarized zone (DMZ)*. From the local network's point of view, the DMZ is considered part of the outside world; it exists to provide an attachment point for the next component, the *bastion* hosts. These hosts provide external connection points for services such as email, the World Wide Web, FTP, etc. From the local network's point of view, these hosts have an intermediate trust level—they are locally administered, but they are not protected by the firewall so may not be completely secure. Ideally there is one bastion host for each external service. This keeps a security problem with one service from becoming a security problem for another service. Bastion hosts should not allow network login access, but instead be managed by directly attached consoles or serial lines. By eliminating the possibility that someone can reach these hosts through the network, you make their security cleaner and simpler to verify.

---

* More information on building and using firewalls can be found in the, *Building Internet Firewalls,* by D. Brent Chapman and Elizabeth D. Zwicky (O'Reilly)

But why do you need the bastion hosts? Why not let the data streams for the desired services flow through the firewall system to servers that are themselves protected by the firewall? The bastion hosts serve as proxies that make communications with the outside world more secure. For example, security holes are regularly found in the UNIX mail daemon known as *sendmail*. If this program is running on all of your UNIX hosts, and your firewall permits direct access from the outside, how much security have you really gained? Absolutely none! Your firewall cannot distinguish between a legitimate email message sent to one of your machines and an attack on one of sendmail's weaknesses. Both appear as valid SMTP data streams. But your attacks on your bastion email server should be less of a concern than attacks on your internal hosts. Perhaps the bastion doesn't run sendmail, so it doesn't share in its problems (though it probably has some of its own). Perhaps it does, but you have taken steps to limit the damage that can be done if this machine is compromised. Since it is dedicated to handling email, you can delete any programs that you don't need to handle email and manage the system. This machine probably does not need a compiler, a Telnet client or server, an FTP client or server, and so on. Once the intruder gets to this machine, there isn't much he can do.

Of course a bastion email system still needs to pass email through the firewall to the internal network securely. There are many ways to do this; each depends on how security conscious you are. You might configure the firewall to allow SMTP connections to and from the bastion email server; a corresponding internal email server can communicate with the bastion server on demand to pass mail in and out. Or you might have the bastion email server hold all mail destined for the inside until the internal email server contacts and retrieves it. This approach is more secure since the bastion email system cannot initiate a connection to the inside, but it is a little more difficult to set up correctly. Either way, though, you have limited the flow of traffic through the firewall to a carefully selected set of endpoints that can be monitored closely, and on which you can concentrate your security efforts. Using this kind of dual-server system creates a security airlock that prevents a machine outside the firewall from using any weaknesses in your email software to break-in to machines in your internal network. Similar kinds of systems can be created to support services like Telnet, FTP, and the World Wide Web. Ideally, each should use its own dedicated bastion host so that security problems with one service do not affect the others.

Moving on, we have the firewall itself. This may be a dedicated, special-purpose device with two or more network interfaces that can be programmed to allow some packets to pass through it based on criteria like the source and destination IP addresses, transport protocols, or the TCP or UDP source and destination ports. Special-purpose firewall devices have the advantage of being specifically designed as firewalls, rather than having some features tacked on as an afterthought. Just as is the case with dedicated routers, this allows them to concentrate all their efforts on this one task. This tends to make a dedicated firewall harder to penetrate than other types of firewalls, and means that any weaknesses they might have are less likely to be widely known. While "security through obscurity" is not usually a good thing to bet your job on, a little obscurity doesn't hurt. Of course, obscurity makes it harder for you and your staff to manage and maintain this critical device; it's yet another piece of equipment, with its own configuration language.

Another option for the firewall system might be a general-purpose computing platform with multiple interfaces; on this system, you run special software that provides packet filtering features similar to the special-purpose firewall described above. Its greatest strengths are that a general-purpose computer is more likely to be familiar to you and your staff, and therefore much easier to manage; in addition, you can upgrade to a faster system by buying a faster computer; you don't have to wait for your firewall vendor.

The third type of firewall, and the most common, is a dedicated router that uses special security features. Often, you already own the router so you can use its packet filtering "for free." Unfortunately, this option is typically the least flexible and poorest choice. A router's job is to route packets, and any filtering detracts from its performance. It may even detract from its performance for packet streams between two internal network segments that do not have to traverse the firewall. One router vendor's equipment has several possible paths that can be taken through the packet switching code. The most efficient of these uses special-purpose hardware accelerations and caches to provide impressive routing performance, quoted at over 200,000 packets per second. However, this switching path cannot be used if complex filters are installed on the router.* When these filters are in place, the code path used now involves the router's CPU, with no special hardware acceleration, and turns in a performance of closer to 20,000 packets per second. While such a performance decrease may only affect packets that must be processed by the filter, there are classes of filters that can cause *every* packet through the router to have to take this slower path.

The potential performance impact on unrelated processing is one reason that any type of firewall should be dedicated to the task of firewalling, and not serve some other function. Furthermore, you want to keep your firewall system simple. A simple security system is much easier to verify. If your firewall is also your email gateway, are you absolutely sure that your email software is secure? If it isn't, it could be used to gain access to your firewall system and compromise security. These other services really should be on your bastion hosts.

---

* Some simple filters can still be processed through the fast code path, with only a slight decrease of performance. However, simple filters are, well, *simple*, and cannot handle all filtering tasks.

But even using bastion hosts on your DMZ network cannot protect you completely. Recall that your bastion hosts may be able to initiate communications with hosts behind the firewall, even if only with a single server. No matter how good the firewall software is, it will do most of its decision making based on the IP addresses of the endpoints involved. This is not ideal, since the firewall's only indication of the IP addresses involved comes from the packet it is processing, and there is no requirement that the sender is telling the truth. IPv6 addresses this issue by providing a digital signature capability; a receiver can ensure that only one machine could possibly have sent the packet. IPv4 has no such mechanism and is vulnerable to spoofing attacks. So what if an intruder sends packets claiming to come from one of your bastion hosts? Can your firewall detect these spoofed packets and discard them? It can if you take one more precaution in the configuration of your firewall setup, but this time the precaution is on your border router.

To prevent spoofing, you can configure your border router to reject any packets that come from the outside world, but claim to come from one of your bastion hosts. With a configuration like this, spoofing attempts will never reach the firewall, which can therefore trust any packets that claim to come from the bastion hosts. This kind of router filtering is not difficult. On the Cisco IOS, you would add these commands to your border router's configuration. Note that `serial 0` is the link to the outside world, and `ethernet 0` is the DMZ Ethernet.

```
! our connection to the outside world - make sure that no one can
! masquerade as one of our bastion hosts on the DMZ from outside
interface serial 0
 description Link to the Internet
 ip address 10.1.1.1 255.255.255.0
 ip access-group 1 in
!
interface ethernet 0
 description Connection to DMZ network
 ip address 192.168.1.1 255.255.255.0
!
! define an access-list that blocks addresses from our DMZ network
access-list 1 deny   192.168.1.0 0.0.0.255
access-list 1 permit 0.0.0.0     255.255.255.255
```

The access list simply denies passage to any packet with a source address on our DMZ network, and permits all others. Applying this access list as an *incoming* filter on the serial interface tells the router to drop any packet that pretends to be from the bastion hosts. With this in place, the firewall need not be as concerned about the validity of packets claiming to be from our external servers.

Once you have established a clear break between your internal network and your bastion hosts, you have eliminated the need for your internal hosts to have globally accessible IP addresses. After all, isn't your firewall supposed to be preventing direct contact from beyond your own network? The only hosts that should be accessing your internal network from the outside are your external servers. Therefore, you may consider using the private addresses from RFC 1918 for your internal network. This has the dual effect of conserving Internet address space and providing additional security to your internal hosts. Using these private addresses makes it more difficult for a would-be attacker to reach the internal machines, since their addresses have no significance outside of your network. If you ensure that your firewall, bastion hosts, and border router all disallow IP source routing, your internal machines are effectively unreachable from outside by direct means, even if your firewall should fail. To disable source routing, add the following command to your Cisco configuration:

```
no ip source-route
```

Is Host Security Really Necessary?

One of the reasons that people seem so fond of network firewalls and other network-based security measures is that they assume they can allow host security to lapse if they secure the perimeter of their network. They reason that it is far easier to keep a single firewall and a half-dozen public (external) machines secure than many thousand. In this, they are correct, but also gravely mistaken.

Most network security is really host security. If host administrators assume that the firewall will protect their hosts from access violations, they are in for a rude awakening. Hosts should protect themselves from network intruders as much as they would from local intruders, if not more. The network can only help host security, not replace it. Securing the perimeter of the network but ignoring internal security measures has been likened to having a piece of candy with a hard, crunchy exterior and a soft, gooey interior. Once the exterior shell is breached, the insides just ooze out. Consider what happens if an intruder gets through your firewall: he or she can easily move from machine to machine causing untold damage, loss of sensitive information, and disruption. If your hosts were providing additional security measures of their own, the damage might be confined to a smaller set of hosts, rather than extending throughout your network.

A firewall also won't help you guard against threats from your own users. Studies show that 90 percent of most corporate security budgets are spent to protect against outside threats, but 90 percent of the damage is done by employees and others inside the company. While you can take action against internal users after the fact, the damage may already be done. Furthermore, internal users often cause problems through ignorance rather than malice. Good host security helps to protect against mistakes as well as intentional attacks.

Finally, consider what happens when a user installs an unauthorized modem on a workstation so he or she can get around the firewall and reach the workstation from home. Security holes like this often go undiscovered until an intruder finds and exploits this trivial way to bypass your firewall.

When you consider these potential internal security threats, the answer to the question, "Is host security still necessary when I have a firewall?" is an unqualified "Yes!" A firewall should be a part of a larger security scheme, not the only security you have. All hosts *must* take responsibility for their own security. So what can you do? Host security is beyond the scope of this book, but there are many excellent books on the topic, such as *Practical Unix and Internet Security, 2nd Edition*, by Simson Garfinkel and Gene Spafford, (O'Reilly). Still, there are a few simple ideas you can keep in mind.

- Keep up with any security patches that your vendor supplies. This is one of the surest ways to avoid a break-in. By the time a vendor releases a security patch, the would-be intruders often know about it and are actively exploiting it. If you don't keep up with security patches, you make yourself a target.

- Disable any services that are not necessary. For example, if a UNIX workstation never has to receive mail from another host, perhaps because all mail is received centrally, then there is no reason it should be running a mailer daemon. Eliminating this unused service closes any security threats that service presents.

- Configure your machines to permit access to themselves only from IP addresses that are properly registered with the DNS. By properly registered, I mean that when you look up the host's name from its IP address, and then look up its IP address from this name, you get back the same IP address, or a list that contains the IP address. Requiring a properly registered address makes illicit attachment to your network without detection more difficult.

- Practice good password security. Encourage users (force them if necessary) to select good passwords, and to change them with regularity. Educate them on the need for keeping their passwords secret, and on seeking assistance anytime they believe their password has been compromised. Password guessing is still one of the most productive avenues of attack. Consider using single-use password systems based on smart cards, thereby making it impossible for eavesdroppers to obtain a usable password. Explore systems like Kerberos (from MIT) that don't send the password across the network in the first place.

- Audit your systems regularly. This implies that you have them performing an appropriate level of logging of various types of activity. At a minimum, they should be creating log entries every time a user logs in, logs out, or performs an action that requires special privileges. In addition, it may be worthwhile to have the machines log all network access attempts, whether successful or not, to show evidence of network probing. I once spotted a student probing security on my network by correlating curious patterns of failed access attempts to several machines. Even if such audit trails do not prevent a break-in from occurring, they may give you the evidence that the break-in did occur, and what was done. This can be valuable when you need to repair the damage, or if you need to take legal action.

Router Access Security

All hosts on the network must protect themselves—they cannot rely exclusively on the network for protection from illegitimate access. If your network devices can be managed in band, using Telnet, SNMP, HTTP, or whatever, they are effectively hosts and must protect themselves, too. You might not think of a router as much of a target; after all, routers contain no sensitive data. But this is a grave mistake. An intruder who gains control of one of your routers may be capable of:

- Punching holes in router-based firewall configurations

- Disrupting proper network operation

- Launching a further attack on other machines using the router's Telnet client

- Sending a copy of every packet, or just *interesting* packets, to a receiving machine for future analysis

The first point may be the greatest weakness of any firewall system. If the firewall itself is compromised, no security guarantees can be made. If your firewall is based on the packet filtering capabilities of your router, defending your routers becomes an absolute necessity. But the second point should concern a network administrator at least as much, if not more. What happens if the intruder takes control of your router at a remote office, disrupts the connection to your main office, and changes the router's password? You may now have crucial business that cannot be conducted, with real cost to your company, until someone can physically regain control of the router. Clearly, this is not tolerable.

The third and fourth possibilities are the most serious. Your router is probably considered an *internal* host for security checking purposes, and may have easy access to your most sensitive systems. Even if it isn't, by taking control of the router, the intruder might be able to make it masquerade as a more trusted host and gain access to systems all over your organization without the benefit of security or password checks. By not securing your routers, you give an intruder a stepping stone to systems where more damage is possible. While eavesdropping on your internal network is not generally feasible from a distance, if an intruder can configure your router to forward copies of packets from your internal network to another system where he can analyze them at leisure, he can easily gather information about passwords, products under development, or anything else he desires. He is only limited by his skill and your router's flexibility; you intentionally chose very flexible routers, didn't you?

Unlike providing good host security for a time-share system, securing a router is not so straightforward. What you can do is limited to what your vendor supplies; you can't add your own security software on top of it. Typically access will be password protected, but passwords are only as secure as you make them. You can seldom replace this password system with something more secure. One thing you can do is restrict access to the router to as small a subset of your network as possible. Ideally, it should only be accessible from your staff's workstations and your management station. This is one place where a router's packet filtering capabilities may be appropriate. For example, if your staff workstations are all on 172.16.24.0/24, and the only machines on that network are your staff workstations, you can configure the Cisco IOS to restrict Telnet access to the router with these commands:

```
access-list 1 permit 172.16.24.0 0.0.0.255
!
line vty 0 4
 access-class 1 in
```

This configuration tells the router that all attempts to gain inbound access to virtual terminals (used for Telnet) 0 through 4 must come from a source address that passes access list 1. While this still suffers from the possibility of IP address spoofing, you have weeded out a large class of casual attackers. By the way, you should make sure that you apply the same access list to *all* of the virtual terminals on a router. You cannot predict which will be used by an inbound Telnet session. Similar controls can be used on other network equipment.

Consider having routers use their packet filtering capabilities to control access to devices that can't do packet filtering on their own. As an example of third-party protection, in my network I have many Ethernet switches that are not capable of blocking unwanted Telnet connections. Since I have the ability to put their management cards all on the same IP subnet of my network, I can use a simple access list on the interface leading to that network to protect them all:

```
interface ethernet 0
 description Ethernet Switch Management Subnet
 ip address 172.16.243.1 255.255.255.0
 ip access-group 1
!
! define an access list that permits my network management subnet and
! my staff subnet access to the switches, routers, etc.
access-list 1 permit 172.16.11.0 0.0.0.255
access-list 1 permit 172.16.15.0 0.0.0.255
```

The access list permits access from the subnet where my network management hosts are located as well as from the subnet where network staff workstations are located. Any other access attempt (including ping) will be denied. Keep in mind that while using a router's packet filtering capabilities to protect itself does little to its performance (the CPU is already processing the packets sent to the router), using it to protect other devices may hurt performance.

Likewise, give serious thought to which machines should have access to your routers and other equipment using SNMP. Version 1 of the SNMP protocol, which is still the most common, has no real security, and the security in Version 2 is generally regarded as a failure. Permission to read or write system configuration variables is based on a simple community string that is included with each request, but is otherwise unprotected. This means that if you use SNMP to manage your network equipment, you should investigate ways to ensure that as few hosts as possible can access the system for writing, and you should guard the community string as if it were a password. You can restrict the set of machines that can change the router's configuration by using an access list, similar to the one used to control Telnet access as shown here. In fact, it may even be the same access list that controls Telnet access.

```
! define the hosts permitted to make SNMP write requests to this router
access-list 1 permit 172.16.24.11  0.0.0.0
access-list 1 permit 172.16.131.57 0.0.0.0
!
! define all hosts in my network so I can restrict SNMP read requests,
! too
access-list 2 permit 172.16.0.0    0.0.255.255
!
! now apply the access lists to restrict SNMP access
snmp-server community secret RW 1
snmp-server community public RO 2
snmp-server trap-authentication
snmp-server host 172.16.24.11 public
```

First, I restricted read-write access to SNMP to two machines. One of these is presumably your network management station, and the other is probably your workstation acting as a backup. Keep the list of machines that can make SNMP write requests to a minimum. Second, I restricted read-only access to hosts on the local network, rather than leaving it wide open. While this may seem odd, it was done to prevent an intruder from gaining helpful information about the network's internal structure. It may also stop a "helpful" remote administrator from steering your less-experienced network staff into exploring a problem that doesn't exist.*

Regardless of who you allow into your routers using SNMP and what privileges you give them, you should include any commands necessary to cause authentication failures to generate SNMP trap messages on your management station. This

---

* Yes, it happened.

can help you determine when someone is attempting to access your routers via SNMP from the wrong place or with the wrong community string. Even if you don't use SNMP, be sure that your routers and other network devices have a valid SNMP configuration, or that you are sure that SNMP processing has been disabled. On my network, we regularly find departmentally operated network hubs and switches that are using the default SNMP configuration that comes on the device, which means that they have SNMP enabled for full access with a default community string. Our current practice is to point out the problem to them, but if a malicious individual found himself in this situation, he might well exploit it.

Finally, if your router supports other in band management mechanisms, such as HTTP, you should restrict access to them as well. Unfortunately, the Cisco IOS does not yet support the same kind of access controls on the HTTP configuration interface. For this reason, it is better to disable this interface if you have security concerns, at least until Cisco gives it the same kind of access controls they have for Telnet and SNMP. HTTP is disabled by default; if you have enabled it or want to be sure that it's disabled, add this to your configuration:

```
no ip http server
```

But if you stop with controlling access, you are asking for trouble. It is common for network configuration files to be stored on a network host and loaded into the routers or other devices using the TFTP protocol. This is extremely convenient, and I even advocate it in an earlier chapter. But use caution around TFTP. By default, Cisco's configuration files contain all their password information in plain text, and TFTP has no real access controls. If you find this to be true for your router, and you use TFTP to load your configuration files, consider running custom software on your TFTP server to limit access to the configuration files to your routers and network devices, or consider using any encrypted password features offered by your vendor. Adding the following line to your configuration encrypts the passwords stored on the router:

```
service password-encryption
```

Displaying your configuration gives you the encrypted string to put in your offline configurations, thereby preventing anyone who might obtain your configurations via TFTP from having your passwords. You should note that this password encryption is reversible, so is not perfectly secure. For your enable password (the one used to gain privileges) you should use:

```
enable secret my-password
```

The encryption scheme used for this password is newer and more robust.

Local passwords for Telnet access and access to privileged commands are not without their disadvantages. Among these disadvantages are the following:

- You have to maintain local passwords on many routers, updating all of them when you change passwords.

- You have to communicate the changed passwords to legitimate users securely.

- It is difficult to give different access levels to different individuals.

- Passwords still traverse the network in clear text.

To deal with these problems, the Cisco IOS allows several alternative methods of validating access to a router and to privileged commands on the router. Briefly, these methods are:

Terminal Access Controller Access Control System (TACACS)
TACACS provides for centralized user password authentication and some minimal accounting. Whenever a user requests some action, the router sends the user name and password to a central server. The server consults its access control database and either permits or denies the requested action. TACACS is the oldest of Cisco's remote authentication mechanisms, and the most limited. If you use TACACS to control access to the router and to control access to the router's privileged commands, any user with access to the router has access to the privileged commands because the TACACS server cannot distinguish a login attempt from a request for increased privileges.

Extended TACACS (XTACACS)
XTACACS attempts to resolve some of the limitations of the TACACS system by providing the server more detail about the action being attempted. For example, where TACACS cannot tell the difference between a login attempt and a request for increased privileges, XTACACS can. It also provides greater detail in its logging capabilities to allow collecting audit trails and accounting data.

TACACS+
TACACS+ is part of Cisco's new *Authentication, Authorization, and Accounting (AAA)* model. AAA provides a framework within which several different protocols can cooperate to provide the services the router needs for authenticating users, authorizing actions, and accounting. TACACS+ was the first of the protocols built within this system, and is an extension of the earlier TACACS protocols. Unlike the earlier TACACS systems, TACACS+ encrypts sensitive information as it crosses the network. Of the three TACACS variants, it provides the most flexibility and control, but is also the most complex.

Remote Access Dial In User Services (RADIUS)
While the original TACACS protocol was an open Internet standard, later enhancements by Cisco made it more of a proprietary protocol. RADIUS is the new attempt by the Internet community to design a remote access and accounting protocol that can handle all kinds of network access requests, as

well as being secure. RADIUS achieves security by using a secret that is shared between the clients and the server. This secret (really an encryption key) is used by the client and the server to encrypt sensitive information as it crosses the network to avoid eavesdropping attacks. While not yet a full Internet standard, RADIUS has been deployed in devices from many different vendors.

Kerberos version 5

As part of their Project Athena, MIT designed the Kerberos authentication system. Kerberos is designed so that a password never crosses the network in plain text. Instead, for each operation, Kerberos generates a ticket that is encrypted with the user's stored password. When the client system receives the encrypted ticket, it uses the user-supplied password to decrypt it. If successful, access is granted. Kerberos is not an Internet standard, but many sites have extensive Kerberos installations controlling access to their multi-user and single-user machines, and might want to use this system to control access to their routers as well.

Whichever system you choose, you will need an appropriate server. This server may be a commercial system, or it may be a homegrown system that allows you to use any number of security enhancing devices such as single-use passwords generated by smart cards. Other than the need for this central server, the main disadvantage of these enhanced authentication systems is that you may find yourself locked out of your router if your server is down or unreachable. You need to balance this risk against your level of paranoia and decide what is appropriate. Unfortunately, since the specifics of configuring any of these remote authentication services are highly specific to your individual situation and to the system chosen, presenting meaningful examples is beyond the scope of this book.

The Effects of External Connectivity

Nearly everyone is aware that a link to the Internet has a major impact on the security of a network; the Internet has millions of users, all of which are potential intruders. Unfortunately, other dangers exist for any kind of connectivity that extends beyond your network. Consider a private link to a neighboring organization. This link may become an avenue for security problems—perhaps an attack from a legitimate user of the neighbor network, or from an intruder there. More likely, the private link may be a path for introducing a computer virus into your network. Just because your neighbor has fewer users than the Internet does not mean security should be any less stringent. It does little good to have a firewall system protecting your front door if your neighbor has access to a back door and has poor security himself. If it is not feasible to provide the same kind of firewall protections on these links, then consider connecting the neighbor to your DMZ network, as shown in Figure 10-2.

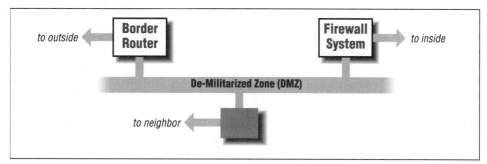

Figure 10-2. Connect your neighbors to your DMZ rather than to your internal network

The biggest disadvantage of this connection point is that you may not be able to give your neighbor a different level of access than you give to the world at large. This depends on the flexibility of your firewall system, but as far as security is concerned, it may be appropriate to put your neighbor on the same footing as the rest of the world.

However, the most often overlooked source of security problems is not your permanent external links. This dubious honor is reserved for your dial-up modem pools. These are often placed at the heart of your network, with little or no security restrictions placed between them and your network. Once you realize that there are far more machines with modems in the world than machines attached to the Internet, you should see why dial-up modems are a major security threat. One network I know was taking great pains to ensure that it wasn't possible to access certain sensitive machines from public access sites elsewhere on the network, yet it had a dial-up modem pool with absolutely no user authentication that was permitted access. The public access sites were far less of a security threat than their own modems, because an intruder working from the public access sites might at least be noticed by witnesses.

To fend off this threat to your network's security, you can do several things. First, *never* allow unauthenticated use of your dial-up modems. At a minimum, have the caller identify himself to the system and provide a password, even if these are never checked. This gives the appearance of security, and may chase off the casual attacker. Better would be to have your dial-up servers validate the user and password, perhaps using one of the remote authentication services listed earlier. But that still may not be enough. When that isn't enough, consider having your dial-up servers call back the user after establishing their identity. This way, even a captured user name and password are only valid from a specific location. However, dial-back modems don't work well if your users are moving around a lot. If none of these solutions are feasible or adequate, your only choice may be to treat your dial-up modems as if they were part of the outside world, and put them outside of your firewall. While inconvenient to your legitimate users, placing a modem pool outside the firewall isolates a major security problem from your network.

Enhancing Privacy

The first thing you should notice about this section is its title. It is not called *Ensuring Privacy*, or even *Providing Privacy*. I chose the word *enhancing* because it underscores the difficulty that providing any assurances of privacy presents. It is nearly impossible, with any reasonable budget, to ensure that your network is absolutely immune to breaches of privacy. Understanding and accepting this reality is one of the hardest aspects of network security for many people. You do your users a disservice if you lead them to believe that their network communications are, in any way, private. They should understand that the privacy of most network installations is more like that of a postcard than a telephone call: once a packet leaves your machine, you have no idea how many eyes might see and read it before it reached its destination.

Second, your own user community is a bigger threat to privacy than those outside your organization. Eavesdropping on network data requires access to the network involved. Snoops outside your network must first gain access to the network in order to listen in; your own users already have access. Network eavesdropping software is readily and freely available for many computer platforms. Some systems even come with such software. Of course, eavesdropping on data exchanges that involve public networks is a different issue, and we'll talk briefly about that below.

So what can you do to enhance privacy? The most powerful way to enhance privacy on your network is to ensure that nothing of interest can be obtained easily by snooping. This may mean that sensitive data (for example, payroll information) is never permitted on the network. If the data is never on the network, it cannot be intercepted. But this is often unreasonable. All kinds of data with varying levels of sensitivity must traverse our networks on a daily basis. After all, that is why the network exists. Instead of forbidding the data, we need to find ways to protect it.

Designing for Privacy

One alternative to forbidding sensitive data is to control where it can go by designing your network carefully. The idea is to keep sensitive data confined to as small a part of the network as possible. For example, if you can structure the network so that payroll information can pass from the personnel department to the disbursements office without crossing through the engineering department, the users in the engineering department have no opportunity to eavesdrop on the transmission.

The problem is that handling all the competing needs for private exchanges can result in a topology that is effectively impossible to build. To understand why, consider three departments, A, B, and C. If A and B need to be able to exchange information that C should not see, they need a path to each other that does not go through department C. One way to achieve this would be to connect A and B to each other, and then connect C to department A. But now what happens if C needs to exchange information with B that department A should not see? Okay, simply move department C's connection to be attached to B rather than A. Problem solved. Except now what happens if A and C have a private exchange need? Well, you could add an extra link to connect A and C directly, but that won't scale well if you have as few as a dozen departments, each with its own need for private communications with other departments.

For most networks, the multi-level star topology (discussed in Chapter 2, *Network Design—Part 1*) presents a reasonable compromise between privacy and practicality. In a multi-level star (See Figure 10-3), the only networks that must be traversed between any pair of departments are the core and distribution components. These components should not have user machines in the first place, so the only privacy threat comes from the network staff. This group is usually small, and (one hopes) professional. At any rate, if you can't trust your staff, you can't provide privacy no matter how you design the network.

When examining the paths sensitive data may take through your network, don't forget any backup or redundant paths you have added to improve reliability. While your primary network paths may keep data from where it is not supposed to be, your backup paths may send this same data exactly where you don't want it. While this may be acceptable when the network is in fail-over mode, you at least need to be aware of the risk and advise users of the threat to privacy during such times.

Sometimes, you can't design around privacy issues. For example, you may need to maintain privacy between a pair of hosts on a single network segment; it's unacceptable for other hosts on the segment to pry, but for various reasons, you can't segregate the hosts that need privacy. In situations like this, there are two options to consider. First, because of the nature of switched networks, data from host A to host B will not be sent on the connection to host C, effectively preventing host C from snooping. While this may be more expensive than doing nothing, it may be far cheaper than other alternatives. The second option is a variant of the first. Many vendors offer security features in their Ethernet hubs. The idea is that the hub learns, or is configured to know, which machines are connected to its ports, and then scrambles the data on the links that should not

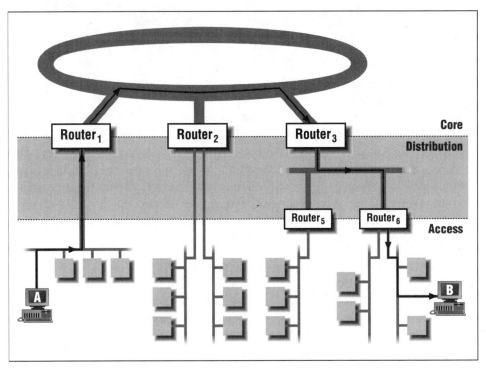

Figure 10-3. A multi-level star facilitates private communications

receive it. This provides similar privacy to that provided by an Ethernet switch, except the machines still have to contend for bandwidth. It is typically much cheaper than an Ethernet switch.

Data Encryption

Designing your network to enhance privacy is fine if you are designing or re-designing it from scratch. But what about established networks that cannot be easily restructured, or, worse yet, private data that must leave the confines of the organization's network and traverse the public Internet? For these situations, data encryption is about the only reasonable option. Encryption can occur at several points in the communications path; each point has advantages over the others. As a general rule, the farther up you move in the communications stack, the more flexible the system can be, but the more information is exposed about the nature of the communication:

- Starting at the bottom of the communications stack, encryption may occur at the link level: all data that cross a single physical link is encrypted. This may mean encrypting the entire packet, or it may be encryption of the link-level payload, leaving the link-level headers in the clear. Regardless of which is used, the encryption must be undone by the link-level recipient, whether the end host or a router, to allow routing decisions to be made. Therefore, this kind of encryption is most often used on a point-to-point link, or for communications between two hosts on the same subnet.

- The second point where encryption may occur is at the network layer. In this kind of encryption, the IP header information is still in the clear, but the IP data payload is encrypted based on the destination machine's address. Because it leaves the IP header in the clear, this kind of encryption lets you route packets across an IP network without requiring each router to decrypt the packet, make its decision, and then re-encrypt the packet for the next hop. This enhances security since the data is only decrypted by the ultimate destination. However, there's a price: information about who is communicating with whom is visible in the non-encrypted IP headers. It is now possible to know that the machine `merlin` is communicating with `arthur`, even if we don't know what was said. In some situations, that's more than you want to reveal.

- Moving farther up the communications stack, you might use encryption at the transport layer. In this case, the application program hands data in the clear to the network software, which encrypts the transport layer data stream before sending it down to IP for routing. In some respects, this is an improvement: encrypting at the transport layer decreases the time that clear text data is available in the end systems by pushing encryption closer to the application program. It is harder for someone snooping around in the operating system buffers to find any unencrypted data for the exchange. However, even more information about the kind of communication is available in the clear. If I know that `merlin` is sending data to TCP port 25 on `arthur`, it is a pretty safe bet that this is email.

- Finally, you can apply encryption at the application level by having the application encrypt the data before it ever hands it to the system. For example, your email program might encrypt the body of your email message, but leave the headers in the clear so that your message can be processed by any intermediate mailers necessary to reach your correspondent. This email may even have to cross some non-IP networks on its way, which would make any lower-layer encryption useless. Application-level encryption is even more immune to exposure on a multi-user host, but even more information is visible. I know you sent email, and I know to whom you sent it.

To do encryption, you can use special hardware that resides within the computer, or is placed between the network and the computer, or you can use software. Hardware solutions lend themselves to encryption points lower on the communication protocol stack, and software solutions lend themselves to points higher on the stack. Hardware solutions also tend to be faster because they don't use the host's CPU, and they may be more robust since operating system errors do not affect security. Hardware encryption also tends to be more expensive than software encryption. To see why, each host that is to participate in a private exchange with any other host requires this hardware device. If you have a thousand machines that must communicate securely in various pairs, you will need a thousand encryption devices. That could be rather expensive. Software encryption has the advantage that not all exchanges need to be encrypted. This is possible with a hardware encryption device, but it requires the device to be much more intelligent. The host system now needs some way to tell the encryption device whether a packet is to be encrypted. With software, the system simply does not encrypt data that does not need to be encrypted.

You may not need host-to-host encryption. Instead, you may need encryption between your network and another organization's network (perhaps a subsidiary), because the link between your two networks is a public network. In this case, a hardware-based solution may be perfect. You would install such a device between your network and the Internet, and the other organization would do the same. Then you would program the devices to encrypt any data being sent to the other, creating a virtual private network. Devices for doing this are becoming more common as the Internet becomes used more heavily for commerce.

As an enhancement to privacy, encryption provides the best assurance against unauthorized data snooping. However, it is not without its weaknesses. You have to make tradeoffs between flexibility, protection, speed, and cost. Furthermore, encryption is not foolproof. Given enough time and processing power, any encryption scheme can be broken. But the goal of encryption is not to ensure that the data is private for eternity. Instead, the goal is to ensure that by the time the data is revealed, it no longer has any value or special sensitivity, or that the cost to decrypt the data is greater than its value. For example, if it takes an industrial spy two years to decrypt your company's formula for a new super glue, but it will only take your company one year to bring it to market, decrypting the formula has little value to the spy's employer.

Even weak encryption has value. Your potential enemy in the data privacy game is more likely to be an insider. These people usually aren't maliciously trying to steal company secrets for the competition. They are more often interested in learning some juicy gossip, or getting some idea what was discussed in a high-level meeting. By applying even the simplest encryption, you make them work for their gossip. This is something most will probably be unwilling to do. In effect, you stop the casual snoop.

Be aware that many governments consider encryption techniques a threat. Some countries have outlawed any encryption scheme that the government is unable to easily break. Others, such as the United States, have stringent regulations about the exportation of encryption hardware and software. While these may not be issues for a company doing business in one area, multi-national corporations need to understand the laws governing their ability to use encryption, even for their own internal activities.

Virtual Private Networks

Recently, *virtual private networks (VPNs)* have been gaining popularity. A virtual private network is a link between two (or more) sites across public data networks, such as the Internet, that has the same kind of security assurances as a privately owned network. It is roughly equivalent to leasing private lines between your sites, thereby ensuring the privacy of the network links, without going to the added expense. Devices at each site establish encrypted tunnels to each other, and then treat these tunnels as if they were private point to point links. Packets that must be securely transmitted to another site served by the VPN are sent to the local device. It encrypts the packet as if it were simply data and places it in the payload of another packet, which is then sent across the public network to the remote device. This device extracts the encrypted data and decrypts it, recovering the original packet, and sends it on to its destination.

The advantage of a VPN is clear. At no point does the sensitive data ever appear in clear text on a public data network. On those links, it is always encrypted; it is only visible on the private networks of either site—just like a dedicated private link! The disadvantages aren't too severe either, the biggest being the need to purchase a device (or software) to form the endpoints of the tunnels. While this can be a significant expense if you need many virtual links, it may still be cheaper than the cost of the private links themselves.

The second disadvantage of a VPN is that both sites need compatible hardware or software providing the tunnels. While this may not be a problem for a large corporation that can send a dozen identical devices to each of its remote offices, for more loosely affiliated organizations with multiple communicating partners, this can mean having a different VPN device for each remote site—not only costly, but a management nightmare. Still, if your data privacy needs are great enough, and the costs are better than for private data lines, a VPN may be exactly the right answer.

Finally, when you consider using a VPN that spans the public Internet, keep in mind that you are competing with other sites and even with your own public traffic for access to bandwidth. While you can almost always buy a faster private link to a remote site, when you are using the Internet, bandwidth is not unlimited. What you get is shared among many users at many sites, and the exact amount of available bandwidth is almost never under your control.

Maintaining Data Integrity

Most people assume that nothing can happen to their data between the time they send it and the time it is received. Would that it were so! How can you be sure that the data you sent into the network is the same data received on the other side? Network protocols ensure that communications are relatively free of error by using checksums on hardware frames, packet headers, and data, but they can't ensure that tampering does not occur at other points in the communications path. For example, an email message could be altered before it left the sending machine, after it arrived on the receiving machine, or while waiting in the mail queues of an intermediate machine. Such tampering is beyond the protection of network protocols. Likewise, there is no way that a machine can ensure that the alleged sender of an email message is, in fact, the person who sent it. Some forgeries may be detectable by a human after careful scrutiny, but few users know what to look for, and forgeries can be quite good.

The best way to ensure data integrity is through the use of a technique known as a *digital signature*. Like a traditional signature, a digital signature is something added to a piece of data, such as an email message, that can be examined to determine the veracity of the message's origin. Unlike a traditional signature, a digital signature is much harder to forge, and thereby provides a higher degree of certainty that the alleged author did, in fact, sign the message. Digital signatures provide another important benefit. Because a digital signature is computed based on the contents of the text being signed, any change in the text will cause the signature checking algorithm to fail. In the case of an email message, a digital signature ensures not only that the alleged sender actually sent the message, but also that the message has not been altered since it was signed.

Fortunately, digital signature software is widely available for many platforms. One such system, *Pretty Good Privacy (PGP)*, is freely available for non-commercial use for UNIX, Microsoft Windows, Macintosh, VMS, and many other systems.* For the cost of the time to obtain, install, and train users in its use, you can verify the content and origin of files, email, or other discrete data. This software system is described in *PGP: Pretty Good Privacy*, by Simson Garfinkel (O'Reilly).

PGP is a wonderful tool for signing and encrypting data at the application level, but it doesn't help with machine-to-machine verification. Unfortunately, IPv4 does not yet have a digital signature capability for general IP communications. However, IPv4 has added digital signatures to some dynamic routing protocol exchanges. To understand why using signatures in routing exchanges is important, consider what

---

* Commercial versions are available from PGP, Inc. See their web site at *http://www.pgp.com* for pricing and availability.

would happen if a malicious (or even careless) user started sending dynamic protocol updates into your network with false information. At best, your network would have mysterious black holes into which packets disappeared, instead of going to their destinations. At worst, packets for some or all of your machines might be sent to some other destination of the perpetrator's choice, where they could be analyzed at his leisure. Digital signature technology can help by allowing your routers to ensure that the routing updates they receive are legitimately from your routers.

If the routing protocol you have chosen supports signed updates, you should seriously consider using them. Configuration is simple. You give the router the authentication key for an interface or a neighbor, and the router takes it from there. For example, to use authentication keys for OSPF you add:

```
interface ethernet 0
 ip address 192.168.1.100 255.255.255.0
 ip ospf authentication-key mysecret
 !
router ospf 1
 network 172.16.0.0 0.0.255.255     area 1
 network 0.0.0.0     255.255.255.255 area 0
 area 0 authentication
```

This fragment tells the router to start an OSPF process, placing interfaces in `172.16.0.0/16` in area 1, and all others in area 0. It then defines an authentication key for interface `ethernet 0` (each interface can have a different key). Finally, it tells the router to use authentication in area 0. Other areas, such as area 1, are not authenticated. Since `ethernet 0` is in area 0, all of the router's updates to area 0 will use the authentication key `mysecret`. If an update arrives on that interface that is not authenticated by this key, the router will reject it. For this reason, all devices participating in an OSPF area must either use authentication keys, or not use them. You cannot mix.

Configuring authentication for BGP updates to neighbors is also straightforward. Simply tell the BGP routing process what password to use for each neighbor:

```
router bgp 101
 network 172.16.0.0
 neighbor 192.168.23.4 remote-as 102
 neighbor 192.168.23.4 password my-secret
 neighbor 10.23.4.109 remote-as 103
 neighbor 10.23.4.109 password his-secret
```

Each neighbor can use a different password, just as each interface could use a different authentication key in OSPF. You can also specify some neighbors that do not use passwords; exchanges with these neighbors are not authenticated.

Unfortunately, most dynamic routing protocols do not support any kind of authentication. In these cases, your only defenses are to configure your routers to exchange routing information only where you must, preferably only with machines under your direct control; to filter out unwanted routing exchanges with some neighbors using administrative distances; and to filter updates received to ensure that they are reasonably sane. For example, if you know that your default route can only come from one of a small set of routers, you should filter the default route from any updates coming from *any* other router, even if it is under your control. All of these techniques are discussed in Chapter 6.

Preventing Denial of Service

The fourth aspect of network security you must address is denial of service. In a denial of service attack, the attacker's goal is not to get into your systems or intercept your data, but to prevent legitimate users from carrying out their tasks. For example, a program that successfully monopolized the CPU resources of a multiuser system would prevent users from getting work done. Any resource is subject to a denial of service attack, but the network opens opportunities for such attacks from outside a single machine or organization. Consider what would happen if a set of machines bombard another machine on the network with packets as fast as they can generate them. If the target machine can't keep up, it could cease functioning on the network, or even crash when it exhausted its resources.

The best defense against most denial of service attacks is to cut off the attacker's ability to reach the resource. If a firewall is in place between your network and the outside world, denial of service attacks against your internal machines must use services that can pass directly through the firewall. Any service that cannot pass through the firewall cannot be used to deny service to an internal machine. It can, however, still affect the ability of the firewall to perform its duties, or consume available bandwidth on your external links.

Another important defense is to take advantage of your vendor support. Many denial of service attacks can be addressed by software patches from the vendor of the affected system. By keeping current with vendor-supplied patches and updates, you may avoid having a system affected, or you may mitigate the effect of a denial of service attack.

Finally, disable services that you do not need; disabled services cannot be used as points of attack. In Chapter 8, *The Technical Side of Network Management*, I said that the TCP and UDP small services such as *echo* and *daytime* are increasingly common targets for denial of service attacks. By default, these services are enabled on your routers, and probably on many of your network hosts. You have to decide whether the diagnostic value of these services is worth more than the potential for attack. Disabling these services in the Cisco IOS is as easy as adding:

```
no service tcp-small-servers
no service udp-small-servers
```

In the end, there will always be denial of service attacks that are unavoidable, no matter how diligent you are. For these, your only course of action is to notice the attack, and then begin the process of tracking it back to its source, or finding a way to stop it. Maintaining a good relationship with the network engineers at your provider or neighbor's site can make this process go more smoothly. Fortunately, really dangerous denial of service attacks are rather rare. Most people lack the resources to have much impact on your network unless they are exploiting a bug in your hosts. If your network connection is a T1 line, an attacker who wants to flood your connection with packets also needs access to a T1 line. Most people with this much money have better things to do.

There are other, less obvious ways to disrupt service on your network. It's relatively easy to send ICMP redirect packets to a router that cause it to override its own routing knowledge (even static routes) and send packets the wrong way. Since a router is supposed to be an *authoritative* source of routing information, routers should not process any ICMP redirects they receive. Fortunately, most router vendors ignore redirects by default (don't confuse commands to *send* redirects with commands to *process* redirects), and some don't even give the option of honoring them. Check your router to be sure.

Sometimes, a router can be attacked by the very methods and protocols we put in place to manage them. For example, consider the effects of a machine trying to walk the entire SNMP MIB on one of your routers. Depending on the packet switching load on the router, it might be able to keep up for a while, but it will eventually get a burst of activity that will push it over the edge into failure. Even if it doesn't, it is spending an awful lot of time dealing with SNMP that should be dedicated to productive routing tasks. This is yet another reason for restricting which machines have access to the SNMP processes on your routers and network devices. If you restrict who can probe your network with SNMP, you minimize the number of people you need to worry about.

Finally, in Chapter 1, *The Basics of IP Networking*, I said it is possible for a machine to send a broadcast packet to a network to which it is not attached. It does this by using the network or subnetwork broadcast address for the remote network, and relying on the routers in the network to route the packet to the remote network using unicast packets; the final router broadcasts the packet to the destination network. This kind of directed broadcast can be useful. However, the potential for abuse, misuse, or just plain error is great. Each such broadcast packet will interrupt all machines on the receiving network segment, even those that do not run IP. Each must examine the packet to determine if it requires processing, and, if it does, to carry out that processing.

Now consider what happens if a machine sends many directed broadcasts. A moderately fast machine can consume a large portion of the bandwidth on the receiving network, interrupting all the machines there without any benefit to your network, and without having to deal with the disruption itself. Do you really want a malicious individual to be able to disrupt your network from halfway around the world? I recommend that you disable directed broadcast processing on some or all of your routers, unless you have an exceptional reason to allow them. (Disabling directed broadcasts does not disable local broadcasts, which are essential to your network.) In the Cisco IOS, add the following statement to each interface:

```
no ip directed-broadcast
```

This statement is part of my default interface configuration. I have yet to find a reason to allow directed broadcasts sufficiently strong that I'm willing to take the risk of them being abused.

Other Security Concerns

Controlling access, enhancing data privacy, maintaining data integrity, and preventing denial of service are the most common network security concerns. But they are not the only concerns you should address. In this section, I'll discuss some concerns that are not directly related to network security, but which should be addressed as part of a company-wide security plan.

Computer Viruses

One extremely common denial of service attack is a computer virus. Viruses are pieces of software that are designed to replicate themselves and spread the "infection" to other machines. They can do this by attaching themselves to binary programs, document files, or by hiding in boot sectors of disks. Their effect may be as benign as printing a message on the screen of the machine that is infected, or as serious as wiping clean a hard drive of all data. Their cousins, Trojan horses, may also capture information such as passwords or network packets and send them to a receiver for later use. Unfortunately, computer viruses and Trojan horses are a part of life for both the computer user and the network administrator. There are now several thousand known viruses and variants, and new ones are being written constantly. But there are steps you can take to prevent infection, or to clean up after.

The first thing you should do is to obtain anti-virus software for the systems that are most readily infected. These are usually your PC and Macintosh machines, but others may be vulnerable, so look around. Anti-virus software typically operates in two modes. The first mode scans to detect infected files and systems before the virus has a chance to replicate. The second mode attempts to detect an infection in progress and prevent it. For example, since some viruses try to change the contents of the boot sector of a system's disk, the anti-virus software may intercept any such attempt and ask the user what to do. If the change is legitimate, the user can allow it. Otherwise, the virus is identified and stopped. Some anti-virus software can help clean up after an infection is detected. If the virus can't be removed safely, it may be necessary to restore the system from backup media, or if that is unavailable or also infected, the system may have to be reinstalled from *write-protected* distribution media. Either approach can take significant effort.

By far the most potent weapon against computer viruses is user education and careful procedures. It should be mandated that all software that a user retrieves from the network, brings in from home, or receives from a friend should go through a careful quarantine. This quarantine should be on a specially designated machine that is not attached to the network and has several different anti-virus software systems installed. Only when it passes all of these anti-virus software scans should it be considered for installation on a user's machine.

Even supposedly blank disks can carry an infection. In some cases, simply inserting an infected diskette can infect the machine; likewise, inserting a clean diskette into an infected machine can infect the diskette. For these reasons, diskettes that have been in infected machines, or are of unknown origin, should be handled carefully. It may be possible to certify them as "clean" after a bulk-erasure process, but with diskettes as cheap as they are, it is safer to destroy them and use new diskettes whenever possible.

Employee Theft

Too often, computer and network administrators go to great lengths to secure their hosts and networks, only to have valuable trade secrets walk out of the company in an employee's briefcase. While this is not technically a network security issue, it should not be ignored. When dealing with data privacy, you must view your own users as the potential enemy. Don't fall into the trap of asking the wolf to guard the sheep! The only way that the network can address employee theft is to provide good data privacy and access controls. If the thief is unable to obtain the data, he cannot steal it. Beyond that, it becomes an issue of ensuring that trusted personnel are trustworthy.

Finally, whatever you choose to implement, the time to think about it and put it in place is *before* you need it. Ideally, you should design security measures into the network when you build it, and coordinate them with a larger company-wide plan. Unfortunately, almost nobody does this. Most network administrators don't worry about security until a problem occurs. Then they rush about madly putting ill-conceived security measures in place in a misguided attempt to prevent a future attack. Of those who do build security into their networks before it is needed, most seem to be affected by a sort of tunnel vision. They focus solely on one particular aspect of security, such as access controls, and completely ignore other potentially more serious concerns. Or they expend a lot of effort securing their networks from the outside world, only to ignore the threat from their own user community until it is too late.

Don't be a member of either group. A well-designed network security plan *must* consider all possible security threats, and all aspects of those threats *before* a breach occurs. While you may not think there is anything of value on your network or systems, someone will, and you may not find out how valuable they consider it until it is too late.

Configuring Interfaces

Without interfaces, there wouldn't be much to IP routing. So what is involved in configuring IP on the interfaces of your router? In fact, very little. Configuring IP on an interface of a Cisco router takes the form:

```
interface type number
  ip address 172.16.52.34 255.255.255.0
  optional IP configuration statements such as proxy ARP
  interface-specific configuration statements
```

The *type* in the `interface` statement is a system-defined name for a class of interfaces such as `ethernet`, `fddi`, or `serial`, and the *number* specifies a particular interface. The IOS counts interfaces from zero, so the first Ethernet interface would be called `ethernet 0`, while the third serial interface would be called `serial 2`. On larger routers, the interface number may take the form *slot/number*, where *slot* represents a slot in the chassis (again, numbered from zero) and *number* represents a particular interface on the card in that slot. So the second Ethernet interface on the card in the first slot of a Cisco 75XX router would be called `ethernet 0/1`. The newest routers in the Cisco 75XX series can use a three-part numbering scheme that takes the form *slot/sub-slot/number*.

After specifying the interface, you assign an IP address and netmask to it using the `ip address` statement. This statement is the minimum required for IP to use the interface, but other IP-related configuration statements can be included. Examples of these would be commands to enable or disable proxy ARP, directed broadcasts, IP multicasts, etc. None of these are required to make IP routing work, but some may change the behavior of your dynamic routing protocol. These statements are discussed in the appropriate chapters elsewhere in this book

Finally, each interface type may have statements that are either optional or required to make the interface work. LAN media such as Ethernet, Token Ring, and FDDI usually need no additional configuration. But a serial interface may need to have its link-level protocol encapsulation set to something like PPP or Frame Relay. An on-demand interface needs rules for when it should connect, when to disconnect, and how to map protocol addresses to destinations to call. Configurations for a Frame Relay or ATM interface are even more involved; you must establish virtual circuits and mappings from protocol addresses to these virtual circuits. Finally, special purpose interfaces such as a mainframe channel attachment require close coordination of information between the router and the host mainframe. The best place to get information about configuring interfaces is your router documentation, but I'll present some of the basics for the more common interfaces here.

Traditional LAN Media—Ethernet, Token Ring, and FDDI

Traditional LAN media, such as Ethernet, Token Ring, and FDDI, give you few configuration choices. This is partly because they are older standards and so well entrenched that the default values are nearly always right. It is also because they are less flexible and don't need the complexity of something like ATM.

Ethernet presents the fewest choices. Your only real decision is which encapsulation method to use for your IP datagrams. Your choices are:

- The standard ARPA Ethernet Version 2.0 encapsulation, which uses a 16-bit protocol type code. This is the default, and is almost always what you want to use.

- SAP IEEE 802.3 encapsulation, in which the type code becomes the frame length for the IEEE 802.2 LLC encapsulation.

- The SNAP method, as specified in RFC 1042, which allows Ethernet protocols to run on IEEE 802.2 media.

The default is the Ethernet version 2 framing with good reason—most devices only support this framing. As such, you will almost never change the encapsulation. Should you need to, insert *one* of the following `encapsulation` statements into your configuration for the Ethernet interface:

```
interface ethernet 0
 ip address 172.16.52.34 255.255.255.0
! for ARPA Ethernet Version 2.0 encapsulation (the default)
 encapsulation arpa
! for IEEE 802.3 encapsulation
 encapsulation sap
! for RFC 1042 SNAP encapsulation
 encapsulation snap
```

Token Ring gives you a few more options, but even those are fairly limited. Token Ring may run at either 4 Mbps or 16 Mbps; some hardware requires you to specify which speed to use. To do so, use the `ring-speed` statement:

```
interface tokenring 1
 ip address 172.16.52.34 255.255.255.0
! specify 4 Mbps speed
 ring-speed 4
! or specify 16 Mbps speed
 ring-speed 16
```

You can also specify whether to allow early token release. Normally, a machine doesn't generate a token until it has received its own frame back from the network, indicating that the frame has completed its trip around the ring. Early token release allows the machine to generate a token immediately after transmitting its frame, but before it has received the frame back from the network. This can result in a higher effective bandwidth, at the cost of missing some error conditions. Enable early release by adding the following statement to your interface configuration:

```
early-token-release
```

FDDI gives the most options, but almost all of them control timers used by the low-level protocols. Unless you know exactly what each timer does and what the results of changing one will be, you should not touch these timers without instructions from Cisco technical support. You can easily make your FDDI ring unusable. The only one I have ever used was the TL-min timer, which controls the timing of the physical layer signaling. When I added a Cisco router to my non-Cisco FDDI ring, I had to slow it down a few microseconds to give the router next to it a little more time to bring the ring up. The configuration below increased this timer to 200 microseconds, just enough time to keep the whole ring happy:

```
interface fddi 2
 ip address 172.16.52.34 255.255.255.0
! slow down some low-level processing to allow the other routers to
! keep up
 fddi tl-min-time 200
```

Permanent Serial Links

Permanent serial links are little more complex than traditional LAN media. Your first decision is what low-level encapsulation method to use on the link. The three most common choices are the Point to Point Protocol (PPP), High-level Data Link Control (HDLC), and Frame Relay. Frame Relay is complex enough that I give it its own section. The biggest difference between PPP and HDLC is that PPP is an open standard defined by the Internet community, while HDLC is an ISO modification to the Synchronous Data Link Control (SDLC) protocol developed by IBM.

Each is capable of handling multiple protocols, and each has some minor strengths over the other. But perhaps the biggest strength that PPP has is that it is more likely to be interoperable with routers from other vendors, because of its status as an Internet standard. If you are working exclusively with Cisco equipment, there is no strong reason to prefer one over the other. HDLC is the default, but you can select PPP using the `encapsulation` statement:

```
interface serial 0
 ip address 172.16.52.34 255.255.255.0
! select PPP as the encapsulation protocol on this interface
encapsulation ppp
```

If you select PPP, you may want or need to run an authentication protocol. You don't really need authentication on a permanent serial line since the other end is well known, but the configuration of PPP is the same whether you use it on a permanent line or an on-demand line. Besides, the remote network administrator may insist that you use authentication to guard against the extremely unlikely event that leased circuits get crossed. For authentication, you have two choices with PPP (and none with HDLC): the Password Authentication Protocol (PAP), and the Challenge Handshake Authentication Protocol (CHAP). PAP is simpler and older, and is still more widely implemented. With PAP, the calling router sends the called router a username and password in order to "login" to the link. The called router validates the information and either accepts the connection or rejects it. CHAP takes a different approach that avoids sending the password. With CHAP, the called router sends a challenge string to the calling router. The calling router encrypts the string with its password, and sends it back to the called router, which also encrypts the challenge with the caller's password. If the encrypted challenges match, the caller is authenticated. To configure PAP or CHAP on your router, include:

```
interface serial 0
 ip address 172.16.52.34 255.255.255.0
 encapsulation ppp
! or use ppp authentication pap
ppp authentication chap
username name1 password secret1
username name2 password secret2
...
```

You need to specify a username and password for each router that might connect to this router, or to which it might connect. Of course, you need not use any authentication. The choice is entirely yours, but if this is an on-demand link with no authentication, you have a glaring security hole in your network.

Whether you select PPP or HDLC, you can use link-level compression to increase effective bandwidth. The compression algorithms available depend on the encapsulation; PPP can use both a predictor compression scheme (the RAND algorithm), or the Stacker compression scheme developed by STAC, Inc. HDLC is limited to the

Stacker algorithm. To enable link-level compression, include one of the following statements in your configuration:

```
interface serial 0
 ip address 172.16.52.34 255.255.255.0
 encapsulation ppp
 compress predictor
! or
 compress stac
!
interface serial 1
 ip address 172.16.53.17 255.255.255.0
 encapsulation hdlc
 compress stac
```

Both ends of the link must use the same type of compression, or none at all. Most Cisco routers do not have any hardware compression assistance—the main CPU must handle all of the compression. If you enable compression, monitor your CPU utilization carefully. If it consistently exceeds 65 percent, disable compression.

On-Demand Links

Dial-on-demand links can use several underlying technologies. Of these, switched synchronous serial, analog dial-up modems, and ISDN are the most common. All have more similarities than differences, so I will discuss them together. To IP, or any other network protocol, dial-on-demand links look the same as a serial interface that is only there when in use. The IP configuration is simple and straightforward. The complexity comes in specifying how to map IP addresses to destination phone numbers,[*] how and when to bring up the link, and when to tear it down.

Mapping from IP addresses to phone numbers is usually handled by a static mapping stored on each router. This can mean a lot of typing if you have many on-demand links, but since much of the information may be shared by many routers, if you maintain your configurations off-line, you may be able to do some simple preprocessing that inserts the map by including a common file. You configure maps by adding dialer map statements to your on-demand interface configuration:

```
dialer map ip 192.168.100.1  5551212
dialer map ip 192.168.100.17 5558891
...
```

This map tells the router that it can reach the IP address 192.168.100.1 by calling 555-1212, and that it can reach 192.168.100.17 by calling 555-8891. If

---

[*] For lack of a better term, I'll use the term "phone number" for the string used to identify the called party to the switching network. It should not be taken to mean that there is a voice telephone.

the on-demand interface is an ISDN line, you can optionally append a call speed parameter to force some calls to be placed at 56 kbps and others at 64 kbps:

```
dialer map ip 192.168.100.1  5551212 speed 56
dialer map ip 192.168.100.17 5558891 speed 64
...
```

The harder part is telling the router how to bring up the link. For an ISDN line, this is handled by telling the router what type of ISDN switch it is connected to, and how to identify itself to the switch. For example, to tell the router that it is connected to a Northern Telecom DMS-100 switch, you would say:

```
isdn switch-type basic-dms100
interface bri 0
 ip address 172.16.52.34 255.255.255.0
 isdn spid1 888555121201
 isdn spid2 888555121301
```

Notice that the switch type is specified *outside* the interface configuration. This is a global configuration statement for the router; all of the ISDN interfaces on a single router must connect to the same type of switch. The configuration also includes the Service Profile Identifiers (SPIDs) for my ISDN line on the interface. Depending on the type of ISDN service you have, you may have zero, one, or two SPIDs. The telephone company will give you the SPIDs—DO NOT make up some numbers! If these numbers are wrong, the ISDN network won't talk to you.

For analog modem lines, configuring how to dial is more difficult. You first have to tell the router that the interface is an on-demand interface by using the `dialer in-band` statement, shown below. This tells the router that it can talk to the modem by sending it commands as part of the data stream. You specify these commands with a chat script that tells the router, in effect, "When the modem sends *this* to you, you send *that* back to it." A chat script presented in the Cisco IOS documentation is:

```
chat-script dial ABORT ERROR "" "AT Z" OK "ATDT \T" TIMEOUT 30 CONNECT \c
```

This statement creates a script called `dial` and then defines expect-send pairs. There are two special expect values. ABORT tells the router to fail the script if the text following the ABORT appears in the input stream from the modem. You can set up as many ABORT conditions as you wish. The other special value is TIMEOUT. It sets a timer that determines how long the router will wait to see the next matching input string before it declares a failure. The default value is five seconds. In all other cases, the pairs create a step-by-step progression for the router to follow. So, in this script, the router first expects to see anything (an empty string), and then sends AT Z to the modem. It should next see the string OK, to which it responds ATDT followed by the phone number to dial (the \T is replaced with the number to call). Next, the router is told to increase its timeout value to 30 seconds to give the remote device time to answer. If the router next sees the string CONNECT, it sends nothing (the \c means to send nothing), and the script completes successfully. Of course, a real chat script is likely to be more detailed than this example. There are many special strings defined for various situations; the dialog with your modem will best be worked out with your modem's documentation and Cisco's documentation, and a bit of trial and error.

Once you have your chat script done, you need to associate it with the on-demand interface attached to the modem:

```
interface async 0
 ip address 172.16.52.34 255.255.255.0
 dialer in-band
 script dialer dial
```

This tells the router that when it needs to use this interface, it should use the script called dial to talk to the modem.* There are many more options for dialer scripts, and even a set of commands to set up login scripts for the remote site. The details are endless, and you'll want to consult current IOS documentation to explore them before you set up an analog modem based on-demand link.

Now we have IP addresses mapped to phone numbers, and we have told the router how to place a call. All that is left is to tell the router when to bring up the link, and when to take it down. To control when the link is brought up, you use an access control list to define a class of packets that should be considered *interesting* enough to bring up the link. This can be a simple access list or an extended access list. A simple access list to bring up the link any time a packet is coming from the subnets 172.16.25.0/24 or 172.16.80.0/23 would look like:

```
interface async 0
 ip address 172.16.52.34 255.255.255.0
 dialer in-band
 script dialer dial
 dialer-group 1
! define what we consider interesting packets
access-list 27 permit 172.16.25.0 0.0.0.255
access-list 27 permit 172.16.80.0 0.0.1.255
! associate the access list of interesting packets with a dialer group
dialer-list 1 list 27
```

After telling the router that the interface is an on-demand link with the dialer in-band statement, we then tell the router what dialer group this interface

---

* The script name is actually a regular expression, which allows you to define a group of scripts that behave similarly, and select any that match. Since a literal string is a regular expression that matches itself, you can always use the chat script name, if you only have one that you want to use.

belongs to. You can have up to ten dialer groups (numbered from 1 to 10). Next, the configuration tells the router what is interesting by defining access list 27, and associates that access list with the dialer group by using the `dialer-list` statement. When any packet that passes access list 27 is to be sent on this interface, the router will dial the phone number for the destination and send the packet. The access list you define can be as complex as you wish. For example, because you can use an extended access control list, you could easily filter by protocol, TCP or UDP port, source and/or destination address, or any combination. For example, an access list that would prevent ICMP from bringing up the link, unless it came from the machine at `172.16.27.34` and was destined for any machine on subnet `172.16.98.0/24` would look like:

```
access-list 127 permit  ip    172.16.27.34 0.0.0.0       172.16.98.0 0.0.0.255
access-list 127 deny    icmp  0.0.0.0 255.255.255.255    0.0.0.0 255.255.255.255
access-list 127 permit  ip    0.0.0.0 255.255.255.255    0.0.0.0 255.255.255.255
```

The first `access-list` statement could just also have specified ICMP for the protocol, but I chose this method because it makes the access list processing faster if the addresses match—recall that access lists exit on the first match. Keep in mind that the dialer access control list places no restriction on what traffic can traverse the link, only what is considered interesting for deciding when to bring it up. Access control is provided by the `ip access-group` statement mentioned in Chapter 10, *Network Security*.

Now all we need to do is to tell the router when to tear down the connection. In the IOS, this is handled by an inactivity timer. Whenever the router sends a packet that is interesting enough to have caused the interface to come up, it resets the timer. If the timer reaches the configured value (120 seconds by default) without seeing any interesting packets, it hangs up the line. You can set the idle timeout period on each interface by adding these lines:

```
! set the idle timeout for this interface to 5 minutes (300 seconds)
dialer idle-timeout 300
```

When there is contention for this interface because a call is in progress and an interesting packet needs to be sent to another site, the router uses a second timer that typically has a much shorter inactivity timeout. This timer is set using the `dialer fast-idle` statement, and defaults to 20 seconds. If your fast idle timer is getting invoked often, you should consider adding more modems. Thrashing between phone calls can hurt network throughput, and may even cost more money in the long run.

Once the link is established, an on-demand link presents the same configuration options as a permanent link. What encapsulation you use, whether you want to use PAP or CHAP for PPP, and link compression all need to be configured. See the section above on permanent serial links for details. There are many ways to fine tune the behavior of your on-demand links. These options are beyond the scope of this book; consult your IOS documentation.

Frame Relay

Frame Relay is not a special type of interface hardware; it is an encapsulation method that can run on top of nearly any serial interface. It is most often used on permanent synchronous serial links. A router or host in a Frame Relay network usually connects to a switch, either privately owned or operated by the telephone company. Frame Relay is a packet switching technology that allows multiple logical data streams to be multiplexed onto a single physical link. These logical data streams are called *virtual circuits* and are identified with a Data-Link Connection Identifier (DLCI). But a DLCI only has local significance in Frame Relay. It can (and generally does) change on each physical link in the Frame Relay network.

Two types of virtual circuits are possible. A permanent virtual circuit (PVC) is manually created by the switch's administrator, and lasts until manually removed. It is essentially akin to a permanent serial link. The other type of virtual circuit is a switched virtual circuit (SVC). An SVC is created on-demand by software, and only lasts until the software determines it is time to remove it, much akin to a phone call. While Frame Relay has been recently extended to use both types of circuits, most Frame Relay networks still only provide and use PVCs. For this reason, I will not cover SVC Frame Relay configuration here.

Because the circuits in a Frame Relay network are multiplexed onto a single physical network link, a Frame Relay interface can operate in one of two modes. In point-to-point mode, the interface is operating like a traditional serial link. The interface talks to a single device on a single virtual circuit, which makes other parts of the Frame Relay configuration simpler, since mapping between network addresses and virtual circuits is straightforward—the other end of the virtual circuit had better be the router or host you are expecting there, or the administrator that configured the virtual circuit has made a mistake. In multipoint mode, a device can talk to one of several different remote devices, each connected to one of a collection of virtual circuits. But each virtual circuit is still just a point-to-point connection. While the device can talk to each remote device in turn, it cannot send a single broadcast packet to all devices without replicating it onto each virtual circuit. This kind of pseudo-broadcast is expensive in terms of both the processing power of the device, as well as in bandwidth on the network—each packet appears multiple times.

Before we can explore Frame Relay configuration, you need to understand a little about sub-interfaces. Some technologies, notably Frame Relay and ATM, allow multiple logical network interfaces to exist simultaneously on the same physical interface. Each of these logical interfaces can have its own IP address, netmask, and so forth. This is different from the multiplexing that occurs in virtual circuits. Each logical interface can have one or more virtual circuits associated with it, but a virtual circuit is normally associated with a single logical interface. To allow independent configuration of multiple logical interfaces, the IOS uses a sub-interface. The name for the sub-interface is the same as the name for the main interface followed by a period (dot) and a number indicating which sub-interface. So for example, `serial 2.3` is the third sub-interface of the main interface called `serial 2`. Notice that it is *not* the fourth sub-interface—sub-interface 0 is essentially the same as the main interface. Sub-interfaces take a little getting used to, especially when you discover that some commands apply only to an interface, and others only to a sub-interface. With practice, the concepts get easy, and the IOS is fairly good at providing help with which commands belong where. Unfortunately, most Frame Relay configurations cannot get away without using sub-interfaces. In the discussion that follows, I will use the generic term *interface* to refer to either. I hope it won't be too confusing.

Besides telling the router about the virtual circuits that are available, the major configuration task is to provide a mapping from IP addresses to DLCIs. How you do this depends on whether the interface is in point-to-point or multipoint mode. Point-to-point interfaces can operate in one of two modes: implicit or explicit. In implicit mode, the router simply assumes that the device on the other end of the virtual circuit must match the IP address it is sending to. This is, in fact, conceptually much like using unnumbered point-to-point links, and a point-to-point Frame Relay interface can be configured as an unnumbered interface. In either case, you need only associate the DLCI with the interface:

```
interface serial 0
! configure the main interface for Frame Relay encapsulation
 encapsulation frame-relay ietf
! now create a point-to-point sub-interface and give it an IP address
interface serial 0.1 point-to-point
 ip address 172.16.52.34 255.255.255.252
! finally, associate DLCI 192 with this sub-interface
! the mapping from IP address to DLCI will be implicit
 frame-relay interface-dlci 192
```

The other option is to provide an explicit map from IP address to Frame Relay DLCI. Here, instead of telling the router that a DLCI is to be associated with the interface, you include a statement to map the IP address to the DLCI:

```
interface serial 0
! configure the main interface for Frame Relay encapsulation
 encapsulation frame-relay ietf
! now create a point-to-point sub-interface and give it an IP address
interface serial 0.1 point-to-point
```

```
  ip address 172.16.52.34 255.255.255.252
! explicitly map the remote IP address to DLCI 192
frame-relay map 172.16.52.35 192
```

It is rare that you would use the explicit mapping option—implicit mapping is simpler to maintain since the IP address of the remote end does not have to be explicitly configured.

When the interface is in multipoint mode, things get more interesting. It is not possible for the router to infer the IP address of the remote device from the DLCI because the interface is associated with multiple DLCIs and multiple remote IP addresses. Again, there are two options. Just as you could explicitly configure the mapping between IP address and DLCI on a point-to-point interface, you can explicitly (and statically) map between the multiple IP addresses on a subnet and the DLCIs on an interface. You do this with repeated frame-relay map statements:

```
interface serial 0
! configure the main interface for Frame Relay encapsulation
 encapsulation frame-relay ietf
! now create a multipoint sub-interface and give it an IP address
interface serial 0.1 multipoint
 ip address 172.16.52.34 255.255.255.0
! explicitly map each remote IP address to the correct DLCI
 frame-relay map 172.16.52.35  192
 frame-relay map 172.16.52.109 314 broadcast
 frame-relay map 172.16.52.212 789 broadcast
```

The broadcast keyword tells the router that pseudo-broadcasts should be sent on this DLCI. By default, broadcasts are not sent on any DLCI. Notice that we don't have to tell the router which DLCIs are available. That is implied by the mapping from IP address to DLCI. But we do have to include a mapping for each remote IP address and DLCI pair, which can be a lot of work for a large Frame Relay network. This is where the alternative method for providing this mapping comes in handy. If we simply tell the router about all of the DLCIs, but don't tell it what IP address to associate with them, it sends an inverse ARP query to the remote device asking it its IP address. From the responses it is able to build a map dynamically:

```
interface serial 0
! configure the main interface for Frame Relay encapsulation
 encapsulation frame-relay ietf
! now create a multipoint sub-interface and give it an IP address
interface serial 0.1 multipoint
 ip address 172.16.52.34 255.255.255.0
! dynamically map each remote IP address to the correct DLCI using
! inverse ARP on these DLCIs
 frame-relay interface-dlci 192
 frame-relay interface-dlci 314
 frame-relay interface-dlci 789
```

Static mapping gives you more control, at the cost of maintaining the static mapping on each router (it is likely to be different on each), while dynamic routing pushes more of the work off to the routers. Which you should use depends on the size of your Frame Relay network, how often it changes, and how much control you need.

A few final points about Frame Relay sub-interfaces. First, all of the sub-interfaces of a main interface must use the same encapsulation. It makes no sense to make serial 0.1 use Frame Relay and serial 0.2 use PPP. This is why the encapsulation statement only applies to the main interface. Second, there is no reason you cannot mix point-to-point sub-interfaces and multipoint sub-interfaces on a single physical interface. However they are treated as distinct interfaces and do not see each others' traffic. Finally, most options set on the main interface apply to its sub-interfaces—but some options may not. Some may also be overridden by commands on the sub-interface. When in doubt, consult the IOS documentation, talk to others with more experience, and experiment in your test network.

Asynchronous Transfer Mode (ATM)

In many ways, ATM looks much like Frame Relay. Many of the concepts, terms, and methods in ATM were borrowed from experience with Frame Relay; for example, ATM is built on the concept of virtual circuits. This is not to say that ATM is superior to Frame Relay (though some will certainly claim it is so). Rather, each has its strengths and is targeted at different parts of the network and has different goals. Frame Relay is primarily intended to be a WAN technology and seeks to make optimal use of the underlying links. ATM, on the other hand, is intended to be both a LAN and a WAN technology, merging the two seamlessly. Its primary goals are speed and quality assurance guarantees.

Other differences exist between Frame Relay and ATM. For example, Frame Relay's basic data unit is a variable size frame, just as traditional LAN media would use. ATM's basic data unit is a fixed size 53-octet *cell*. This small size was chosen to be handled quickly and efficiently. Unfortunately, because of its small size, a single IP packet must be mapped onto multiple cells. If any one of these cells is lost, the entire packet must be discarded. ATM networks must be designed to avoid cell loss as much as possible.

Unlike Frame Relay, an ATM interface is a special piece of hardware—Frame Relay simply used any suitable serial interface. This hardware is connected to an ATM switch using one of several physical media and at various speeds. Common media and speed combinations are:

- Fiber optics at 622 Mbps (OC-12)

- Fiber optics at 155 Mbps (OC-3)

- Category 5 twisted copper at 155 Mbps

- Fiber optics at 100 Mbps (TAXI)

- Coaxial cable at 45 Mbps (DS-3)

There is also a 25 Mbps standard over category 4 twisted copper, but it does not seem to be attracting much interest. Perhaps this is because it is not significantly faster than switched Ethernet, and is more expensive than Fast Ethernet at 100 Mbps. Regardless of the media type and speed, the configuration of the router is the same.

ATM virtual circuits are identified by two numbers. The first of these, the virtual path identifier (VPI), identifies a bundle of virtual circuits that may be switched as a unit by some switches in the network. Most software and systems expect the VPI to be 0 for most common applications, so you should stick with this value unless you know exactly what you are doing. The second number is the virtual channel identifier (VCI). It identifies the circuit within the bundle identified by the VPI. VCI numbers below 32 are reserved for special well-known uses by the ATM Forum, the body responsible for ATM standards. We'll deal with two of those a little later. The VPI/VCI numbers for a virtual circuit, like the DLCI in Frame Relay, only has significance on a single physical link of the network—either between a host and a switch or between two switches. It can (and usually does) change on each physical link. This means that while router A identifies a circuit to router B as 0/32, router B might see it as 0/67, but it is still the same circuit.

Virtual circuits in ATM also come in two flavors—permanent virtual circuits (PVCs) and switched virtual circuits (SVCs). PVCs are most often used in wide-area ATM, though they may also be used in local-area ATM. As with Frame Relay, they must be manually created on each ATM switch by an administrator, and exist until manually removed. SVCs are most often used in local-area ATM. Here they are convenient because software can create them on demand, and remove them when they fall idle. This frees the administrator from configuring an ever-changing array of circuits as communications needs change. Few wide-area ATM networks support SVCs.

Okay, enough background. Let's explore the configuration. ATM can (and usually does) use sub-interfaces to allow multiple logical subnets to exist on a single ATM network with only one physical attachment to the router. One router in my network currently has more than 60 sub-interfaces defined on its lone ATM interface. Each sub-interface can have its own IP address, and each can use PVCs or SVCs independent of the others. I'll show examples of each. ATM also defines two ways for IP datagrams to be carried across the ATM network. The first (and older method) is Classical IP over ATM, defined in RFC 1577. The second is an ATM Forum standard called LAN Emulation (LANE). I'll talk about both.

Classical IP can be used with either PVCs or SVCs. When used with PVCs, you need to tell the router about the virtual circuits that exist in the network, and how to map IP addresses to these virtual circuits. To tell the router about virtual circuits, you add commands to the interface configuration:

```
interface atm 1
 ip address 172.16.52.34 255.255.255.0
 ! create the PVCs to be used by this interface - one line for each
 atm pvc 1 0 32 aal5snap
 atm pvc 2 0 45 aal5snap
 ...
```

Each `atm pvc` statement informs the router of one PVC. The first number is used to refer to the virtual circuit elsewhere in the configuration. It must be unique, but is otherwise arbitrary. The second and third numbers indicate the VPI/VCI pair for this circuit. In this example, virtual circuit 1 is assigned VPI/VCI 0/32, and virtual circuit 2 is assigned 0/45. The final keyword on each PVC definition tells the router what kind of encapsulation to use. The one shown, `aal5snap`, is the most common; both ends of the virtual circuit must use the same encapsulation. Once all the circuits are created, the router must be told the mapping between virtual circuits and IP addresses. To do so, you create a map list, and associate it with the interface:

```
interface atm 1
 ip address 172.16.52.34 255.255.255.0
 ! create the PVCs to be used by this interface - one line for each
 atm pvc 1 0 32 aal5snap
 atm pvc 2 0 45 aal5snap
 map-group my-map
 ! define a mapping between protocol addresses and virtual circuits
 map-list my-map
  ip 172.16.52.77   atm-vc 1
  ip 172.16.52.198 atm-vc 2 broadcast
```

The `map-list` statement and those following it define a map list called `my-map`. The first `ip` statement says that the address `172.16.52.77` can be reached on virtual circuit 1, which is assigned VPI/VCI 0/32. The second does likewise for `172.16.52.198`, but also tells the router that broadcasts should be sent to this device. Since ATM is not a broadcast technology, the router handles broadcasts by replicating each packet on each virtual circuit marked for broadcast reception. Pseudo-broadcasting is expensive in terms of router CPU and link bandwidth.

PVCs and static mappings work fine when there are only a few hosts in the network. But if there are many hosts, there are a lot of IP addresses to map to a lot of PVCs. One alternative that makes this a little more dynamic is to use inverse ARP to discover the mapping. Instead of providing the router with a static mapping between addresses and virtual circuits, we tell it to ask the device on the other end of each PVC what its address is:

```
interface atm 1
 ip address 172.16.52.34 255.255.255.0
 ! create the PVCs to be used by this interface and set them for
 ! inverse arp
 atm pvc 1 0 32 aal5snap inarp 5
 atm pvc 2 0 45 aal5snap inarp 5
...
```

In this example, I have told the router about its virtual circuits, as before. But now I have also told it to use inverse ARP on each of the virtual circuits sending a request every five minutes. From the responses it can build a map from IP address to virtual circuit, and can even keep up with changes to the IP addresses associated with a virtual circuit. But even here, a large number of virtual circuits can mean a lot of configuration, and if the circuits change frequently, configuration can become a nightmare.

This is where SVCs can help. SVCs are created on demand by software. Therefore, it is not possible to map an IP address to a switched virtual circuit. Instead, the router must map an IP address to the ATM equivalent of an address. This equivalent is called an Network Service Access Point Address (NSAPA). It is a 20-octet hexadecimal value. When a device creates a virtual circuit, it tells the ATM network the NSAPA of the destination, and waits for the network to tell it that the circuit is in place. It does this over a specially designated PVC used for signaling; this PVC is assigned VPI/VCI 0/5, and must exist in any SVC configuration. In addition, the network needs a way to figure out where each NSAPA is located. To do this, each device carries out a small dialog with the switch when it attaches. It asks the switch what the first 13 octets of its NSAPA should be, appends the last 7 from its own configuration, and informs the switch of the resulting value. Aggregation of NSAPAs happens automatically, because each switch has its own unique 13-octet prefix. This exchange is carried out over a second specially designated PVC with VPI/VCI 0/16. Both these PVCs will appear in all of our SVC examples.

There are two ways that the router can map an IP address to an ATM NSAPA. The first is using static maps, similar to those used in the PVC example. This configuration looks like:

```
interface atm 0
 atm pvc 1 0 5 qsaal
 atm pvc 2 0 16 ilmi
 !
interface atm 0.1
 ip address 172.16.52.34 255.255.255.0
 atm esi-address 0987.1189.0034.13
 atm map-group my-svc-map
 ! create a mapping from IP address to NSAPA - circuits will be created
 ! on-demand
 map-list my-svc-map
  ip 172.16.52.77  atm-nsap BC.CDEF.01.234567.890A.BCDE.F012.3456.7890.1334.13
  ip 172.16.52.198 atm-nsap BC.CDEF.01.234567.890A.BCDE.F012.3456.7890.1224.12
```

There is a lot of new stuff in this example. First, the two PVCs needed for signaling and ILMI are defined and marked to use the appropriate protocols. The encapsulation QSAAL indicates to the router that this virtual circuit is used to signal the switch about SVCs the router would like to have set up. Similarly, the encapsulation ILMI tells the router to use this circuit to exchange management information with the switch such as to register its NSAPA. These circuits are associated with the main interface—all sub-interfaces that need to do signaling or ILMI exchanges with the switch will use them. Next, sub-interface atm 0.1 specifies an ESI (End Station Identifier) address for itself. This is the last 7 octets of the router's NSAPA, and should be assigned by the local ATM administrator to ensure that it is unique among all devices attached to a single ATM switch. The router will use the ILMI virtual circuit to retrieve the 13-octet switch prefix, append its ESI to it to form the 20-octet NSAPA for this router, and then register this value with the switch again using the ILMI virtual circuit. The resulting NSAPA *must* be unique within the network.[*] Uniqueness is guaranteed by assigning a unique prefix to each ATM switch, and a unique ESI to each device attached to the switch. The switch prefix, configured by the ATM administrator, can either be assigned to the organization by the ISO or an ATM service provider, or, for private ATM networks, selected arbitrarily. Finally, I created a new map list called my-svc-map that maps IP addresses to NSAPAs, and associates it with the sub-interface. This means that each sub-interface may have its own map.

While using SVCs helps matters greatly, it is still a mess to configure. Each router still needs to be configured with the NSAPA of all other devices in the ATM network. It would be so much easier if the routers could not only create virtual circuits on demand, but could also dynamically discover the NSAPA associated with each. Since ATM is not a broadcast technology, a router cannot just broadcast an ARP request and have the remote device answer. Instead, it must rely on an ATM ARP server. When an ATM ARP server is used in the network, each router is told the server's NSAPA. They then open an SVC to the server and tell it their IP address and NSAPA. They must refresh this information every 20 minutes. Then, when any device wants to contact another device, it asks the ARP server which NSAPA is associated with the device's IP address. When the server responds, the device opens an SVC to the destination and sends its packets. When the circuit falls idle for 20 minutes, it is closed. Here is the configuration for an ATM ARP server:

```
! the configuration for an ATM ARP server
interface atm 1
 atm pvc 1 0 5 qsaal
 atm pvc 2 0 16 ilmi
```

---

[*] In fact, the first 19 octets must be unique. The 20th octet only has meaning to the local device and is not used by the switches in call routing.

```
!
interface atm 0.1
 ip address 172.16.52.34 255.255.255.0
 atm esi-address 0987.1189.0034.13
 atm arp-server self
```

We still need the signaling and ILMI PVCs, and we still need to tell the router its ESI address so that it can properly register with the switch (and later with the ARP server). But to run the server, all we need to do is to tell the router that it is the ATM ARP server for this subnet. I did this with the `atm arp-server self` statement. Now here's the configuration for an ARP client:

```
! the configuration for an ATM ARP client
interface atm 1
 atm pvc 1 0 5 qsaal
 atm pvc 2 0 16 ilmi
!
interface atm 0.1
 ip address 172.16.52.34 255.255.255.0
 atm esi-address 0987.1189.0034.13
 atm arp-server nsap BC.CDEF.01.234567.890A.BCDE.F012.3456.7890.1334.13
```

We need to tell the client where the server is located by using the `atm arp-server nsap` statement. While the NSAPA of the ATM ARP server must still be replicated into each device on the network, at least the NSAPAs of other devices don't need to be explicitly mapped. Since the ATM ARP server is configured per sub-interface, it is possible for a router to be the ARP server for one subnet on one sub-interface, and an ARP client for another subnet on another sub-interface. It is even possible for the router to have yet another sub-interface where it uses PVCs. It all depends on each subnet's needs.

The other way to send IP across ATM is LAN Emulation (LANE). LANE attempts to hide the underlying ATM network from the network protocol as well as from edge devices such as ATM-connected LAN switches. It does this by encapsulating entire LAN frames from whatever medium is being emulated (Ethernet and Token Ring are defined), and sending those across the ATM network instead of raw network layer packets. This has the advantage of supporting non-IP protocols transparently. But there is more to emulating a Token Ring or Ethernet than simply sending complete LAN frames through the network. One of the biggest problems is dealing with broadcasts. ATM is not a broadcast technology; it uses point-to-point virtual circuits. But LAN media are broadcast technologies, and network protocols expect to be able to send broadcasts over the network. LANE must also decide where to send the unicast frames that it receives. It could just flood them everywhere in the network, but that is wasteful. It would be better to identify which ATM device needs to see the frame, and send it there. This requires that the devices participating in the LANE environment must be able to map from an Ethernet or Token Ring MAC address to a virtual circuit or NSAPA.

The solution to both problems is to create a set of servers. The first and most important server that LANE defines is the LAN Emulation Configuration Server (LECS). The LECS is the central repository for information about the entire LANE setup. As such, there can be only one LECS in an ATM network (though redundant LECS are being addressed in the next version of the standard). When a LANE device first initializes its ATM interface, it contacts the LECS to find out where the other servers for the Emulated LAN (E-LAN) are. The LECS responds by sending back the NSAPA of the LAN Emulation Server (LES) that the device asked for, or a default if one was not supplied.

The LES is responsible for controlling membership in the E-LAN, and for keeping track of who is where. In effect, it becomes both the guardian of admission and the ARP server for the E-LAN. There is one LES for each E-LAN in the ATM network. Whenever a device in the E-LAN needs to know where a specific LAN MAC address is, it sends a LANE ARP to the LES to obtain the appropriate NSAPA. While it is waiting for the response, rather than discard or even hold the frame it wants to send, it transmits the frame to the third server in the LANE framework, the Broadcast and Unknown Server (BUS). This server is responsible for handling both broadcast frames that need to be flooded to all parts of the E-LAN, and frames where the mapping from LAN MAC address to NSAPA is not yet known. These are also flooded. But rather than using pseudo-broadcasts with all their expense, the BUS has a point-to-multipoint virtual circuit opened. This kind of virtual circuit has one sender, and many listeners. When a packet is sent on this circuit, the switches in the network replicate the cells at the optimal points in the network to ensure that every listener gets them, and that the packet does not cross the same link twice. Because it is closely linked in function with the LES, the LES and BUS are a single monolithic server in current versions of the IOS.

The final component of the LANE framework is the LAN Emulation Client (LEC). While there is only one LECS for the entire ATM network, and one LES/BUS for each E-LAN, there is an LEC on each device in the E-LAN, and a device participating in multiple E-LANs will have multiple LECs (not to be confused with the LECS). It is the LEC that handles the exchanges between the device and the servers for an E-LAN, and, once it knows the mapping from a LAN MAC address to an ATM NSAPA, it opens a virtual circuit directly to the remote device's LEC. Thereafter packets flow directly between the two LECs bypassing the LES/BUS.

There are a lot of pieces, and the concepts take a little time to sink in. But the configuration of a LANE network is not that difficult. First, some device in the network (it can be one of your routers) must be configured as the LECS. Since it must have knowledge of where each LES is located, it has a potentially long list of NSAPAs to deal with, but they are only recorded in this one router's configuration:

```
! define the NSAPA of the LES for each E-LAN
lane database my-lane
 name elan1 server-atm-address 47.00918100000000613E5D0301.00603E0DE841.01
 name elan2 server-atm-address 47.00918100000000613E5D0301.008876EF0356.08
 name elan3 server-atm-address 47.00918100000000613E5D0301.0060344982DB.01
 name elan4 server-atm-address 47.00918100000000613E5D0301.00E4409DE642.0C
 default-name elan1
 !
interface atm 0
 atm pvc 1 0 5 qsaal
 atm pvc 2 0 16 ilmi
 ! attach the LANE database to this interface, and use the default LANE
 ! addresses
 lane config my-lane
 lane auto-config-atm-address
```

In this example, I have listed four E-LANs in the LECS database called `my-lane`. They are named `elan1`, `elan2`, `elan3`, and `elan4`. Each has an NSAPA listed for its LES. The default E-LAN for any client that does not know what E-LAN it should join is `elan1`. In this example, I have left the membership in the E-LANs unrestricted. If you want to restrict membership, consult the IOS documentation for the specifics. It does result in a *much* larger LECS database, but if you feel you need the protection, then do so. After you create the database, you must bind it to an ATM interface, *not* a sub-interface, using the `lane config` statement. Finally, the `lane auto-config-atm-address` statement tells the router to use the default algorithm specified by Cisco for determining the NSAPAs to use on any LANE sub-interfaces.

With the LECS configured, we can now move on to the LES/BUS and LEC configurations. Rather than show these separately, the next example uses two sub-interfaces to show the possibilities. The first sub-interface, `atm 0.1`, is configured for use as the LES/BUS for `elan1`. It also has a client for this E-LAN, since we want it to be a full participant. If we had not included the LEC, the LES/BUS would function normally, but the router would not join the E-LAN itself and so could not route for it. The second sub-interface only has an LEC for `elan2`—the LES/BUS is on another device. Both of these E-LANs are emulating Ethernets, though one could easily have been a Token Ring, if I had desired. We don't tell the router where the LES/BUS is. Instead, it will ask the LECS (which happens to be running on the same router, but would not have to be) where the LES is.

```
! this sub-interface has both the LES/BUS and an LEC for elan1
interface atm 0.1
 ip address 172.16.52.34 255.255.255.0
 lane server-bus ethernet elan1
 lane client ethernet elan1
 ! this sub-interface only has an LEC for elan2 - the LES/BUS is
 ! elsewhere
interface atm 0.2
 ip address 172.16.87.3 255.255.254.0
```

```
lane client ethernet elan2
```

I did not tell either sub-interface what NSAPA to use for itself. Because I included the `lane auto-config-atm-address` statement on the main interface, the sub-interface will generate unique addresses using an algorithm provided in the IOS. This is a much easier way to get unique NSAPAs than maintaining them manually.

So should you use LANE or Classical IP in your ATM network? It depends. LANE by nature is multi-protocol. Since the native LAN medium's frames are sent transparently across the ATM network, it doesn't matter if the frame contains IP, AppleTalk, IPX, or any other LAN protocol. It also integrates traditional LAN media with your ATM network and can serve as a transitional step between traditional LANs and native ATM, though there is no reason it should not be a more permanent part of your network. Classical IP, on the other hand, has the advantage that it can use a larger MTU than LANE. Since LANE is emulating an Ethernet or a Token Ring, it is confined to the MTU specified for those media. The MTU for Classical IP is 9180 octets, which can yield better performance. Also, because LANE attempts to hide the ATM network from the attached devices, ATM's quality of service guarantees are no longer available. Classical IP may have access to the full range of ATM features. In the end, the best answer to which you should run is "both." You can use classical IP on subnets (and sub-interfaces) where all the devices can use the native ATM features, for example between your routers on an ATM backbone, and you can use LANE on subnets (and sub-interfaces) where you are supporting ATM-connected LAN switches. Both will co-exist peacefully. However, a single subnet or sub-interface must use one or the other.

B

Where and How to Get New RFCs

RFCs are the official standards documents for the IP protocol family. They're available from many repositories, using just about any technique: www, FTP, email, and so on. Probably the most convenient way to get RFCs is via the Web site maintained by the RFC editor. The URL for this site is: *http://www.isi.edu/rfc-editor/*; in addition to the repository itself, this site has a (somewhat crude) searchable index. Another Web site with a more friendly searchable index is *http://ds.internic.net/ds/dspg1intdoc.html*.

The two most common places to obtain RFCs via FTP are *ftp://ftp.isi.edu/in-notes/rfcnnnn.txt* and *ftp://ds.internic.net/rfc/rfcnnnn.txt*, where *nnnn* is the number of the RFC you want. Always use a four-digit number.

It's often convenient to retrieve RFCs using email. To get RFCs from *isi.edu* using email, send a message to *rfc-info@isi.edu* with the body:

```
Retrieve: RFC
Doc-ID: RFCnnnn
```

where *nnnn* refers to the number of the RFC (always use 4 digits—the DOC-ID of RFC 822 is RFC0822). The *rfc-info@isi.edu* server provides other ways of selecting RFCs based on keywords and such; for more information send a message to *rfc-info@isi.edu* with the message body:

```
help: help
```

To get RFCs from *ds.internic.net* using email, send a mail message to *mailserv@ds.internic.net* and include any of the following commands in the message body:

```
document-by-name rfcnnnn
```

where *nnnn* is the RFC number;

```
file /ftp/rfc/rfcnnnn.yyy
```

where *nnnn* is the RFC number and yyy is txt or ps;

```
help
```

to get information on how to use the mailserver.

There are many other sites that provide RFCs, some of which may be more convenient for users outside of the US. To get a complete list, retrieve the file *ftp://ftp.isi.edu/in-notes/rfc-retrieval.txt*.

C

Obtaining Internet Drafts

The Internet Drafts are the *working documents* of the Internet Engineering Task Force. As such, they should be considered works in progress, and should only be cited as such. Most Internet Drafts will never make it beyond the draft stage. These represent ideas that either did not generate the interest that the original author had anticipated, or were deemed to be undesirable by consensus opinion. Other drafts will ultimately become Internet Requests for Comment (RFC), where they will either be informational in nature, or put on the standards track where they may ultimately become Internet standards.

In any event, an Internet Draft is only valid for six months from the date of its publication. At that time, it must either be resubmitted (presumably with revisions), be submitted for consideration as an RFC, or withdrawn. As such, it is important that if you retrieve and read an Internet Draft, you keep in mind that the information contained in it is *not* a standard, does *not* represent a proposed standard, and may *never* get beyond the draft stage. Still, drafts are valuable if you want to see what topics are currently being discussed within the IETF, and perhaps provide some comment or insight to an Internet Draft's author.

Internet Drafts are available electronically via several different means. To obtain the drafts via anonymous FTP, FTP to one of the following sites and login with the name anonymous. Then, *cd* to the */internet-drafts* directory. There, in addition to the Internet Draft documents themselves, you will find the files *1id-abstracts.txt*, which lists the current Internet Drafts, their titles, pathnames, authors, dates of publication, and abstracts; and *1id-index.txt*, which contains an abbreviated listing of Internet Drafts (the document title, filename, and posting date).

Region	Host	IP Address
Africa	*ftp.is.co.za*	196.4.160.8
Europe	*nic.nordu.net*	192.36.148.17
Pacific Rim	*munnari.oz.au*[1]	128.250.1.21
US East Coast	*ds.internic.net*	198.49.45.10
US West Coast	*ftp.isi.edu*	128.9.0.32

[1] The Internet-Drafts on this machine are stored in UNIX compressed form (i.e., the .Z file extension).

The Internet Drafts are also available via electronic mail from *ds.internic.net*. To retrieve a file, mail a request to *mailserv@ds.internic.net* with a subject of anything you want (it will be ignored). In the *body* of the message, put one or more commands of the form:

```
FILE /internet-drafts/1id-abstracts.txt
PATH jdoe@somedomain.edu
```

where PATH lists the e-mail address where the response should be sent. If you have the *mpack* utility or a MIME-compliant mail reader, you may want to use the additional command:

```
ENCODING mime
```

This command results in the information being returned in a MIME message.

Internet Drafts are also available from the World Wide Web. The IETF itself claims that this service is constantly evolving, so check it frequently. The URL for Internet Drafts is *http://www.ietf.org/1id-abstracts.html* and the IETF home page can be found at *http://www.ietf.org/home.html*.

D

Obtaining IP Addresses

If at all possible, you should obtain your IP address space from your Internet provider, or from the private address blocks defined by RFC 1918. Address space is at a premium, and this is the best way to ensure that you get an adequate address space while still preserving address space for future requests.

If you decide that you *must* have address space that is portable, you should understand that it is not guaranteed to be routable by either the Internet Assigned Numbers Authority (IANA) or any of the IP registries. It may even be that your Internet provider will choose not to route it, and will, instead, insist that you use address space that it provides.

Who you contact to obtain portable address space depends on what part of the world you are in. Please refer to the section below that best describes your location.

Asian-Pacific Rim

The regional registry for the Asian-Pacific Rim is the Asian Pacific Network Information Center (APNIC). Retrieve the file */apnic/docs/Contents* from the anonymous FTP server at *ftp.apnic.net*, and review it to determine which template form you need from the */apnic/docs* directory on that server. Once you have completed the appropriate form, email it to: *ip-request@rs.apnic.net*. You can submit the form by fax to: +81-3-5500-0481; or via postal mail to:

> Asia Pacific Network Information Center
> Tokyo Central Post Office Box 351
> Tokyo, 100-91, Japan

The APNIC states plainly that submission by email is preferred, and postal mail should be used only as a last resort. It does not accept requests via telephone. If you have any questions regarding this form, contact the APNIC via email at *hostmaster@apnic.net* (preferred), fax at the above number, postal mail at the above address or via telephone at +81-3-5500-0480.

Europe

European IP addresses are assigned by the RIPE NCC. Obtain the file */ripe/forms/netnum-appl.txt* via anonymous FTP from *ftp.ripe.net*, or from your Internet Service Provider. In addition, obtain a copy of the file */ripe/forms/netnum-support.txt*. Read both files carefully, and follow the instructions contained in them for submitting your request.

Contact the RIPE NCC at:

> RIPE NCC
> Kruislaan 409
> 1098 SJ Amsterdam
> The Netherlands
>
> tel: +31 20 592 5065
> fax: +31 20 592 5090
> email: *hostmaster@ripe.net*

Canada

The regional registry for Canada will soon be provided by the Canadian Association of Internet Providers (CAIP). However, at this time, they are not ready to handle requests. Until they are, requests should be sent to the US registry using the form */templates/canadian-ip-template.txt* obtained from the anonymous FTP server on *rs.internic.net*. Submit this form to the US registry according to the instructions for US sites, *not* according to the instructions contained in this form.

United States, the Americas, and Other Locations

IP address assignment for the United States, the rest of the Americas (except Canada), and other locations not covered by another regional registry, are handled by the InterNIC Registration Service, whose address is:

Network Solutions
InterNIC Registration Services
505 Huntmar Park Drive
Herndon, VA 22070
USA

This is the registry of last resort. If you have a regional registry, the InterNIC will redirect you to them, costing you time and money. The InterNIC has gotten *very* strict in their requirements that requesters work with their Internet Service Providers to obtain address space. If you attempt to bypass your ISP, the InterNIC will probably send you back to them, unless you can justify why your case is an exception.

To request an IP address from the US InterNIC, obtain the file */templates/internet-number-template.txt* via anonymous FTP from *ds.internic.net*. Fill it out and email it to *hostmaster@internic.net* (preferred), mail a hard-copy to the above postal address, or FAX it to (703) 742-4811.

If you do not have access to FTP, you can write the InterNIC at the above address requesting the form, or you can call them at (703) 742-4777. Using a postal request or making a phone request will result in some delay; retrieving the file yourself is most efficient.

Index

Numbers

1s broadcast systems, 11
0s broadcast systems, 11

A

ABORT value, chat scripts, 292
access attempts, logging, 266
access control
  bastion hosts, 261–262, 264
  border routers, 264
  external connections, 272–274
  firewalls, 262–265
  host security, 265–267
  private addresses, 264
  router access, 267–272
  security concerns, 257, 259–260
  (see also access lists)
access lists
  AS path filtering, 250–252
  backup static routes and, 148
  changing, 226–227
  dial-on-demand interfaces,
    configuring, 293–294
  filtering routing updates, 156–160
  IGPs, using for external routing, 243
  router access security, 268–270
  (see also access control)
access network component, 30, 79, 118,
    119
access-group statement (Cisco IOS), 148

access-list statement (Cisco IOS), 148, 248,
    294
adaptability, routing, 116–117
address resolution, 203, 207, 212–214
  (see also ARP)
Address Resolution Protocol (see ARP)
address spaces
  base address/bit count notation, 6–7
  holes in, 20
  IP addresses, 3–4
  provider-assigned addresses, 237
  subnest 0 and subnet 1, 68, 76
  variable length subnet masks and, 64
  (see also aggregation)
address statement (Cisco IOS), 287
addresses, 2
  address-mask pairs, in network
    statements, 134, 153
  (see also address spaces)
administrative distances (Cisco IOS),
    144–145, 153–155
advertisements, suppressing, 151–152,
    252–253
agents, SNMP definition, 209
aggregation
  classless routing protocols, 70
  hybrid routing schemes and, 120
  network topology and, 56-57, 68–70
  OSPF areas and, 138
  (see also address spaces)
Alarm RMON monitoring group, 190

About the Authors

As an undergraduate at Baylor University, **Scott M. Ballew** was fascinated by the idea of two computers communicating with each other instead of acting independently. But it was during his second year of graduate study at Purdue, when he was given the opportunity to be the sole administrator for the Cypress Network—an experimental long-haul packet switching network—that he discovered his love of networking. Scott is now a member of Purdue University Computing Center's network engineering group where he manages a network of over 20 routers and more than 250 subnets using such varied technologies as switched and shared Ethernet, Fast Ethernet, FDDI, HiPPI, ATM, Frame Relay, and several wide-area links to the university's regional campuses.

When he is not busy working on (or writing about) his network, Scott enjoys quiet evenings at home with a good movie or a good book, playing games with friends, and remodeling and redecorating his house.

Colophon

Our look is the result of reader comments, our own experimentation, and feedback from distribution channels. Distinctive covers complement our distinctive approach to technical topics, breathing personality and life into potentially dry subjects.

The animal on the cover of *Managing IP Networks with Cisco Routers* is a donkey, or ass. Relatives of horses, today's domesticated asses are descendants of the African wild ass, making them the only domesticated animal, with the possible exception of the cat, with origins in Africa. Wild asses have been kept as beasts of burden since ancient times, and by 2500 B.C. domestic asses were depicted in Egyptian art.

Donkeys make excellent beasts of burden for several reasons. They are capable of very sure footing, and can live in mountainous areas. Unlike most animals, donkeys can survive on brackish water. And, despite their reputations for stubborness, they often have placid dispositions. To enhance their natural qualifications, asses can be bred with horses, producing either a mule (a cross between a jackass and a mare) or a hinny (a cross between a jenny ass and a stallion). These hybrid offspring are always sterile.

Edie Freedman designed the cover of this book, using a 19th-century engraving from the Dover Pictorial Archive. The cover layout was produced with Quark

XPress 3.3 using the ITC Garamond font. Whenever possible, our books use Rep-Kover™, a durable and flexible lay-flat binding. If the page count exceeds Rep-Kover's limit, perfect binding is used.

The inside layout was designed by Edie Freedman and Nancy Priest and implemented in FrameMaker 5.0 by Mike Sierra. The text and heading fonts are ITC Garamond Light and Garamond Book. The illustrations that appear in the book were created in Macromedia Freehand 7.0 by Chris Reilley. This colophon was written by Clairemarie Fisher O'Leary.

More Titles from O'Reilly

Network Administration

Using & Managing PPP

By Andrew Sun
1st Edition October 1998 (est.)
436 pages (est.), ISBN 1-56592-321-9

This book is for network administrators and others who have to set up computer systems to use PPP. It covers all aspects of the protocol, including how to set up dial-in servers, authentication, debugging, and PPP options. In addition, it contains overviews of related areas, like serial communications, DNS setup, and routing.

Virtual Private Networks

By Charlie Scott, Paul Wolfe & Mike Erwin
1st Edition February 1998
184 pages, ISBN 1-56592-319-7

This book tells you how to plan and build a Virtual Private Network (VPN), a collection of technologies that creates secure connections or "tunnels" over regular Internet lines. It starts with general concerns like costs and configuration and continues with detailed descriptions of how to install and use VPN technologies that are available for Windows NT and UNIX, such as PPTP and L2TP, the AltaVista Tunnel, and the Cisco PIX Firewall.

TCP/IP Network Administration, 2nd Edition

By Craig Hunt
2nd Edition December 1997
630 pages, ISBN 1-56592-322-7

A complete guide to setting up and running a TCP/IP network for practicing system administrators. Beyond basic setup, this new second edition discusses the Internet routing protocols and provides a tutorial on how to configure important network services. It now also includes Linux in addition to BSD and System V TCP/IP implementations.

sendmail, 2nd Edition

By Bryan Costales & Eric Allman
2nd Edition January 1997
1050 pages, ISBN 1-56592-222-0

sendmail, 2nd Edition, covers sendmail Version 8.8 from Berkeley and the standard versions available on most systems. This cross-referenced edition offers an expanded tutorial, solution-oriented examples, and new topics such as the #error delivery agent, sendmail's exit values, MIME headers, and how to set up and use the user database, mailertable, and smrsh.

sendmail Desktop Reference

By Bryan Costales & Eric Allman
1st Edition March 1997
74 pages, ISBN 1-56592-278-6

This quick-reference guide provides a complete overview of the latest version of sendmail (V8.8), from command-line switches to configuration commands, from options declarations to macro definitions, and from m4 features to debugging switches—all packed into a convenient, carry-around booklet co-authored by the creator of sendmail. Includes extensive cross-references to sendmail, Second Edition.

DNS and BIND, 2nd Edition

By Paul Albitz & Cricket Liu
2nd Edition December 1996
438 pages, ISBN 1-56592-236-0

This book is a complete guide to the Internet's Domain Name System (DNS) and the Berkeley Internet Name Domain (BIND) software, the UNIX implementation of DNS. This second edition covers BIND 4.8.3, which is included in most vendor implementations today, as well as BIND 4.9.4, the potential future standard.

Network Administration

Getting Connected: The Internet at 56K and Up

By Kevin Dowd
1st Edition June 1996
424 pages, ISBN 1-56592-154-2

A complete guide for businesses, schools, and other organizations who want to connect their computers to the Internet. This book covers everything you need to know to make informed decisions, from helping you figure out which services you really need to providing down-to-earth explanations and configuration instructions for telecommunication options at higher than modem speeds, such as frame relay, ISDN, and leased lines. Once you're online, it shows you how to set up basic Internet services, such as a World Wide Web server. Tackles issues for PC, Macintosh, and UNIX platforms.

Networking Personal Computers with TCP/IP

By Craig Hunt
1st Edition July 1995
408 pages, ISBN 1-56592-123-2

This book offers practical information as well as detailed instructions for attaching PCs to a TCP/IP network and its UNIX servers. It discusses the challenges you'll face and offers general advice on how to deal with them, provides basic TCP/IP configuration information for some of the popular PC operating systems, covers advanced configuration topics and configuration of specific applications such as email, and includes a chapter on on integrating Netware with TCP/IP.

Windows NT System Administration

Managing the Windows NT Registry

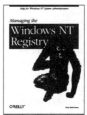

By Paul Robichaux
1st Edition April 1998
470 pages, ISBN 1-56592-378-2

The Windows NT Registry is the repository for all hardware, software, and application configuration settings. This is the system administrator's guide to maintaining, monitoring, and updating the Registry database. A "must-have" for every NT system manager or administrator, it covers what the Registry is and where it lives on disk, available tools, Registry access from programs, and Registry content.

Learning Perl on Win32 Systems

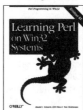

By Randal L. Schwartz,
Erik Olson & Tom Christiansen
1st Edition August 1997
306 pages, ISBN 1-56592-324-3

In this carefully paced course, leading Perl trainers and a Windows NT practitioner teach you to program in the language that promises to emerge as the scripting language of choice on NT. Based on the "llama" book, this book features tips for PC users and new, NT-specific examples, along with a foreword by Larry Wall, the creator of Perl, and Dick Hardt, the creator of Perl for Win32.

Windows NT Desktop Reference

By Æleen Frisch
1st Edition January 1998
64 pages, ISBN 1-56592-437-1

A hip-pocket quick reference to Windows NT commands, as well as the most useful commands from the Resource Kits. Commands are arranged ingroups related to their purpose and function. Covers Windows NT 4.0.

Windows NT System Administration

Windows NT in a Nutshell

By Eric Pearce
1st Edition June 1997
364 pages, ISBN 1-56592-251-4

Anyone who installs Windows NT, creates a user, or adds a printer is an NT system administrator (whether they realize it or not). This book features a new tagged callout approach to documenting the 4.0 GUI as well as real-life examples of command usage and strategies for problem solving, with an emphasis on networking. Windows NT in a Nutshell will be as useful to the single-system home user as it will be to the administrator of a 1,000-node corporate network.

Windows NT User Administration

By Ashley J. Meggitt & Timothy D. Ritchey
1st Edition November 1997
218 pages, ISBN 1-56592-301-4

Many Windows NT books introduce you to a range of topics, but seldom do they give you enough information to master any one thing. This book (like other O'Reilly animal books) is different. *Windows NT User Administration* makes you an expert at creating users efficiently, controlling what they can do, limiting the damage they can cause, and monitoring their activities on your system. Don't simply react to problems; use the techniques in this book to anticipate and prevent them.

Windows NT SNMP

By James D. Murray
1st Edition February 1998
464 pages, Includes CD-ROM
ISBN 1-56592-338-3

This book describes the implementation of SNMP (the Simple Network Management Protocol) on Windows NT 3.51 and 4.0 (with a look ahead to NT 5.0) and Windows 95 systems. It covers SNMP and network basics and detailed information on developing SNMP management applications and extension agents. The book comes with a CD-ROM containing a wealth of additional information: standards documents, sample code from the book, and many third-party, SNMP-related software tools, libraries, and demos.

Essential Windows NT System Administration

By Æleen Frisch
1st Edition February 1998
486 pages, ISBN 1-56592-274-3

This book combines practical experience with technical expertise to help you manage Windows NT systems as productively as possible. It covers the standard utilities offered with the Windows NT operating system and from the Resource Kit, as well as important commercial and free third-party tools. By the author of O'Reilly's bestselling book, *Essential System Administration*.

Windows NT Backup & Restore

By Jody Leber
1st Edition May 1998
320 pages, ISBN 1-56592-272-7

Beginning with the need for a workable recovery policy and ways to translate that policy into requirements, *Windows NT Backup & Restore* presents the reader with practical guidelines for setting up an effective backup system in both small and large environments. It covers the native NT utilities as well as major third-party hardware and software.

Windows NT Server 4.0 for NetWare Administrators

By Robert Bruce Thompson
1st Edition November 1997
756 pages, ISBN 1-56592-280-8

This book provides a fast-track means or experienced NetWare administrators to build on their knowledge and master the fundamentals of using the Microsoft Windows NT Server. The broad coverage of many aspects of Windows NT Server is balanced by a tightly focused approach of comparison, contrast, and differentiation between NetWare and NT features and methodologies.

Windows NT System Administration

MCSE: The Core Exams in a Nutshell

By Michael Moncur
1st Edition May 1998
424 pages, ISBN 1-56592-376-6

MCSE: The Core Exams in a Nutshell is a detailed quick reference for administrators with Windows NT experience or experience administering a different platform, such as UNIX, who want to learn what is necessary to pass the MCSE required exam portion of the MCSE certification. While no book is a substitute for real-world experience, this book will help you codify your knowledge and prepare for the exams.

MCSE: The Electives in a Nutshell

By Michael Moncur
1st Edition September 1998 (est.)
550 pages (est.), ISBN: 1-56592-482-7

A companion volume to MCSE: The Core Exams in a Nutshell, MCSE: The Electives in a Nutshell is a comprehensive study guide that covers the elective exams for the MCSE as well as the Internet requirements and electives for the MCSE+Internet. This detailed reference is aimed at sophisticated users who need a bridge between real-world experience and the MCSE exam requirements.

System Administration

termcap & terminfo

By John Strang,
Linda Mui & Tim O'Reilly
3rd Edition April 1988
270 pages, ISBN 0-937175-22-6

For UNIX system administrators and programmers. This handbook provides information on writing and debugging terminal descriptions, as well as terminal initialization, for the two UNIX terminal databases.

Volume 8: X Window System Administrator's Guide

By Linda Mui & Eric Pearce
1st Edition October 1992
372 pages, ISBN 0-937175-83-8

This book focuses on issues of system administration for X and X-based networks—not just for UNIX system administrators, but for anyone faced with the job of administering X (including those running X on stand-alone workstations).

System Performance Tuning

By Mike Loukides
1st Edition November 1990
336 pages, ISBN 0-937175-60-9

System Performance Tuning answers the fundamental question: How can I get my UNIX-based computer to do more work without buying more hardware? Some performance problems do require you to buy a bigger or faster computer, but many can be solved simply by making better use of the resources you already have.

System Administration

Essential System Administration

By Æleen Frisch
2nd Edition September 1995
788 pages, ISBN 1-56592-127-5

Thoroughly revised and updated for all major versions of UNIX, this second edition of *Essential System Administration* provides a compact, manageable introduction to the tasks faced by everyone responsible for a UNIX system. Whether you use a stand-alone UNIX system, routinely provide administrative support for a larger shared system, or just want an understanding of basic administrative functions, this book is for you. Offers expanded sections on networking, electronic mail, security, and kernel configuration.

Using & Managing UUCP

By Ed Ravin, Tim O'Reilly,
Dale Dougherty & Grace Todino
1st Edition September 1996
424 pages, ISBN 1-56592-153-4

Using & Managing UUCP describes, in one volume, this popular communications and file transfer program. UUCP is very attractive to computer users with limited resources, a small machine, and a dial-up connection. This book covers Taylor UUCP, the latest versions of HoneyDanBer UUCP, and the specific implementation details of UUCP versions shipped by major UNIX vendors.

Managing NFS and NIS

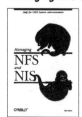

By Hal Stern
1st Edition June 1991
436 pages, ISBN 0-937175-75-7

Managing NFS and NIS is for system administrators who need to set up or manage a network filesystem installation. NFS (Network Filesystem) is probably running at any site that has two or more UNIX systems. NIS (Network Information System) is a distributed database used to manage a network of computers. The only practical book devoted entirely to these subjects, this guide is a "must-have" for anyone interested in UNIX networking.

How to stay in touch with O'Reilly

1. Visit Our Award-Winning Web Site

http://www.oreilly.com/

★ "Top 100 Sites on the Web" —*PC Magazine*
★ "Top 5% Web sites" —*Point Communications*
★ "3-Star site" —*The McKinley Group*

Our web site contains a library of comprehensive product information (including book excerpts and tables of contents), downloadable software, background articles, interviews with technology leaders, links to relevant sites, book cover art, and more. File us in your Bookmarks or Hotlist!

2. Join Our Email Mailing Lists

New Product Releases

To receive automatic email with brief descriptions of all new O'Reilly products as they are released, send email to:
listproc@online.oreilly.com
Put the following information in the first line of your message (*not* in the Subject field):
subscribe oreilly-news

O'Reilly Events

If you'd also like us to send information about trade show events, special promotions, and other O'Reilly events, send email to:
listproc@online.oreilly.com
Put the following information in the first line of your message (*not* in the Subject field):
subscribe oreilly-events

3. Get Examples from Our Books via FTP

There are two ways to access an archive of example files from our books:

Regular FTP

- ftp to:
  ftp.oreilly.com
  (login: anonymous
  password: your email address)
- Point your web browser to:
  ftp://ftp.oreilly.com/

FTPMAIL

- Send an email message to:
  ftpmail@online.oreilly.com
  (Write "help" in the message body)

4. Contact Us via Email

order@oreilly.com
To place a book or software order online. Good for North American and international customers.

subscriptions@oreilly.com
To place an order for any of our newsletters or periodicals.

books@oreilly.com
General questions about any of our books.

software@oreilly.com
For general questions and product information about our software. Check out O'Reilly Software Online at **http://software.oreilly.com/** for software and technical support information. Registered O'Reilly software users send your questions to: **website-support@oreilly.com**

cs@oreilly.com
For answers to problems regarding your order or our products.

booktech@oreilly.com
For book content technical questions or corrections.

proposals@oreilly.com
To submit new book or software proposals to our editors and product managers.

international@oreilly.com
For information about our international distributors or translation queries. For a list of our distributors outside of North America check out:
http://www.oreilly.com/www/order/country.html

O'Reilly & Associates, Inc.
101 Morris Street, Sebastopol, CA 95472 USA
TEL   707-829-0515 or 800-998-9938
          (6am to 5pm PST)
FAX   707-829-0104

Titles from O'Reilly

International Distributors

UK, EUROPE, MIDDLE EAST AND NORTHERN AFRICA (EXCEPT FRANCE, GERMANY, SWITZERLAND, & AUSTRIA)

INQUIRIES
International Thomson Publishing Europe
Berkshire House
168-173 High Holborn
London WC1V 7AA
United Kingdom
Telephone: 44-171-497-1422
Fax: 44-171-497-1426
Email: itpint@itps.co.uk

ORDERS
International Thomson Publishing Services, Ltd.
Cheriton House, North Way
Andover, Hampshire SP10 5BE
United Kingdom
Telephone: 44-264-342-832 (UK)
Telephone: 44-264-342-806 (outside UK)
Fax: 44-264-364418 (UK)
Fax: 44-264-342761 (outside UK)
UK & Eire orders: itpuk@itps.co.uk
International orders: itpint@itps.co.uk

FRANCE
Editions Eyrolles
61 bd Saint-Germain
75240 Paris Cedex 05
France
Fax: 33-01-44-41-11-44

FRENCH LANGUAGE BOOKS
All countries except Canada
Telephone: 33-01-44-41-46-16
Email: geodif@eyrolles.com
English language books
Telephone: 33-01-44-41-11-87
Email: distribution@eyrolles.com

GERMANY, SWITZERLAND, AND AUSTRIA

INQUIRIES
O'Reilly Verlag
Balthasarstr. 81
D-50670 Köln
Germany
Telephone: 49-221-97-31-60-0
Fax: 49-221-97-31-60-8
Email: anfragen@oreilly.de

ORDERS
International Thomson Publishing
Königswinterer Straße 418
53227 Bonn, Germany
Telephone: 49-228-97024 0
Fax: 49-228-441342
Email: order@oreilly.de

JAPAN
O'Reilly Japan, Inc.
Kiyoshige Building 2F
12-Banchi, Sanei-cho
Shinjuku-ku
Tokyo 160-0008 Japan
Telephone: 81-3-3356-5227
Fax: 81-3-3356-5261
Email: kenji@oreilly.com

INDIA
Computer Bookshop (India) PVT. Ltd.
190 Dr. D.N. Road, Fort
Bombay 400 001 India
Telephone: 91-22-207-0989
Fax: 91-22-262-3551
Email: cbsbom@giasbm01.vsnl.net.in

HONG KONG
City Discount Subscription Service Ltd.
Unit D, 3rd Floor, Yan's Tower
27 Wong Chuk Hang Road
Aberdeen, Hong Kong
Telephone: 852-2580-3539
Fax: 852-2580-6463
Email: citydis@ppn.com.hk

KOREA
Hanbit Media, Inc.
Sonyoung Bldg. 202
Yeksam-dong 736-36
Kangnam-ku
Seoul, Korea
Telephone: 822-554-9610
Fax: 822-556-0363
Email: hant93@chollian.dacom.co.kr

SINGAPORE, MALAYSIA, AND THAILAND
Addison Wesley Longman Singapore PTE Ltd.
25 First Lok Yang Road
Singapore 629734
Telephone: 65-268-2666
Fax: 65-268-7023
Email: daniel@longman.com.sg

PHILIPPINES
Mutual Books, Inc.
429-D Shaw Boulevard
Mandaluyong City, Metro
Manila, Philippines
Telephone: 632-725-7538
Fax: 632-721-3056
Email: mbikikog@mnl.sequel.net

CHINA
Ron's DataCom Co., Ltd.
79 Dongwu Avenue
Dongxihu District
Wuhan 430040
China
Telephone: 86-27-83892568
Fax: 86-27-83222108
Email: hongfeng@public.wh.hb.cn

ALL OTHER ASIAN COUNTRIES
O'Reilly & Associates, Inc.
101 Morris Street
Sebastopol, CA 95472 USA
Telephone: 707-829-0515
Fax: 707-829-0104
Email: order@oreilly.com

AUSTRALIA
WoodsLane Pty. Ltd.
7/5 Vuko Place, Warriewood NSW 2102
P.O. Box 935
Mona Vale NSW 2103
Australia
Telephone: 61-2-9970-5111
Fax: 61-2-9970-5002
Email: info@woodslane.com.au

NEW ZEALAND
Woodslane New Zealand Ltd.
21 Cooks Street (P.O. Box 575)
Waganui, New Zealand
Telephone: 64-6-347-6543
Fax: 64-6-345-4840
Email: info@woodslane.com.au

THE AMERICAS
McGraw-Hill Interamericana Editores, S.A. de C.V.
Cedro No. 512
Col. Atlampa 06450
Mexico, D.F.
Telephone: 52-5-541-3155
Fax: 52-5-541-4913
Email: mcgraw-hill@infosel.net.mx

SOUTH AFRICA
International Thomson Publishing South Africa
Building 18, Constantia Park
138 Sixteenth Road
P.O. Box 2459
Halfway House, 1685 South Africa
Telephone: 27-11-805-4819
Fax: 27-11-805-3648